WORDS THAT WON THE WAR

London: Humphrey Milford
Oxford University Press

One of Howard Chandler Christy's Memorable Posters

WORDS THAT WON THE WAR

The Story of
The Committee on Public Information
1917-1919

By
JAMES R. MOCK
AND
CEDRIC LARSON

PRINCETON
PRINCETON UNIVERSITY PRESS
1939

Composed by Princeton University Press
and printed in the United States of America

TO OUR PARENTS

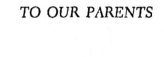

PREFACE

On July 6, 1937, trucks rolled up to The National Archives in Washington, bringing to their last resting place 180 cubic feet of records which for the previous sixteen years had been all but lost in the Munitions Building basement at 20th Street and Constitution Avenue. The precious cargo represented virtually all that is left of the files of the Committee on Public Information, the so-called Creel Committee of the World War. Here in these papers is the story of America's first "propaganda ministry," and its dynamic leader, George Creel.

This book goes to press at a moment when no one can say that America will surely avoid facing once more the issues and problems of 1917-1919. The lessons of the Creel Committee are calling aloud for recognition in this tense year of 1939. Therefore, this book attempts whenever possible to consider not only the actual mechanics and the work of the CPI but also the larger and more gravely urgent questions which are with us today—or may be tomorrow.

France and England have become, at least for the time being, "totalitarian democracies," and Americans ask themselves what may happen to this country if it is sucked into the maelstrom. As this book attempts to demonstrate, the advance of censorship power can be silent and almost unnoticed as wave follows wave of patriotic hysteria. If the record of the last war is to be taken, American resistance to repressive measures may not be great. The question arises whether, in the event of a new war, America would feel like indulging in the luxury of some "Creel Committee" to stand as buffer between military dictatorship and civil life.

As to the foreign work of the CPI—about which little has been written and not all of that in entire candor—the world problem was in many respects so similar to that of today that Americans can turn back with the highest profit to these newly available records of relations between the United States and the Allies in opposition to German militarism.

From June 30, 1919, until the files were placed in the custody of the Archives, they shrank to less than a quarter of their former bulk—partly because of the ministrations of the "Useless Papers Committee" and partly for unexplained reasons

But the papers that remain—hundreds of thousands of them—provide an historical source of the first importance to the American people. Letters, memoranda, cablegrams, printed documents, Military and Naval Intelligence reports, slides, movie films, posters—all these are waiting to tell their story.

The Committee was so widespread in its ramifications that the collection touches nearly all phases of American and world affairs for the years 1917 to 1919. The authors have consciously restricted themselves to intensive study of these files, though fully realizing that words alone did not win the war. The "strategic equation" of military language recognizes four factors (combat, economic, political, and psychologic), and this book is concerned only with the last and obviously with only some of its aspects A similar study might be oriented about the forensic activities of Woodrow Wilson, the work of the Military Intelligence Branch, or any of a number of other points of interest But the Committee on Public Information touched all of these, and a complete understanding of its work would be essential to appreciation of other work on "the psychologic front"

At the end of his *Propaganda Technique in the World War*, Harold D. Lasswell says. "To illuminate the mechanisms of propaganda is to reveal the secret springs of social action." This book can hope to make no such thoroughgoing contribution to human knowledge, but it is in that spirit that it has been written

As Dr. Lasswell also says "In the Great Society it is no longer possible to fuse the waywardness of individuals in the furnace of the war dance, a new and subtler instrument must weld thousands and even millions of human beings into one amalgamated mass of hate and will and hope. A new flame must burn out the canker of dissent and temper the steel of bellicose enthusiasm The name of this new hammer and anvil of social solidarity is propaganda. Talk must take the place of drill, print must supplant the dance. War dances live in literature and at the fringes of the modern earth, war propaganda breathes and fumes in the capitals and provinces of the world."

And in describing the specific objectives of war propaganda, Dr. Lasswell gives this list

1. To mobilize hatred against the enemy
2. To preserve the friendship of allies.
3. To preserve the friendship and, if possible, to procure the cooperation of neutrals.
4 To demoralize the enemy

The reader will see how perfectly the work of the Committee on Public Information follows this formula, thus making the record of its activity not only significant as a chapter in American history but an especially apt illustration of how all war propaganda works

As to previous knowledge of the Committee, it appears that, except for partial use in two doctoral dissertations, no scholar had been through the files until Dr Frank Hardee Allen of the National Archives had completed his conscientious and useful classification of the material Heretofore, the principal sources have been the *Complete Report of the Chairman of the Committee on Public Information* and the popular *How We Advertised America*—both written by George Creel with his customary verve and loyal pride in the organization, but far from complete because of hasty and chaotic liquidation of the Washington office while Mr Creel was at the Peace Conference.

Accordingly, much material which George Creel himself could not get at in 1919 has been available to the authors, and the majority of the documents in this book have never been published before. A number of them will necessitate reinterpretation of certain statements in George Creel's books and in the recollections set down in print by his associates

Nevertheless, it is obvious that only a portion of the total evidence is presented here, and that nothing less than a small library could do justice to the fascinating story of the Creel Committee. What the authors have attempted to do is to suggest the Committee's implications for democratic government and its lessons for future national emergencies, and, through selected examples, to describe its impact on the American people and world affairs

A few of the documents have been used in other form for the authors' articles in the *Public Opinion Quarterly*, the *Quarterly Journal of Speech*, and the *Journalism Quarterly*. In each case we are grateful to the editors for permission to reprint

The authors realize how futile this undertaking would have been without the sincere interest and generous cooperation of a large group of individuals including former members of the CPI, historians, librarians, and archivists. First and foremost, the authors wish to thank the staff of the National Archives for patient, helpful and courteous service in making accessible the files of the Committee on Public Information and the archives of contemporary federal agencies

They also wish to express their profound gratitude for the many and unsurpassed research facilities afforded them by the Library of Congress, including study cubicles, periodicals, newspapers, and books of the various collections.

To the following institutions a debt is acknowledged in the writing of this book, either directly or indirectly the Hoover War Library, Stanford University, Carnegie Endowment for International Peace and its library, Washington, D.C.; the Public Library, Washington, D C ; Libraries of the Army War College and of the Army Industrial College, Division of Cultural Relations, Department of State, Signal Corps, U.S.A ; Navy Department Recruiting Service, and Princeton University Library.

Participants in the activities described in the following pages who have been of assistance, through personal interviews in a majority of cases, are: George Creel, Josephus Daniels, Carl Byoir, E. S. Rochester, Captain Henry T. Hunt, Wallace Irwin, Eugene White, Lee B. Wood, Lawrence Rubel, and Judge Charles E. Douglas.

The writers wish to thank especially Professor Harold D. Lasswell for his active interest in this study, and the Princeton University Press for its constant understanding and help. For unfailing editorial cooperation and advice the authors are deeply indebted to Mr. and Mrs. Datus C. Smith, Jr. To Miss Bess Glenn of The National Archives the authors are indebted for her assistance in indexing this volume.

Many specific personal acknowledgments appear elsewhere in the book.

The National Archives,
Washington, D.C.
September 15, 1939.

J. R. M. AND C. L.

TABLE OF CONTENTS

Preface   vii

Part I. The Creel Committee and Its Background

1. The American Mind in Wartime   3
2. The Coming of Censorship   19
3. George Creel's Improvisation   48

Part II. "Holding Fast the Inner Lines"

4 Fighting with Printer's Ink· Words and Pictures   77
5. Broadcasting Before Radio: Four-Minute Men   113
6. A Barrage of Film· Mobilizing the Movies   131
7. Clio Joins the Colors: Scholars and the Schools   158
8. The People's War: Labor and Capital   187
9 Deleting the Hyphen: the Foreign-Born   213

Part III. Advertising Our Mission Abroad

10. "The Fight for the Mind of Mankind"   235
11. Crossing the Enemy Lines   248
12. In the Land of the Neutrals   263
13. Educating Our Comrades in Arms   285
14. The CPI and Russian Chaos   300
15. Below the Rio Grande   321

Part IV. The Future

16. Blueprint for Tomorrow's CPI   337

Notes   349

Index   359

LIST OF ILLUSTRATIONS

	PAGE
Fight or Buy Bonds	*frontispiece*
Don't Talk	14
The Censorship Board	44
George Creel Shortly Before the War	45
Three Creel Title Pages	58
Spies and Lies	64
Halt the Hun	65
Army Censorship Order on Tanks	87
Battle News Manufactured in New York	90
Stopped, Delayed, or Otherwise Dealt With	91
Two Phases of the "Official Bulletin"	95
The German Idea	98
A Famous Gibson Drawing	103
Bulletin for Cartoonists	108
Slide Announcing Four-Minute Speakers	114
Four-Minute Men Bulletin	119
The Movie Industry Joins Up	133
The Fate of "The Caillaux Case"	148
The Most Famous of the "Hate" Pictures	149
Four CPI Pamphlets	163
Bachelor of Atrocities	169
Not Too Academic	174
National School Service	182
For Mobilizing the Nation's Schools	184
Beware of German Traps	192
Why Does Drifting from Job to Job . . .	192
Let Us Remember Russia	194
Help from the National Association of Manufacturers	204
The Hand That Threatens	207

Dr. Uncle Sam   207
The Cartoon That Aroused Creel's Anger   212
Hyphenated Americans Are Asked to Buy   220
Germans Learn How the War Came to America   227
An American "Paper Bullet"   250
To Encourage German Defeatism   254
Invitation to German Deserters   260
Special Inducements Were Sometimes Needed   270
Agent's Report from Santander   273
Releasing Propaganda-Laden Balloons   296
"Shoulder Arms" and "America's Answer"   297
The German-Bolshevik Conspiracy   318
One Blueprint for Tomorrow's CPI   344

Part I

THE CREEL COMMITTEE AND ITS BACKGROUND

"It is given to every man either to eat his cake or to keep his cake, but it is given to no man to do both. A country can choose to be a great military power, and to remain in peace times constantly upon a military footing, subtracting from education and religion and progress all along the line the cost of it; or it can choose to be a great democracy of hope and peace and progress, and knowing well beforehand that if it chooses to be this latter, it must muddle and suffer infinitely in men and money when war is forced upon it. Each nation can choose one of these two things. Nobody can choose both."—Senator *John Sharp Williams in a letter to George Creel, April 4, 1918.*

Chapter 1

THE AMERICAN MIND IN WARTIME

WE had gone to war We had decided to send our boys over to France to save democracy. But even as indignation against Germany had surged higher and higher in those last tense days before 3·12 a.m , April 6, 1917, no one could say just what the American people would do after their eloquent leader had urged them into war

The great majority of Americans, it seemed, wanted to fight, but people wondered anxiously how large and how determined the minority might be Minorities are dangerous when the fate of civilization is hanging in the balance. Who felt quite easy with Senator LaFollette and his "little group of wilful men" still in Congress? How could we count on the millions of Germans, Austrians, Hungarians, Poles, Russians and other "aliens in our midst"? Wasn't there something very disquieting in the widely quoted opinion of Dr Aleš Hrdlicka that the Melting Pot had failed to melt? How many people still believed there was such a thing as being too proud to fight? How many remembered the President's statement that there was no essential difference in the expressed war aims of the belligerents? What of enemy spies, of whom there were said to be 100,000 or more at large, and their allies, the pacifists, Socialists, and labor agitators? What about the success of Wilson's campaign slogan, "He kept us out of war"? What about warnings against entanglement in Europe's quarrels which still echoed in countless homes?

And what, above all, about the unknown thousands of Americans who might not feel very strongly one way or the other but thought Europe was a long way off and might find it too much bother to make the sacrifices which a modern war demands of the entire population?

[3]

We had pledged "our lives, our fortunes, and our sacred honor," but could we fulfill that pledge? When a peaceful nation, jealous of individual liberty and proud of its freedom from militarism, attempted to mobilize its men, money, resources, and emotions for one mighty effort, even a rather small minority could bring disaster "Widespread cooperation" was not good enough when the nation's life was at stake Nothing less than complete solidarity would do

America was not unified when war was declared. The necessary reversal of opinion was too great to be achieved overnight. The agonizing question in official Washington, the question on which hung the fate of the country's entire wartime effort, was whether the inner lines at home would hold as effectively as the lines in France

The Committee on Public Information was assigned the staggering task of "holding fast the inner lines." The story of how it fulfilled that mission is a dramatic record of vigor, effectiveness, and creative imagination. The Committee was America's "propaganda ministry" during the World War, charged with encouraging and then consolidating the revolution of opinion which changed the United States from anti-militaristic democracy to an organized war machine. This work touched the private life of virtually every man, woman, and child, it reflected the thoughts of the American people under the leadership of Woodrow Wilson, and it popularized what was for us a new idea of the individual's relation to the state.

President Wilson created the Committee on Public Information by executive order dated April 13, 1917, and appointed George Creel as civilian chairman, with the Secretaries of State, War, and Navy as the other members. Mr Creel assembled as brilliant and talented a group of journalists, scholars, press agents, editors, artists, and other manipulators of the symbols of public opinion as America had ever seen united for a single purpose It was a gargantuan advertising agency the like of which the country had never known, and the breathtaking scope of its activities was not to be equalled until the rise of totalitarian dictatorships after the war. George Creel, Carl

[4]

Byoir, Edgar Sisson, Harvey O'Higgins, Guy Stanton Ford, and their famous associates were literally public relations counsellors to the United States government, carrying first to the citizens of this country and then to those in distant lands the ideas which gave motive power to the stupendous undertaking of 1917-1918

Whether or not one accepts the interpretation of Charles Beard, the Nye Committee, Walter Millis, or someone else, it is clear that *ideas*, for whatever reason they were held, took us into the war and kept alive the fiercely burning fires of industrial and military and naval activity. Without the driving force of those ideas there would have been no A.E.F. in France, no destroyer squadron at Queenstown, no sub-chasers in the Mediterranean, no "Bridge of Ships" spanning the Atlantic, no Liberty Bonds, no Draft Law, no food rationing, no coal shortage, no seizure of railroads and ammunition plants, no abridgment of free speech and free press

And it was the Committee on Public Information that both mobilized and expressed the thoughts and emotions supporting these extraordinary dislocations of peaceful life The story of its career holds a strategic place in the history of the war, and it presses for current attention as America anxiously considers what it will do in the current European War.

Through every known channel of communication the Committee carried straight to the people its message of Wilson's idealism, a war to end war, and America to the rescue of civilization "Fireside chats" via radio did not in that day give national leaders the present easy avenue of approach to the family circle, but the Committee was nevertheless able to address itself directly to the minds and hearts of Americans, however isolated they might appear to be from the main stream of martial activity.

If they included misinformation in their complex of ideas about the war, at least it was misinformation shared with them by editors and college professors, the country's greatest intellectual and spiritual leaders, and by public figures in the shadow of the White House History had not yet separated true and false, and many things were believed in 1918 that scholars would deny today. But there was little expressed difference of opinion. It was illegal to express dissent of certain kinds, but for most people no law was necessary. The Committee on Public Information had done its work so well that there was a burning eagerness to believe, to conform, to feel the exaltation of joining in a great and selfless enterprise.

When facts were known or convictions held by any considerable number of the people they were common to all—to simple folk on the edge of the prairie, to department store clerks and subway guards in the metropolis, to lumbermen deep in the forests of the Northwest, and to maintenance men set down in squalid huts along a desert right-of-way. Americans stood close together in the comradeship of battle in 1917 and 1918, and it was largely the doing of the Committee on Public Information.

Consider the case of one mid-western family. They lived on a quarter-section of farmland a dozen miles from the railroad, telegraph, and postoffice. The nearest daily newspaper was published at the far end of the next county, seventy-five miles away. No through road passed near their farm, they had seen pavement only a few times in their lives, and they had no phone. Normally they paid scant attention to public affairs. Their only aim in life, so it seemed, was to bring in the golden harvest.

Yet when this simple, uneducated family, far from urban centers of information and five thousand miles across sea and land from the battlefields of France, sat down to a threshers' supper in the summer of 1918 they were more conscious of the World War than many more literate people had been of any war since fighting began.

And every item of war news they saw—in the county weekly, in magazines, or in the city daily picked up occasionally in the general store—was not merely officially approved information but precisely the same kind that millions of their fellow citizens were getting at the same moment. Every war story had been censored somewhere along the line—at the source, in transit, or in the newspaper office in accordance with "voluntary" rules issued by the CPI. The same mimeograph machines furnished most of the Washington news, and the same cable censorship had passed all items from abroad.

Patriotic advertising in all of these papers had been prepared by the CPI, and even commercial announcements had a patriotic twist which had been suggested by someone in the Committee office Cartoons were those inspired by the Committee staff At the state fair the family viewed war exhibits under Committee sponsorship, and the movies at the county seat began with one of the Committee's patriotic films and paused briefly for oratory by one of the Committees Four-Minute Men, who had gained his ideas for the talk from the Committee's "suggestions "

At the township school the children saw war photographs issued by the Committee, recited war verse from a Committee brochure, learned current events from a Committee newspaper, studied war maps with a teacher who had acquired her knowledge of international politics through the Committee's pamphlets, and when they came home at night bore more literature for their parents

The postoffice bulletin board was adorned with copies of the Committee's *Official Bulletin*, and posters in the general store and on telephone poles up and down the countryside were those designed by the Committee's artists, the same pictures appearing again and again with the persuasive insistence of modern cigarette advertising Both the children and their mother read war stories suggested or actually briefed by the Committee. On Sunday the pastor thanked Providence for blessings that had been listed by one of the Committee's copywriters, and prayed for achievement of an objective glowingly described by another. When the Ladies' Aid held its monthly meeting, the program was that suggested by the Committee's division of women's war work, and the speaker came bearing credentials from the Committee's speakers' bureau He delivered an address which he thought was his own but which actually paraphrased one of the Committee pamphlets, and his

[7]

talk was illustrated with lantern slides which the Committee had prepared.

Some people in the community were of foreign extraction, some unable to read English, but that did not make them ineligible to join the crusade against despotism, in fact it seemed to single them out for special attention. Their foreign-language newspapers carried translations of the same news the rest of the community was reading in English, and many of the pamphlets were also given in a number of tongues. Some of these people belonged to the Friends of German Democracy, others to the John Ericsson League of Patriotic Service, the American-Hungarian Loyalty League, and so on, according to their several countries of origin—and almost all of these groups were either openly or secretly supported by the CPI.

Everyone wore the same patriotic buttons, put up the same window stickers, passed the same clichés, knew the same rumors The wool buyer who visited the various farms in the spring had carried a little pamphlet, which the Committee had designed especially for travelling men, enabling him to speak with the exciting authority of inside information, and everyone assumed that the stories must be true because salesmen who stopped at the general store brought with them the same thrilling narrative

Uniformity of testimony is convincing

And testimony seemed nearly uniform not only in the heart of the Great Plains country but throughout the nation. Dissenters merely intensified the vigor with which their fellow citizens presented the prevailing view of the war, of international morality, and of world politics Scholars will long discuss the precise division of "real opinion" in America when war was declared, but there can be no uncertainty regarding articulate opinion as it was expressed in newspapers, books, pamphlets, cartoons, and public addresses—it was overwhelmingly and wholeheartedly on the side of the Allies and in favor of our belligerence.

Search for the reasons behind this has engaged the energy of many brilliant investigators, and they offer varying interpretations. But all seem agreed that in the years of our neutrality, as the calendar turned through 1915, 1916, and the first fatal months of 1917, there was a steady and progressively rapid solidifying of opinion around the concepts which President Wilson was to present in their familiar aspect only as the country stood at the very brink of the abyss These concepts of a "War to End War" and "Make the World Safe for Democracy" had taken form slowly at first, but as our actual entry neared there was a coagulation of opinion, and this process was hastened by many forces, such as economic interest, Anglo-American friendship, British propaganda, exposure of German plots in America, the uplifting sweep of President Wilson's eloquence, America's Big Brother complex, the hope of making a better world, and so on

Many agencies were at work to bring more and ever more American citizens within the magnetic field of the war spirit. The National Security League, the American Defense Society, the Navy League, General Leonard Wood, many of the leaders of the League to Enforce Peace—all these and many more undertook deliberate campaigns for military preparedness. Most of them also favored war at least a year before our entry.

Almost from the invasion of Belgium in 1914, a growing number of Americans believed that France and England were fighting our battle These people set about converting their fellow citizens Friends of Germany, anglophobes, pacifists, and isolationists attempted to check this movement, but they lost ground steadily. More and more Americans came to believe that defeat of the Allies would mean eventual doom for democracy everywhere, many feared actual and immediate armed invasion or at least bombardment of North America Special economic interests both nurtured and exploited these fears, and every sensational development in Germany's submarine warfare, in the occupation of Belgium, or in the inept German plotting in this country was used by all of the war groups—the idealists as well as the special interests—to gain

[9]

new supporters for their contention that German military might must be struck to earth.

Through it all rang the voice of Woodrow Wilson, a clear call to the American people, lifting them to heights of spiritual excitement from which they were not to descend until the back-to-normalcy days of President Harding

When war was declared there was a sharp intensification of feeling, a speeding up in the process of unifying opinion, but there was not the sharp break with the past that we sometimes think of From August 1914 to April 1917 a host of disparate groups had carried the burden of propaganda and education which the Committee on Public Information assumed under George Creel when war actually came.

The Committee performed an almost incredible task in the marshalling of opinion, in building strong walls of national solidarity. But it is important to realize that the Committee was no inner clique imposing unwanted views on the general public. Scarcely an idea may be found in all the work of the CPI that was not held by many Americans before war was declared The Committee was representative of the articulate majority in American opinion.

What the Committee did do was to codify and standardize ideas already widely current, and to bring the powerful force of the emotions behind them It is true that the whipping-in of stragglers through application of social pressure held a vitally important place in the work, but the greatest effort was directed toward vitalizing convictions already held and toward developing the will to fight for ideas already familiar.

The job was to keep the Wilson program before the people and to make it seem like something worth dying for.

With the CPI viewed in this light, George Creel's selection for the post of chairman was natural He had been a Wilson man "before 1912"; for years he had expressed in the language of front-page journalism very much the same sort of thing that President Wilson expressed in the language of the library and the pulpit. Mr. Creel has given the authors his own report on the reasons for his selection:

[10]

"As editor of the *Rocky Mountain News* in Denver, I advocated Woodrow Wilson's nomination as early as 1911, and had correspondence with him throughout his first administration. Going to New York in 1913, I played a rather important part in the 1916 campaign, contributing syndicated articles to the press and also publishing *Wilson and the Issues*. After the election he asked me to come to Washington as a member of his official family, but my finances would not permit acceptance of the offer When we entered the war on April 6, 1917, and the papers carried the news that some rigid form of censorship would be adopted, I wrote a letter of protest to the President in which I explained to him that the need was for expression not repression, and urged a campaign that would carry our war aims and peace terms not only to the United States, but to every neutral country, and also in England, France, and Italy As for censorship, I insisted that all proper needs could be met by some voluntary methods. He sent for me and after approving my proposal, drafted me to act as active chairman No other person was considered for the place."

Mr. Creel suggests here not only his political kinship with Wilson but also his determination to carry out the work of the CPI along Wilsonian lines—by bold appeal to the people

Two methods of handling public opinion were available to the United States. An ironclad censorship could be established, with a great bureaucracy attempting to judge the "loyalty" of every item in every newspaper, every word in every conversation—to probe, in fact, into the innermost thoughts of every citizen. On the other hand, a policy could be adopted whereby the hand of censorship was held back but the channels of communication were literally choked with official, approved news and opinion, leaving little freeway for rumor or disloyal reports.

George Creel took the affirmative line.

Consistently to the end of the war, he placed his faith in a censorship which was at least technically voluntary. The newspapers accepted this censorship, though they also contributed in full measure the expected criticism of Mr. Creel himself He was one of the most disliked and traduced members of the national government while the war was in progress, and the 1918 caricature of him carries over to the present day.

This picture is unfair, as the reader will discover, but Mr Creel was in a sense hoist with his own petard. For he, more than any other one man aside from the President, helped to produce the 1917 temper in which the tossing about of symbols became a substitute for an intellectual transaction, and in which people thought together and thought in stereotypes.

Truth, George Creel knew, is the first casualty in war, but he shared with his chief and with millions of their fellow citizens the hope that "this war will be different." As the story of the CPI unfolds it will be clear in how many ways George Creel attempted to protect truth. But the emotional climate in which Ora Buffington, a Pennsylvania attorney, urged the CPI to import for public exhibition some of the Belgian children whose hands had been cut off was the very climate that Mr. Creel had to maintain for the support of President Wilson's most ennobling political ideals.

The CPI hoped that it could direct the nation's emotional energy into channels of constructive patriotism, not hysteria, but it was not always successful Though only too well aware of how hysteria begins and grows, the Committee was forced to deal constantly with the material of panic, fear, and intolerance.

Preposterous or frightening evidences of "national jitters" were continually received

Joseph P. Tumulty, the President's secretary, had been imprisoned as a German spy . . . he had been shot. . . .

Five Americans, former prisoners of war with their tongues cut out, were in a hospital ship lying in the Potomac. . . .

The assistant to the chairman of the U.S. Shipping Board protested against the cover of the *Hog Island News*, a shipbuilder's house organ, which showed a huge porker carrying an American flag—he thought it might be used for German propaganda. . . .

Newspapers reported a TEUTON PLAN TO TORTURE CAPTURED SAMMIES . . .

U-boat captains were believed to have landed on the Atlantic Coast and then to have made their way inland, poisoning wells en route. . . .

Suspected pro-Germans were lynched . . .

A report was syndicated that a man in a training camp near Chillicothe, Ohio, had never received any mail Shortly after this publication, he received 1,200 letters, nineteen special-delivery messages, and fifty-four packages. . . . "As it happens," the tired postmaster reported to Washington, "—— can neither read or write He is not just right and was not accepted by the army but refuses to leave. . . ."

All of this was socially unwholesome It was also dangerous During the Spanish-American War, as at other times, civilian hysteria had forced the United States to change its disposition of forces and threatened strategical plans. But the CPI was caught in a dilemma. It was forced to return again and again to the methods of arousing opinion which brought the very atmosphere of hate and fear which might endanger national safety and was surely incompatible with the consecrated mission on which President Wilson was leading the country.

George Creel has been charged with being too eager, too impetuous and flamboyant. Each of these adjectives is properly applied to him. Evidence is abundant, however, that countless citizens wished public opinion to be whipped to higher and higher fury The independent patriotic groups such as the National Security League, perhaps jealous of government interference with private enterprise, frequently charged the CPI with malingering Even more sober observers feared public apathy and called ever and again for more dramatic action

In August 1917, for instance, Grosvenor Clarkson, secretary (later director) of the Council of National Defense, wrote to a number of prominent men, calling attention to lack of war enthusiasm and asking their opinions Clarkson sent copies of the replies to Creel

"The Mood for Spy Hunts"
A Poster Displayed in Boston by a Military Intelligence Office

Roy W. Howard of the Scripps papers and United Press, who had just returned from the Pacific Coast, concurred in Clarkson's judgment and said: "This weakness must be remedied before the nation will go to war with its heart as well as its hands and feet." Frederick Dixon, editor of the *Christian Science Monitor* "The country is not awake . . invaluable time is being wasted." Frank Cobb, editor of the *New York World*. "There are plenty of soap-boxes and some of them might well be occupied by men who believe in the United States and in the justice of its cause." R. J. Cuddihy, treasurer of Funk and Wagnalls. "The churches of the country should be counted on to reach the spiritual and emotional side of our people, and . . . this is the side that must be fully awakened."

Typical of many letters that came to Creel through all the months of the war was one from S. H. Church, president of Carnegie Institute of Technology. In January 1918 he wrote that the CPI must emphasize "in season and out of season, the fact that we are engaged in a bloody and remorseless war with the most pitiless and despicable nation that has ever attacked the peace and dignity of civilization, and that this high note of raging battle ought to be sounded throughout the world until we shall receive a definite assurance that peace is within our grasp and upon our own terms."

The "high note of raging battle," however, produced not only the will to fight Germany but also the mood for spy hunts. Spies there undoubtedly were, but their number was infinitesimal compared with the excitement they caused. After the war John Lord O'Brian, head of the War-Emergency Division of the Department of Justice, said that "No other one cause contributed so much to the oppression of innocent men as the systematic and indiscriminate agitation against what was claimed to be an all-pervasive system of German espionage." Captain Henry T. Hunt, head of the Military Intelligence counter-espionage section during the war, has told the authors that in addition to unfounded spy stories innocently launched there were many started with the apparent object of removing or inconveniencing political, business, or social rivals. As an illustration of the complexity of charges and counter-charges, he reports that on one occasion two of his own men were taken into custody by the Department of Justice, while seeking to determine the loyalty of the headwaiter in a Washington hotel.

The nervousness illustrated by this incident was exploited and turned to devious uses Professor S H. Clark of the Department of Public Speaking at the University of Chicago, for instance, wrote to Creel· "Many public men and many of our prominent newspapers who have always bitterly fought socialism, the I.W W.'s, and even labor unions, are taking advantage of the present crisis in an effort not purely patriotic to squelch all of these more or less radical organizations without regard to the effect upon the future of our country, to say nothing of the effect in the present war "

One man who emphatically agreed with this was the famous I.W.W. agitator, Big Bill Haywood, who wrote to Creel from Cook County Jail· "Perhaps some day when the pendulum swings back, when a war-mad world can assume something of a normal attitude of thought, when the ideas and ideals of a New Freedom will not be misinterpreted, I may ask you to do something for us I still hate autocracy and Russian Oligarchy from the bottom of my heart, but even more the Industrial Oligarchy so rapidly developing in this country— which must be fought after the World War if democracy is to endure."

From the very opposite end of the social and economic scale—from Thomas W Lamont, the Morgan partner who had just purchased the *New York Evening Post*—Creel received yet another letter showing appreciation of what happens in wartime: "There is altogether too great a tendency to call people names just because they happen to talk intelligently on certain topics. I have heard people dubbed Socialists just because they happened to be students of sociology and, looking forward, were convinced that in the future labor would have to have an even squarer deal than it has had in the past. I have heard other people called pro-Germans just because they expressed the hope that the war would not last forever. . . . I think we are apt, in time of war, to fall into a mood of more or less intolerance, if the other fellow doesn't agree with us."

But perhaps the most interesting of all the letters which came to George Creel on this subject was that from the wealthy but radical lawyer and publicist, Amos Pinchot, whose political position lay somewhere between Big Bill Haywood and Thomas Lamont. He wrote

"Has Wilson changed? Is he going back on himself and on us? Has he seen a new vision of a world peace, founded on things un-American, based on old-world imperialist aggression, which he so lately condemned? Have we got to die tomorrow for principles that yesterday the President told us were wrong?

"What has changed Wilson? Who has put it over on him?

"We have got to remember that before we went into the war, the Administration, and the liberal press, the Scripps papers, the Cloverleaf syndicate, the N E A, and even much of the reactionary press, for two solid years carried on an anti-war propaganda They were pro-Ally, but they said that we had no business in it At the end of this period the President went to the country on the issue that he kept us out of war—and won. . . .

"Considering our approaches to the war, the President's own attitude, his distinct downright repudiation of the Allies' annexation policies, the anti-imperialist feeling in America, it seems fairly evident that even for Wilson the task of swinging the public into line for the present war aims of the Allies would be too big a task, even if it were a right and necessary course

"If the President attempts it he will fail. He will fall as an American leader, and fall farther and harder than any modern liberal statesman "

There is no evidence of a reply from Creel, but from many other records we know what he would have said He would

[17]

have granted the change in the President's attitude toward the war, granted the perils of entanglement in European politics, granted the dangers to democracy which militarism had brought to this country. But he would have said that we were fighting not for Europe's war aims but for Wilson's, and that the hope of a new world, of universal democracy, and of permanent peace made any temporary concessions richly justified.

Creel did not, however, push from his mind the knowledge of how "patriotism" was being turned to selfish uses, and how much work remained to be done for democracy at home. In March 1918 he wrote to Joseph E. Davis "I shall support every necessary measure directed to the supreme end of defeating . . the unholy combination of autocracy, militarism, and predatory capitalism which rules Germany and threatens liberty and self-government everywhere. . . [But] I ask and expect only support of those who believe that for the sake of political liberty and social progress, America must win this war while it consolidates at home every position won from the forces of reaction and political bigotry"

George Creel, as Woodrow Wilson, faced the tragic dilemma of a war on behalf of democracy In the record of the Committee on Public Information one may find evidence of their success or lack of success in meeting it. This book can present only part of the evidence, but the files of the CPI contain some of the most important material of American history. For it is not only George Creel that is to be judged but the entire national policy of a democracy at war The problem boils down to this· Can any wartime compromise be "temporary"? Can modern war, a war of populations, be waged without permanent loss of some of the things for which America entered the World War in 1917?

Every observer will have his own answer to these questions, but no one can afford to evade them

Chapter 2

THE COMING OF CENSORSHIP

A MERICA went under censorship during the World War
without realizing it. Debate was energetic and inspiring
while it lasted, but after the opponents of censorship
had won a single major engagement in the campaign they
thought the enemy had retired from the field They were
wrong The enemy quietly occupied the abandoned positions
and then, at a convenient opportunity, swarmed into defenseless territory behind the lines

An account of these maneuvers is essential to an appreciation of the CPI, for though the Committee's chief function
was to distribute affirmative propaganda it was likewise intimately concerned with the negative phases of public opinion
management—with suppression of speech or publication inimi-
cal to the doctrines for which America believed it was fighting.
The fact that the censorship power was employed with moderation does not detract from its significance in American history If the Administration had wished, it might have imposed
an almost complete censorship on the utterances and publications of all Americans during the war

"If the Administration had wished" really means "if George
Creel had wished," for in censorship as in affirmative propaganda he held the key. Knowledge of the political and emotional background of the Espionage Act of June 15, 1917, thus
sharpens understanding of the later work of the CPI.

As interpreted by the courts, the Espionage Act pressed hard
against the limits of constitutionality set by the First Amendment. Minority critics asserted in 1918, as more will grant
today, that in its final form the act violated the guaranty of
free speech and free press established in the Bill of Rights, but

[19]

a unanimous decision of the Supreme Court in 1919 denied the claim.

Even with the Espionage Act on the books, as well as the later Trading-with-the-Enemy Act of October 6, 1917, and the so-called "Sedition Act" of May 16, 1918, the Committee on Public Information lacked the authority for censorship enforcement, as that power rested with the Department of Justice and the Post Office Department. But both through official liaison and through Mr Creel's persuasive powers of personal influence the Committee held a position of strategic importance Mr Creel was officially a member of the Censorship Board, and his contact with the Department of Justice was continuous. He enjoyed the fullest cooperation of Military Intelligence, Naval Intelligence, and of certain Post Office officials R. L. Maddox, chairman of the Censorship Board, was in the most intimate relationship to Mr. Creel throughout the period, and the intelligence branches of the two fighting arms looked to the CPI for leadership and direction in many matters pertaining to civilian censorship. Contact with government offices gave still other means of direct and indirect pressure, all supported by law

Without specific powers of enforcement, the CPI thus enjoyed censorship power which was tantamount to direct legal force, although this was energetically denied by the Committee during the war. The CPI insisted that it was merely an intermediary between law-enforcement bodies and the people The Committee's representatives and agents did not make arrests—not often did they even threaten—but any individual or publication failing to play the game of secrecy and patriotism according to wartime standards could be handed over to one of the other agencies for appropriate action.

Authority for this action came in the first place from the history-making Espionage Act. The law went on the books practically without public notice, and with the majority of the public ignorant of the authority for civilian censorship which it contained Weeks of violent debate preceded this anticlimax, however, and the story is revealing both for an understanding

[20]

of the CPI and for an appreciation of the issue which will confront America in the event of our participation in another war.

On February 5, 1917, four days after Germany had resumed unrestricted submarine warfare and two days after President Wilson electrified America by telling a joint session of Congress that passports had been handed to Ambassador von Bernstorff, a bill was introduced in the House and Senate "to define and punish espionage." This particular bill was to die with the lame duck session of the 64th Congress on March 4, but it was destined to make history through its legacy to the new session

This measure introduced in February 1917 is worth attention for its hint of coming innovation in American law and for its indication of how the lines of debate were to be drawn when we were actually at war.

At the beginning of 1917 America had no law on the books permitting the federal government to interfere seriously with the rights of free speech and free press True, there was a 1911 statute forbidding improper acquisition and communication of information relating to facilities of national defense, and this was useful in dealing with actual enemy agents But there were no means of controlling the utterances of people who might not be actual spies or traitors but nevertheless were regarded as extremely dangerous in the existing national emergency—pacifists, Socialists, German-Americans reluctant to take up arms against the Fatherland, agitators for Irish independence, and plain well-meaning people who merely liked to indulge in the traditional American activity of belaboring the "guv'ment."

The First Amendment of the Constitution says that Congress shall make no law "abridging the freedom of speech or of the press; or the right of the people peaceably to assemble and to petition the government for a redress of grievances " But if these popular rights should be granted without any let or hindrance whatsoever, it appeared to many people that the national safety would be imperilled

More than a century earlier America had attempted regimentation of opinion through the famous Sedition Act of

1798, but the measure had been employed for political persecution, helping to bring about the defiant Virginia and Kentucky Resolutions, and in its unpopularity had been a factor in the Federalist overturn of 1800 The Sedition Act expired automatically in 1801, and now, as America moved inexorably toward a new war in the opening months of 1917, there were no legal means of suppressing speech or publication if the offending act fell much short of out-and-out trading in military secrets. Before America was finished with the World War, new laws would come into being which in certain respects exceeded in severity the hated measure of 1798. And the first steps were taken in this direction while we were still at peace

On February 5, 1917, Lee S. Overman, Democrat of North Carolina, introduced in the Senate, and Edwin Yates Webb, also a Democrat of North Carolina and chairman of the House Judiciary Committee, introduced in the House, similar bills "to define and punish espionage." One purpose was to modernize the phraseology of the 1911 statute (for instance to cover invisible writing and spying from airplanes), but in sections 2 and 3 may be found the first shadowy suggestion of a new kind of restriction—new at least since an angry populace had swept the Federalists from office in 1800 and had allowed the Sedition Act of 1798 to die an unmourned death

In the Webb-Overman bill as originally introduced life imprisonment was ordered for anyone who in wartime and without lawful authority should "collect, record, publish, or communicate" certain broadly defined types of military information "of such a nature as is calculated to be, or might be, directly or indirectly, useful to the enemy." And, more important, the same drastic penalty was to pay for the crime of wartime communication or publication of false reports or statements, "or reports or statements likely or intended to cause disaffection in, or to interfere with the success of, the military or naval forces of the United States "

Senator Overman's bill was referred to his own committee, and on February 8 was reported out with "amendments," which consisted of thirteen other bills relating to passports, internment, neutrality, and other problems arising out of America's tense relations with Germany This omnibus measure passed the Senate February 20, and two days later hearings were held by the House Judiciary Committee.

Norman Thomas, pastor of the East Harlem Church, New York, appeared before the committee on behalf of the American Union Against Militarism, which represented a considerable body of Socialist and pacifist opinion. Mr. Thomas was not impressed with the assurance, frequently given by supporters of the bill, that sweeping powers should be granted but that they would not be employed against essentially loyal citizens. He said. "It [the bill] certainly could be used to muzzle such conscientious objectors as the Quakers and other good souls, although treason would be the last thing to enter their minds."

Criticism was also offered by Dr Robert L. Hale, instructor in economics at Columbia University, by John D Moore, national secretary of the Friends of Irish Freedom, and by Arthur E Holder, former president of the Iowa State Federation of Labor and at the time Washington lobbyist of the American Federation of Labor. Charles T. Halloran quoted newspaper interviews with the President's secretary, Joseph P Tumulty, in an attempt to persuade Congressmen that this was not an "Administration bill"—i.e. that they could oppose or amend it without fearing White House reprisals Chairman Webb's reply made it clear that although amendment was expected the Department of Justice was behind the bill.

Nevertheless, the Webb-Overman bill, though passed in the Senate, did not come to a vote in the House As the old Congress ended at noon on March 4 the question of censorship and control of opinion was still unsettled

On April 2, the very day on which President Wilson delivered his War Message to the joint session of the 65th Congress, Representative Webb introduced a new bill which, after nine and a half weeks of public and legislative debate and a checkered career of amendment and counter-amendment, became the law of the land An identical measure was introduced in the Senate by Charles A. Culberson, Democrat of Texas and chairman of the Senate Judiciary Committee of which Senator Overman was one of the most prominent and active members The purpose was "To punish acts of interference with the foreign relations, the neutrality, and the foreign commerce of the United States; to punish espionage, and better to enforce the criminal laws of the United States, and for other purposes."

This new bill received public notice far exceeding that given to the earlier measure, which had received no discriminating public attention. That earlier bill, in the popular view, was merely an improved means of dealing with the 100,000 German spies who Senator Overman and many other people said were honeycombing our country, engaging in sabotage, espionage, and insidious propaganda It occurred to few, apparently, that the bill might have any effect on the speech or publication of loyal American citizens When the *Literary Digest* presented in its issue of March 10 a summary of press opinion of that earlier bill the caption was "To Make Us Spy-Proof and Bomb-Proof" and there was scarcely a suggestion of opposition to it The *Chicago Tribune* granted that there might be a great deal of nonsense in the talk of espionage, but only the *New York Evening Post*, owned by the liberal pacifist, Oswald Garrison Villard, was quoted as stressing the importance of freedom to criticize. In fact, the *Digest* said, the *Post's* Washington correspondent (presumably Mr. Villard himself) reported that the American Union Against Militarism was the only organization opposing the bill.

There is reason to believe that the new Espionage Bill would have encountered even less opposition than the old one if it had not been for a new and direct threat to the freedom of the press. This threat, at one time placed in section 4, Title I, of the bill, was opposed by natural newspaper desire for independence, but was advanced by a mounting tide of public excitement.

Patriotic hysteria had been rising during March, and both individuals and organizations which formerly had opposed either militarism or certain militaristic threats to traditional American procedure came to realize that in war—even a "People's War"—normal civil liberties must be curtailed. In some cases the former dissenters became convinced of the justice of the American cause, in others it was a hasty and undignified scramble for the bandwagon. But in either event uniformity of opinion was becoming more fashionable.

Back as early as the first week in February, immediately following the dismissal of Ambassador von Bernstorff, German-American organizations had commenced their eager professions of loyalty to the United States, and in the middle of the month it was reported that 50,000 citizenship applications had been received in a single day This movement continued, and C J Hexamer, president of the German-American National Alliance, pledged the support of his suspected organization if war should come, and was reported (inaccurately) to be forming German-American regiments to take the field against the Fatherland. Immediately after the declaration of war the *Literary Digest* reported that "unequivocal loyalty is the keynote of articles in the German-American press," though a certain hesitancy in discussing the President's War Message was noted in some cases.

The great wartime schism in the ranks of the Socialists did not occur until the middle of April, but all during March the press had carried stories reporting the conversion of individual Socialists who previously had opposed entrance into what they regarded as an imperialist war Certain pacifist groups, notably the flying squadron of speakers led by Chancellor-Emeritus David Starr Jordan of Stanford University, continued their energetic but futile efforts to stem the tide of war, and the Emergency Peace Federation was frequently in the news But heckling and sometimes mob violence were making the profession of pacifism more and more uncomfortable, at the same time that many onetime pacifists, through change of conviction, had "joined up" for the duration of the war, announcing that the surest way to peace lay through military victory for the just cause of the Allies.

Labor groups, many of which were eyed with suspicion because of their supposed disinclination to prosecute the "Capitalists' War," as agitators called it, were similarly eager to display their patriotism. The four Railroad Brotherhoods announced on March 10 that their threatened strike would be called off in the event of war.

Nicholas Murray Butler, president of Columbia University and director of the Carnegie Endowment for International Peace, became an advocate of the use of military force, and a few weeks later the Endowment suspended its normal activities and turned over its facilities and personnel to the government. The Committee on Public Information, incidentally, was one of the beneficiaries, receiving use of the Endowment's building rent free.

Even the churches joined the procession, making ready to effect their famous compromise between warfare and religion. The *Literary Digest* reported that on March 11, at the suggestion of the New York Federation of Churches, "War Sunday" was celebrated. The magazine said, "In flag-draped pulpits the pastors of New York, men of peace, sounded the call to arms "

The day before this warlike sabbath, a "council of war" was reported to have included such a strange assortment as Theodore Roosevelt, J P Morgan, and Billy Sunday, the diversity of their interests and attributes suggesting the importance of national solidarity

All of these and countless other indications that patriotic Americans were managing to forget minor differences and set aside petty insistence on individual rights helped make the ideas of the Espionage Bill seem reasonable and necessary. But possibly the most significant event in the chain of circumstances facilitating public acceptance of the Espionage Bill in the new Congress was a notorious Senate filibuster in the old one The filibuster was concerned with "armed neutrality," not censorship, but it takes an important place in the pattern of 1917 opinion relating to free speech.

On February 26 President Wilson asked Congress for authority to arm merchant ships for self-defense against submarines; he said he could order this without seeking legislative permission, but he wished to feel that Congress was behind him "in whatever it may become necessary for me to do." The Armed Ship Bill passed the House by the overwhelming vote of 403-13. But in the Senate it was talked to death. Senator Robert M. LaFollette, Sr., of Wisconsin led the filibuster. Talking against time, he and his handful of associates prevented passage by prolonging debate from the morning of February 28 until noon on March 4, when the 64th Congress came to an end. And this was in spite of the fact that Senator Hitchcock presented a statement of seventy-six Senators (more than three-fourths of the total) that they would approve the measure if only it could be brought to a vote.

President Wilson angrily called the filibusterers "a little group of wilful men, representing no opinion but their own," and said that they had "rendered the great government of the United States helpless and contemptible." On March 9 the President ordered the arming of the ships anyway, and the eleven men who had opposed this act of self-defense were subjected to bitter denunciation. Charges of treason were freely passed, and roar upon roar of approval greeted the Rev. Lyman P. Abbott when, in a patriotic mass-meeting sponsored in New York by the American Rights League, he called the eleven Senators "Germany's allies."

The general press was nearly unanimous in its excoriation of the offenders, and several state legislatures passed resolutions of rebuke. When Senator Stone (who admitted opposition but denied that he had engaged in filibuster) said "Many telegrams of applause have reached me," the New York Sun retorted, "No doubt, but were they written in English?"

On March 8 the Senate, by a 76-3 count, adopted cloture, providing that debate might be limited by a two-thirds vote. A chorus of approval came from the press. Means had been found to close the mouths of noisy dissenters.

Limitation of parliamentary debate is obviously very different from general censorship, but to the average American in 1917 it must have seemed all of a piece: the "thwarting of the national will" by a few long-winded orators illustrated the danger of allowing unlimited free speech, whether within or without the walls of Congress.

So much of America's articulate public opinion was thus friendly to the general idea of the espionage legislation—seemed, in fact, reconciled to its most sternly repressive measures—that the new bill, introduced after the President's War Message, might easily have become enacted into law without protest if it had not been for newspaper alarm at indications of a coming press censorship. Administrative departments of the government were already withholding information which the press thought it should have. On April 6 President Wilson authorized seizure of wireless establishments, and four days later Secretary of the Navy Daniels issued an appeal for voluntary censorship on news of ship movements. The newspapers of April 15 carried the story of establishment of the CPI which, as often as not, was regarded as merely a censorship bureau.

We noted in Chapter I how George Creel was dismayed at reports of the coming censorship. He was far from being the only journalist similarly alarmed. Editor & Publisher, most influential journal of the press world, said editorially in its issue of April 7: "It is becoming obvious that if the freedom of the press to usefully serve the nation is to be preserved, its preservation must be the work of the newspapermen themselves. The constitutional guarantee seems to weigh very lightly with some of our public servants."

Not everyone was so uncompromising, as many people believed censorship of some sort was inevitable and that the important thing was to ensure its intelligent administration. Thus the April 14 issue of Editor & Publisher carried a leading article by Frederick Roy Martin, assistant general manager of the Associated Press, urging that a "newspaperman should direct censorship," and the American Association of Teachers of Journalism adopted a resolution of the same import.

Memorials from individual editors and publishers and from various groups continued to reach Congress, however, and the American Newspaper Publishers Association adopted a resolution asserting that "the proposed legislation strikes at the fundamental rights of the people, not only assailing their freedom of speech but also seeking to deprive them of the means of forming intelligent opinion. . . . Its possible consequences in restricting liberty of the press are full of peril to free institutions."

The reason for this suddenly increased solicitude for the First Amendment may be found in the fact that the part of this bill dealing specifically with espionage, contained proposed legislation in sections 3 and 4, which newspapers interpreted as a potential threat to the freedom of the press. When a powerful minority in the Senate took the cue from the Administration that section 4 was too mild, and more than a score of attempts were made to amend it, a general hue and cry of alarm was raised in the press of the nation about its rights.

These amendments would be too detailed to examine individually, but one or two typical ones may be noticed. On April 19, Senator Cummins introduced an amendment which provided that the President was authorized to prescribe and promulgate reasonable rules and regulations "not abridging the freedom of speech or of the press, for the purpose of preventing the disclosure to the public, and thereby to the enemy" of movements of the nation's armed forces, or plans of military or naval operations A more drastic proposal was offered by Senator Kirby on May 9 "A press censorship is hereby established, for the period of the war, with the Secretaries of the Navy and War as directors thereof." They were empowered either jointly or singly to issue a written order and "summarily suspend' for thirty days any newspaper or magazine giving vital and prohibited military information.

The newspapers of course fought this sort of thing tooth and nail but—paradoxically enough—in June when the country became enveloped in the whirl and excitement of the First Liberty Loan and the Draft, neither the papers nor the readers seemed to know or care about the passage of the espionage legislation which became law on the 15th of that month. The outline of the tortuous course of this bill will be traced in the remaining pages of this chapter.

At the hearings before the House Judiciary Committee on April 12, the opponents of the bill were not of the sort to win the approval of patriotic Americans. They included Harry Weinberger of the Free-Speech League of America, Gilbert E Roe, onetime legal associate of Senator LaFollette; Arthur E Holder, the A F. of L lobbyist, Jane Addams, president of the Women's Peace Party of America, John Reed, identified in the press only as "war correspondent"; and John D Moore, secretary of the Friends of Irish Freedom.

Professor Horace A Eaton, chairman of the English Department at Syracuse University, told the Committee "I am wondering whether it would not be possible, since some of you gentlemen have already said so, to insert in the bill a definite phrase saying that it shall in no way infringe upon the civil rights granted to citizens of the United States under the Constitution" And Emily Green Balch, professor of civics at Wellesley College and in future years to become the founder of the Women's International League for Peace and Freedom, put the same thought more bluntly. "I want to see a war which is intended as a war for democracy . carried through without any Prussianizing here. . ."

In response to criticism such as Professor Eaton's, the Senate added a limiting amendment, which, however, was subjected in turn to a proviso of its own, the result at one stage being. "Provided, That nothing in this section shall be construed to limit or restrict, nor shall any regulation herein provided for limit or restrict, any discussion, comment, or criticism of the acts or policies of the government or its representatives, or the publication of the same; Provided, That no discussion, comment, or criticism shall convey information prohibited under the provisions of this section."

Even with this and other provisos, however, the newspapers were unsatisfied with the bill, and they continued their bombardment. Congressman William L. Igoe, St Louis Democrat, said "We are informed by the Attorney General that a large delegation of newspapermen conferred with him in regard to sections 2 and 3 and were satisfied with them." But on April 19, for instance, the *New York Times* said, under the head "SENATORS RIDDLE ESPIONAGE BILL"·

"It is becoming increasingly evident that the portion of the Administration which has fallen into bureaucratic ways is willing to override the provision of the Constitution concerning freedom of speech and the press in order to gratify prejudices." And again, the next day, the *Times* referred to "the Administration measure which has been construed as unduly limiting the freedom of the press," and declared, "Both the constitutionality and the public policy of the provision have been brought under a sustained fire from all parts of the country, and Senators on both sides of the aisle, both yesterday and today, directed that fire against the measure at close quarters."

On the following day the heading "SENATE MODIFIES ESPIONAGE BILL," covered a story reporting that "Even this amended provision to the minds of some Senators, carried lurking dangers to the liberties of the press. . . ." But the most impressive evidence of press reaction to the projected censorship came in the *Times* of Sunday, April 22, when a canvass of editorial opinion from many states was presented under the heading·

OPPOSE CENSORSHIP
AS NOW PROPOSED

The *San Francisco Chronicle* called the bill "the Russian method of excision" The *Los Angeles Times* termed it "a Kaiserism." It was attacked by the *St. Louis Globe-Democrat* on the grounds that it "would prevent proper criticism and keep people from knowing what they are entitled to know." The *Pittsburgh Post* said· "It behooves Congress to be on guard against members who have felt the smart of just criticism of the press and would be glad to make the censorship provision the vehicle for their spite." The *Philadelphia Public Ledger* declared "America will never submit to the suppression of information to which the people are plainly entitled." The

Hartford Courant reminded Congress that "the American people are not accustomed to wearing muzzles." And Creel's old paper, the *Rocky Mountain News* of Denver, warned that "If the National Administration insists upon a gag law in the name of press censorship it will be the first to suffer."

The *Seattle Post-Intelligencer* was a little more friendly "While a war is in progress little good can come from bushwhacking the men we have placed in positions of responsibility." And the *Baltimore Sun* took a moderate position. "It is better to have a law, drawn as definitely as possible, which will apply to all alike and do away with the temptation to print a piece of doubtful news in order to score a beat on a competitor, than no law at all." But the *Omaha World-Herald* spoke for the great majority when it said. "If there is anything sacred to the average American it is a free press, and any encroachment upon it is sure to be received with aversion."

But America was really in the war now. An American with the Canadians at Vimy Ridge had carried the stars and stripes into battle just a few days before, unofficially suggesting the untruth that it would not be long before our troops would invade France in force. On April 19, the anniversary of Paul Revere's Ride, "Wake Up America" parades were held all over the country, electrifying many who had been at least apathetic before. On April 21 the Balfour Mission arrived from England, and three days later saw New York's thrilling welcome to Viviani and Joffre, who was called the "hero of the Marne"

Simultaneously fear of spies and of non-conforming opinion was steadily rising. Allegedly careful histories of German machinations on American soil were being issued by a dozen presses, and it was generally believed that Germany had made pacifists and radicals serve an un-American cause. In the very week that Congress met to declare war the *Literary Digest* was reporting "Opponents of war against Germany are apparently by no means silenced. Pacifist petitions pour in upon Congressmen, anti-war advertisements fill pages of the newspapers, pacifist orators draw crowds, circulate handbills, and hamper recruiting." And the *New York World* added: "The real pacifists are

[32]

outnumbered by militarists in open sympathy with an enemy country"

At about the same time it was learned that the Emergency Peace Federation ("of morally obtuse women and their consorts," as a famous scholar described their membership) had transferred its pacifist energies from the unsuccessful effort against war to a campaign against conscription A little later newspaper readers learned that the Germans had planned a Negro insurrection in the South, and the Socialist Party "emergency convention" in St. Louis brazenly declared that the American people had been "plunged into this war by the trickery and treachery of the ruling class." Upton Sinclair, one of the apostate Socialists who broke with his party on the issue of war, was reported to have told the government that mines had been laid to inaugurate a reign of terror when conscription went into effect, and he had it on the authority of Emma Goldman that rioting would be "almost civil war" A cartoon in a United Mine Workers' publication, showing The People squeezed between the Kaiser and Allied capitalists, was widely reproduced, raising new fears of a labor revolt or, at the least, destructive sabotage.

The Eddystone Ammunition Plant had been blown up on April 10, apparently the terrifying result of design, not accident, and military guards at bridges, aqueducts, and other facilities throughout the country suggested the imminent occurrence of similar tragedies It is difficult to find a newspaper published in April 1917 that did not have on every other page some reference to the malevolent work of "the enemy within" Some of these stories were based on authentic facts regarding enemy activity, but more were purely imaginary.

The press itself was the most important agency in spreading fear of espionage, and at the same time was attempting to limit the provisions of the Espionage Bill This was clearly revealed somewhat later when two articles in a single issue of the *Literary Digest* were devoted, respectively, to an attack on George Creel and press censorship, and to an exciting exposé of the dark figures and darker deeds in "Treason's Twilight Zone," the *Digest* slanting the stories to show support for the press quotations in each case.

Apparent inconsistency of this sort was seized upon by supporters of the bill. No patriotic, law-abiding American need fear the Espionage Bill, they said; it was aimed only at the country's enemies. The press did not so interpret the press-censorship section, and a hardy band of legislators, Congressman Fiorello LaGuardia among them, retained skepticism regarding various parts of the bill.

As introduced, section 3, of the part of the bill on espionage, read "Whoever, in time of war, shall wilfully make or convey false reports or false statements with intent to interfere with the operation or success of the military or naval forces of the United States or to promote the success of their enemies; and whoever in time of war shall wilfully cause or attempt to cause disaffection in the military or naval forces of the United States shall be punished by imprisonment for not less than twenty years or for life."

Severity of the penalty is most noteworthy here, for the maximum under the hated Sedition Act of 1798 was $5,000 or five years or both, and the maximum for this offense under England's Defense of the Realm Act was £100 or six months

The vagueness of making "intent" the criterion of guilt was attacked by some of the legislative opponents of the bill, and also was an issue in many of the court cases under the act as finally passed, but this nicety went generally unnoticed in the newspaper press during the parliamentary phases of the debate

Far from contemplating tricky phraseology, the House Judiciary Committee claimed that the word "intent" had been included "to avoid making innocent acts criminal." The committee said: "The criminality of the act is made to depend upon the knowledge, intent, or reason to believe that the information obtained or transmitted concerning our national defense is to be used to the injury of the United States." But Congressman Martin B. Madden, Chicago Republican, spoke for the dissenters, as well as for fellow party members who feared a possible political use of the censorship power, when he said that the bill "affects the liberties of the people of the United States to an extent that they have never been affected before in all our history." To which Chairman Webb promptly replied that the bill was not quite so important as some people supposed: "I think it has been magnified somewhat by a lot of misinformation that has been printed about it in the newspapers, and they have created the impression that the committee or somebody was undertaking to unduly abridge the freedom of press and the freedom of speech."

All during May the debate surged back and forth with everyone eager for an espionage act to apply to the country's enemies but few people, apparently, believing that any part of the bill except the press-censorship section carried any threat to the civil liberties of the general population The standard case for the bill was presented in a speech of Congressman Dick Thompson Morgan, Oklahoma Republican, on May 2.

"Then let us approach this bill with the proper attitude of mind. The object is not to restrict an American citizen in any just right he has under the Constitution and laws of this nation On the other hand, it is to guard and protect those rights, to maintain the honor of the United States, . . . to conserve and protect our American free institutions and insure the perpetuation of the Nation. . .

"Now what is the source of this measure? It comes from three great departments of this government—from the Attorney General, the Secretary of War, and the Secretary of the Navy. .

"This is to be a criminal statute largely. Who is it to affect? The law-abiding citizen? Not at all. It is intended only to affect the criminal classes. . . . Here in the United States also are several thousand aliens, citizens of foreign nations. We have the right to assume that some of these aliens are unfriendly to the United States in the great struggle in which we are now engaged. Now, then, it is to control and subdue these criminal classes, these men who are unfriendly to the United States, these men who perhaps are not citizens and who would not hesitate to hinder our success in the war. I repeat, it is the

[35]

criminal classes that this act is intended to deter from crime, and to punish if they violate the law."

Lack of public comprehension of the Espionage Act is partly explained by the number of tremendous events clamoring for newspaper attention, and by the highly intricate parliamentary history of the bill. It is impossible to describe in a few words the tortuous path on which the measure proceeded through the legislative mill, but an indication of the difficulty encountered by newspaper readers (and apparently editors also) may be found in the relation between the House and Senate versions, and in the maneuvers relating to the press-censorship provisions of section 4.

With respect to the latter, one of the most interesting events took place on May 4 On that day, by a vote of 220-167, the House decided to eliminate section 4. Here, it would appear, was a smashing victory for the anti-censorship forces. Immediately, however, Congressman Warren Gard, Ohio Democrat ("taking advantage of empty seats," it was charged later), introduced a substitute section 4 which was adopted a few minutes later by a vote of 190-185.

The Gard Amendment provided "During any national emergency resulting in a war in which the United States is a party, or from imminence of such war, the publication wilfully and without proper authority of any information relating to the national defense that is or may be useful to the enemy is hereby prohibited," and the President was authorized by proclamation to determine the character of information prohibited and the existence of the national emergency. Defendants were to be entitled to a jury trial.

With the Gard Amendment and others, the Espionage Bill was passed by the House on May 4, the count being 260 to 105, with 62 not voting and 3 "present." The following day the bill went to the Senate, where it was amended by the drastic process of striking out the entire measure following the enacting clause and substituting the Senate's own amended bill. This was a matter of parliamentary convenience, not necessarily indicating fundamental difference of opinion, but here again the

[36]

public failed to understand The reference to "wholesale amendment" must have led many people to believe that the Senate intended to pull the teeth of the Espionage Act.

This was far from the Senate's intention, but debate was extended, certain of the opponents expressing anew their fear that the law, if passed, would be used to protect the Administration from criticism Senator Hiram Johnson had warned that "We may well pause lest in our tenderness for democracy abroad we forget democracy at home " And even some of President Wilson's fellow party members were eager to preserve freedom of criticism Henry Fountain Ashurst, Democrat of Arizona, alluded to "the golden stream of $7,000,000,000" which soon was to proceed from the Treasury representing taxes laid upon the people. He granted that if he were in the Cabinet he would try to conceal his mistakes, but it was in the public interest that the newspapers should be free to discuss "how and when and by whom" the war funds were to be spent.

Incidentally, Senator Ashurst brings us closer to the main subject of this book in another part of the same speech· "I do not know who the censor is that has been appointed," he said. "I was told the other day, I have forgotten. I am going to assume that the censor who has been appointed is a man of the highest character, but when I assume that I am not bound still further to assume that he is the wisest man, the most circumspect man, in all our country." Mr. Ashurst was not the only American who, while debating whether or not the United States should have a censorship law, referred to George Creel as a censor already in action. The 1917 newspaper reader must have been in some confusion as to what the new law proposed to do and why it was wanted

Of the fact that the Administration wanted it, however, there could be no doubt, for on April 25 President Wilson had written a letter to Arthur Brisbane assuring him of the fairness with which the law would be used "I shall not expect or permit any part of this law to apply to me or any of my official actions, or in any way to be used as a shield against criticism " But he did want the Espionage Act, and White House pressure to ensure passage was applied in various ways. On May 22, for instance, he wrote Chairman Webb that he regarded censorship as embodied in the recent House action as "absolutely necessary to the public safety", passage was "imperative."

By the time this second Presidential letter was written the Senate, by a vote of 77 to 6, had passed its version of the House bill, without specific press censorship. That occurred on May 14, and the issue was being fought out in conference. On May 23, the day after Mr. Wilson wrote to Congressman Webb, he received the senate conferees at the White House, urging "the imperative necessity that a censorship be established to prevent information of the movement of American ships and other war moves being conveyed to the enemy." (Just a week earlier the destroyer squadron had arrived at Queenstown, and the press widely reported that the harbor had been mined in obvious foreknowledge of the squadron's arrival) The President told the Senators that he wanted a "mild form of censorship" to impose "more than a moral obligation upon any newspapers that might tend to print news by which the enemy might profit." A conference report was returned to the two chambers with press censorship included.

The first conference report with respect to section 4 modified the Gard Amendment which had already passed the House, and which has been previously discussed The modified section 4 described specifically the character of information useful to the enemy which should not be published and made it unlawful to publish it. It left out the part of the Gard proviso which authorized the President by proclamation to determine the character of information prohibited, and the existence of the national emergency, but authorized the President by proclamation to declare the character of such prohibited information which was not useful to the enemy, and which therefore might be published lawfully.

But on May 31 the defiant House voted, 184 to 144, to send the Espionage Bill back to conference a second time with orders to revamp section 4. The second conference report adopted section 4 virtually as it had been introduced originally on April 2, which merely stated that if two or more persons conspired to violate sections 2 or 3 of the espionage title they would be punished in accordance with the respective sections, and other offenses covered by the title were to be punished according to a penal law of 1909. Thus the danger of having the President state what might be or what might not be published was swept away, with only section 3 covering the field. The newspapers felt that in the defeat of the Gard Amendment and the altered first conference report of section 4, they had gained the day, and they ceased to decry censorship further. And it was thus in the shape of the second conference report that the entire espionage bill passed the House June 7, the Senate June 12, and secured President Wilson's signature June 15.

At least a suggestion of public reaction to the bill may be obtained by following the *New York Times* news stories and editorials through the last month of its parliamentary history.

When the Senate passed the bill without the Cummins censorship amendment the *Times* headlined its May 15 story:

SPY BILL PASSES; NO CENSORSHIP

Amendment for Press Supervision Is Beaten by Vote of 48 to 34.

EMBARGO PLAN RETAINED

The President's letter to Chairman Webb was printed May 23 with the heading "WILSON DEMANDS PRESS CENSORSHIP." And when the President summoned the senate conferees on May 23 the story was covered the next morning both in the news columns and on the editorial page,

where the paper said "Does the Administration really feel that
this Prussian edict would be a proper return for the services
the newspapers have rendered to the authorities in Washington?"

Encouraged on May 25, the *Times* said "Although no
accurate forecast could be made, the impression at the Capitol
today among leaders in both houses was that the censorship
legislation desired by President Wilson was doomed to defeat. . . In both houses there is a deep-rooted conviction
that censorship is not needed, that the newspapers of the
country may be depended upon not to print news that would
be of advantage to the enemy"

The future newspaper habit of attacking Mr. Wilson by the
indirect method of criticizing George Creel was presaged in
the same issue· "President Wilson has been told by some
Senators with whom he has discussed the censorship situation
that until the appointment of George Creel as head of the
Bureau of Public Information congressional opposition to censorship was not so strong as at present. The President is said
to have expressed full confidence in Mr. Creel's ability and
discretion."

In the next issue the headline was "CONFEREES OFFER
CENSORSHIP BILL WITH JURY TRIAL," and on the
following day, "NEW CENSORSHIP PLAN ADDS
POWER OF SUPPRESSION." On the 29th the *Times* reported, "HOUSE TO DEBATE CENSORSHIP TODAY.
DEFEAT INDICATED," and at the bottom of the article,
"CREEL FOR CENSORSHIP BASED ON COOPERA-
TION." And in a two-column editorial the paper struck home
with "Apart from its unconstitutionality, censorship may be
set down as a futility in the present situation of the United
States Our journals cannot reach the enemy until from two to
six weeks after publication, and they might be withheld
altogether from the outgoing mails rather than deprive our
own people of legitimate information "

On May 30 the *Times* carried a three-column story on the
National Conference of Foreign Relations at Long Beach, L I ,

where vigorous criticism of censorship was a feature of the program. The next day increased opposition to the bill was reported from Washington, together with the renewed activities of Administration leaders to put the legislation across: "Democratic leaders have been working with Representatives in the last few days, endeavoring to persuade them to fall into line with the President and vote for censorship. . . . If enough of them can be won over to the President's viewpoint, censorship will pass the House.

"Postmaster General Burleson, who worked indefatigably among the Democratic Representatives three weeks ago, when the first censorship vote was taken, was conspicuous in the House lobby early this week He talked with many Democratic Representatives, impressing upon them the necessity of giving the President the power over the newspapers that he asks."

But on the next day, June 1, the *Times* reported triumphantly, "HOUSE DEFEATS CENSORSHIP LAW BY 184 TO 144 Spy Bill Goes Back to Conference, with Orders to Eliminate Press Gag"

That last headline may be taken as a fair measure of public understanding of the Espionage Act Aside from the defeated section 4 it was only a "spy bill"—not only to the *Times* but to many other papers as well. As soon as the specific measure for press censorship had been killed the newspapers lost practically all interest. When the conference report was finally accepted, and when President Wilson's signature was affixed to this outstandingly important legislation, the event was almost unreported in the general press

Interest was by then entirely absorbed in the Draft Act, the raising of the first Liberty Loan, initial operations of the Food Administration, plans for an American expeditionary force, and battle news from abroad Both *Current History* and the *Literary Digest*, which are normally excellent sounding boards of press opinion for the period, chronicled passage of the Espionage Act with scarcely a suggestion of its relation to free speech and free press The *Digest*, in its weekly summary of important events, reports for June 15 "President Wilson signs . . . the Espionage Bill . . . thus giving the executive power to place an embargo on all exports "

As observed earlier in this chapter, only two of the twelve titles of the Espionage Act are directly relevant to a discussion of free speech, but apparently the great bulk of Americans did not know that *anything* affecting the civil liberty of ordinary citizens remained in the bill at its passage.

Yet in section 3 of Title I and in Title XII was the authority used by the Department of Justice in prosecuting approximately 2,000 cases, in only some of which the defendants were anything like the "spies and enemy agents" against whom the public thought the bill was directed. In its final form in 1917, section 3 of Title I read:

"Whoever, when the United States is at war, shall wilfully make or convey false reports or false statements with intent to interfere with the operation or success of the military or naval forces of the United States or to promote the success of its enemies, and whoever, when the United States is at war, shall wilfully cause or attempt to cause insubordination, disloyalty, mutiny, or refusal of duty in the military or naval forces of the United States, or shall wilfully obstruct the recruiting or enlistment service of the United States, to the injury of the service or of the United States, shall be punished by a fine of not more than $10,000 or imprisonment for not more than twenty years, or both."

This is what gave teeth to the Committee on Public Information. Without questioning the loyalty of the great majority of American newspapers, it may fairly be said that this was the big stick behind the "voluntary" censorship of the press. In certain cases it was actually used for control of the press, and in countless others the shadow of its authority fell across the desks of the country's editors. The CPI was no agency of prosecution, but law-enforcement bodies were always prepared to use this section of the act to force compliance with the Committee's wishes. This is the section most frequently in mind when reference is made to "conviction under the wartime Es-

[42]

pionage Act," and the names of many famous defendants are associated with it—Victor L. Berger, Eugene V. Debs, Big Bill Haywood and ninety-two others in the mass trial of the I.W.W , Max Eastman (two mistrials) , Scott Nearing (acquitted) , Kate Richards O'Hare, Rose Pastor Stokes, and hundreds of others. Sentences of five, ten, and twenty years were imposed with a liberal hand, though only the shortest of these were served to completion, for President Harding freed many of the offenders and President Coolidge ordered release of the "last political prisoner" on December 15, 1923.

Power over the press was found not only in the section just quoted but also in Title XII, where it was declared that any matter violating the Espionage Act was non-mailable. Oswald Garrison Villard, an issue of whose *Nation* was excluded for an attack on Samuel Gompers until Secretary Franklin K Lane and Joseph P. Tumulty came to his support, has charged that the measure was used for the persecution of insignificant publications while the Department of Justice feared to attack more important journals. Mr. Villard reports that when he published the internationally embarrassing text of the Secret Treaties in the *New York Evening Post* he was not even asked where he had obtained the inflammatory material—which may indicate either naive ignorance of its importance or reluctance to tackle a paper with such influential Washington connections as the *Post* then had

One other part of the Espionage Act is relevant here—Title XI, under which the government seized the motion picture *The Spirit of '76*, which had been in production before war began but, unhappily for the owners, was released at an awkward time from the point of view of patriotism. The movie film was impounded because, in its portrayal of the American Revolution, it showed British soldiers practising atrocities on non-combatants.

The validity of the Espionage Act was not finally established by the Supreme Court until the war was over. When the time came, four months after the Armistice, however, the Court placed its stamp of approval on the broad interpretation which

[43]

almost all judges except Learned Hand and Charles F. Amidon had given to the act. One of the most important cases was that of *Schenck v. United States*, decided March 3, 1919, in which Schenck, an officer of the Socialist Party, was held to have violated the law through printing and distributing leaflets which might have deterred drafted men from doing their duty —and the Court did not require proof that the leaflets had actually influenced conscripts

Most striking of the many interesting aspects of the Schenck case is that the decision was rendered, for a united Court, by the famous liberal, Oliver Wendell Holmes He rejected unequivocally the possible plea of protection under the First Amendment, denying that free speech is an absolute right, and in effect warning all dissenters that they cannot expect protection from the courts in a time of great stress such as the World War.

"When a nation is at war," Justice Holmes said, "many things that might be said in time of peace are such a hindrance to its effort that their utterance will not be endured so long as men fight, and that no court could regard them as protected by any constitutional rights."

In this and other cases it was decided that words alone constitute an overt act, that "to obstruct" means not only "to prevent" but also "to make difficult," and that for most offenses it is unnecessary to prove actual injury to the United States if the acts' remote tendencies be considered injurious (Professor Zechariah Chafee, Jr., calls this similar to a charge of attempted murder for firing a rifle at a man forty miles away.)

But broad as was this interpretation of the Espionage Act, that was not the only source of censorship power In the Trading-with-the-Enemy Act of October 6, 1917, censorship of messages between the United States and any foreign country was authorized. By use of powers granted by this act, the President established a Censorship Board, of which George Creel was a member, and because of the importance of transatlantic news this placed one more powerful weapon in Creel's hands.

And in section 19 of the act was a provision which enabled

George Creel Shortly Before the War

the government to whip into line the entire foreign-language press of the United States. No one could mail a magazine or newspaper containing any article or editorial in a foreign language "respecting the government of the United States or of any nation engaged in the present war, its policies, international relations, the state or conduct of the war, or any matter relating thereto," unless a sworn translation were filed with the postmaster. But there was a strategic proviso the President might issue revocable permits removing these onerous restrictions from specific publications as long as they behaved themselves Critics called it a form of blackmail

Even with these laws on the books, however, the government sometimes felt that it lacked sufficient power, and several frightening examples of mob violence against supposed offenders persuaded the Department of Justice that orderly law-enforcement required improvement of the language of the Espionage Act—notably to make clear that *attempts* to obstruct the recruiting service and opposition to the Liberty Loan were covered Attorney General Gregory asked Congress to make the required amendment. The Senate Judiciary Committee not only complied with the request but in a burst of patriotic fervor proceeded to establish nine new offenses. This thoroughgoing amendment, which is known as the Sedition Act of 1918, was passed by Congress and signed by the President on May 16, 1918, with little public notice—an illustration of the consuming speed with which a tendency toward restrictive legislation can proceed in wartime.

Among other new offenses which the so-called Sedition Act of 1918 (actually it was only an amendment of the Espionage Act) made punishable by penalties up to $10,000 and twenty years was the wilful writing, utterance, or publication of any "disloyal, profane, scurrilous, or abusive language about the form of government of the United States, or the Constitution of the United States, or the military or naval forces of the United States, or the flag of the United States, or the uniform of the army or navy of the United States, or any language intended to bring the form of government of the United States,

[45]

or the Constitution of the United States, or the flag of the United States, or the uniform of the army or navy of the United States into contempt, scorn, contumely, or disrepute" The Sedition Act also changed Title XII of the original statute, allowing the Postmaster General upon evidence satisfactory to him (i.e. without trial) to return mail addressed to anyone violating the Espionage Act.

Thus, in spite of newspaper elation back in May 1917 that "SPY BILL PASSES: NO CENSORSHIP," in a few short months editors might be punished in a variety of ways for publication of matter believed to have even remotely bad tendencies—by exclusion from the mails (and in the case of foreign-language papers by withdrawal of permits without which it was difficult if not impossible to do business), and by severe personal penalties of fine and imprisonment

Although none of these extraordinary powers was vested in the Committee on Public Information, George Creel's membership on the Censorship Board and his support by Military and Naval Intelligence, and the Department of Justice and similar establishments made his word almost as good as law. And he used that law with a sober sense of responsibility. Mr. Creel merits criticism for many of his impetuous actions and "horseback decisions" during the war years, he was wrong many times, he caused more dissension than necessary with other branches of government, and he may have taken too much pride in the CPI. But the more complete one's knowledge of wartime history the more certain does it become that there was appreciably more press freedom in the United States than in the warring nations of Europe, and that the largest share of credit for this belongs to Mr Creel

If the censorship was not quite as voluntary as many Americans believed it was during 1917-1918, it was very largely self-administered. The CPI set down the general principles, and, without legal action, the great majority of American newspapers followed these rules under their own interpretation Hints of political use of the CPI were of course constantly offered during the war. In a sense they were justified, for if it is difficult

[46]

to distinguish between the President as politician and the President as statesman in peacetime, it is practically impossible when the country is at war The CPI was naturally used to the advancement of Mr Wilson's ideas, but in the narrower sense of seeking aggrandizement for the Administration's political party George Creel's committee has a remarkably clear record. Some of the Committee's most responsible positions were filled by Republicans, and Mr. Creel set his face against involvement in local politics even when the "patriotic" excuse for it seemed pressing to some of his friends

Censorship, too, was employed "politically" in so far as the term covers suppression of arguments against the Wilsonian system of ideas, but it was never successfully charged that Mr Creel used his censorship authority for strictly partisan advantage or to advance his personal or political fortunes. Even charges of outright disloyalty he received without calling on the government for protection.

But the power was there. It was there in abundance, and it is easy to imagine how logically and effortlessly, supported by wave upon wave of patriotic emotion, George Creel might have continued to expand his powers and tighten his grip on the American press. That he did not is the strongest evidence of his sincerity in advocating "expression not repression." The positive side of the CPI story will be examined in later chapters In the meantime, who was this remarkable man who, in spite of having more than a fair share of mercurial temperament, carried his liberalism through the hatred and hysteria of war, and what was the vast and unparalleled organization that he built up?

Chapter 3

GEORGE CREEL'S IMPROVISATION

THE structure of the Committee on Public Information defies blueprinting It was developed according to no careful plan It was improvised on the job, and the job was never completed From the moment of its birth in April 1917 until it passed into history half a year after the Armistice, the Committee's organization, activities, and personnel changed incessantly. The staff was always coming and going in important haste, and the work itself underwent continual change of scope and direction

Main objectives were fixed, but two hours never passed without a new idea for achieving them Bureaus were thrown together in an evening on the flash of someone's four o'clock inspiration, and on some other day might be as speedily closed down, merged with another office, or directed to assume entirely new duties.

Three of Woodrow Wilson's Cabinet members had presented the germ of an idea, and Presidential proclamation had ordered its development, but it was the brilliant and restless mind of George Creel that took this idea and created a vast and complex organization of which the President and his advisers could not have dreamed when they inaugurated the CPI in the first week after declaration of war.

Mr Creel was called in to rectify an appallingly bad and chaotic system of government news release which had tried the patience of working newspapermen and at the same time had failed to satisfy federal officials. The press could not get as much information as it wanted, yet the State Department and the war-making divisions of the government were angered by publication of some of the news that the papers had secured

[48]

What the papers took to be routine information, or at the worst a harmless little scoop, appeared to some officials as dangerous.

Thus the original purpose of the CPI was to supervise the handling of government news, and that was why George Creel was summoned to Washington.

Not only did he do this primary job of directing the release (or sometimes the suppression) of news of the American people at war, but he moved into the far less restricted field of opinion management, invented new techniques and perfected old ones, and first to last built up a stupendous propaganda organization that was to make President Wilson's theories known at every village crossroads in this country and in remote corners of foreign lands

The background of the CPI is described in a recent letter to the authors from Josephus Daniels, who became Ambassador to Mexico under President Franklin Roosevelt but was Secretary of the Navy (and therefore a member of the CPI) under President Wilson. He writes

"When we entered the World War, the President, Mr Baker and I particularly—all the members of the Cabinet also agreeing—were very anxious that we should not fall into the stupid censorship which had marked the action of some countries in dealing with war news Immediately upon our entrance into the war I called in all the newspapermen in Washington, and particularly the representatives of the press associations, and told them that we would have no censorship but that the President and his Cabinet wished them and all newspapermen in America to impose self-censorship, that we would give them freely the information that would let them know what was going on and request them from time to time to publish nothing which might fall into the hands of the enemy or embarrass war operations. Ninety-nine per cent of them patriotically accepted this suggestion but we soon found that now and then the zeal for scoops outran patriotism. Determined to have no censorship and to give the public all information possible, we

[49]

decided to establish the Committee on Public Information. No other name was suggested as the executive head of that committee except that of Mr. Creel. . . . Lansing, I think, would have preferred a sort of censorship and never warmed up to Mr. Creel or to the work of the Committee. Baker, saying that I was a journalist by profession, largely turned over to me the work of the Committee, and never a week passed that I was not in consultation with Mr. Creel.

"I had known Mr. Creel before. The President had for him a sincere friendship and admiration, and in turn Mr Creel was devoted to the President."

The well known "zeal for scoops" may have posed the most urgent problem, but the Cabinet members also had some understanding, even that early in the war, of the part that public opinion was to play in the struggle. On April 13, one week after America declared war, the Secretary of State, the Secretary of War, and the Secretary of the Navy sent the following letter to President Wilson.

Dear Mr. President

Even though the cooperation of the press has been generous and patriotic, there is a steadily developing need for some authoritative agency to assure the publication of all the vital facts of national defense Premature or ill-advised announcements of policies, plans, and specific activities, whether innocent or otherwise, would constitute a source of danger.

While there is much that is properly secret in connection with the departments of the government, the total is small compared to the vast amount of information that it is right and proper for the people to have.

America's great present needs are confidence, enthusiasm, and service, and these needs will not be met completely unless every citizen is given the feeling of partnership that comes with full, frank statements concerning the conduct of the public business.

It is our opinion that the two functions—censorship and publicity—can be joined in honesty and with profit, and we recommend the creation of a Committee on Public Information. The chairman should be a civilian, preferably some writer of proved courage, ability, and vision, able to gain the understanding cooperation of the press and at the same time rally the authors of the country to a work of service. Other members should be the

Secretary of State, the Secretary of War, the Secretary of the Navy, or an officer or officers detailed to the work by them.

We believe you have undoubted authority to create this Committee on Public Information without waiting for further legislation, and because of the importance of the task, and its pressing necessity, we trust that you will see fit to do so.

The committee, upon appointment, can proceed to the framing of regulations and the creation of machinery that will safeguard all information of value to an enemy, and at the same time open every department of government to the inspection of the people as far as possible Such regulations and such machinery will, of course, be submitted for your approval before becoming effective

Respectfully,

Robert Lansing
Newton D. Baker
Josephus Daniels

On the next day the President issued Executive Order 2594 (dated April 13, 1917), establishing the Committee in exact accordance with the recommendation of this letter·

"I hereby create a Committee on Public Information, to be composed of the Secretary of State, the Secretary of War, the Secretary of the Navy, and a civilian who shall be charged with the executive direction of the Committee.

"As civilian chairman of the Committee I appoint Mr. George Creel.

"The Secretary of State, the Secretary of War, and the Secretary of the Navy are authorized each to detail an officer or officers to the work of the Committee."

Lansing, Baker, and Daniels had told the President that the civilian chairman of the CPI should be a man "of proved courage, ability, and vision" Mr Wilson selected George Creel, and it is hard to see how he could have made a better choice Mr Creel's knowledge of journalism, his vivid personality, his devotion to Wilsonian political doctrines, his creative and vigorous mind, and the emotional drive which urged him on in every job he undertook—all of these characteristics proved invaluable. Without them the Committee

[51]

would not have become the impressive testimonial to his ability which it now is.

But only by the most careful exploration of the CPI files can one appreciate the overwhelming importance of that other requisite mentioned by the Cabinet members—courage—and the degree to which Mr. Creel was required to display it Courage was needed above all else for the thankless task of trying to mobilize opinion yet safeguard democracy, to preserve liberalism in the essentially illiberal undertaking of warfare and at a time when people from the White House on down were finding the ways of liberalism too slow or too uncertain for that critical hour.

The chairman of the CPI came by his liberalism honestly, not by 1912 conversion for the sake of political expediency He had been a believer in the ideas of the "New Freedom" before Woodrow Wilson had used the term, and even before Mr. Wilson came to the governorship of New Jersey had been as energetic in its advancement on the plane of journalism and practical politics as the future President had been on the plane of political philosophy.

George Creel was forty-one when he became head of the CPI He had been born in Lafayette County, Missouri, the son of a Confederate officer who migrated from Virginia after the Civil War. While George was a boy the family moved to Kansas City, and it was there that he was educated in the public schools, attracting some local attention by his sharp-penned contributions to the high school paper. Then he worked briefly for the *Kansas City World* until, according to legend, refusal to pry into the life of a bereaved family ended his first job and interrupted for the time being his career in journalism He left for New York on a cattle train and had a perilous time keeping himself alive for the first few months in the East. He sold jokes and shovelled snow that first winter in New York, and eventually got a job on the *New York Journal.*

While on the staff of the *Journal*, at the age of twenty, he and Arthur Grissom decided that Kansas City could, and by all means should, support a semi-literary weekly So George Creel went back to Kansas City, travelling this time, however, as a customer of the passenger department, not the stock-handling division. He and Grissom established the *Independent* Later he bought his partner out and for a decade ran the paper successfully by himself

The *Independent's* Volume 1, Number 1, appeared March 11, 1899. The paper sold for three cents and was published each Saturday. A serial, "The Servant of the Prince," by Arthur Grissom started in the first issue, as did a column of jokes, verse, and philosophical anecdotes captioned "Cap and Bells" and signed GEO. EDW CREEL. This column was renamed "Vagrant Chords," and again "Original Humor," and before long the signature had contracted to GEORGE CREEL.

With the May 2, 1903, issue, the cover blossomed forth with "George Creel, Editor and Publisher," and such legends as "Brilliant Articles," "Clever Comment," and "All That Is Best in Poetry and Prose" One other slogan underwent an interesting metamorphosis, changing from "A Clean Paper for Clean People" in 1903 to "A Clean, Clever Paper for Intelligent People" in 1904—whether denoting a change in the product, the clientèle, or merely the sales appeal the evidence does not show.

Creel contributed every sort of literary work to his periodical—articles, verse, and stories, including one production entitled "A Study in Soul-Strife. the Story of a Murder Mystery." He attacked indecent plays and erring politicians, and he wrote popular songs, one of which, "Every Jack Must Have His Jill," he gave full-page advertising on the back cover Only a writer with the omniscience of a latter-day columnist would attempt to cover so wide a variety of topics.

From the beginning of his proprietorship of the *Independent*, Creel dedicated a considerable share of his great energy to social and economic problems On October 31, 1903, the reading public was advised that the paper was "Devoted to the Interests of Employer and Independent Employee," and he often launched the *Independent* on crusades looking toward one or another of the objectives of the yet-to-be-announced "New Freedom" One number in 1907 carried an article by another contributor which Creel gave prominent display under the heading·

HOPES FOR WOMEN
HOW SOCIALISM WILL TEND TO
ELEVATE THE GENTLER SEX

In 1909 Creel relinquished his editorship to K(atherine) M. Baxter, and the paper increased its attention to the theater and turned to gentler crusades, such as "Abolish the French Heel." The magazine, incidentally, after various changes of name, is published today as *The Independent· Kansas City's Weekly Journal of Society*, directing its efforts to the publication of débutante pictures and similar material. It still carries the line "Established March 11, 1899," though as long ago as 1917 Creel's connection seems to have been forgotten. When he became chairman of the CPI, the *Independent*, alas! appeared unaware of the distinction conferred upon its founder

Creel left Kansas City to move farther west, but before going an important event occurred in his literary career· he published his first book. It was called *Quatrains of Christ*. It was in a precious, gift-book binding and consisted of 121 stanzas after the fashion of Omar. Edwin Markham referred to this work of "the brilliant young editor of the *Independent*" as "one of the four or five best books of verse among the many that have come to me from the younger American writers." The *Denver Post*, to the services of which paper Creel was shortly to be called, went farther, throwing caution to the winds: "A masterpiece . . . which, had it been printed before the translation of Omar, would have ranked higher than it in English literature." A sample stanza from these reflections on the life of Jesus·

> God gave us mind and will; we are the free
> Unfettered masters of our destiny,
> And not as He did make us will He judge,
> But as His word has meant that we should be.

[54]

Some of Creel's friends chaffed him about the *Quatrains of Christ* during the war years, and he appears to have taken the badinage good-naturedly. But the high purpose and religious spirit which Creel revealed in these lines was to have an important place in the work of the CPI.

When "the brilliant young editor" left Kansas City to join the editorial staff of the *Denver Post* the Colorado city was in the thick of a political battle. A campaign for a public water system was won and attacks were launched against the city's political machine. Initiative, referendum, and direct primary were important issues of the day, and Creel's signed editorials on these and other subjects attracted a great deal of attention Once a state legislator sued Creel and his paper for libel, but the bold editorial writer took the witness stand and won over the jury According to reports, when Creel was urged to say that he spoke figuratively when describing certain people as fit to be hanged, he made the courtroom ring with "No, I meant it. The hemp! The hemp!"

A short time later Creel became interested in a county election campaign, lending support to a reform ticket backed by Judge Ben B. Lindsey. This was important for the future because it forced Creel to withdraw from his job and enter magazine journalism, and it committed him more definitely than ever before to the liberal side of important social issues. Creel thought that the *Post* was guilty of treachery to the reform ticket, so he resigned from the paper, devoting the last few days before election to campaigning for what proved to be the losing side But he had won the lasting friendship of Ben Lindsey and it turned him toward a wider public. Without a position and without funds he visited his friend Warden Jim Tynan at the state prison at Canyon City, and from there went to New York He was delighted to find a ready sale for magazine articles, and he might have continued in the "muckraking" field had he not received, in the summer of 1911, a letter from Senator T. M. Patterson, owner of the *Rocky Mountain News*, to come back to Denver and do some honest-to-goodness muckraking of a practical sort—to help put over a commission form of government

He went and the campaign was successful But before the victory he had an exciting interlude as a member of the Fire and Police Board. He directed certain reforms such as depriving policemen of clubs, and he tried to end brutal treatment of radicals who, he thought, were only encouraged to more violence when subjected to police cruelty He attempted to deal with the problem of commercialized vice and venereal disease. Finally, he forced an undercover political fight into the open and was dismissed by the mayor for his pains. But the Commission Government Movement which he led, and which he had continued to support through editorials in the *Rocky Mountain News*, triumphed by a two-to-one vote at the polls

At one point Creel was asked to be a candidate for commissioner but refused, giving as excuse the principal charge of his many opponents during the CPI experience—that he was temperamentally unsuited for public office

But he was temperamentally suited to rough-and-tumble journalism, and his editorial pen was never quiet. Through the autumn of 1912 the entire first page of section 5 in each Sunday issue of the *News* was given over to Creel, who discoursed on a bewildering variety of subjects—"The Volcanic Balkans," Margaret Sanger and sex hygiene, the direct primary, the Payne-Aldrich tariff, and "The Secret of Charm"

When President-elect Woodrow Wilson visited Denver on October 8, 1912, the *Rocky Mountain News* burst forth with a three-column photograph and this headline

> HURRAH WILSON! COLORADO   (red)
> MONSTER CROWDS GO WILD   (black)
> OVER TOUR OF BOSSES' FOE   (red)

Creel had performed a great deal of political service for Wilson during the campaign, and after the election continued to train his guns on the forces of privilege and monopoly. With increasing frequency his byline appeared at the head of leading articles in *Everybody's*, *Pearson's*, and other magazines, and usually in support of some phase of the "New Freedom" In the March 1915 issue of *Pearson's* was his article "How Tainted Money Taints," suggesting that millionaires made their huge gifts to philanthropic and educational institutions "to chloroform public opinion." He did not hesitate to name names and incidents in his campaign against "Monopolized Altruism," and this may go far toward explaining many of the charges of radicalism which were brought against him when appointed to the CPI

In a letter to the *New Republic* of March 27, 1915, Creel said, "For fifteen years I have devoted myself to a task of agitation in politics and industry, always trying to stay close to what may be termed the 'underdog.' During this time I have seen oppression, exploitation, corruption, treachery, and betrayal in all their forms, and it may well be that these experiences have made me less than judicial, overquick to suspect and denounce."

A year before this letter, Creel's name had appeared as coauthor on the title page of an important new book, once more revealing the development of his social conscience and his eagerness "to suspect and denounce" The book was *Children in Bondage*, "a complete and careful presentation of the anxious problem of child labor—its causes, its crimes, and its cure," published by Hearst's International Library Company. The authors were Edwin Markham, Ben Lindsey, and George Creel. It was ruthless in its attack on "the great American cancer."

In 1913 Creel left the *Rocky Mountain News* and, while engaged in various journalistic tasks, continued to expand his already wide acquaintance in the fields of politics, literature, and the arts. In the last category he was greatly aided by his wife, who was the actress Blanche Bates, star of *The Darling of the Gods* and other well known vehicles When Creel went to the CPI, it was reported that her friendship for Margaret Wilson, the President's daughter, helped reinforce the close ties between Creel and Mr. Wilson

[57]

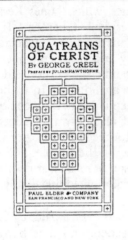

QUATRAINS
OF CHRIST
By GEORGE CREEL
PREFACE BY JULIAN HAWTHORNE

PAUL ELDER & COMPANY
SAN FRANCISCO AND NEW YORK

CHILDREN IN
BONDAGE

A Complete and Careful Presentation
of the Anxious Problem of Child Labor
—its Causes, its Crimes, and its Cure

BY

EDWIN MARKHAM,
BENJAMIN B. LINDSEY, AND GEORGE CREEL

WITH AN INTRODUCTION BY

OWEN R. LOVEJOY
SECRETARY NATIONAL CHILD LABOR COMMITTEE

"Jesus called a little child unto him, and said, Whoso
shall offend one of these little ones ... it were
better for him that a millstone were hanged about his
neck, and that he were drowned in the depth of the sea."

HEARST'S INTERNATIONAL LIBRARY CO.
NEW YORK   1914

Everybody's Magazine
NUMBER TWO   FEBRUARY 1917   VOLUME XXXVI

1918
1919
1920
1917

THE NEXT FOUR YEARS
An interview with the President
By George Creel

CARTOONS BY ROLLIN KIRBY

THE people of the United States were
not belied by the promise of a full
dinner-pail, nor were they frightened by the fear of war. Their in-
tent, I believe, was to consolidate the ethical
gains of the last four years. The vote was
an approval of progress, a victory for for-
ward-marching policies."

This is the meaning of November seventh
as gathered by the President. It is upon
the conviction that he will prevail.

It was shortly after election that I talked
with him, yet the day was already remote
in his thought. Instead of elation there
was a certain boisterousness, or if not that ...

During the campaign the question was
raised as to the proper conception of the
Presidency. It was urged against Mr. Wilson that he did not look upon the President
merely as the administrative head of Government, but as presently the political leader and lawmaker of the nation. So he did
so he said. It is a duty laid upon the President by the Constitution to propose "such
measures as he shall judge necessary and
expedient," and not only does Mr. Wilson
mean to make such proposals, but he in-
tends to further them by every legitimate
force at his command.

WILSON
AND THE ISSUES

BY

GEORGE CREEL

NEW YORK
THE CENTURY CO.
1916

Three Creel Title Pages and an Important Magazine Article

To aid Wilson in the reelection campaign of 1916, Creel wrote the book *Wilson and the Issues*, which James Kerney says "had mightily pleased" the President Chapter VII in that book was "The Case of Josephus Daniels," a detailed defense of the Secretary of the Navy and future member of the CPI. On the final page of the volume the author said:

"Are these hard-won heights to be abandoned? In its hour of greatest hope is democracy to surrender? Are the people of the United States so lost to the spirit of Henry and Jefferson and Lincoln that they prefer chains to freedom? Is it possible to build a government of the people, by the people, and for the people, or must humanity, by reason of its own stupidities, blindnesses, incapacities, and cowardice yield inevitably to the rule of the self-elected few?"

This loyalty to the President's ideals was repaid by Mr. Wilson's loyalty to Creel It was needed, and it is beyond doubt that if the President had not stood by him Mr. Creel would have been out of office on any one of a dozen occasions when newspaper or Congressional ire was directed against him. We have already seen in Chapter II some indications of how his appointment to the CPI was received. The *New York Times* spoke for many lesser papers when it said on April 16

"Mr. Creel may have been unjustly criticized in Denver, but we are unable to discover in his turbulent career as a municipal officer there, or in his qualities as a writer, or in his services to the Woman Suffrage Party in New York, any evidence of the ability, the experience, or the judicial temperament required 'to gain the understanding and cooperation of the press,' as the three Cabinet officers put it. That he is qualified for any position of authority over the press is made further doubtful by his publicly expressed hostility toward certain newspapers.

"As to 'rallying the authors of the country,' the other function assigned to Mr Creel, those estimable and gifted ladies and gentlemen can doubtless be made useful in various ways, but essential to the information of the public during the war will be not pleasing fictions prepared by imaginative writers but facts, even painful facts, accurately described by conscientious and competent reporters."

More than a year later the *Times* said again "George Creel had been a radical writer, an editor of the *Rocky Mountain News*, to whose columns he contributed editorials savagely denouncing the United States government. . . . Whatever may have been the rights or the wrongs of his controversies, his career had been one of turbulence and mud-spattering; he had denounced and been denounced His name stood for acrimonious contention " To this Creel replied in an unpublished letter to the *Times*, in which he said· "I enclose a clipping which strikes me as being very unfair. In none of my editorials did I ever 'savagely denounce the United States government' I was an advocate of the initiative and the referendum, and all my considerations were directed to the support of these measures The feeling of the people in Colorado was indicated by the tremendous majorities given in favor of the reform, and also to every other measure that I proposed during my three years' stay in Denver. . ."

Creel went on to say, "My career has not been one of 'turbulence and mud-spattering.' . . . Any mud-spattering in Denver was due to the very villainous activities of the corrupt men that I fought and defeated."

But note the final sentence of the letter· "I do not write this with the expectation or desire of any correction, but simply to let you know the truth "

That interchange between Creel and the *Times* is perhaps as impressive testimony as can be given of the way in which "Censor Creel" used his power. The head of the mighty Committee on Public Information wrote in answer to a personal attack not "with the expectation or desire of any correction, but simply to let you know the truth."

If Mr. Creel had been disposed to bring reprisals against his critics he would have been kept busy, for they were legion His eagerness and zeal and his tempestuous spirit would have ensured him a considerable number of enemies under any circumstances, but it is clear that Congress thoroughly enjoyed the sport of "jumping on George," as it was called. It was a safe and convenient way of attacking the national administration without the political dangers incurred by direct criticism of Wilson

He was asked if he was an I.W.W and a Socialist, and he was forced to say that all CPI personnel was under the surveillance of Military Intelligence (Captain Rupert Hughes was one of the investigators) before this particular kind of criticism stopped.

The most famous incident in the Congressional campaign against the CPI came in May 1918 In the course of a New York speech Creel had been asked whether he thought all Congressmen were loyal. Without hesitation he replied, "I do not like slumming, so I won't explore into the hearts of Congress for you"

Both houses of Congress were of course immediately up in arms, and there was a chorus of demands that Creel be forced to resign. Claude Kitchin said that the chairman of the CPI was "unworthy of the respect of any decent citizen." Creel issued a public letter of apology but even then the cries of rage did not stop. Ray Stannard Baker believes that it was on this occasion that Wilson refused Creel's proffered resignation, saying that one indiscretion would not be allowed to outweigh a year of useful service. And once when a group of Senators called on Wilson to ask for Creel's head the President replied "Gentlemen, when I think of the manner in which Mr. Creel has been maligned and persecuted I think it a very human thing for him to have said"

On still another occasion Mr Creel recalls that the President called him on the telephone while he was under attack and said "If necessary I will go up there myself as your counsel" But the chairman of the CPI was marked for punishment, and when, in June 1918, Congress voted on the 1918-1919 appropriation it cut nearly in half the sum for which Creel had asked One useful by-product of this incident was the Congressional hearing at which the CPI was asked to justify itself, with Creel, Byoir, Ford, and others reading important information into the record. But the attack on the CPI resulted not only in curtailing operations of certain divisions but in entire abandonment of two of them and, in the foreign field and at home, a weakening of prestige.

Congress might be criticized by the press, but the newspapers agreed with the legislators on the subject of George Creel. From the very first announcement of his appointment until the present day he has been the target for "inkpotshots" from the press as well as from opponents of his social and economic ideas, from people jealous of the power placed in his hands, and from thousands of citizens who had no particular grudge against the man but resented the invariable appearance of his name on government publicity and were taught by the newspapers that he was to blame for their woes In addition to being accused of manufacturing one important and several minor news hoaxes in the CPI itself, Creel's traducers attempted to link him with the Naval Oil Leases and various other scandals.

Five years after the war Mr. Creel wrote an article, "The 'Lash' of Public Opinion," in which he delivered himself of the following sad reflections "It is these joined causes—the indecencies of partisanship, the noise and unintelligibility of a large portion of the press, the lack of trustworthy information, the dreary routine of mud-slinging that passes for political discussion—that have killed public opinion, or rather deafened it, confused it, bored it, disgusted it. Cynicism, indifference, disgust, disbelief, confusion, bewilderment—these are some of the reasons why false servants are not lashed into obscurity and, in fact, are never called to pay proper penalty."

In spite of the frequency of personal attacks during the war, Mr Creel felt unable to go into the courts to defend his honor because of the expense and his fear of the courts' delay But "not all the attacks of twenty years have given me a protective callousness, and every lie has seen me die a thousand deaths." Even if suits could have been won, there was no time during the war to worry about personal reputations. The country was engaged in a death struggle with autocracy, and the anger of the CPI leader was reserved, in public at least, for the slacker, the Kaiserite, the enemy within.

Commander George Barr Baker, naval censor at New York and after the war Calvin Coolidge's publicity director for the 1924 campaign, expressed Creel's own thoughts when he wrote him in January 1918. "I don't think that the hard pull or the worries and perplexities of our positions are doing us any harm. If we live through them we will probably have done what we dreamed of doing—giving faithful service towards Democracy If we work ourselves to death we will at least have gone the very best kind of way Figuring it this way, we should be happy."

Mr. Creel's entire conception of "giving faithful service towards Democracy" was summed up in his unwavering loyalty to Wilson The CPI leader, like his chief, enlarged the "New Freedom" into the "New Patriotism," a logical extension to world affairs of the program which both had advocated at home for many years. This "New Patriotism" can be defined in many ways, but an understanding of its significance to Americans while the war was in progress comes best not through the sober terms of political philosophy but in the flaming words of a famous wartime speech which was gradually evolved by Carl Vrooman of the U.S. Department of Agriculture. His high-voltage oratory was in constant demand, it expressed what millions of Americans were thinking, and Mr. Creel said that he had read the speech "with joy and profit." The following brief passage from Vrooman's "New Patriotism" speech expresses Creel's own ideas exactly, if in language more baroque than the chairman of the CPI was accustomed to use:

"We are going to extirpate the hell-born spirit of conquest and break and crush its votaries once and for all time We are in a crusade not only for liberty and democracy but for a peace that must never again be jeopardized by the crazy dreams of world conquest of a war-mad Kaiser surrounded by a war-mad conclave of Hindenburgs, Ludendorffs, Tirpitzes,

[63]

and Crown Princes We mean to demonstrate so that a thousand years from now people will read, and rejoice in the fact, that in our generation *civilized nations by the use of civilized methods* were able to defend themselves against terrorism, Tirpitzism, Zeppelinism, and the blood-red Moloch of materialism."

George Creel did not throw words around as Vrooman did, but that is what he believed.

In the February 1917 issue of *Everybody's* he wrote "The Next Four Years an Interview with the President," illustrated with cartoons by Rollin Kirby Here was renewed proof of his intimacy with the President As the *New York Times* pointed out after the issue appeared, the article was strikingly similar to Wilson's "Peace Without Victory" speech of the day before In the article Creel said that he was presenting certain propositions regarding world affairs "that have come to be convictions with the President, and that he set down for me."

The next issue of *Everybody's*, appearing just before declaration of war, carried Creel's article, "Four Million Citizen Defenders," advocating universal military training as "a health insurance policy for America." And the June 1917 issue contained his article "The Sweat of War," probably written in March, emphasizing the importance of mobilizing all national resources, not merely armies. That ended Creel's writing as a private citizen until after the war. From then on he spoke and wrote and acted not as an individual but as a spokesman of the Wilson administration and public relations counsel to the American people.

Events in the month of April 1917 moved with lightning swiftness, even for a man used to the pace of Denver journalism. The first job of the CPI was of course the orderly dissemination of government news, and that was first on the order of business when Creel assumed office But other needs pressed themselves on the chairman's attention almost from the start. It was immediately evident that he intended no passive rôle for his committee· he proposed to make the news

Spies *and* Lies

German agents are everywhere, eager to gather scraps of news about our men, our ships, our munitions. It is still possible to get such information through to Germany, where thousands of these fragments—often individually harmless—are patiently pieced together into a whole which spells death to American soldiers and danger to American homes.

But while the enemy is most industrious in trying to collect information, and his systems elaborate, he is *not* superhuman—indeed he is often very stupid, and would fail to get what he wants were it not deliberately handed to him by the carelessness of loyal Americans.

Do not discuss in public, or with strangers, any news of troop and transport movements, or bits of gossip as to our military preparations, which come into your possession.

Do not permit your friends in service to tell you—or write you—"inside" facts about where they are, what they are doing and seeing.

Do not become a tool of the Hun by passing on the malicious, disheartening rumors which he so eagerly sows. Remember he asks no better service than to have you spread his lies of disasters to our soldiers and sailors, gross scandals in the Red Cross, cruelties, neglect and wholesale executions in our camps, drunkenness and vice in the Expeditionary Force, and other tales certain to disturb American patriots and to bring anxiety and grief to American parents.

And do not wait until you catch someone putting a bomb under a factory. Report the man who spreads pessimistic stories, divulges—or seeks—confidential military information, cries for peace, or belittles our efforts to win the war.

Send the names of such persons, even if they are in uniform, to the Department of Justice, Washington. Give all the details you can, with names of witnesses if possible—show the Hun that we can beat him at his own game of collecting scattered information and putting it to work. The fact that you made the report will not become public.

You are in contact with the enemy *today*, just as truly as if you faced him across No Man's Land. In your hands are two powerful weapons with which to meet him—discretion and vigilance. *Use them.*

COMMITTEE ON PUBLIC INFORMATION
8 JACKSON PLACE, WASHINGTON, D. C.

George Creel, Chairman
The Secretary of State
The Secretary of War
The Secretary of the Navy

Contributed through Division of Advertising

United States Gov't Comm. on Public Information

Creel Committee Advertising in the "Saturday Evening Post"

As the War Progressed
A Well Known Poster by Henry Patrick Raleigh

division merely the basis for a kaleidoscopic variety of other activities which would serve to bring the war home to the American people, teach them the significance of the Wilson program of reconstruction, and inspire each of them with some part of the emotional patriotism of Creel himself.

By the end of the war, opinion was nearly as important in the business of the CPI as the staple commodity, news. The use of symbols assumed greater and greater importance, and a number of the CPI divisions were concerned exclusively with symbol-manipulation.

It is indicative of the impromptu organization and development of the Committee that no one can draw a definitive outline of its work. As mentioned before, bureaus and divisions sprang up overnight and were modified, amalgamated, divided, extended, or entirely demobilized with a frequency and intricacy which typified the feverish atmosphere of official Washington. A "come at once" telegram would be dispatched to some journalist, scholar, or public figure, he would catch an afternoon train, and presto! the next dawn would break on a brand new unit of the CPI. As would be expected, a great deal of Creel's time was occupied with personnel administration, and especially with regretfully declining the proffered services of eager patriots who thought that they, too, could make some unique contribution toward saving civilization. Some of the Committee's most useful men arrived unheralded, but the majority were summoned because someone already in the work knew their particular talents and the help that they could give

In spite of the structural confusion and the resulting inaccuracy of any attempt to explain details of the Committee's set-up, a quick overall picture of its functions will be helpful before proceeding to closer examination of certain phases in the work. The Committee was divided into two main sections —Foreign and Domestic. Between them they had more than a score of special divisions, which maintained offices on Jackson Place (near the White House) or elsewhere in Washington, or in other cities. In the following paragraphs most of these divisions are described very briefly, as they receive closer

[65]

attention in later chapters. It must be borne in mind that this classification is in many respects artificial, and that with nearly equal logic a breakdown could be made into either more or fewer divisions.

THE COMMITTEE ON PUBLIC INFORMATION

EXECUTIVE DIVISION In addition to Mr. Creel, this division included the associate chairmen, the Committee secretary, and their staff. It carried payroll and expenses not assigned to other units and adopted, permanently or temporarily, such orphan bureaus as could not find a place elsewhere. The associate chairmen were Edgar Sisson, Harvey J. O'Higgins, and Carl Byoir, the secretary was Maurice F Lyons

Mr. Sisson was a onetime reporter and dramatic critic who had become city editor of the *Chicago Tribune*, managing editor of *Collier's* and editor of the *Cosmopolitan*. He was a registered Republican though supposed to have Progressive leanings. Mr. Creel sent him to Russia in an attempt to stem the tide of Bolshevism, and on his return he became director of the CPI Foreign Section.

Mr. O'Higgins was an author and playwright who, according to Mr. Creel, made $15,000 a year by his pen before coming to the CPI He worked closely with the Division of Syndicate Features, and under his own name wrote the famous pamphlet *The German Whisper* which tried to lay to rest the rumors of inefficiency and industrial breakdown which the Germans allegedly had started.

Mr. Byoir, who was called a "multiple director" by Creel because of his interest in all branches of the Committee work, came to the CPI from the office of circulation manager of the *Cosmopolitan*, of which Sisson was editor. Previously he had been interested in the Montessori system of pre-school education, and had been co-founder of the children's publication *John Martin's Book* Following the war he became a corporation executive, and in 1930 founded the famous public-relations firm of Carl Byoir and Associates.

[66]

Carl Byoir's widely celebrated public relations projects have included the "United Action Campaign" of the American Legion, the President's Birthday Balls, the campaign, on behalf of the Great Atlantic and Pacific Tea Company, against chain-store legislation and the effort for consumer support in attacking "hidden-taxes " As was revealed in testimony before the Dickstein Committee some years ago, one of his important accounts at that time was the German Tourist Information Service.

Compensation for members of the Executive Division, as for most members of the CPI organization bore some relation to the need of the individual, and frequently division heads cheerfully accepted less than was given to a number of their subordinates. Salaries for the executives were Creel $8,000, Sisson, $6,000, O'Higgins $6,000, and Byoir $5,200

BUSINESS MANAGEMENT. This office was created in October 1917 to relieve the Executive Division of many details, and to take over from N P Webster, disbursing clerk in the White House, the handling of finances C. D. Lee was director. Altogether the Committee received $9,675,670.23 (of which $5,600,000 came from the President's National Security and Defense Fund, $1,250,000 by direct appropriation from Congress for the year 1918-1919, and $2,825,670 23 from earnings such as film rentals, sale of publications, and so on). A large sum was returned to appropriations, and this deduction, plus Committee earnings, reduced the net cost of the entire undertaking to $4,464,602 39.

Two other divisions were in close relation to Business Management: the *Division of Stenography and Mimeographing* and the *Division of Production and Distribution*. The latter was under the direction of Henry Atwater and was organized June 1917, the initial job being nationwide distribution of the pamphlet *The War Message and the Facts Behind It*. At first, all production was by the Government Printing Office, but as demand increased it became necessary to let contracts to private houses, and this division set up offices in New York.

Division of News. This rock-bottom essential of any committee on public information came into being automatically with formation of the Committee. John W. McConaughy was its first director, and he was succeeded by Leigh Reilly. In all more than 6,000 releases were issued, and Mr. Creel estimated that these were published to the extent of about 20,000 newspaper columns per week.

Official Bulletin This was the official daily newspaper of the United States government, serving to eliminate a great deal of correspondence for the purpose of interdepartmental intelligence, to disseminate government news throughout the country, and also to preserve "without color or bias" a record of the nation's participation in the war. The journal reached a peak circulation of 118,008, and the cost of the venture was over $650,000. The first issue appeared May 10, 1917, and the last, as a government organ, March 31, 1919 E S Rochester was editor.

Foreign Language Newspaper Division. William Churchill was director of this division, which was formed in April 1917 and eleven months later was absorbed into the Division of Work with the Foreign Born. It followed closely every foreign-language paper printed in this country (especially with reference to the special permits required under the Trading-with-the-Enemy Act), translated Committee pamphlets into foreign languages, and provided a translating service for other units of the C.P.I.

Civic and Eucational Cooperation. Guy Stanton Ford was director of this division, which prepared 105 publications, most of them written by nationally famous scholars. Circulation amounted to 75,000,000. In the last few months of the war the Division also issued a sixteen-page paper, *The National School Service*, which was said to reach 20,000,000 homes through distribution to school children.

Picture Division. This division was merged with the Film Division (see below) in March 1918, both branches having been established five months earlier by the President's executive order. The Picture Division and the later *Bureau of War Photographs* issued permits "to open up the war activities of the nation to the exploitation of the camera" Once the pictures were made, they were given wide distribution. A *Department of Slides* was part of the Bureau of War Photographs, taking over the production work from the Signal Corps Laboratory and distributing more than 200,000 slides.

FILM DIVISION. At first this unit limited its work to distribution of Signal Corps movies, but eventually the division acquired an Educational Department and a Scenario Department, working closely with commercial producers and also making pictures on its own account. Charles S. Hart was directing genius of the Division which spent $1,066,730 59, but recovered more than three-quarters through film rentals.

BUREAU OF WAR EXPOSITIONS. Twenty cities saw exhibits of the machinery of war and trophies captured from the Germans. Admission receipts exceeded by more than $400,000 the $1,006,142 80 of expenses The showing of the exposition on the Chicago Lake Front, under the direction of Samuel Insull, was the greatest of all, bringing in receipts of $583,731.24 and having a total attendance of more than two million (224,-871 in one day). Parades and other special events helped stir enthusiasm, and there was a daily sham battle on land and in the air, employing the services of 3,000 soldiers, sailors, and marines and a British-American squadron of fourteen war planes. The fascination of the War Expositions is revealed by a front-page story of part two from the Chicago *Herald and Examiner* of September 1, 1918·

"Go and see the 'German 77's,' the favorite field piece of the Hun army, captured in battle, battered and made useless by allied shells.

"See the big torpedo, captured by the British navy, and known to be a mate to the one with which the Germans sank the *Lusitania*.

[69]

"Look on the 6,000-pound anti-aircraft gun captured by American troops, and notice how they perforated and riddled it with steel before they took it.

"See official French photographs of Hun atrocities. See the official photographs, which cannot be denied

"Walk through the trenches, and look at the dugouts in which our boys live, the helmets and gas masks they must wear, the weight of the packs they must carry, and try to imagine the hum of bullets, the roar of exploding shells, and the smash of showers of shrapnel aimed at them   .

"Go down to the War Exposition and picture to yourself that hail of shell, that smudge of poison gas, that shower of machine-gun bullets, all the atmosphere of treachery and hate and unfair fighting our boys had to face.

"When you get that realization you will be readier to do your full share here at home. And THAT is the sole reason for the exposition."

BUREAU OF STATE FAIR EXHIBITS This bureau, under the protection of the CPI Executive Division, put on a different type of display, with conservation the principal "message" but with war equipment again as the best drawing card. Exhibits were shown at sixty fairs and attracted an estimated 7,000,000 people. Captain Joseph H Hittinger, assigned by the War Department, handled the CPI end of the program, in cooperation with the Joint Committee on Government Exhibits of which Frank Lamson-Scribner of the Department of Agriculture was chairman.

INDUSTRIAL RELATIONS. Roger W. Babson, counsellor of businessmen, was given CPI office space at 16 Jackson Place in the late winter of 1918 and outlined a full-fledged division to bring labor into line A publishing program was inaugurated, but most of the plans did not materialize under the aegis of the CPI. After a month the work of the division was transferred to the Department of Labor

The *Alliance for Labor and Democracy,* Robert Maisel, director, bore an intimate relation both to the CPI and to Mr.

Babson's other work, but technically it was an independent organization headed by Samuel Gompers.

In view of the form of the Alliance and the brief life of Mr. Babson's division, the formal record gives the utterly wrong impression that the CPI was not interested in labor. Actually, as the reader will discover, labor was uppermost in the Committee's thought a great deal of the time.

LABOR PUBLICATIONS DIVISION Robert Maisel was director not only of the Alliance but also of this CPI unit which served it Offices were at 51 Chambers Street, New York, and the chief work was to distribute patriotic literature designed to appeal to labor. Later, field agents did a great deal of contact work with industry.

SERVICE BUREAU. Members of the CPI were entertained in the early months when citizens observed the word "information" in the Committee title and wrote in or telephoned in search of exactly that commodity Later, as the number of requests mounted, amusement declined It was decided to establish a regular information bureau, and this was done by executive order dated March 19, 1918. Professor Frederick W. McReynolds of Dartmouth, who was serving as CPI counsel, was director. Beginning May 1, information booths were established in the Union Station and elsewhere and a central office at 15th and G Streets, across from the Treasury Building Records were kept of "the function, location, and personnel of all government agencies," and 86,000 queries were answered. The need for the work was dramatically presented by one questioner whose exclamation, reminiscent to every Washington visitor, was "Can you give me some information, but for heaven's sake don't send me to another man " Arthur J. Klein was Professor McReynolds's chief assistant, and after February 1, 1919, the directorship was held successively by former Congressman Martin A Morrison (later Civil Service Commissioner and assistant chief counsel of the Federal Trade Commission), and Mary E Schick

PICTORIAL PUBLICITY Charles Dana Gibson was head of this unit, which was established April 17, 1917, and maintained headquarters at 200 Fifth Avenue, New York. The division cost the CPI only $13,170.97, and its posters and other illustrations are vividly remembered to this day by millions of Americans.

BUREAU OF CARTOONS. This was one of the offices taken in by the Executive Division. Under the direction of Alfred M. Saperston, a *Weekly Bulletin for Cartoonists* was sent to every known worker in the field

ADVERTISING. William H Johns was director of this division, which was established in December 1917 Carl Byoir served as Washington liaison officer. Headquarters were in the Metropolitan Tower, New York, and the work consisted not only in directing some of the most famous patriotic advertising campaigns of the war but also in obtaining contributions of free space

FOUR-MINUTE MEN. More than 75,000 volunteer speakers gave their four-minute talks in movie houses, theaters, and other public places from Maine to Samoa Donald Ryerson, creator of the division, was succeeded in the directorship by William McCormick Blair and then by William H Ingersoll

SPEAKING DIVISION Arthur E Bestor was director of this division, which was created in September 1917 and merged with the Four-Minute Men a year later It served as lecture bureau for all government speakers.

SYNDICATE FEATURES. "The volunteer services of the leading novelists, essayists, and short-story writers" were enlisted, L. Ames Brown, first director, was succeeded by William MacLeod Raine, and Harvey O'Higgins, associate director of the CPI, was actively interested. Circulation of the division's features was believed to be 12,000,000 a month.

WOMEN'S WAR WORK. Mrs Clara Sears Taylor was director of this attempt at "informing and energizing the women of the country." Mrs. William A Mundell ("Caroline Singer") was assistant director, and she made news-coverage of the War Department her particular field, while Mrs. Taylor covered the Women's Division of the Council of National Defense. This latter group, which included such well known women as Ida Tarbell, Dr. Anna Howard Shaw, and Carrie Chapman Catt, took over the work of "Mrs. Taylor and her broken-hearted associates" when Congressional budget-slashing forced the CPI unit out of existence on June 30, 1918. Before that, however, the Division had prepared 2,305 news stories and 292 pictures regarding women in the war, and had sent 50,000 letters to wives and mothers who had written to the government in agitation about conscription, conservation, or some other aspect of the war which touched them personally.

WORK WITH THE FOREIGN BORN "The alien in our midst" received CPI attention from the very first, but the formal division was not set up until May 1918 The director was Josephine Roche, and she had a number of bureau heads responsible for ensuring the patriotism of specific nationalities.

Activities of this unit in the CPI's Domestic Section dovetailed at many points with that of the Foreign Section

FOREIGN SECTION

The Foreign Section commenced operations in earnest in October 1917, and the last of its field offices abroad did not close until June 1919. At first George Creel himself had personal charge of the work but later the directors of the Foreign Section were, successively, Arthur Woods, Will Irwin, Edgar Sisson, and H N. Rickey Carl Byoir was "associate general director of the Foreign Section" under Sisson Much of the work gave support to, or was supported by, our regular diplomatic representatives, and nearly all of it was closely coordinated, at least in theory, with Military and Naval Intelligence, and the War Trade Board.

Details of the work are given later, but for the purposes of this "catalog" of CPI divisions, it may be said that there were three distinct units of the Foreign Section

WIRELESS AND CABLE SERVICE With the help of the CPI News Division daily dispatches were prepared, and with the help of Naval Communications and commercial cables this service was sent to nearly every country in the world, some of it even appearing in German papers

FOREIGN PRESS BUREAU. Under the direction of Ernest Poole, this division sent to our agents abroad a great profusion of feature articles, photographs, cuts, and mats, calling on the assistance of the Domestic Section's Division of Syndicate Features and Division of Pictures for much of this material

FOREIGN FILM DIVISION This unit handled export of movies from the Domestic Division of Films, using the export-license device to compel commercial distributors to take CPI movies whenever sending their own entertainment films abroad. Jules Brulatour and John Tuerk were in active charge.

* * *

Such, in broadest outline, was the improvisation of George Creel Many and brilliant were the famous Americans working under him, but the mighty propaganda machine of the CPI was his creation. He was the director of strategy in the "fight for the mind of mankind"

Mr. Creel's post-war career has been interesting. In addition to magazine articles, he has written eight books (including a story of the CPI in *How We Advertised America*). He has recently been United States Commissioner to the San Francisco International Exposition. He has been chairman of the San Francisco Regional Labor Board and chairman of the National Advisory Committee of the Works Progress Administration. And he was Upton Sinclair's opponent in the Democratic primaries during the EPIC campaign for the governorship of California.

For some men this might constitute a career in itself, but for George Creel it was anticlimax He will be remembered for his work of almost a generation ago His contribution to the winning of the war and his remarkable achievements as innovator and administrator of propaganda techniques seem destined to influence social thinking and action for years to come. The CPI was wiped out of existence on June 30, 1919, but the work that it did is still evident today as America considers the possibility of entanglement in a new European War.

[74]

Part II

"HOLDING FAST THE INNER LINES"

Chapter 4

FIGHTING WITH PRINTER'S INK: WORDS AND PICTURES

NEWS was the life-blood of the CPI—news from the front, from training camps, from the White House, from farms and factories, from worker's homes, from every place that had a story to tell regarding the American people in the war. This news had to be selected, interpreted, cast into new form, translated into different languages, expressed through new media, but without it there would have been no Committee on Public Information. Dean Ford and his corps of scholars, Charles Dana Gibson and his world-famous illustrators, William Johns and his advertising men, Ernest Poole and his Foreign Press Bureau—none of these would have had material with which to work if it had not been for the spade work by the News Division, the primary source of information about the war.

As George Creel and many other people have repeatedly emphasized, press cooperation with the CPI and its support of the war rested on a "voluntary" basis, but the reader has seen in Chapter II that impressive legal authority lay behind it This authority was gradually extended, by Congressional and Presidential action, as the war progressed, and by the time of the Armistice the government's potential control of the press was nearly complete. A self-denying ordinance by Mr Wilson and Mr. Creel was all that stood in the way of an attempt to impose a harsh, rigorous, and thoroughgoing censorship.

Even before the CPI, an agreement for voluntary censorship had been reached by representatives of the press and of the Departments of State, War and Navy. Then, on April 16, 1917, ten days after declaration of war and three days after

[77]

creation of the CPI, Mr. Wilson backed this up with a warning proclamation regarding "Treason and Misprision of Treason," stating, among other things, that the courts had found to be treasonable "The performance of any act or publication of statements or information which will give or supply, in any way, aid and comfort to the enemies of the United States "

A new system of general surveillance was also brought into being, for on April 25 J. C. Koons, First Assistant Postmaster General, issued an order to all postmasters to report "suspicious characters, disloyal and treasonable acts and utterances, and anything which might be important during the existence of the present state of war "

Three days later the President clamped down on all cable, telephone and telegraph messages entering or leaving the United States. Wireless establishments had already been seized by the Navy, so that after April 28 no electrical communication could go in or out of the United States without government approval. The President's order was put into "instant effect" as it applied to the Orient and Latin America, though transatlantic communication was not censored until July 25 "out of a desire to learn the workings of the French and British censorships in order to assure effective cooperation without duplication "

Commander David W Todd, director of Naval Communications, was placed in charge of cable censorship and Brigadier General Frank McIntyre given supervision of telephone and telegraph lines at the Mexican border Both offices were in constant touch with the CPI, which also served as clearing house for the coordination of Military and Naval Intelligence with all other branches of the government. Elaborate rules were prescribed and frequently amended: only certain codes could be used; acknowledgment of receipt of messages was forbidden, for some circuits, codes were entirely outlawed, every attempt was made "to ease the situation of the American trader and correspondent, consistent with military safety," but all cablegrams were accepted at the sender's risk and with the knowledge that they might be "stopped, delayed, or otherwise dealt with at the discretion of the censor, and without notice to the sender." That meant the end of unrestricted news from the theater of war.

Domestic news was not censored yet, at any rate On May 24, à propos of a telephone call from George Creel regarding an editorial on "Defective Shells," the *Washington Herald* published a two-column, front-page editorial blast: "The tremendous influence of President Wilson is behind the campaign to shackle the press while the war is being fought, to rob it of the right guaranteed by the Constitution, to establish an autocratic menace to those organs of public opinion which may have the courage to criticize the conduct of the great struggle upon which the nation is engaged " All of this had to do with publication of a story regarding a tragic explosion on the *Mongolia*, and the controversy raged for several days The *Herald's* charges of bad ammunition, which Creel declared to be "baseless," were properly recognized as weakening public confidence in the Navy.

While the *Mongolia* discussion was at its height, the Navy Department announced, on May 26, that the time of arrival of the American destroyers at Queenstown, Ireland, had been known in Berlin four days in advance Secretary Daniels accordingly issued a statement reminding editors of the pervasiveness of the German spy system and adding.

"The premature publication of ship movements is particularly a source of danger The Department, while realizing that newspapers did not give this information, would be pleased if the fact were brought to the attention of editors, by way of showing that extreme care is required in shielding military information from the enemy "

President Wilson, as the reader knows, had favored adequate censorship power all along, but for the first fifty-three days of the war (that is, from April 6 to May 28) selection of news was very largely a matter of the editor's individual discretion He was subject to laws against treason and his good sense normally told him what might and what might not be

[79]

published Then on May 28 came the "Preliminary Statement," in which the CPI codified rules but still depended upon existing laws for its authority

On June 15 the President signed the Espionage Act, as described in Chapter II, and through the summer of 1917 that law provided the threat of force behind the press censorship

Under the powers conferred upon him by the Trading-with-the-Enemy Act President Wilson issued an executive order on October 12, 1917, which among other things set up a Censorship Board which actually possessed more power than envisioned in the ill-fated Kirby Amendment of the previous May. It was, however, supposed to be concerned chiefly with international communications, outgoing and incoming foreign mail, and the like. The members of this new board included George Creel and representatives of State, War, Navy, Post Office, and War Trade Board. It had control of communication with foreign countries and through the Post Office Department it had power over the mailing privilege of any disloyal publication.

Finally, on May 16, 1918, the so-called "Sedition Act" amending the Espionage Act brought a wholesale extension in the categories of seditious information, including various forms of "disrespect" offenses which were subject to great latitude in interpretation.

With all of these laws on the books, not to mention the prevalence of an excited wartime spirit, George Creel at last held a whip hand over the editors of the country, but his administration was not greatly different from what it had been on May 28, 1917, when he issued the "Preliminary Statement"

This latter document was issued as a pamphlet and reproduced in the *Official Bulletin* of June 2, 1917 It carried on the cover a quotation from President Wilson's letter to Arthur Brisbane "I can imagine no greater disservice to the country than to establish a system of censorship that would deny to the people of a free republic like our own their indisputable right to criticize their own public officials. While exercising the great powers of the office I hold, I would regret in a crisis like the one through which we are now passing to lose the benefit of patriotic and intelligent criticism." Page 2 carried a quotation from President Monroe's message of December 2, 1823, in support of the same doctrine. Then in an italicized foreword Mr Creel set forth the policy of the CPI.

"Belligerent countries are usually at pains to veil in secrecy all operations of censorship. Rules and regulations are issued as 'private and confidential.' Each pamphlet is numbered, and the recipient held to strict accountability for its safe and secret keeping. The Committee on Public Information has decided against this policy, and the press is at liberty to give full publicity to this communication. . . ."

The purpose of the announcement, Mr. Creel said, was not only to state what news should be withheld, but also to remove "needless misapprehensions which have led the conscientious many to omit matters freely open to discussion," and to put an end to "such misrepresentations as have served to shelter the unscrupulous few." Special injunctions in the foreword included a warning against possible insults to our comrades in arms, and prohibition against unsigned dispatches from "our special correspondent," and against exaggerated or unverified reports capable of leading to panic.

Reckless journalism, said Mr. Creel, is bad enough in peacetime, but "is a positive menace when the nation is at war."

He added "In this day of high emotionalism and mental confusion, the printed word has immeasurable power, and the term traitor is not too harsh in application to the publisher, editor, or writer who wields this power without full and solemn recognition of responsibilities."

Then came the "Regulations for the Periodical Press of the United States during the War." News fell into three categories —Dangerous, Questionable, and Routine.

"Dangerous" news included stories of naval and military operations in progress, movement of official missions; threats and plots against the life of the President; news regarding secret

[81]

service and confidential agents; movements of alien labor. Naval information in the forbidden category included the position, number, or identification of Allied or American warships, certain data pertaining to lights and buoys, mention of ports of arrival or departure; any details of mines or mine traps, signals, orders, or wireless messages to or from any warship, all phases of submarine warfare, facts regarding drydocks Forbidden military information included any relating to fixed land defenses; movements of American or Canadian troops; assignment of small detachments; concentration at ports; aircraft and equipment that was, or might be, in the process of experimentation

"Questionable" matter, which might be published but only with the greatest caution and usually only with the approval of the CPI, was not exhaustively described, but three illustrations were given· naval and military operations, including training-camp routine; technical inventions; and sensational or disquieting rumors, such as those of an epidemic, without the most painstaking verification.

The great bulk of news, however, the Committee realized to be in the "Routine" category. Writers and editors were urged to submit articles if they had any doubt as to the propriety of publication, and the CPI promised speedy consideration of all such submitted copy. If approved it was stamped either "Passed by the Committee on Public Information," signifying merely that it could be published safely, not necessarily that it was accurate; or "Authorized by the Committee on Public Information," which meant that it had been carefully investigated and officially approved.

In general, editors were warned against feeling that because facts were generally known in a local district it was therefore safe to give them publication. Editors were also charged to examine, with the same care that they devoted to news, the contents of advertising copy, and even paid reading notices. And of course everyone was to guard against indiscriminate publication of maps, charts, and pictures

But after all of these "don'ts," the "Preliminary Statement" wound up with a declaration of the CPI's positive function.

[82]

"The Committee on Public Information was given its name in no spirit of subterfuge, but as an honest announcement of purpose." The primary aim was to make news accessible, and to present it without coloring or bias

Editors were asked to report infractions of the rules to the CPI, and many of the papers passed on this invitation to their readers. The *Literary Digest*, for instance, concluded a long article on treason with the announcement that "Readers are invited to clip and send us any editorial utterances they encounter which seem to them seditious or treasonable." Most of the readers were naturally unfamiliar with precise rules and frequently urged suppression of papers guilty of no impropriety.

Then, too, some of the newspaper associations gave their organized assistance, as when the Pittsburgh Press Club developed an intelligence bureau not only to disseminate information but also to keep twenty-seven Pennsylvania counties under surveillance for the Department of Justice. On top of all this, the Department of Justice itself extended official recognition to a national organization of amateur detectives known as the American Protective League This group seemed clothed with at least semi-official authority yet lacked official discipline and sometimes even knowledge of the laws It was never accused of lacking diligence in its purpose of "securing information and conducting investigations of complaints which do not appear to require immediate investigation by agents of the Department."

Thus not only enforcement agencies but a host of civilian investigators were alert for disobedience of Mr. Creel's rules. The "Preliminary Statement" was widely distributed, and few of the rules could be broken without the Committee learning about it.

Understandably, this new journalistic code was not received in newspaper offices with cordiality, but its provisions were generally followed

To the very end of the war, however, individual papers broke over the traces from time to time—sometimes the same paper repeatedly—bringing a rebuke from Mr. Creel or, less frequently, a visit from an enforcement officer. In the matter of censorship, as has been pointed out, Mr. Creel lived a sort of Jekyll-and-Hyde existence. As chairman of the CPI he could dictate his favorite paragraph, which is incorporated in many of his letters:

"The Committee on Public Information is without the slightest authority to decide what constitutes seditious utterances or disloyal attitudes, Congress having specifically vested these powers in other departments and in the courts of the land. At all times we have refused to assume this authority, or to be put in the position of usurping functions of the prosecutory and judicial branches of government. Only in cases of absolute misstatement of fact have we ever intervened, scrupulously avoiding all appearance of control over opinion."

But as a member of the Censorship Board, backed by the might of the United States government and in many respects not even obliged to seek action from the courts, Mr. Creel had the power to crack down on any newspaper or periodical, suggesting that the Department of Justice prosecute its editor or that the publication itself be excluded from the mails. He could have brought petty reprisals against it all along the line, and he even had the ability, through liaison with the War Trade Board, to cut off the supply of newsprint.

To the newspapers, many of the CPI decisions about publishable news seemed unreasonable, but in the great majority of cases the Committee was able to present a good argument. It seemed natural to many editors, for instance, to mention the name of the vessel and master when describing the exploits of armed merchantmen which attacked or sank submarines. But the CPI recalled the celebrated 1916 case in which Charles Fryatt, captain of a British merchantman, was captured, court-martialled, and shot for "a franc-tireur crime against armed German sea-forces" because a year earlier the House of Commons had publicly commended him for attempting to ram the U-33. The case had been alluded to in the CPI rules, but in the first week in June various papers forgot the censorship agreement and carried dispatches from France telling of the victory of the *Silver Bell* over a submarine. So on June 15 the Navy Department issued a "formal request on the press for restoration of the agreement to its original force."

Even news items far less dramatic than tales of submarine warfare might have an important effect on the outcome of the war. As an indication of the indirect influences which Mr. Creel was obliged to keep constantly in mind, here is a letter to Commander Todd, who was in charge of cable censorship· "The closing of American packing houses in Buenos Aires is compelling the Allies to send ships to America for meat supplies As far as cable censorship is concerned this news must be suppressed, as Mr. Hoover states that publication would send up meat prices at once. Will you please issue the necessary order?"

Through the entire CPI experience Mr. Creel tried to be reasonable, but he was not prepared to be easygoing. Indication of this comes in many records such as an exchange of letters with Hugh J Hughes, editor of the Minneapolis magazine *Farm, Stock and Home*. Mr. Hughes wrote in January 1918:

"Do you think we are concealing anything from Germany when we withhold from publication the approximate number of men now in France? Isn't that number quite as well known to Wilhelmstrasse as to Washington? Is not the location of American units on the front perfectly well known to Germany, likewise the ports of entry in France?"

Mr. Creel replied: "I tell you quite frankly, as the Secretary testified, that Germany does not know how many men we have in France, or does not know their location On the theory that the Germans are bound to find out everything, and that therefore there is no point in attempting any secrecy, we might as well send advance information of our plans in carbon to the German War Office and have done with it Merely because we may fail in some essential of secrecy is not a reason why common prudence should be thrown to the winds."

Never throughout the war, however, was there complete, 100 per cent conformity with the CPI rules. Certain newspapers flouted the censorship again and again, though it must be said that in nearly all of these cases the transgression was that of publishing "dangerous" news not of "disloyalty" or encouragement of disaffection. A few examples may be given from the summer of 1918, one from a Sunday supplement and three from different issues of the same daily.

On Sunday, August 4, the Hearst-owned *San Francisco Examiner* carried a two-page spread in its feature section "The American Weekly," with the title.

WHY THE U-BOATS CAN'T GET OUR TROOPSHIPS

The article was illustrated and even showed diagrams purporting to reveal how mines were set and exploded, the position of British minefields, and the organization of a large convoy.

On August 16 Creel sent personally the following telegram·

> EDITOR EXAMINER
>
> SAN FRANCISCO CALIFORNIA
>
> YOUR ISSUE OF AUGUST FOURTH CONTAINS [TWO] PAGE ARTICLE ENTITLED WHY U BOATS CANT GET OUR TROOP SHIPS PLEASE WIRE AT ONCE WHERE YOU SECURED THIS MATERIAL AND PHOTOGRAPHS AND BY WHAT AUTHORITY YOU PUBLISHED IN-FORMATION ABSOLUTELY PROHIBITED BY LAW
>
> GEORGE CREEL

Since the "American Weekly" supplement appeared in most Sunday papers owned by Hearst, it is not entirely clear why Mr. Creel wired to the *Examiner*. Perhaps protest had also been lodged with other papers (some of which had carried the story a week earlier), but if so, no record remains.

Another example of disregarded censorship rules related to the new tank developed in France by Renault. On July 26, 1918, Colonel Marlborough Churchill of Military Intelligence issued through the CPI a confidential memorandum to all editors asking for "great caution in the use of pictures and articles concerning tanks" The memorandum pointed out that the tank was undergoing rapid evolution and that the French Ministry of Armament had taken great care to prevent publication of pictures or specifications. Recently, however, a French illustrated paper had carried one of the forbidden pictures and it was found that this was reproduced from an American periodical "which reached France and presumably Germany." Churchill "strongly urged" a closer guard on information about tanks.

But the August 10 issue of the *Washington Post* carried a page 1 story, replete with details, under the headlines:

FRENCH TANK MARVEL

Brigadier General Churchill (recently promoted) on the 29th wrote to Edward B. McLean, editor of the *Washington Post*: "It is my painful duty to inform you that your paper has ignored one of the few appeals that General Pershing has made to the press. His specific and earnest statement . . . was followed by the article on your front page August 10, entitled 'French Tank Marvel,' signed by the pseudonym 'Ryley Grannon.' . . . I should be obliged for an explanation of your action in this matter, and a statement as to your attitude toward such requests in general."

Mr. McLean came to the Military Intelligence office and satisfied the authorities that the tank rule had been overlooked, not intentionally disregarded. Soon after that, orders of the Chief Military Censor were given on special colored cards printed as shown in Order No. 1 reproduced below:

WAR DEPARTMENT

No. 1.   OFFICE OF THE CHIEF MILITARY CENSOR   Sept. 17, 1918.
Washington

To All Correspondents, Editors and Publishers:

NOTICE: Memoranda of this nature are sent on cards of this size and color for the convenience of those concerned. It is suggested that they be filed for observance until the receipt of a similar card cancelling the request.

Memorandum on Tanks

Editors are requested to refrain from disclosing the strength of the personnel of the Tank Corps; from disclosing the number of its members overseas; from disclosing the number of tanks built or building in the United States; and from publishing descriptions or photographs of American tanks.

No objection is interposed to publicity designed to promote the recruiting campaign of the Corps, provided that in all such publicity the above request is observed.

The request to refrain from publication of photographs and descriptions of British and French "Whippet" tanks is withdrawn.

M. CHURCHILL,
Brig. Gen., Gen. Staff, Director of Military Intelligence, Chief Military Censor.

But the *Post* was in continual difficulties. On August 22, before the exchange with General Churchill on tanks, the paper had published another page 1 story, signed by Albert W. Fox, in contravention of the rules. The heading was "FOUR VESSELS SUNK," and the story told of the depradations of a German raider. This notation appears on the dossier of this case in the CPI file: "Much of the attached article by Fox was in violation of Admiral Benson's injunction of secrecy in rel. these details. Commander Foote had Fox on the carpet in rel this."

And still the *Washington Post* was unchastened On August 30, in a confidential note to the press, Secretary of the Navy Daniels had said: "The publication of any reference to naval guns on the Western Front or of any detail of such guns is absolutely unauthorized, and it is highly desirable that no publication of the kind be made at present. The press is requested not to print anything in regard to these guns until publication is officially authorized." Yet on September 21, 1918, the *Washington Post* published another story of Albert W Fox under the head "MEAN DOOM OF METZ," telling how American long-range "9-inch guns and guns of larger caliber, were bombarding the forts around Metz"

All these were "stunt" stories. More clearly indicative of the fact that Creel did not push to the edge of his power is the tremendous number of newspaper stories and editorials sharply critical of the Administration; exposing alleged inefficiency and stupidity, protesting against government rules on food, fuel, prices, and the mobilization of industry; and always, always taking those "inkpotshots" at the CPI and its chairman. The *New York Evening Post*, as mentioned before, published the text of the Allies' secret treaties; the same paper was able to attack the authenticity of the Sisson Documents regarding Russia (see Chapter XIV); Former President Theodore Roosevelt and Senator Henry Cabot Lodge had a good press for their scarcely covert attacks on President Wilson, General George W. Goethals was able to bring into the open many of his charges regarding first the shipbuilding program and later aircraft production; and the left-wing press was allowed what seems even today to have been remarkable latitude in discussing many (though not all) of the questions regarding the war. When Creel's opinion was solicited by the Department of Justice, for instance, he wrote of the *New Republic* "It is very independent in its criticisms, somewhat radical in its attitude, but its support of the Administration in the prosecution of the war has been very able and effective"

As this shows, if Mr Creel thought a paper was fundamentally loyal to Wilson's war aims, he did not quibble about criticism on minor points. He was as ready as anyone else to use "disloyalty" as a stick for beating the men whom he considered Wilson's real opponents, but he was rarely petty.

He could afford to overlook unimportant details in a small number of papers because all the rest of the press was pounding out an anvil chorus of patriotism under the direction of the CPI. Nearly all the papers were publishing the stories streaming out from the Committee's News Division in such a flood that obstructions were swept along with it

The News Division of the CPI was in one respect like a great city desk serving all of the newspapers in the country. But that suggestion that it was able to *command* publication is not accurate As Mr Creel explained when on the griddle before the House Committee on Appropriations in the spring of 1918, CPI releases were tested for their news value by the soundest of all methods—they were placed on the desk of all Washington correspondents, and those gentlemen could do with them as they pleased. The only thing they could not do was to break a release ("Newspapers that fail to observe the release will be deprived in future of the privilege of receiving statements issued by the Committee in advance of the date of release") With that exception they were entirely on their own responsibility as to disposition of the stories—they could file them with the telegraph operator or the trash man at their own discretion

In the overwhelming majority of cases the correspondents wished to use the CPI stories, and their home offices wished to print them. The average publication of CPI material, Mr. Creel estimated after the war, filled more than 20,000 columns per week. Leo Rosten, in his book *The Washington Correspondents*, gives the CPI period as the origin of that remarkable journalistic phenomenon known as the "handout."

More than 6,000 releases were issued during the life of the Committtee.

The Division of News never closed its doors. It was open twenty-four hours a day, seven days a week, and between its reporters and its wire connections it was in constant touch with war developments throughout the world. In Washington it had men constantly digging in government departments for facts which would make good newspaper copy, and its rewrite men were continually busy on stories coming in from other parts of the country or from abroad.

J. W McConaughy, who had formerly been editorial writer for *Munsey's Magazine* and the *New York Evening Mail*, was first director of this key division of the Committee Records are not complete as to other personnel in the early months, but in June 1918 Leigh Reilly became director, coming from the post of editor of the *Chicago Herald* At that time eighteen other people were in the Division. Mr. Reilly was paid $5,200 per year, and his ranking assistants, receiving $3,900, were Marlen E Pew, subsequently editor of *Editor and Publisher*, and Arthur W. Crawford, Washington correspondent for the *Chicago Herald*. Among the other employees was Kenneth Durant, regarding whom Mr. Creel told the House Appropriations Committee·

"Mr. Durant was a Philadelphian who was in London before our war. He was engaged over there in English propaganda work. He then came to this country for the British commission on the state of American public opinion Sir Gilbert Parker, when he was here, recommended Mr. Durant to me as one of the best men he knew, and Mr. Durant is now in the News Division sitting on this desk."

In addition to ferreting out publishable news items from Washington offices, the division also prepared releases on

WAR DEPARTMENT
OFFICE OF THE CHIEF OF STAFF
Washington

May 8, 1918.

Mr. George Creel,
Chairman, Committee on Public Information,
10 Jackson Place, Washington, D. C.

My dear Mr. Creel:

    Enclosed you will find an article which appeared in the New York American with the cable date line of April 30, 1918. Copies of dispatches furnished by the press censor show that this cable never passed through the censorship office. In other words, if it came through, it came in a way to avoid censorship. It appears to this office from the reading of the dispatch that apparently it was written in the United States, being a "grape vine," as newspaper men call it, or a story written on some little fragment of fact secured from another source. If this be true, of course, it is a case of manufacturing news.

    [possible] for you to have one of your men take this office in New York? The suggestion is that the the basis that the dispatch is a legitimate one ship has been evaded. This probably would either e censorship had been evaded, or would bring out ispatch is a fictitious one written in this coun-

    [woul]d like to have this matter cleared up and the news articles preceded by cable dispatch lines e one of the duties of an attache of the censor- ether changes have been made in cable dispatches e them, also to determine if there are censorship [manu]facturing of cable dispatches.

    [kind] enough to return to us the enclosed clipping [purp]ose?

Yours very sincerely.

M. E. Van Deman
Colonel, General Staff,
Chief, Military Intelligence Branch,
Executive Division

By: Henry T. Hunt
Captain, Inf., U. S. N.A.

Battle News Manufactured in New York

Captain Hunt of Military Intelligence Sends Mr. Creel Evidence of a
Spurious "Foreign Dispatch" to the "New York American"

WESTERN UNION
CABLEGRAM

PRESS

NEWCOMB CARLTON, PRESIDENT   GEORGE W. E. ATKINS, FIRST VICE PRESIDENT

Received at 16 BROAD STREET, NEW YORK

33W BBP MAR 20 18

WASHINGTON DC COLLECT DBR

POSTERITY

LONDON

MARCH 20 IN EDITORIAL IN KANSAS CITY STAR ROOSEVELT W
. . . . STAY . . . . .
IS NOT MAKING WAR ON TURKEY STOP ANSWER OF RUSSIAN BOLSHEVIKI TO
PRESIDENTS MESSAGE WAS ROOSEVELT SAYS QUOTE EXAMPLE OF MEAN AND STUPID
IMPERTINENCE STOP THERE WAS NO GRATITUDE NO APOLOGY FOR THEIR BETRAYAL
OF AMERICA AND OF CAUSE OF LIBERTY AND NO EXPRESSION OF HOSTILITY TO
THEIR GERMAN MASTERS BUT THERE WAS GRATITUDE AND INSOLENT ZEAL FOR
FOR CLASS WAR IN AMERICA QUOTE STOP THERE IS NOW IN ROOSEVELT OPINION
NO REASON FOR OURSELVES TO DRAW DISTINCTION BETWEEN BOLSHEVIKI

WESTERN UNION
CABLEGRAM

Form No 7

MAR 20 1918

NEWCOMB CARLTON, PRESIDENT   GEORGE W. E. ATKINS, FIRST VICE PRESIDENT

Received at 16 BROAD STREET, NEW YORK

4/33W CCZ POSTERITY LONDON

IDEAS AND ENERGY TO TAKE CHARGE OF INDUSTRY AND REGULATE DIRECT AND ACCELE-
RATE IT TO MAXIMUM OF PRODUCTION QUOTE STOP THERE EXPRESSES THAT MANY PERSONS
HAVE DEMANDED THAT IS CREATION OF AIR MINISTRY OR AT LEAST PLACE UNDER SINGLE
CONTROL WORK THAT IS NOW SCATTERED STOP THIS AGITATION FOR AIR MINISTRY
WILL UNDOUBTEDLY HAVE GOOD EFFECT EVEN IF MINISTER IS NOT APPOINTED STOP
BUT THAT PUBLIC KNOWS THAT IS WRONG IT WILL BRING UPON REFORM AND REFORM
IN CONDUCT OF WAR HAS ALWAYS FOLLOWED AGITATION IT WAS ONLY WHEN PUBLIC
KNEW SHIP BUILDING PROGRAMME WAS NOT BEING CARRIED OUT THAT ONE WAS ACCEL-
ERATED AND SAME THING HAPPENED WHEN WAR DEPARTMENT FELL BEHIND IN PRODUCTION
OF GUNS STOP STATES HAS FACILITIES TO TURN OUT AEROPLANES IN LARGE NUMBERS
IF ONE IS PROPERLY SYSTEMIZED AND PLACED IN HANDS OF MEN WHO KNOW THAT IS
REQUIRED AND ARE GIVEN UNHAMPERED AUTHORITY

LON 12869

"Stopped, Delayed, or Otherwise Dealt With . . ."
First and Last Sheets of an Outgoing Four-Page News Dispatch

Pershing's communiqués, casualty lists, interviews with Cabinet officers, and every other kind of material which ingenuity might devise. It also relayed to the newspapers special requests from various departments, such as this one which the Department of Agriculture wished published in twenty-four states where, in September 1917, there was found to be an excess of perishable fruits and vegetables The Department asked:

"1. Publication by you daily for a period of three weeks or more of a short popular article dealing with some phase of the problem of perishables.

"2 Publication also of a short box giving instructions for conservation.

"3. Such editorial comment in support of this campaign as you may deem proper and advisable

"4. Assignment by you of a reporter to conduct a daily local campaign "

Still another form of press communication was the *War News Digest*, sent upon request to 12,000 country editors When Mr. Reilly succeeded Mr McConaughy, the latter became editor of the *War News Digest*, holding that post until his departure for South America on a special CPI mission. A news service under Reilly's division was established with the A.E F. and Maximilian Foster was the official CPI representative in France.

In the last months of the war the News Division added yet one more to its duties by preparing a nightly digest of world news which was sent by wireless to all naval vessels and transports.

As to general policy in this division, Mr. Creel's final report declares "A special and painstaking effort was made to present the facts without the slightest trace of color or bias, either in the selection of the facts to be made public or in the manner in which they were presented. Thus the News Division set forth in exactly the same colorless style the remarkable success of the Browning guns on the one hand and, on the other, the facts of bad health conditions in three or four of our largest camps."

In order to provide an extra check against inaccuracy, all articles by the CPI were submitted for approval to the chief of the department in which the news originated—which newspapermen will recognize as beneficial not only in keeping faith with the public but also as having the "political" advantage of preventing sniping at the CPI from other departments. Both Mr. Creel and Dr Guy Stanton Ford have stated that of the 6,000 releases only three were ever called into question as to accuracy, and that the only error alleged with any foundation in fact (the airplane shipment incident) occurred through acceptance at face value of a statement by a war-making division.

Whether or not a post-war examination of all the CPI releases would leave this almost incredible record intact, only a casual glance at the Committee's work is needed to see that no newspaper office carried on its work with a greater sense of responsibility and sobriety in the handling of news

From first to last the Division of News cost only $76,323.82, which is not only an extremely modest sum in comparison with that for some of the other divisions, but is infinitesimal in relation to the mighty and pivotal job which it performed. The CPI never became quite the super-agency for which Mr. Creel hoped, because a number of the old-line departments and even some of the large emergency establishments, such as the Food Administration, the War Trade Board, and the Council of National Defense maintained their own publicity offices. But the CPI had a monopoly on the news that really counted—that from most branches of the army and navy, from the State Department, and the White House, and from many other offices.

Official Bulletin

And in one important respect the CPI had the field entirely to itself It published the first official daily newspaper in the history of the United States This country, unlike many others, had no governmental gazette such as it now maintains in the Federal Register There was no one authoritative medium for publication of government news, the text of orders and proclamations, reports, and so on. As things stood in the first part of 1917, each newspaper could decide for itself whether to publish such documents in full, to give the contents in brief paraphrase, or to omit the material altogether; in many cases important items were entirely ignored.

The *Official Bulletin* was therefore established primarily to give a place for official publication of these important papers. But two other objects were also in view reduction in the amount of correspondence necessary to maintain interdepartmental intelligence, and preservation of "a faithful record of the part played by the government of the United States in the World War . . . so that the people of the world might know and enjoy a better understanding as to what was being done, the objects sought, and the reasons actuating the government in its operations."

So the *Official Bulletin* (later called *Official U S. Bulletin*) was founded, and its first issue appeared May 10, 1917. The editor was Edward Sudler Rochester, who was managing editor of the *Washington Post* for seven years and after the war was to serve as Special Assistant to the Attorney General and secretary of the Federal Conservation Board. He is and was a Republican and is known for his books on President Harding and President Coolidge. Mr. Rochester was paid $5,200 a year. The associate editor, who received $2,340, was John D. Neel, former city editor of the *Washington Post* The rest of the staff included reporters, clerks, messengers, and copyreaders.

The *Bulletin* was 9 x 11 in format. The number of pages grew from eight in May 1917 to thirty-two and sometimes more in the winter of 1919 Publication was daily except Sunday. Daily average circulation increased without exception each month from 60,000 in May 1917 to 115,000 in October 1918 It declined rapidly from the high point to a low of 33,000 in March 1919

Distribution of the *Bulletin* was free to "public officials, newspapers, and agencies of a public or semi-public character equipped to disseminate the official information it will contain." It was posted in every military camp and in each of the 54,000 postoffices

Individual subscriptions cost $5 a year—a fairly high figure for a government publication but purposely fixed there to allay the fears of newspapers that the government was trying to take business away from them. These fears were groundless, for paid circulation was never important. On December 31, 1918, Mr. Rochester estimated that total subscription revenue had amounted to $80,000 (which would be the equivalent of only 16,000 one-year subscriptions).

Total cost of the *Bulletin* cannot be fixed exactly, but in June 1918 Carl Byoir told Congress that in its first year the daily had cost $194,609.40, and that he estimated its average cost in the last few months to have been about $21,000 a month.

The *Bulletin*, of course, was never a real newspaper; it was a glorified release sheet. But renewed explanation of this fact was necessary, as in this statement in the May 23, 1917, issue. "Exclusive publication is neither the thought nor ambition It will not interfere with the legitimate functions of the press in any manner, nor will official news be delayed or withheld in order to give the *Bulletin* any special news significance." But sticking to its own conception of its job the *Bulletin* performed an invaluable service not only for the government during the World War but for present-day students of that exciting period

The post-war history of the *Official Bulletin* is interesting Mr. Rochester has told the authors that he made every effort to have it continued as a governmental publication, but Congress refused to authorize the expense, and the paper came out for the last time as a government publication with the appearance of No. 575 on March 31, 1919. But Roger W. Babson, who had been establishing contact with business and industrial leaders through his work with the CPI, the Department of Labor, and his own Wellesley Associates, thought he saw the chance for a successful commercial venture. He was allowed to take over the mailing list and good will of the *Official Bulletin*, and for a considerable time the legend "Official Gov't News" appeared on the paper. (This formed the basis of one of the charges against Creel—that he had allowed Babson to take a government asset—but Mr. Creel was at the Peace Conference when all this happened.)

The "*Official Bulletin*" as Published under the Creel Committee and (below) in the Process of Becoming a Commercial News Letter under Roger W. Babson

Mr. Babson retained Mr. Rochester as editor, changed the title to *United States Bulletin*, moved to a twice-weekly and eventually to a weekly schedule, and boosted subscription rates to $10 a year. He thus became one of the first in the now busy field of publishers of Washington news-letters. Commencing with the March 22, 1920, number, all issues were marked CONFIDENTIAL, and subscriptions for individuals were raised to $52 a year. After a few months Mr. Rochester left the enterprise. In the spring of 1921 the *United States Bulletin*

[95]

Service, as it was then called, was merged with other publications of the Babson Institute.

Two other "legacies" from the ideas of the *Official Bulletin*, though entirely unconnected with it, have followed the original more closely than Mr. Babson's news-letter They are the private *United States Daily* (now *United States News*) published by David Lawrence and valued for the speed with which it furnishes governmental reports more complete than are available in many newspapers; and the governmental *Federal Register*, established on July 26, 1935, under the jurisdiction of a committee of which the Archivist of the United States, Dr. R D W. Conner is chairman, to publish proclamations and other documents which the President determines have general application and legal effect or which Congress requires to be published.

ADVERTISING DIVISION

The News Division and the *Official Bulletin* took care of the news columns of the nation's press, but it was inevitable that the possibilities for patriotic work through advertising should also be exploited. Plans for the CPI's Advertising Division were announced at a meeting in the Hotel McAlpin, New York, on December 18, 1917, in pursuance of an executive order by the President setting up the division.

William H. Johns of the George Batten Advertising Agency, president of the American Association of Advertising Agencies, and subsequently president of Batten, Barton, Durstine & Osborn, was appointed director of the division. Others on the board of directors included Thomas Cusack, leader in the field of poster advertising; William D'Arcy, president of the Associated Advertising Clubs of the World, O. C. Harn, chairman of the national commission of the Associated Advertising Clubs of the World; Herbert S. Houston of Doubleday, Page & Co., and onetime president of the A.A.C.W , Lewis B. Jones of the Eastman Kodak Company and president of the Association of National Advertisers; and Jesse H. Neal, secretary of

[96]

Associated Business Papers, representing 500 of the major trade and technical publications

Carl Byoir, associate chairman of the CPI, was continually interested in the work of this division, giving it energetic assistance throughout its career, and also serving as Washington liaison, since the division's headquarters were maintained in the Metropolitan Tower, New York.

Virtually every advertisers' and publishers' association was in formal cooperation with the division, and generous help came from hundreds of individual advertising agencies and thousands of newspapers and magazines.

The most memorable of the publicity campaigns of the World War were conceived and executed by this division. The list of "clients" includes the Liberty Loans, U.S. Shipping Board, War Savings Stamps, Food Administration, War Department, Training Camp Activities, Department of Agriculture, Council of National Defense, Department of Labor, Fuel Administration, United War Work Drive, Red Cross, and many others.

At first the CPI disclaimed all intention of soliciting contributions of advertising space from publishers Mr. Creel wrote Edward Percy Howard, editor of the American Press, on January 2, 1918 "You are mistaken if you assume that we are going to ask the newspapers of the country for any free advertising space. This is not my idea, nor will it be done. The advertisers of the United States organized themselves of their own volition, and have absolute control of their own affairs, only touching government through this Committee. Their principal endeavor, as I understand it, will be in the direction of influencing the advertisers, not the papers "

But in this respect, as in certain others, Mr. Creel was not able to keep complete control over the actions of an independent body which had been given governmental authority and prestige. The same end that Mr. Creel had disclaimed in his letter to Mr Howard was achieved by the Division of Advertising through indirection. publishers' associations, frequently

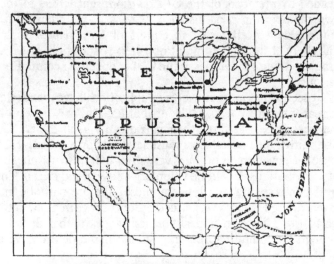

THE GERMAN IDEA

SHALL this war make Germany's word the highest law in the world?
Read what she expects. Here are the words of her own spokesmen.
Then ask yourself where Germany would have the United States
stand after the war.

Shall we bow to Germany's wishes—assist German ambition?

No. The German idea must be so completely crushed that it will
never again rear its venomous head.

It's a fight, as the President said, "to the last dollar, the last drop
of blood."

THE AMERICAN IDEA

The President's Flag Day Speech, With
Evidence of Germany's plans. 32
pages.
The War Message and the Facts Behind It. 32 pages.
The Nation in Arms. 16 pages.
Why We Fight Germany.
War, Labor and Peace.

THE GERMAN IDEA

Conquest and Kultur. 160 pages.
German War Practices. 96 pages.
Treatment of German Militarism and
German Critics.
The German War Code.

COMMITTEE ON PUBLIC INFORMATION
8 JACKSON PLACE, WASHINGTON, D. C.

Contributed through Division of Advertising, United States Governm't Committee on Public Information

George Creel, Chairman
The Secretary of State
The Secretary of War
The Secretary of the Navy

This space contributed for the Winning of the War by

The Publisher of

Advertisement in the "American Magazine." Cities on the Map Bear
Such Names as Heineapolis and Ach Looey. Note the
"American Reservation" in the Southwest

headed by members of the CPI division, sent letters to their own membership For instance, here is a quotation from a mimeographed letter sent to editors of farm papers on the stationery of the Agricultural Publishers Association, of which Frank E Long (a member of the CPI cooperating committee) was president.

"It seems that most all worthy publications have manifested a great interest by regularly contributing, and it is now up to the farm papers to show their patriotism and liberality. The Committee for Farm Papers must act on its own initiative, because the government ruling is very strict in its instructions that all contributions should be voluntary and that aid of this kind must come spontaneously from those who are patriotic and have a desire to help It is perfectly proper for each group interest to make its own appeal for assistance in this direction through its committee, but not in the name of the government"

Copy prepared by the Advertising Division was often given a special slant according to the public it was supposed to reach. The layout "Bachelor of Atrocities" (see Chapter VII) was for college papers and alumni magazines, and special appeals of other sorts were prepared for farmers, laborers, businessmen, and many other groups. Sometimes the patriotic message could be joined with a commercial appeal. This was the case with advertising carried by the Wear-Ever Magazine of the Aluminum Cooking Utensil Company at New Kensington, Pennsylvania. Space was offered in this house organ, and several hundred demonstrating salesmen were urged to distribute patriotic literature and display cards, and also to help put across the government's message during their demonstrations In a typical issue the Wear-Ever Magazine started off with a war poem, "The Service Flag," proceeded through an article "How Wear-Ever Utensils Are Helping to Win the War," and then came to an article entitled "Patriotism and Profit" reading in part

"It is possible and entirely practical for you, as a Wear-Ever dealer, to demonstrate and advertise Wear-Ever aluminum utensils in a way that will greatly aid the U S. Food and Fuel Administrations—and at the same time realize a profit from which to buy Liberty Bonds, pay war taxes, and contribute to the Y.M C.A. or Red Cross.

" 'To save food is as important as to raise it.' If, therefore, you have printed over your name in your local newspaper or newspapers the canning and preserving advertisements reproduced in this connection—or if you have proofs of the advertisements printed and mailed with statements or letters, or distributed from house to house—you can at once realize a profit and render a distinct, patriotic service . . . thereby . . . helping to make certain that 'Food Will Win the War.' "

Through whatever means of pressure or patriotic inspiration, publishers were induced to donate advertising space in such abundance that it is almost impossible to pick up a periodical of the war years without finding one or more pages devoted to the message of the CPI. Advertisers themselves bought space from the papers and then donated it to the CPI, and private individuals also contributed. An obviously incomplete summary of donated space shows the following:

Type of Advertising	Insertions	Circulation	Amount
General magazines	1,512	351,409,159	$895,108 29
Farm papers	1,443	134,279,895	361,221.84
Trade and miscel-			
laneous pubs.	4,353	41,377,554	238,102.47
House organs	831	14,386,475	52,727.50
Outdoor display	7	. . . .	8,550 00
Newspapers	653	6,272,636	17,567.60
College papers	377	1,107,429	12,337.01
Book jackets			
(amount est)	116	. . . . . .	7,700 00
Theater curtains	75	. . . .	1,500 00
Total	9,367	548,833,148	$1,594,814 71

Outdoor advertising valued at thousands and thousands of dollars is not included here, nor are the 60,000 window displays, many of them elaborate and costly, prepared by the national war service committee of the International Association of Display Men.

Advertising copy turned out by the Division was powerful, as the few examples shown in this book suggest. This copy restated in vivid, memorable terms the concepts behind President Wilson's war program, news items from the front, or scholarly interpretations given by the CPI Division of Civic and Educational Cooperation. But the phase of CPI advertising which is remembered most clearly today is the brilliant work of illustration which frequently told the entire story and required only two or three words of copy. This was the work of the Division of Pictorial Publicity.

Pictorial Publicity

On April 17, 1917, the Society of Illustrators was meeting at the Hotel Majestic, New York, to consider how American artists might help their country. Many were already hard at work through the patriotic group known as The Vigilantes, but they wanted to do something more and did not know just what it should be While the meeting was in progress, Charles Dana Gibson was handed a telegram from George Creel asking him to appoint a committee of artists to help the government with pictorial publicity.

On April 22, Mr. Gibson met Mr. Creel at the latter's house, and the CPI Division of Pictorial Publicity was launched just nine days after George Creel himself started work.

Charles Dana Gibson was an ideal leader for the division He had talent, professional prestige, and a burning desire to serve his country. As America's most famous illustrator and outstanding contributor to *Life* (at that time the American counterpart of *Punch*) he would have been widely known in any event, but there was a special reason for his popularity· the Gibson Girls which he drew had become part of our culture, and there must have been few literate Americans in 1917 who did not know Charles Dana Gibson and his work.

Frank De Sales Casey was chosen by Gibson as his assistant and held the offices of vice-chairman and treasurer. The job as treasurer was a sinecure The artists insisted on presenting their paintings to the government without compensation, and Gibson himself not only contributed his own expensive talent and his administrative ability but, for a long period, paid the division's operating expenses out of his own pocket. Both he and Casey paid their travelling expenses for a long time. Later the government assumed this expense, and carried the payroll of the one-man office force, but the whole great picture campaign, from beginning to end, cost the government only $13,170 97.

The list of associate chairmen serving under Gibson was a Who's Who of American art—Herbert Adams, E H. Blashfield, Ralph Clarkson, Cass Gilbert, Oliver Dennett Grover, Arthur T. Matthews, Joseph Pennell, Edmond C. Tarbell, Francis C Jones, and Douglas Volk Most of these were incumbent or past presidents of such distinguished groups as the National Academy of Design or the Society of American Artists and had a tremendous following both within and without the profession. The division included landscapists, portrait painters, etchers, lithographers, architects, illustrators, cartoonists, and apparently every other branch of the profession.

Gibson and Casey, who had their office at 200 Fifth Avenue, New York, travelled extensively, and some of the associate chairmen set up branch organizations in their own cities—Grover in Chicago, Tarbell in Boston, and Matthews in San Francisco Competitions were never held because it was felt that the great mass of entries would be worthless, causing a mountain of extra work and probably resulting in injured feelings. Each job was assigned, usually by Casey.

"Casey knows every artist in town," was Gibson's proud boast.

The method of translating ideas to the drawing-board or easel was explained by Gibson in a *New York Times* magazine article on January 20, 1918:

"We have a meeting every Friday night. This takes place at

our headquarters, 200 Fifth Avenue, where we meet men who are sent to us with their requests by the different departments at Washington. The meeting is adjourned to Keene's Chop House, where we have dinner.

"Suppose we have with us someone from the Food Administrator's office, sent to us so that we can get more clearly in mind the needs of his division through personal contact. Casey, once having got the suggestion, picks out two of the best men he thinks can be found for the work, and at dinner he places them on each side of the official emissary. In the course of the dinner

A Famous Gibson Drawing, Widely Reprinted from "Life"

views are exchanged on all sides, and we come to understand one another pretty thoroughly."

Every week Casey journeyed to Washington with a 75-pound container of drawings—the newest products of America's Blashfields and Pennells and Christys and Flaggs—and when he returned he brought a new list of the requirements of the United States Government

This was the campaign that has been called "The Battle of the Fences," and although there were many soldiers in that battle none was carried along on a wave of higher idealism than Gibson himself. It has been said that no artist has ever produced a grander figure of Uncle Sam than Gibson's—"tall, stalwart, and muscular in his starry coat and striped breeches, a figure of homely, Lincolnesque dignity." Even before our entry into the war, Gibson's cartoons, prominently displayed in the pro-Ally *Life*, helped build the spirit which was now predominant in American life. His Miss Columbias became "the noblest types of Gibson Girl," and the vicious drawings of the Kaiser, the Crown Prince, and the whole Junker class are the pictures of those men that remain in the minds of many people today—"The thin, cruel hauteur of the Crown Prince. The Kaiser, hollow-eyed, despicable with cringing bravado, his hands bloody, the mark of Cain on his forehead. A more damning caricature has never been drawn." Thus wrote Gibson's biographer, Fairfax Downey, who added.

"The war had moved him as politics never had been able to do. The scorn, the elation, the passionate conviction which make a great cartoonist now were his Color for a time was forgotten in the power which surged genii-like from his ink bottle Never had he drawn with such vigor and verve His soldiers fixed bayonets and leapt into action. Columbia's robe swept back outlining her beautifully molded body as she rushed forward toward victory"

Gibson constantly urged his co-workers to make their posters represent ideas, not things. A drawing that drew his special anger was a food-conservation poster with the representation of a garbage can and the exhortation to cheat the garbage can and beat the Kaiser. In his *New York Times* article he said.

"We have been looking at this matter [war posters and war art] heretofore too much from the material side. We must see more of the spiritual side of the conflict. We must picture the great aims of this country in fighting this war They already have been pictured in words by the President, and I want to say now that he is the greatest artist in the country today, because he is an idealist. He is the great Moses of America He points out the promised land, the milk and honey. The work of the artist will be made easy by putting into pictorial form the last message of the President"

The division served virtually every government department and relief organization, and was of course in a very special relationship to the CPI Division of Advertising. Shortly after the advertising unit was set up, Carl Byoir wrote to its director, William Johns, suggesting that the two branches of the CPI should work together On January 28, 1918, Mr Johns replied "We are already in active cooperation"

In the *Complete Report* of the CPI it is revealed that Mr Gibson and his associates made 700 poster designs, 122 carcards, 310 advertising illustrations, and 287 cartoons Thousands of other patriotic works were executed independently of the CPI. Not included in this calculation but taking an important place in the whole CPI program were the nineteen seals and buttons which brought in a new era of "outdoor advertising worn on the person"

One of the great undertakings of the Division of Pictorial Publicity was a huge canvas, 90 x 25 feet, in front of the New York Public Library, painted in the presence of great crowds to stimulate sales of Liberty Bonds. From outlines blocked on the canvas the artists painted allegorical figures representing the different branches of the service and the Allied nations.

Henry Reuterdahl and N. C. Wyeth worked on another 90 x 25 painting at the Subtreasury Building for the Third

Liberty Loan, and Lieutenant Reuterdahl made three paintings, each more than 20 feet in height, for the promotion of the Fourth Liberty Loan drive in Washington.

In the United War Work Campaign the same plan was adopted, and seven artists worked in shifts on a large painting at the Public Library and the Metropolitan Museum.

Joseph Pennell was authorized by the government to make a series of war lithographs of munitions factories, navy yards, military camps, and so on, similar to the series he did for the British government in the book *War Work in England*. The United States series appeared in the volume *Joseph Pennell's Pictures of War Work in America*.

Pennell was invited to do the same thing for France, but was unable to finish the work However, on request from General Pershing, Mr. Gibson and a committee chosen from his division selected eight men who were given captain's commissions and ordered to join the A.E.F They were J André Smith, Walter J. Enright, Harvey Dunn, George Wright, William J Aylward, Harry Townsend, Wallace Morgan, and Ernest C Peixotto. Nearly 300 of their works were sent back to this country, and were widely exhibited and reproduced in magazines and elsewhere This collection was one of the highlights in the great Allied War Salon, arranged by Albert E Gallatin at the American Galleries

A small number of the works of art turned out by the Division of Pictorial Publicity are reproduced in this book. Many others will never fade from the memory of Americans who saw them. Even during the war their artistic value was widely recognized, and the hobby of collecting war posters was common. Today they have the additional value of historical documents and the library with a full collection is fortunate indeed. But the perfect tribute to the Division of Pictorial Publicity, the most accurate chronicle of "The Battle of the Fences," is found in Wallace Irwin's poem·

THOUGHTS INSPIRED BY A WARTIME BILLBOARD
By Wallace Irwin

I stand by a fence on a peaceable street
  And gaze on the posters in colors of flame,
Historical documents, sheet upon sheet,
  Of our share in the war ere the armistice came

And I think about Art as a Lady-at-Arms;
  She's a studio character most people say,
With a feminine trick of displaying her charms
  In a manner to puzzle the ignorant lay.

But now as I study that row upon row
  Of wind-blown engravings I feel satisfaction
Deep down in my star-spangled heart, for I know
  How Art put on khaki and went into action.

There are posters for drives—now triumphantly o'er—
  I look with a smile reminiscently fond
As mobilized Fishers and Christys implore
  In a feminine voice, "Win the War—Buy a Bond!"

There's a Jonas Lie shipbuilder, fit for a frame,
  Wallie Morg's "Feed a Fighter" lurks deep in his trench;
There's a Blashfield's Columbia setting her name
  In classical draperies, trimmed by the French.

Charles Livingston Bull in marine composition
  Exhorts us to Hooverize (portrait of bass).
Jack Sheridan tells us that Food's Ammunition—
  We've all tackled war biscuits under that class

See the winged Polish warrior that Benda has wrought!
  Is he private or captain? I cannot tell which,
For printed below is the patriot thought
  Which Poles pronounce "Sladami Ojcow Naszych."

There's the Christy Girl wishing that she was a boy,
  There's Leyendecker coaling for Garfield in jeans,
There's the Montie Flagg guy with the air of fierce joy
  Inviting the public to Tell the Marines.

[107]

And the noble Six Thousand—they count up to that—
  Are marshalled before me in battered review.
They have uttered a thought that is All in One Hat
  In infinite shadings of red, white, and blue.

And if brave Uncle Sam—Dana Gibson, please bow—
  Has called for our labors as never before,
Let him stand in salute in acknowledgment now
  Of the fighters that trooped from the studio door.

BUREAU OF CARTOONS

Closely allied to the Division of Pictorial Publicity (though not in organizational tie-up) was the Bureau of Cartoons, which was established May 28, 1918, to "mobilize and direct the scattered cartoon power of the country for constructive war work." The bureau was under the general direction of the CPI's Executive Division and was headed by Alfred M. Saperston until his enlistment in the marine aviation service, when he

COMMITTEE ON PUBLIC INFORMATION

GEORGE CREEL, *Chairman*
THE SECRETARY OF STATE
THE SECRETARY OF WAR
THE SECRETARY OF THE NAVY

Bureau of Cartoons   *Bulletin No. 25*

BULLETIN FOR CARTOONISTS
NOVEMBER 30, 1918

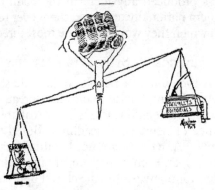

was succeeded by Gretchen Leicht George J. Hecht, a non-salaried volunteer, established the division in the first place and always had unofficial supervision of the work.

The major activity of the bureau was publication of the *Weekly Bulletin for Cartoonists*, which had a mailing list of 750 of the leading American cartoonists, to whom it dispatched ideas and captions for drawings to support ideas which some branch of the government wished emphasized at that particular time As an illustration, here are some of the captions suggested for the sale of War Savings Stamps in 1918·

"Stamp" Out the Kaiser
Make Thrift Your Buy-Word
Insure Prosperity for Posterity by Buying War Savings
    Stamps
He Also Serves Who Stays and Saves
Some Give Their Lives—Will You Loan Your Savings?
Invest Your Money and Divest the Kaiser

Through the *Weekly Bulletin* it was possible to gear "the nation's cartoon power" directly to whatever national drive was under way at the moment—conservation of food or fuel, Liberty Bonds, no Sunday motoring, Red Cross, no profiteering, and so on. Thirty-seven different agencies forwarded their ideas to cartoonists through the medium of the *Bulletin*.

In addition to this work, the Bureau of Cartoons took the best drawings produced anywhere in the country and either syndicated them nationally or turned them over to the particular agency to which they would give the most direct help

Division of Syndicate Features

Presumably even illiterate people could understand the message of the Advertising Division and the Bureau of Cartoons, and most people who could read at all were capable of grasping the significance of newspaper headlines But the CPI recognized that many Americans are not habitually careful readers of news columns, or, even if they are, are incapable of making interpretation: for many people the closest approach to knowledge and understanding of the forces behind current events came through Sunday supplements and similar feature material. Even for citizens on a higher plane of literacy, fiction rather than news was frequently a more customary means of contact with the outside world.

With all this in mind, the CPI set up the Division of Syndicate Features in August 1917, placing L. Ames Brown in the post of director and calling on the services of fifty leading writers, many of whom had previously done similar work with the private group known as The Vigilantes. The list of CPI feature writers included some of the best and most expensive bylines in America, among others Samuel Hopkins Adams, Booth Tarkington, Ellis Parker Butler, Meredith Nicholson, Mary Roberts Rinehart, Wallace Irwin, John Erskine, Rex Beach, and many others. Harvey O'Higgins, associate chairman of the CPI, made this division his special pet Mr. Brown, the first director of this division, had been White House correspondent of the *New York Sun*, and after the war was president of Lord & Thomas and Logan. When he left the CPI to become chief intelligence officer of the Shipping Board, he was succeeded by W. McLeod Raine, a Denver newspaperman and novelist whose present-day bibliography includes fifty-two full-length books, mostly "westerns." In addition to Mr. Raine the staff of the division included Patrick Gallagher, Donald L. Breed, James Collins, and Arthur E. McFarlane.

In testimony before the House Appropriations Committee, Carl Byoir gave a perfect example of the way in which the Division of Syndicate Features was able to reach a tremendous public inaccessible through regular news channels

"Take the Lichnowsky memoir, which was probably the most damning document in proof of the fact that Germany started the great war It had very little newspaper circulation originally; it was confined to one great metropolitan newspaper in the original announcement. Through the syndicate features, we furnished that important document to every Sunday paper in the United States, and it got wide circulation. It gave any minds where there might have been doubt the story from Germany's own ambassador to England as to the fact that Germany had not tried to meet England's efforts to prevent the war."

Another example was given by Mr Creel in testimony before the same committee "Mrs [Mary Roberts] Rinehart, who has a son in the Army and is, I think, one of the best writers in the country, was going on a summer vacation. I said to her, 'Why not visit the cantonments and the fleet, telling the people what you see?' Her standing precluded even the thought of an attempt to influence her observations. She gave up her vacation and did the work as a contribution to government" The story ran in daily and Sunday papers and was sent by boilerplate to more than 12,000 weekly publications.

In addition to soliciting the work of novelists, short-story writers, and essayists for broadcast distribution by the CPI, the Division also furnished facts and ideas for a number of articles, books, and works of fiction to be published independently This was done only "where the writers are so high class that we know they are not going to put out any trashy or stupid stuff "

The Division of Syndicate Features was a popularizer, on a plane of easy understanding and high reader interest, of the material both from the News Division and from the Division of Civic and Educational Cooperation Under the best bylines obtainable, it presented in easily assimilable form information regarding not only the movement of events but also regarding the broad social, political, and philosophical ideas which animated the national leaders The features were believed to reach 12,000,000 people per month, before work was necessarily curtailed by the cutting of the CPI budget after June 30, 1918.

*   *   *

So the fighting with printer's ink was carried on vigorously on many fronts during the war, with George Creel as editor-in-chief of the whole great publishing venture. Unless a person chanced upon one of the rare "disloyal" publications, any news story, feature, picture, cartoon, poster, book, short-story dealing with the war either carried the official seal of the CPI, or carried no less clearly, to our latter-day eyes, the stamp of CPI influence.

But the Creel Committee made its approach to the people not only through the eye but also through the ear. The Four-Minute Men organization, America's "broadcasting network" during the World War, is the subject of the next chapter.

Chapter 5

BROADCASTING BEFORE RADIO FOUR-MINUTE MEN

PRESIDENT WILSON delivered his war message to Congress three years before KDKA sent out the first radio broadcast and six years before the beginning of networks Yet George Creel's Committee on Public Information maintained daily contact with the American people through a device as ingenious and effective for its day as broadcasting systems are for ours.

The famous Four-Minute Men served as America's "nationwide hookup" during the World War. Instead of the voice of a single speaker carried through the ether to distant points, there was a mighty chorus of 75,000 individual voices scattered through the country but united under CPI leadership for coordinated and synchronized expression of Wilsonian doctrine These voices were of many timbres, representing many personalities, but at any given moment each Four-Minute Speaker dealt with the same subject and exhorted his audience toward the same goal. The Four-Minute Men were so many separate loud-speakers, reproducing with greater or less fidelity the words of Woodrow Wilson as interpreted by the CPI.

George Creel said that the Four-Minute Men were "carrying the flaming arrow into every corner of America" Their oratory was a nightly feature in virtually every movie house, and eventually in every place where Americans gathered for a communal purpose.

The movie theater, however, was the real center of activity. Movie advertising in local papers gave each day not only the name of the cinema attraction but also the name of the Four-Minute Man assigned to that particular theater At the movie house itself, when the hero and heroine had walked hand in hand into the sunset, ending the "first show" of the evening, the pianist might shift from "Hearts and Flowers" to "Over There," a slide would be thrown on the screen and one of Mr. Creel's Four-Minute Men would take the stage.

```
┌─────────────────────────────────────┐
│                                     │
│      ④ MINUTE MEN ④               │
│         Copyright, 1917 Trade Mark   │
│                                     │
│          JOHN DOE                   │
│                                     │
│    Will speak four minutes on a     │
│    subject of national importance   │
│                                     │
│   He speaks under the authority of  │
│      THE COMMITTEE ON               │
│      PUBLIC INFORMATION             │
│                                     │
│        WASHINGTON, D. C.            │
│                                     │
└─────────────────────────────────────┘
```

In some future national emergency, a speaker's group like the Four-Minute Men may not be necessary, thanks to the radio, although it will be remembered that the technique was used in many localities during the effort to arouse patriotic enthusiasm for the inauguration of NRA. But during the World War the four-minute speech was a brilliant substitute for a means of communication which technology had not yet devised.

The beginning of this unusual branch of the CPI is engagingly described by Mr. Creel in *How We Advertised America*:

"In the very first hours of the Committee, when we were still penned in the Navy Library, fighting for breath, a handsome rosy-cheeked youth burst through the crowd and caught my lapel in a death-grip. His name was Donald Ryerson. He confessed to Chicago as his home, and the plan that he presented was the organization of volunteer speakers for the purpose of making patriotic talks in motion-picture theaters.

[114]

He had tried the scheme in Chicago, and the success of the venture had catapulted him on the train to Washington and to me."

With a speed of decision typical of Mr. Creel in any circumstances but the almost invariable rule during the exciting life of the CPI, he gave his assent in ten minutes and the handsome rosy-cheeked youth "rushed out" carrying appointment as director of a new speaker's service to be called the Four-Minute Men.

The background of Mr Ryerson's eager approach to Mr. Creel was given in the historical number of the *Four-Minute Men News·*

"In March 1917 a group of young businessmen in Chicago, headed by Donald M Ryerson, following a suggestion of Senator Medill McCormick, conceived the idea of forming themselves into a patriotic committee for the purpose of sending speakers into the motion-picture theaters of Chicago to lay before the people the urgent reasons for new military service requirements as proposed at that time in the Chamberlain Bill .

"Mr. Donald M Ryerson acted as president of the original organization, to which the title of Four-Minute Men was given in dual reference to the Minute Men of the Revolutionary War and to the time limit necessarily imposed . This organization was incorporated under a state charter on April 28, 1917. . Mr. Ryerson himself made the first four-minute speech at the Strand Theater, Chicago, about April 1 or 2 . ."

When the Chamberlain Bill was pushed aside in favor of some form of Selective Draft, Mr Ryerson came to Washington to confer with the Council of National Defense on how his group could help, and it was thus that he met Mr. Creel.

The chairman of the CPI gave him authority to go ahead with his plan on a nationwide basis, and he was catapulted on another train back to Chicago where, for a few weeks, national headquarters of the Four-Minute Men were maintained and where the first four of the *Four-Minute Men Bul-*

letins were published. Headquarters were moved to Washington about June 10, 1917.

By the time of the First Liberty Loan campaign the Four-Minute Men had a national organization of 1,500 speakers—which seemed an impressive number at the time, but was only a beginning. Mr. Ryerson's first idea of organization by Federal Reserve Districts was changed for a state-by-state set-up, but in most other important particulars except size the Four-Minute Men idea came to the CPI in finished form.

Contact with the army of speakers was maintained through the *Four-Minute Men Bulletin*, in the first issue of which Mr. Ryerson gave instructions·

GENERAL SUGGESTIONS

The speech must not be longer than four minutes, which means there is no time for a single waste word

Speakers should go over their speech time and time again until the ideas are firmly fixed in their mind and can not be forgotten This does not mean that the speech needs to be written out and committed, although most speakers, especially when limited in time, do best to commit.

Divide your speech carefully into certain divisions, say 15 seconds for final appeal, 45 seconds to describe the bond, 15 seconds for opening words, etc., etc. Any plan is better than none, and it can be amended every day in the light of experience.

There never was a speech yet that couldn't be improved Never be satisfied with success. Aim to be more successful, and still more successful. So keep your eyes open. Read all the papers every day, to find a new slogan, or a new phraseology, or a new idea to replace something you have in your speech

For twenty-five days the steadily growing number of speakers devoted their oratorical energy to the First Liberty Loan; then, for seven days, the national Red Cross Drive, and so on through thirty-six distinct drives—everything from purely hortatory material to induce a desired state of mind to specific appeals for conservation of food and fuel, investment in war loans, or donation of binoculars to the Navy.

The First Liberty Loan, with an announced goal of $2,000,-000,000, had been 52 per cent oversubscribed, and the Four-Minute Men were justified in the claim that they had contributed importantly to this remarkable showing. From the time of that triumphant first experience on a national scale, the Four-Minute Men program was certain of success. Increasing cooperation came from theater owners, from government departments, and from volunteer speakers.

Liberty Loan committees were helpful in getting speakers during the early stages, though later on men already enrolled were the most effective in bringing in recruits In many cases the Four-Minute Men worked through State Councils of Defense, asking the governor in each state to select a state director and to make the speaking program part of the Council's regular work.

Local chairmen were named for most towns, and often were self-nominated, though before receiving official recognition they were required to present written endorsements from "three prominent businessmen, bankers, professional, or public men " A small sum of money had to be raised for local expenses, but Washington supplied slides and literature.

The most important job for the local chairmen was to choose the speakers. In this connection they were warned against local spellbinders. "Well known speakers are too accustomed to longer speeches with room for anecdotes and introduction, and should be avoided for this service in favor of young lawyers and businessmen who will present messages within the four-minute limit forcefully, rather than originate speeches "

Chairmen were told to rotate assignments to theaters so that speakers would not go stale with the audience. They were warned, also, not to break in on a photoplay, but to speak during the first intermission occurring after 8.00 p.m.

There was no dearth of applicants for speaking jobs. Mr Creel says· "Men of the most unlikely sort had the deep conviction that they were William J Bryans, and when rejected by local organizations many of them travelled clear to Washington for the purpose of delivering a four-minute speech to me in order that I might see for myself the full extent of the injustice to which they had been subjected." But if men of this sort were admitted to the organization through error, every effort was made to eliminate them: "The ax fell heavily whenever a speaker failed to hold his audiences, or injected a note of partizanship, or else proved himself lacking in restraint or good manners."

And in spite of the effort to keep high standards, the number of Four-Minute Men grew and grew. In September 1918 it had reached 40,000 and in only two months more had nearly doubled, reaching the final total of 75,000 In its final development this division of the CPI had 7,629 formally established branches, including 217 colleges and 51 granges, and covering not only every state in the union but also Alaska, Panama Canal Zone, District of Columbia, Guam, Hawaii, Philippine Islands, Porto Rico, and Samoa!

But, with all of these speakers and local chairmen, the plan would not work without the help of the theaters. Most managers wanted to be patriotic and cooperative, but some feared that if they let in the Four-Minute Men other patriotic groups would ask the same privilege. The CPI found it useful, therefore, to have the endorsement of the National Association of Motion Picture Industry, which named the Four-Minute Men as the official and authorized representatives of the United States Government in the movie theaters of America. This endorsement was obtained through William A. Brady, president of the trade group, on condition that the government departments name the CPI as their official speaking bureau. On June 16, 1917, Mr. Creel announced receipt of such statements from R. W. Wooley, director of publicity for the Liberty Loan, and from Herbert Hoover, director of the Food Administration Two days later similar authorization came from Henry P. Davison, national chairman of the Red Cross, and from then on the entire support of exhibitors was secured.

Donald Ryerson, who had cradled the idea of the Four-Minute Men, did not stay long in the directorship. Early in June he took up his commission in the Navy, from which he had secured a brief furlough for the CPI work. He was succeeded by William McCormick Blair, under whom the division had its period of greatest development With boundless energy he perfected the state organizations, inaugurated the

[118]

inspection service to weed out poor speakers, made changes in the *Four-Minute Men Bulletin*, and set up a National Advisory Council including Professor S. H. Clark of the Department of Public Speaking at the University of Chicago, the novelist Samuel Hopkins Adams, and other distinguished men.

COMMITTEE ON PUBLIC INFORMATION   DIVISION OF FOUR MINUTE MEN

February 18, 1918   Bulletin No. 24

The Danger to Democracy

Front Page of a "Four-Minute Men" Bulletin

In a tribute by Mr. Blair's successor, it was said: "A splendid, straight-standing young American is Blair. . . . More than

[119]

an incident is his smile—the sort that mirrors a conscience which has not been clouded and a body full of health. I like to think of Blair as the type which only the free institutions of America can produce "

When Blair left for Camp Zachary Taylor as a volunteer on August 31, 1918, William H. Ingersoll took his place. The new director had been one of the first members of the National Advisory Council and had written several of the most important *Bulletins*. He held the post until the division was demobilized December 31, 1918

In hearings before the House Appropriations Committee, when it was suggested that the Four-Minute Men might be used for partisan purposes, Mr. Creel said to the Congressmen: "I feel that is a very real danger, but quite fortunately those in charge of the Four-Minute Men [Ryerson and Blair] are of the opposite political faith and voted for Mr Hughes I feel that that in itself is a balance and a check."

The scope and variety of the great work done by the Four-Minute Men is best represented through the titles of the forty-six *Bulletins*. Ten of them were concerned with organization details, but the remaining thirty-six represented specific campaigns. Here is the list (with corrections not in Mr Creel's *Complete Report*):

Bulletin No	Topic	Period 1917
1-2	Universal Service by Selective Draft	May 12-21
3-4	First Liberty Loan	May 22-June 15
5-6	Red Cross	June 18-25
7	Organization	————
8-10	Food Conservation	July 1-14
11	Why We Are Fighting	July 23-Aug. 5
12	The Nation in Arms	Aug. 6-26
13	The Importance of Speed	Aug. 19-26
14	What Our Enemy Really Is	Aug. 27-Sept. 23
15	Unmasking German Propaganda	Aug. 27-Sept. 23

16	Onward to Victory	Sept. 24-Oct 27
17	Second Liberty Loan	Oct 8-28
18	Food Pledge	Oct. 29-Nov. 4
19	Maintaining Morals and Morale	Nov. 12-25
20	Carrying the Message	Nov 26-Dec. 22

1918

21	War Savings Stamps	Jan 2-19
22	The Shipbuilder	Jan 28-Feb. 9
23	Eyes for the Navy [appeal for binoculars]	Feb. 11-16
24	The Danger to Democracy	Feb. 18-Mar 10
25	Lincoln's Gettysburg Address	Feb 12
26	The Income Tax	Mar 11-16
27	Farm and Garden	Mar 25-30
28	President Wilson's Letter to Theaters	Mar. 31-Apr 5
29	Third Liberty Loan	Apr 6-May 4
7A	Organization (Republished)	Apr 23
30	Second Red Cross Campaign	May 13-25
31	Danger to America	May 27-June 12
32	Second War Savings Campaign	June 24-28
33	The Meaning of America	June 29-July 29
34	Mobilizing America's Man Power	July 29-Aug. 17
35	Where Did You Get Your Facts?	Aug 26-Sept. 7
36	Certificates to Theater Members	Sept. 9-14
37	"Register!" National Registration Day	Aug. 21
38	Four-Minute Singing	Sept. 10
39	Fourth Liberty Loan	Sept. 28-Oct. 19
40	Food Program for 1919	Oct. 20-Oct. 26
41	Fire Prevention	Oct. 27-Nov. 2
42	United War Work Campaign	Nov. 3-Nov. 18
43	Red Cross Home Service	Dec 7
44	What Have We Won?	Dec. 8-14
45	Red Cross Christmas Roll Call	Dec. 15-23
46	A Tribute to the Allies	Dec. 24

Through these *Bulletins* the CPI had means of guidance, if not of positive control, of its far-flung network of speakers Besides assigning dates and subjects and giving a great deal of material for the speeches, the central office continually offered suggestions about how the actual talks should be given. Reminders about the four-minute rule appeared repeatedly, and an attempt was made to dissuade speakers from bombast and the higher flights of inspirational oratory. For instance in the *Four-Minute Men News*, which supplemented the *Bulletin*, one could read in November 1917·

THE WRONG IDEA

"Take as an example of strong rhetoric that appeals only to those already more than convinced a speech which was submitted to us for approval. An excerpt follows.

> While the attainment of the complete surgery of this dread disease may be contemplated with satisfaction, yet such result will fall far short of full and final compensation for the deliberate and dastard wrongs committed upon innocent victims of German treachery and design The bottomless pit itself is not deep enough to hold the crimes so perpetrated, and when the rolls thereof shall have been written the totals will be paralyzing to the minds of men and the indignation thereat will rise to such heights that blindfolded Justice herself will demand and insist upon ultimate human penalty established by both law and religion, "an eye for an eye," "a tooth for a tooth," and "blood for blood"

"We are unable to recognize any relation between thoughts as expressed above and the inspiring sentiments that breathe through every word uttered by our President.

"Nor are we reminded of any material in our bulletins that bears remotely on this speech. . . . Originality in speakers is certainly to be encouraged . . . but if a government speaker wanders from his subject to express freely personal viewpoints he defeats his own purposes. . .

"A statement only of patent facts will convince those who require argument more readily than 'doubtful disputations.'"

This admonition in the *News* was summed up "No hymn of hate accompanies our message."

But the Four-Minute Men, at least a little later, were specifically encouraged to use official atrocity stories, and the *Bulletin* for January 2, 1918, listed sixteen different examples of *Schrecklichkeit* from which the speaker could choose his illustrations for a talk on War Savings Stamps.

As an example of what the CPI thought the Four-Minute Men should say, here is the complete text of an "Illustrative Four-Minute Speech," one of which set the tone for each of the nationwide campaigns:

While we are sitting here tonight enjoying a picture show, do you realize that thousands and thousands of Belgians, people just like ourselves, are languishing in slavery under Prussian masters?

Driven into slavery, after they were lured back home by Prussian promises—Prussian scraps of paper

Read the stories of deliberate governmentally ordered brutalities as told in the book, German War Practices, recently published by the Government's Committee on Public Information

Read how the Prussian war lords robbed Belgium, pilfered and stole. How they extorted fines of millions of francs for trivial reasons—e g 5,000 francs [5,000,000?] ($1,000,000) in Brussels because of an attack by a policeman; 200,000 marks at Tournai for refusal to send a list of citizens Taxes went to 50,000 francs a month and more in Belgium.

Prussian "Schrecklichkeit" (the deliberate policy of terrorism) leads to almost unbelievable besotten brutality. The German soldiers—their letters are reprinted—were often forced against their wills, they themselves weeping, to carry out unspeakable orders against defenseless old men, women, and children, so that "respect" might grow for German "efficiency" For instance, at Dinant the wives and children of 40 men were forced to witness the execution of their husbands and fathers

Now, then, do you want to take the slightest chance of meeting Prussianism here in America?

If not, then you'll have to help in summoning all the resources of this country for the giant struggle. For resources will win the war

Here's the way you can help save our resources Instead of throwing money away on unnecessary things, buy Thrift Stamps, 25 cents, and War-Savings-Stamps, $4.12, worth $5 in five years, 4 per cent compound interest. They're good as government money, like a mortgage on the U S A

Here's one of the War-Savings Certificates, and here's a Thrift Card Ask at any post office, any bank, or store wherever you see a W S.S sign
It is up to us We, *the people*, must win the war.

As the work of the Four-Minute Men progressed, various new wrinkles were developed, and perhaps the most important of these innovations was "Four-Minute Singing," officially introduced through *Bulletin* 38 in September 1918.

"Let us get it going with a swing," was the slogan, and the *Bulletin* advised that if the official Four-Minute Man could not himself lead the music he should secure a qualified substitute and "be among the others to sing heartily." The industrial army of the inner lines, it was believed, would be kept at a "white heat" of patriotism through the program of song. "The Singing Army, whether it be a fighting army or a working army, cannot be beaten," said the Four-Minute Men, to the delight of music publishers

Special slides were prepared for Four-Minute Singing, and the list of songs which could be thrown on the screen in this way included·

America	There's a Long, Long Trail
Star Spangled Banner	Keep the Home Fires Burning
Columbia the Gem of the Ocean	Pack up Your Troubles
	When You Come Back
Battle Hymn of the Republic	Tramp, Tramp, Tramp
	Saving Food
Dixie	Helping On
When Johnny Comes Marching Home	America the Beautiful

While the main idea of the Four-Minute Men was enjoying its phenomenal success in the movie theaters, the plan was extended to many other kinds of meetings, and various specialized units were formed.

A Women's Division was organized to cover matinee performances in many theaters, as well as meetings of women's clubs.

A Junior Division was also set up and a special *School Bulletin* established. Four issues were published, devoted to War

[124]

Savings Stamps, Third and Fourth Liberty Loan, and the Red Cross Christmas Roll Call Contests for the best junior speeches were held in 200,000 schools, either as part of the regular public-speaking work or as an extracurricular activity, and the winners received government certificates.

The College Four-Minute Men were organized in September 1918, usually with public-speaking teachers as chairmen. Undergraduates studied the regular *Bulletins* and other material and delivered at least one speech each semester, most frequently to their fellow students but sometimes off the campus as well.

Gradually the work was extended to cover more and more kinds of meetings—churches, synagogues, Sunday Schools, lumber camps, lodges, labor unions, social clubs, and even gatherings of the Indian tribes. Soldiers were not exempt for, as part of the morale program, a system of Four-Minute Speeches was devised for the cantonments, with officers delegated to speak to the men. Three *Army Bulletins* were issued by the CPI division—"Why We Are Fighting," "Insurance for Soldiers and Sailors," and "Back of the Trenches."

Wherever an American might be, unless he lived the life of a hermit, it was impossible to escape the ubiquitous Four-Minute Men. Judging from the estimated theater and movie audience in the fall of 1918, they must have reached several million daily.

In New York City alone, 1,600 speakers addressed 500,000 people each week—in English, Yiddish, or Italian.

In final estimate, based on incomplete figures but no unreasonable deductions from them, Mr. Creel set the total number of speeches at 1,000,000 and the total audience at 400,000,000.

Government outlay for all of this was only $140,150 40, and Mr. Creel believed that free newspaper publicity alone had given the Four-Minute Men nearly seven times this value at regular advertising rates. One clipping bureau alone showed 900,000 lines of free publicity in eighteen months. In his *Complete Report* Mr. Creel attempted to give a dollars-and-cents estimate of the value of the Four-Minute Men, showing a breakdown of this sort.

Contributed expenditures	$2,564,970
One million speeches at $4 each	4,000,000
"Rent" of theaters, etc., to deliver above	2,000,000
Speeches (331) of travelling speakers	8,275
Publicity contributed by press	750,000
Grand total	$9,313,245

A more Wilsonian statement of value was given, shortly after the Armistice, when the President sent a congratulatory open letter to the Four-Minute Men, saying in part "May I say that I, personally, have always taken the deepest and most sympathetic interest in your work, and have noted, from time to time, the excellent results you have procured for the various departments of the government. Now that this work has come to its conclusion and the name of the Four-Minute Men (which I venture to hope will not be used henceforth by any similar organization) has become a part of the history of the Great War, I would not willingly omit my heartfelt testimony to its great value to the country, and indeed to civilization as a whole, during our period of national trial and triumph."

The Speaking Division

A new unit, the Speakers' Bureau, joined the Four-Minute Men Division of the CPI in September 1918, with J. J. Pettijohn as its head. But for nearly a year before this it had been functioning as the Speaking Division, a separate branch of the CPI, under the direction of Arthur E. Bestor, president of the Chautauqua Institution. The members of the Speaking Division might be called the Four-Hour Men, because in an emergency they were good for that period.

The division was originally established in accordance with a letter from President Wilson dated September 25, 1917, in an effort to bring order out of the conflicting effort of more than a dozen speaking bureaus representing various government departments.

Under Mr Bestor the Speaking Division became a great federal lecture bureau "to offer a national clearing house for speaking campaigns " A card catalog of more than 10,000 speakers was maintained, and a selected list of 300 of the best was constantly in use. Engagements by Vice-President Marshall and Cabinet officers were regularly made by the division. Liaison was maintained not only with government offices but also with groups having ready-made audiences, such as Rotary Clubs, chautauquas, literary societies, and so on The United States Chamber of Commerce was liberal in its help, not only aiding in securing lecture engagements but deluging its local branches with advance newspaper material for each address Direct relationship was established with the Treasury Department, Department of Labor, Council of National Defense, Food Administration, Red Cross, and other groups. It worked closely with organizations such as the Friends of German Democracy, and it scheduled speakers from the British War Mission, the French High Commission, the Italian Embassy, and the Belgian Legation.

A series of *Speakers Bulletins* was inaugurated in January 1918, but was abandoned shortly to avoid duplicating the work of the regular *Four-Minute Men Bulletins*

War conferences, for the instruction and inspiration of speakers, were planned by the CPI Speaking Division, though usually held under the formal sponsorship of State Councils of Defense; forty-five conferences were thus held in thirty-seven states. And in April 1918 a much larger project was undertaken in the National Conference of American Lecturers at Washington, with a program largely controlled by the CPI. Forty-five speeches were given at this meeting, and opportunity provided for consultation with government officials and with representatives of the Allies.

Some of the most colorful work of the Speaking Division was in connection with the American lecture tours of men and women from across the ocean. Fifty men from the A.E F. were sent back to this country by General Pershing to aid the Speaking Division in the Third Liberty Loan, and 344 Belgian soldiers returning from Russia via the U.S. had their transcontinental journey conducted by the Division.

A company of French Chasseurs—"Blue Devils"—toured the larger cities in picturesque triumph under the chaperonage of the Speaking Division, and many prominent officials of both the French and British missions made their appearances under the same auspices.

The dashing and fascinating Captain Paul Perigord (now professor of French civilization, University of California at Los Angeles), was lionized as "the warrior priest" wherever he went on a seven-months tour of the entire country. The Marquis and Marquise de Courtivron and the Marquis and Marquise de Polignac toured the South and found that the American liking for titles strengthened the appeal of their own charm and the message they had to deliver.

But the most sensational lecture tour arranged by the Speaking Division was that of Wesley Frost, former American consul at Queenstown, Ireland, who had taken testimony from survivors of eighty-one submarinings, including the *Lusitania* and the *Arabic*. His speech, given in numerous cities in 1917 and 1918, was usually called, "The Tragedy of the Lusitania," but drew its material from all of the many atrocities which he ascribed to U-boat commanders—"the Jackals of the Sea." Frequently his talks were illustrated with slides, and sometimes he spoke for the benefit of specific war charities or drives— Liberty Loan, beds for war hospitals, and so on.

Frost's own sense of drama would have assured him of a good press in any event, but through the cooperation of the CPI, the State Department, and the United States Chamber of Commerce, local newspapers received a perfect bombardment of publicity before Frost's arrival. Gradually it came to be believed that Frost was not merely a reporter of tragedy, but that he had actually participated in it. When the former consul

[128]

arrived in Butte, Montana, the *Daily Post* of that city captioned its picture on page 1:

WESLEY FROST, THE GOOD SAMARITAN
OF THE U-BOAT WAR, COMES TO BUTTE

Mr. Creel's old employer, the *Rocky Mountain News*, said "A thousand Denverites sat in the Auditorium last night and alternately sobbed and cheered." The *Cleveland Plain Dealer* reported that Frost had described "A Satan's carnival—the loathesome tomfoolery of a troop of orang-outang gorillas." Here is a passage from Frost's *Lusitania* speech·

"It was quite black out there on the Atlantic, and in the blackness the life-boats alternately rose on the crests of the waves and sank into the black valley between The boats carried women and children whose hair hung in icicles over their shoulders and their half-frozen bodies yielded to the rolling and pitching of the frail boats. Now and then a half-dead passenger uttered a shriek of pain or of anguish as she realized that a friend or relative had died in her arms Meanwhile, in the dark hull of the German submarine, the captain watching through the periscope finally turned his head away. Even this man, agent of Prussian cruelty, had witnessed a scene upon which he did not care to gaze."

These are merely dramatic examples of the men and women who spoke under the auspices of the Speaking Division. It provided more simple fare also, holding charter, as it did, from several government departments concerned with less lugubrious subjects than submarinings But whatever the nature of the talks, whether inspirational or merely informative, the CPI Speaking Division was the master lecture bureau of the war.

* * *

The Four-Minute Men and the Speaking Division together cost the government $210,994.14. There is no doubt that speakers formed the very spearhead of the CPI assault on indifference and civic apathy. In this respect the Four-Minute Men program was one of the most amazing experiments in public-opinion management that the world had seen.

Professor Bertram G Nelson, associate director of the Four-Minute Men Division, expressed it during the war.

"There are a surprisingly large number of people in every community who do not read, there are others who read no English; and a still larger number who read nothing but the headlines. The most enthusiastic, patriotic meetings get together 5,000 people in a city of 500,000, for every one who goes and thrills and applauds there are five hundred who stay at home, passive and ofttimes indifferent. These silent ones eat sugar, bacon and wheat; their vacant minds become the ready recipient of German lies; their tongues become the ready transmitters of German propaganda, their grumblings are heard by the quick ear of the politician; they are ofttimes 'the menace within the walls.' Yet their sons must help do the fighting, their minds, wills, and hearts must become attuned to our national purposes

"How can we reach them? Not through the press, for they do not read; not through patriotic rallies, for they do not come. Every night eight to ten million people of all classes, all degrees of intelligence, black and white, young and old, rich and poor, meet in the moving picture houses of this country, and among them are many of these silent ones who do not read or attend meetings but who must be reached."

Professor Nelson spoke of what the Four-Minute Men could do when Reel 7 came to its end, the theater lights went on, and one of his delegates took the stage. But he would have granted that films themselves held a vital place in patriotic education on the same social and intellectual plane of which he was speaking.

Chapter 6

A BARRAGE OF FILM: MOBILIZING THE MOVIES

AMERICA was thrilling to Theda Bara's "special super de luxe photoplay," *Her Greatest Love*, when war was declared, and Mae Murray was "stampeding a continent" in *A Mormon Maid* On the legitimate stage, Ruth Chatterton was playing *Come Out of the Kitchen*, and in vaudeville Eva Tanguay was convulsing tremendous audiences, while Tin Pan Alley, having discovered the Hawaiian Islands, made the spurious grass skirt and the paper lei familiar accompaniments of the hula dance from Eastport to San Diego. George M. Cohan had just made his movie début in *Broadway Jones*

And then in a few months a great new field was opened to the entertainment world. War themes took the center of the stage "Yacki Hacki Wicki Wacki Woo" gave place to "Hinky Dinky Parley Voo"; "Indianola" was pushed aside for "Over There", and the bugle and drum supplanted the ukulele and the steel guitar. Writers, actors, and musicians still tried to make people laugh, and sometimes cry, but now it was for a higher purpose and in an ennobling common cause.

No field of entertainment felt the effect of war more strongly than the movies, and none was of greater interest to the CPI. Next to the products of Tin Pan Alley—the war songs which are still familiar though meaningless to young Americans—the movie film was both the easiest way of presenting propaganda in the form of entertainment and one of the important items in a broad program of civilian morale.

The CPI did not enter the movie field in a formal sense until July 1917, and the Division of Films was not set up until September of that year, but an observant American, even during the years of our neutrality, might have guessed that sooner or later the United States Government would find itself in the business of producing and distributing movies. Long before our declaration of war the medium had proved itself to be one of the most convenient channels of propaganda.

During those pre-war years, of course, the government had nothing to do with the movies, but partisans of both the Allies and the Central Powers were hard at work. The most terrifying and the most famous of these propaganda films before we entered the war was *The Battle Cry of Peace*, showing in blood-curdling scenes what would happen to America during the coming German invasion of the country. It was based on Hudson Maxim's theories of world politics and German atrociousness, and it made the country's hair stand on end; tremendous support was given to the campaigns for preparedness and belligerence carried on by such groups as the National Security League.

Other films used this bludgeon technique of driving home a point, but the indirect approach was also employed. Geraldine Farrar was quoted in the *Exhibitor's Trade Review* for March 31, 1917: "I knew when I played Joan of Arc for Mr DeMille's picture that it would be, as it is, the greatest of all pro-Ally propaganda."

By that fatal first week in April 1917 a dozen or more films were practically ready for release to do their part in the preparedness campaign. Most of these were pushed through to completion and, though originally planned for a nation officially at peace, became the first of our actual "war pictures."

One of these was *How Uncle Sam Prepares*, made by the Hanover Film Company "by authority of and under the direction of military experts." An allegorical introduction preceded scenes of the Army and Navy in various kinds of operations, and the *Boston Post* called the picture, "a stupendous effort on the part of the government to stimulate recruiting and increase demand for universal training." Then there were preparedness serials such as *Liberty* in twenty episodes and *Uncle Sam at Work* in eleven

Most of this early war-minded activity was a hit-or-miss exploitation of the most thrilling and absorbing subject of the moment. It was not yet a concerted effort in behalf of patri-

What Is Your Liberty Worth To YOU?

¶ The Liberty of the American people is in jeopardy. The cry of liberty or death heard in 1776 is echoed in 1917. Every American industry is contributing huge funds for preparedness — to strengthen the sinews of the government in this hour when upon the test of our force and endurance depends the future independence of our people.

¶ What is the great Motion Picture Industry going to do?

¶ What are *you* going to do?

¶ The Associated Motion Picture Advertisers, Inc., has offered its services to the government to assist in attracting a patriotic activity in behalf of the country in the grave crisis that confronts it, and to stimulate interest in enlistments in the various defensive branches of the government by attractive posters and slides, and by compelling advertising and publicity. These services have received the support of Active men in the United States Service.

¶ But to accomplish the vital results for which we are striving, we must have *funds!* Unfortunately the members of the Associated Motion Picture Advertisers, Inc., haven't a great deal of money. But they are doing their share.

¶ Are *you* going to help?

¶ Funds from one cent to a thousand dollars will help—will enable us to do as much for the government as we would by going out to stop a bullet. Checks, money or express orders should be sent to

ASSOCIATED MOTION PICTURE ADVERTISERS, Inc.
Finance Committee,
B. P. SCHULBERG, Chairman,
485 Fifth Ave., N. Y.

P. S.—*This trade-paper has, with a fine patriotic impulse, contributed this page, gratis, for the purpose of this fund. It means money to Exhibitor's Trade Review. Will YOU do as much?*

The Movie Industry Joins Up
Advertisement in "Exhibitor's Trade Review," April 7, 1917

otism But in the April 7, 1917, issue of *Exhibitor's Trade Review* (which must have gone to press several days before declaration of war), the advertising division of the industry announced its mobilized effort to aid the government in the preparedness program.

Then in the April 21 issue appeared editorials identifying the movie industry still more closely with the government program. One impressed upon the producers their lofty mission in sustaining morale during "the time of strife and turmoil, of suffering and sorrow that is approaching" Movie makers were urged to "have ready and waiting on their shelves pictures of happiness, pictures of cheerfulness, and pictures that show the brightness and sunshine of life."

But on the 28th a warning followed this exhortation to cheerfulness· "Motion picture producers who are contemplating productions with war as their theme will do well to see to it, before those pictures are released, that they are not likely in any particular to exert an influence prejudicial to the government's prosecution of the present war. . . . There is every indication that the federal authorities will suppress such pictures without hesitation. . . . There is no time now to discuss a producer's abstract right to make and market any kind of picture he pleases Probably he possesses that right. But public right takes precedence over any private right, especially in time of war"

Trade papers such as *Exhibitor's Trade Review* helped give encouragement to the movies' enlistment in the patriotic cause, but the industry itself was not slow to act In response to a request from Secretary of the Treasury McAdoo, William A Brady, famous producer and president of the National Association of the Motion Picture Industry, called a meeting of important movie people on May 23, 1917, and a committee was appointed to help arouse public interest in the government borrowing program.

This group swung into action immediately, and devised plans for theater support in the First Liberty Loan drive. The American Banker's Association, through Mr. Brady's committee, paid for 30,000 Liberty Loan slides to show on the movie screens of America, and each was delivered with a letter from Secretary McAdoo to the theater manager. Many ingenious publicity plans were concocted, including an early version of "Bank Night," with $700 in Liberty Bonds distributed at certain theaters each week.

From the beginning and right on through the Victory Loan, movie stars were among the most effective salesmen for Liberty Bonds. Theda Bara took in $300,000 in one day at a booth in front of the New York Public Library, Douglas Fairbanks chartered a special train and, after a whirlwind tour of the country, came back with proceeds from $1,000,000 worth of bonds that he had sold; Mary Pickford was credited with bringing in $2,000,000 on a brief tour of California. The list goes on and on like that, and each of these movie people bought eye-filling amounts of bonds for himself, and helped the government and the relief agencies in countless other ways

This shows the patriotic spirit prevalent in the film centers, but it was not exploitation of the films themselves for the winning of the war. The most important step in that direction was taken on July 11, 1917, when William A Brady and other members of the industry's War Cooperating Committee came to Washington to confer with government officials Their first appointment was with George Creel, who presented a plan whereby the War Cooperating Committee would assign a delegate to each government department to discover how the motion picture industry might help meet its needs.

This plan was adopted by the War Cooperating Committee, which included, besides Mr Brady, such other well known figures as William Fox, D W Griffith, Thomas H. Ince, Jesse L. Lasky, Carl Laemmle, Marcus Loew, Joseph M Schenck, Louis J. Selznick, and Adolph Zukor.

Thus it was through the patriotic eagerness of the movie people themselves that the commercial phase of the wartime cinema program was launched with little more than a suggestion from the government. But there was still a vast field of movie work untouched, and Mr Creel proceeded to exploit it.

As Mr. Creel told the investigating Congressmen in 1918.

"We went to the Signal Corps and explained to them our view that since new pictures were being made for the historical record, there was no reason why these war pictures could not be used to good purpose in the United States, so that the people could see the war going on We worked with them in securing the best photographers in the United States Those men went to France and made pictures over there, and the pictures were sent back to this country.

"Then, we sent Army and Navy photographers around to the cantonments, to the factories, and to the fields; we sent them to the training camps and tried to make a photographic record, as far as we could, representing democracy's preparation for war. Those pictures we put into single-reel and two-reel releases, and even up to eight-reel features, and released them all over the United States We had the captions put in many languages and sent these pictures to all parts of the world so that other peoples might see what our country is, what our institutions are, and how America is rallying to the colors."

This entire program, described only in part in Mr. Creel's statement, was under the supervision of the CPI Division of Films, which was set up by Presidential order on September 25, 1917 Charles S Hart was appointed director. He had been advertising manager of *Hearst's Magazine* at a reported $10,000 a year and came to the CPI at $3,900, having been lured away from a possible Ordnance Department commission by Mr. Creel and Mr. Byoir. Starting from scratch, he built up in eight months a staff that included more than forty-five people, and that by the end of the war was even larger. The head office was in New York, another office in Washington, and many members of the staff were continually on the road

Dr. Guy Stanton Ford said of Mr Creel in 1918· "Here was a man who saw what others had not seen clearly enough in the past, that such a thing has infinite possibilities for good if it is organized in the right way, and that you can teach through the eyes and through these pictures what neither the printed or

spoken word can teach. He caught the idea, and he pushed
it. . . ."

Under Mr. Hart's aggressive administration the CPI Division of Films had five distinct functions:

1. Cooperation with photographers of the Signal Corps and the Navy in preparing and handling pictures they had taken.

2 Writing of scenarios and issuance of permits for commercial films about government work.

3 Production of the documentary films made entirely by the CPI, most of which were finished after the Armistice.

4 Distribution and promotion of war films whether taken by our own government, the Allies, or private producers.

5. Cooperation with the Foreign Film Division in the export of pictures to CPI agents abroad.

The original idea was to make "documentaries" which would not compete with the regular trade and would be shown in public meetings of various kinds but not in movie theaters except for benefit performances. But as the need for longer and more elaborate films became evident, documentaries of feature length were turned out and the problem of distribution became highly involved.

Through the division's educational department, under Clare de Lissa Berg, the CPI furnished movies to army and navy meetings, patriotic rallies, and educational institutions either gratis or at the under-cost figure of $1 per reel per day Although the educational department was kept busy, free distribution came to occupy a less and less important place in the whole undertaking

In three states—California, Michigan, and North Dakota—theaters received CPI films through the respective State Councils of Defense, but everywhere else the pictures were handled by regular commercial distributors on the percentage basis normally followed by the trade. Pathé, First National, and World Film handled the most important of the reels.

Charges to the theaters were fixed according to a sliding scale so that the same film might be obtained for a few dollars

[137]

a week by a crossroads theater but $3,000 a week by a Manhattan picture palace.

One of the particular problems in distribution was the *Official War Review*, a propaganda newsreel prepared by the British, French, and Italian governments and released in this country by the CPI. The Allied countries wished to sell their service to the highest bidder, and this was done for a while, Hearst-Pathé making the top bid. But eventually Mr Creel insisted on making the film available to all four of the chief newsreel companies—Universal, Mutual, Gaumont, and Hearst-Pathé. Each of these services received 2,000 feet at a flat rate of $5,000, which the Allies thought an outrage, but which the CPI persuaded them to accept The CPI also issued to the four companies a weekly allotment of 500 feet of diversified war film of other sorts.

In the production end of the business, the Film Division went through several phases First of all, the CPI laid its hands on whatever war films the Signal Corps might have available. Next, both the CPI cameramen and those of the Signal Corps made a number of "short subjects" of the type supposed not to compete with theaters. The list included

The 1917 Recruit	Labor's Part in Democracy's
The Second Liberty Loan	War
Ready for the Fight	Annapolis
Torpedo Boat Destroyers	Ship Building
Submarines	Making of Big Guns
Army and Navy Sports	Making of Small Arms
The Spirit of 1917	Making of Uniforms
In a Southern Camp	Activities of the Engineers
The Lumber Jack	Woman's Part in the War
Medical O.R C. in Action	Men Who Are Doing Things
Fire and Gas	The Conquest of the Air

Then, as it was decided that the government must accomplish an actual invasion of the movie houses if it was to make full use of the film's patriotic possibilities, the feature-picture program was inaugurated.

[138]

Pershing's Crusaders, seven reels, was the first of these, and it was followed by *America's Answer*, five reels, *Under Four Flags*, five reels; and a quartet of two-reelers called the *U.S.A. Series* A special appeal to the Negro population was made through *Our Colored Fighters*.

While the later of these films were being made and *Pershing's Crusaders* was already on the screen, the Film Division acquired a new unit, the Scenario Department, which was established June 1, 1918, under the direction of Rufus Steele. Up to this time the government had encountered some reluctance on the part of commercial producers to make the kind of documentary film that the departments desired The movie people thought that propaganda films of this sort had no box-office value As a result, the government found it necessary to pay for making the pictures, and then had to enter into further contracts to secure distribution for the films.

The CPI believed that documentaries of the government at work—"the American people in the war"—could be made to have genuine audience appeal Mr. Steele's assignment, therefore, was to prepare scenarios which would interest the movie-goer and yet would put across the message in which the government was interested After discussion, producers agreed to assume the cost of making one-reel subjects, in return for which the CPI wrote the scenario and issued permits allowing cameramen to make the necessary pictures. The film remained the property of the producer and the government derived no income from it. Under this system, eighteen one-reelers were prepared:

Paramount-Bray Pictograph—the "Says Uncle Sam" Series. *Keep 'Em Singing and Nothing Can Lick 'Em, I Run the Biggest Life Insurance Company on Earth; A Girl's a Man for a' That, I'll Help Every Willing Worker Find a Job.*

Pathé Company—*Solving the Farm Problem of the Nation* (U.S Boys' Working Reserve) ; *Feeding the Fighter*

Universal Company—*Reclaiming the Soldiers' Duds, The American Indian Gets into the War Game.*

C L. Chester—*Schooling Our Fighting Mechanics, There Shall Be No Cripples, Colored Americans, It's an Engineer's War, Finding and Fixing the Enemy, Waging War in Washington, All the Comforts of Home; Masters for the Merchant Marine, The College for Camp Cooks; Railless Railroads.*

Private producers also made longer pictures in accordance with the Scenario Department's suggestions. Several of these were abandoned part way through production when the Armistice was signed, but two were finished—*The Miracle of Ships*, a six-reel feature made by C. L. Chester; and the Hodkinson Company's *Made in America*, an eight-reel picture finished long after the Armistice, showing the growth of the citizen army from start to finish.

The work of the Scenario Department was so satisfactory that by the end of the summer of 1918 the CPI decided to go into production on its own Six two-reelers were made, though none of them was shown before the Armistice and two of them never at all. The titles of these last CPI films:

If Your Soldier's Hit	*Making the Nation Fit*
Our Wings of Victory	*The Storm of Steel*
Our Horses of War	*The Bath of Bullets*

Whether the pictures were made by the CPI, the Navy, the Signal Corps, or private companies, the Film Division was tireless in its promotion efforts. The domestic distribution department had seventeen sales representatives in the principal cities to lend support to the commercial distributors, and both these field men and the New York and Washington offices gave continual help in the way of publicity. Besides advance material for newspapers, the division sent posters, subway cards, and window displays, and personal pressure was applied to civic leaders to help boost the films. For instance, George Bowles, manager of the feature film division, sent telegrams to thirty prominent men in St. Louis when *Pershing's Crusaders* opened there in May 1918, asking their "personal cooperation and influence" in the name of the United States Government

And when *Pershing's Crusaders* had had its première in Cincinnati on April 29, every theater critic in town received a personal letter and the managing editors of the *Enquirer*, *Tribune*, *Times-Star*, and *Post* received telegrams

Advertising directed to the moviegoer was but part of the campaign, and the trade papers were filled with announcements designed to engage the interest and arouse the enthusiasm of theater managers For the CPI film *America's Answer*, for instance, the *Moving Picture World* of September 21, 1918, carried a two-page spread regarding this thrilling picture "filmed at the gates of hell and brought back through submarine-infested seas"

This promotion work brought results. *Pershing's Crusaders* and *America's Answer* each had more than 4,000 bookings, and the thirty-one weekly issues of the *Official War Review* had a total of nearly 7,000. In spite of a great deal of free distribution and in spite of (or perhaps because of) the reasonable rental charges and the "proportionate selling plan," the Film Division came close to paying its own way. Total expenses, including disbursement from earnings, came to $1,066,730 59, and more than three-quarters of this was covered by income from films The gross income from sale or rental of films was given in the *Complete Report*.

Pershing's Crusaders	$181,741.69
America's Answer	185,144.30
Under Four Flags	63,946.48
Official War Review	334,622.35
Our Bridge of Ships	992.41
U.S.A. Series	13,864.98
Our Colored Fighters	640 60
News Weekly	15,150.00
Miscellaneous Sales	56,641.58
Total Sales of Films	$852,744.39

This does not include the great cooperative venture of the Film Division with the CPI's Foreign Section (Foreign Film Division) in sending American war pictures to other countries

Under the supervision of Lieutenant John Tuerk, assigned by the War Department, and Jules E. Brulatour, a pioneer figure in the movie industry, more than 6,200 reels went abroad. And this effective propaganda material went everywhere from the banana republics of Central America to the sprawling onetime empire of the Tsar. Details of the work, including some of its difficulties, are given in later chapters of this book, but it is important to note here the device through which the CPI was able to persuade foreign distributors to take American propaganda films.

The Trading-with-the-Enemy Act, which we have already encountered in connection with press censorship, also provided that no film could be exported except by license from the War Trade Board. In practice that meant that no film could leave the country without permission from the CPI, for every export license was submitted to the Committee for approval or rejection. And the decision of the CPI was that no one could export entertainment films unless he agreed to send along with it a certain amount of CPI material The result, as George Creel put it, was that "Charlie Chaplin and Mary Pickford led *Pershing's Crusaders* and *America's Answer* into the enemy's territory and smashed another Hindenburg line."

Lieutenant Tuerk was in charge of the export board of review, and he was supported not only by the general provisions of the Trading-with-the-Enemy Act but also by the action of the War Trade Board in July 1918 when film was placed on the export conservation list Thus, in addition to making a positive requirement that CPI film must accompany each export, the Committee was also able to encourage the kind of commercial pictures which would help the cause—"wholesome views of American life," with emphasis on democracy, fairness to labor, equal opportunity, and so on The main object was to dim the picture of Uncle Shylock which had been deeply etched by German propagandists and even by our own Allies. Limitation of film export caused many practical difficulties in the field, but at home it increased government control over the movie industry.

Everything was not smooth going in connection with film export, however. Sometimes films passed by our government would prove unacceptable to some other, and often a picture with a deceptively patriotic title would contain material believed to have been inspired by the enemy. As Colonel Ernest J. Chambers, Canada's chief press censor, wrote to George Creel, on January 29, 1918 "Many motion picture plays are being submitted . . which, while containing titles damning the Germans up and down, actually feature Germans in the pictures as beings of peculiar benevolence, valor, and ability. . . There has been an unusual crop of motion picture plays entered here for censorship which represent England and Englishmen in a most objectionable light . . I wonder whether these pictures are not due to the suggestion of the wily German who would like to belittle an Allied nation in the eyes of the American people."

Colonel Chambers, however, was carrying coals to Newcastle when he addressed Mr. Creel on this subject, for the CPI had more than sufficient experience with suspected pictures The most famous of all these was *Patria*, and its bizarre history is worth examination both for its suggestion of how the movies can be turned to strange uses and for the interest of the story itself, which has never been adequately reported.

Patria was a fifteen-episode "serial romance of society and preparedness," starring Mrs Vernon Castle, one of the top "money names" of the industry The excellent cast also included Milton Sills, Warner Oland, and others who had a large following. The story carried the byline of a well known Hearst writer, Louis Joseph Vance, the director was Leopold Wharton, and the picture was produced by Hearst's International and released on January 14, 1917, by Pathé, which a short time earlier had become the outlet for Hearst pictures.

For weeks the Hearst newspaper and periodical press had laid down a noisy barrage of advance publicity, including a comprehensive campaign of advertising and news stories, a novelized version of the photoplay for the newspapers, and announcements in every Hearst magazine from *Good House-keeping* to *Motor and Motor Boating.*

When the picture was first released we were not yet at war with Germany, and ostensibly it was merely furthering President Wilson's preparedness campaign But as the contents of the story became known, and as its phenomenal popularity continued after declaration of war, more and more government officials became interested The whole enterprise was swathed in red, white, and blue, but that did not prevent the authorities from making the quick discovery that the shooting in *Patria* was not directed at Germany but at a nation which, in at least a formal sense, was a "comrade in arms"—Japan

Amid *Patria's* successive incidents of exploding munitions plants, derailed trains, kidnaping, death-defying leaps from cliffs, horses, and automobiles, stood the sinister figure of Baron Huroki (Warner Oland), an agent of Japan's secret service The name of the character is noteworthy in view of the fact that General Kuroki was a fire-breathing commander in the Russo-Japanese War Not only did the film accuse a friendly power of the Black Tom Explosion and the incitement of labor violence, but in Episode 14 it showed the Japanese leading an invasion in force against America from the soil of Mexico, another supposedly friendly nation.

Patria Channing (Mrs. Castle), who had been bequeathed $100,000,000 to be used "for American preparedness," eventually assumed command of the disorganized United States army, directing gunfire from an airplane, and, when the Japanese-Mexican forces had been routed, ended up safely in the arms of Captain Parr, U S Secret Service!

All of this was good movie business, but gradually through 1917 and 1918 evidence was pieced together indicating that Mr. Hearst's well known dislike for the Japanese and his supposed opposition to the war might not be the only thing behind *Patria.*

German propaganda agents entered the picture.

In the December 1917 issue of *Everybody's*, Samuel Hopkins Adams, a member of the CPI Syndicate Features Division, had an article, "Invaded America," discussing various German attempts to stir up anti-Japanese feeling in this country. In one passage he said·

"In the fall of 1914, Maximilian Foster, well known as a fiction writer and with some experience in the dramatic field, was approached by a go-between with an offer to write a play on the order of *An Englishman's Home*, Americanized.

"The financial consideration was liberal, not to say generous. $5,000 on the completion of the scenario, and an equal amount upon the delivery of the finished manuscript.

" 'What's the idea?' inquired the author.

" 'Anti-Japanese,' explained the go-between. 'It's to be the Japanese invasion of California: yellow peril and all that sort of thing.'

"Suspicion began to dawn upon the writer's mind 'Who's paying the money?'

" 'That'll be all right,' he was assured. 'Any sort of guarantee you want.'

" 'But I want to know where the money comes from.'

" 'What difference does that make so long as—'

" 'See here! Does this offer originate in the German Foreign Office?'

"The other denied it, but so haltingly that Mr. Foster's suspicions were confirmed. With considerable emphasis and disgust he bade the agent tell his principals to go elsewhere with their offer—and even specified a decidedly uncomfortable elsewhere

"Later the go-between turned up as the recipient of German propaganda money; he was a suborned pro-German 'accelerator of public opinion.' "

Colonel Chambers, the Canadian press censor, saw Adams's article and wrote to Creel:

"I am strongly of the opinion that *Patria* was made to order of enemy agents and that a well known individual identified with a number of publications at present forbidden circulation in Canada [Hearst] was at the bottom of the whole scheme or acted as the agent of the German propagandists

"If I could establish a connection between this individual [Hearst] and those who approached Mr Foster, and also those responsible for the production of *Patria* in its original objectionable form, it would enable me to take a strong stand in connection with a proposal which has been made for restoration of their Canadian circulation to a number of publications whose attitude is, as far as it dare be, anti-Ally"

Creel turned the letter over to Adams, who in reply expressed his confidence in Foster's loyalty and named Edward Lyell Fox as the German agent Fox was a newspaperman, but it was known that he had been in touch with Ambassador von Bernstorff, he had written *New York American* stories of Russian atrocities against Germany (so convincing that the German ambassador wired back to Berlin to learn more about them), and he had written a letter to Captain Franz von Papen, German military attaché and future chancellor of the Second Reich, advocating production of a film play to turn the American people against Japan.

All of this came out in the exciting hearings before the Senate Judiciary Committee when it was attempting to trace lines of influence between German propaganda and the brewing and liquor interests in December 1918 Captain George G. Lester of the Military Intelligence Division of the General Staff told what he knew about the mysterious origins of *Patria* Fox had denied that he meant to go through with the film plan, but Captain Lester said "The fact is that Mr. Hearst, through the International Film Service Corporation, put out a film in 1916 called *Patria* which exploited the very idea which was set forth generally in Fox's statement." The letter to Von Papen, the expelled military attaché, was adduced. Vance, the supposed author of the photoplay, may have allowed use of his name in connection with *Patria* without actually writing the scenario.

[146]

Possibly a complete unravelling of the *Patria* story will never be made, but Captain Lester's final judgment was:

"*Patria* had a story with three barrels. Its principal excuse was 'preparedness.' But by the time the first episodes were released the country was already committed to that. Therefore the only other two elements, anti-Mexican and anti-Japanese propaganda, remained active"

President Wilson saw the film, according to Captain Lester's testimony, and in a personal interview with Hearst demanded that everything reflecting on the Japanese be deleted. The order was carried out The characters continued to wear Japanese uniforms, but Mexican names were conferred upon them, and all of the sins previously charged to the agents of the Mikado were now dumped on Mexico! The film was held up in various places by federal and state authorities while these changes were being made, but then was allowed to run, to the delight of several million people

Another case, similar to that of *Patria* in that the film reflected upon an Allied country, was that of *The Spirit of '76*. This was produced by Robert Goldstein, who had been associated with D. W Griffith in making *The Birth of a Nation* and wished to give the same treatment to the Revolutionary War that Griffith had given to Reconstruction Goldstein's picture was finished just before the war, following a year and a half of production.

One of the scenes, the Wyoming Massacre, showed British soldiers killing women and children and carrying off young girls Naturally, a dramatic presentation of war with a nation now our ally was unlikely to excite official enthusiasm in 1917. But the offense was greatly aggravated, in the opinion of federal officers, because in the censors' preview the massacre scene was omitted, and then later restored to the film; and also because Goldstein was charged with appealing to German-American anglophobes in attempting to finance the production In any event, the reels were seized under Title XI of the Espionage Act, the company went into bankruptcy, and Goldstein was sentenced to ten years in the federal penitentiary.

Still another instance of American solicitude for the feelings of the Allies is found in the record of *The Caillaux Case*, produced by Fox, and protested by the French representatives in this country. The dénouement of this involved censorship story is succinctly presented in the letter, reproduced here, from Philip Patchin of the State Department to George Creel.

These and other incidents in connection with entertainment films were not so frequent, however, as the various contretemps relating to documentary films of our own war work. In many of these cases rival distributors charged that the CPI Film Division, heavily weighted with former Hearst employees, was giving the Hearst services an inside track. There was no denying that Byoir, Sisson, Hart, and a number of other CPI men had once been on the Hearst payroll, but conclusive evidence of favoritism was never offered.

It was charged by Universal, for instance, that while Hearst-Pathé was showing pictures of American tanks in action all other companies were denied the privilege of even photographing them It developed later, however, that permits were issued simultaneously to Hearst and to Universal to take pictures of tanks at a certain place; the Hearst cameramen hurried out to take their pictures, but Universal delayed until the War Department had changed its mind about the whole project and refused to honor the permit. When this was brought to the attention of the CPI, Hearst was ordered to recall the film.

Again, Creel was charged with rigging a Hearst monopoly of war newsreels, but this proved to be the highest-bidder complication alluded to above Hearst was the highest bidder, but eventually the CPI forced the Allies to give the *War Review* to all companies.

These incidents of the tank pictures and the newsreels were made public in connection with a much more serious charge of Hearst influence, the CPI suppression of Universal's film *The Yanks Are Coming*, made at the plant of the Dayton-Wright Airplane Company. The movie concern claimed that the pic-

DEPARTMENT OF STATE
WASHINGTON

In reply refer to
Inf

September 8, 1918.

Dear George:

I return herewith your letter to MacBride and the other correspondence in connection with the Caillaux Film. I agree with you that they have done a great deal in cutting out the objectionable feature of the film. Now that they have it finished I find myself wondering what they are going to do with it. The only good stuff was objectionable and I am afraid there is not much left. It was a 7,000 foot film, or thereabouts, and it seems to me that fully 2,000 feet must have been titles with all the fireworks illuminated. It seems to me that patrons of the Fox Film Company might be saved a lot of trouble if the Company would simply print the titles, give them to their customers and let it go at that.

Sincerely yours,

George Creel, Esquire,
    Committee on Public Information,
        10 Jackson Place,
            Washington, D. C.

The Fate of "The Caillaux Case"

Philip Patchin of the State Department Tersely States the Results of Censorship on a Movie Which Had Been Protested by French Representatives in This Country

Advertisement of the Most Famous "Hate" Picture

ture had been made in cooperation with the War Department and that when shown in a Washington preview had "received the highest praise from officials of the War Department and the Signal Corps." Mr. Creel's representative, however, disapproved of the film, and the CPI refused to pass it.

The chairman would not budge from his position, but the picture was nevertheless advertised to open in New York on June 23, 1918. Carl Byoir was in the ticket line at the Broadway Theater that night, and Department of Justice men were reported to be scattered through the house in case the theater should try to show the forbidden films. Instead, this sign was hung in the lobby:

THE YANKS ARE COMING
advertised to be
tonight
Stopped by the
CREEL-HEARST COMMITTEE

And the next morning's *New York Times* headlined its story in column 1, page 1:

WAR FILM STOPPED;
HEARST INFLUENCE
ON CREEL BLAMED

R. H. Cochrane, vice-president of the Universal Film Company, issued a public statement giving his version of the whole case and once more charging Creel with submitting to Hearst. Some of the supposed "Hearstlings" proved not to be such, and Mr. Cochrane was obliged to admit that permits for the photographing had not been obtained. He said, however, that Mr. Creel was "peeved" at being ignored, and also because one of Universal's men had testified against the CPI before the House Ways and Means Committee on the subject of the newsreel monopoly. It was at just about this time that Dr. James A. B. Scherer, chief field agent of the Council of National Defense,

[149]

resigned because, he said, Secretary Baker had tried to keep him from denouncing Hearst, thus adding still more color to Mr Cochrane's theory of Hearst influence in Washington.

But we know from Ray Stannard Baker's last volume of *Woodrow Wilson. Life and Letters* that the President was very chary of boastful publicity about plane production because he knew how false most of the claims were and feared the reaction of public disillusionment. It is possible that Creel was following specific orders from the White House. In any event the CPI chairman told the papers:

"The motion picture, *The Yanks Are Coming*, was refused the necessary official sanction because every detail of the film's making was in open disregard and even defiance of established procedure No photographs may be made in any factory doing government war work without formal permits, issued after investigation. The Universal did not have these permits, and made no effort to get them. Also, after making the pictures without permits, the Universal planned a commercial exploitation of the film for its own profit, a privilege denied every other motion picture producer in the United States at one time or other.

"The only question in issue is whether private greed shall have power to nullify the government's efforts to protect its military secrets. The charge of Hearst influence is merely an attempt to muddy the water, and is as absurd as it is indecent. No one in connection with this organization had responsibility in the matter save myself. The decision was my own, and others merely carried out my explicit instructions."

Secretary Baker stood by the CPI, and the last we hear of *The Yanks Are Coming* in the CPI files is in correspondence in which Creel, Baker, and Colonel Churchill of Military Intelligence decide to let the Dayton-Wright Company show the films to its own employees, and to bring a print to Washington for the Bureau of Aircraft Production. Everyone agreed that the pictures should not be left "kicking around." A print is now in The National Archives.

Other films were held up or suppressed, too, but they were few in number when compared with the hundreds of privately produced war pictures which were passed without question by the CPI.

The American cinema during the war years turned out some of the most amazing productions that an amazing industry has ever given to its tremendous audience, and it is probable that the strictly "entertainment" films were more important for carrying America's message to the people than the frankly propagandist documentaries issued under the CPI.

Some of these war films are monuments in the development of movie art. Charlie Chaplin's *Shoulder Arms* is considered by many competent people to be one of the great moving pictures. It was not released until October 30, 1918, and cannot be said to have had an important part in the winning of the war If it had appeared earlier, however, it would undoubtedly have been one of the most useful, though one of the most indirect, of the pictures helping the American people to accept the dislocations of war. Charlie is followed from his induction into the army as a rookie, through his inadvertent penetration of the German lines, to his eventual return with a pretty French girl as his companion and the Kaiser and the Crown Prince as his captives

Then there were *Mutt and Jeff at the Front* and many other comedies, and dozens of soul-gripping dramas such as *The Prussian Cur*, for which people in Springfield, Massachusetts, stood in a long line with the thermometer at 103; *To Hell with the Kaiser*, which in Lowell, Massachusetts, required a riot detail to quell a mob seeking admission, and *Wolves of Kultur*, a fifteen-episode thriller by Western Photoplays.

The greatest of all these "hate" pictures, however, was the incomparable *The Kaiser, the Beast of Berlin*, a "sensational creation" written by Elliott J Clawson, directed by Rupert Julian, and made by Jewel Productions. An inadequate idea of this story may be obtained from the synopsis exactly as it appeared in the *Moving Picture World* for April 20, 1918:

[151]

"Marcas, a mighty man, is a peace-loving blacksmith in Louvain, while in the palace in Berlin lives the Kaiser. A captain of the guard, chided for the appearance of his men, in anger knocks the Kaiser down and then commits suicide. The Kaiser soon after starts the world war. Louvain is invaded; the blacksmith, though wounded, saves his daughter from a German soldier. Later, the *Lusitania* is sunk. The commander of the submarine is decorated and then goes mad In an interview with Ambassador Gerard the Kaiser says he will stand no nonsense from America after the war. Then follow further incidents and happenings leading up to the declaration of war by the United States, and Gerard secures his passports Scenes of America's military and naval preparations are shown; then the scene shifts to the close of the war The principal allied generals are gathered in the palace in Berlin, the Kaiser is a captive and is turned over to the King of Belgium, who appoints the blacksmith as his jailer."

An Omaha dispatch to *Exhibitor's Trade Review* said. "Fourteen thousand people—the largest number that ever saw a motion picture in Omaha in one week—saw *The Kaiser* [*The Beast of Berlin*] at the Auditorium in that city last week Eight hundred children attended a 'kid matinee' on Saturday afternoon and the sixteen-piece orchestra that furnished the music could not be heard above the din they made. . . Wild cheering marked every show when the young captain soaked the Kaiser on the jaw. Patriotic societies boosted the picture because of its aid in stirring up the country to war. Street car signs were used, huge street banners swung over the crowds in the downtown district, and a truck paraded the streets with the Kaiser hanging in effigy and a big sign 'All pro-Germans will be admitted free ' None availed himself of the invitation."

The film ultimately received the final apotheosis of any photoplay—a two-reel travesty, *The Geezer of Berlin*.

Ambassador Gerard's book *My Four Years in Germany*, on which all patriotic writers were drawing to prove the Kaiser's evil intentions toward the United States, was turned into a

[152]

movie by First National, and an attempt was made to do the same thing with *Ambassador Morgenthau's Story* regarding Turkey However, as Ray Stannard Baker has shown, President Wilson disapproved of these translations to the screen, not only asking the author, Henry Morgenthau, Sr., to withhold permission, but refusing the request of Harper and Brothers to allow a film version of his own *History of the American People.*

Bureau of War Photographs

President Wilson's executive order of September 25, 1917, had created a Division of Pictures, a Division of Films, and a Division of Publications. In practice, Films and Pictures overlapped, and in March 1918 the two were combined, a Bureau of War Photographs in the Division of Films succeeding to the duties of the abandoned unit.

The Bureau of War Photographs handled official still pictures in the same way that the Division of Films handled movies. In addition, it had charge of censorship for both types of picture, the number of items to be considered running to 700 a day. George Creel said of this censorship "There is no law for it [actually the Espionage Act could have been made to cover it], but we have secured a voluntary agreement with the industry that all still photographs, no matter by whom made, and all motion pictures that deal in any manner with the war and with American aims, shall be submitted to this committee for censorship. In its work it keeps in the closest touch with the Army, the Navy, and the State Department."

Pictures taken by the Signal Corps and other Army and Navy photographers were received by the Bureau of War Photographs and, if considered safe for general distribution, were released to the press Prints were sold at 10 cents each, which was far below the normal cost. The Photographic Association was an important channel of distribution, its members, such as Underwood and Underwood, Harris and Ewing, Brown Brothers, and Western Newspaper Union, taking the pictures

[153]

in great numbers. Schools and libraries ranked next in importance.

An important function of the Bureau of War Photographs was to handle permits for photographing military, naval, and other governmental establishments and equipment. Every applicant was investigated and if he were not considered discreet and patriotic the privilege would be denied. Lawrence E. Rubel was in charge of permits and kept in close touch with Military and Naval Intelligence, which had the veto power over his decisions.

In the whole undertaking the effort was to gain the greatest patriotic use of the camera and the drama and human interest it could convey, without endangering military secrets As an indication of how the rules worked in practice, here is one of many cases covered in the CPI files G. L R. Masters, assistant to the president of the Standard Aircraft Corporation of Elizabeth, New Jersey, wrote to Creel on July 2, 1918·

"At this writing, I am endeavoring to get you on the telephone but in case I am not successful would ask that you give the following matter your consideration

"We are, as you know, to have the official flight of the first Handley Page aeroplane on Saturday, July 6, and as a souvenir to the invited guests, we wish to distribute cards approximately the size of a postal on which will be a photograph of this machine On the reverse side, we desire to give a slight description of the plane in question. For your information we desire to put on the following.

"Weight, approximately 14,000 lbs. fully equipped
"Speed, approximately 100 miles per hour
"Wings, spread, 100 ft
"Fuselage length, 62 ft 10 in.
"Crew of five men
"Bombs carried, approximately 1,800 lbs
"Gasoline carried, approximately 400 gallons
"Gasoline consumed, approximately 60 gallons per hr.
"Climbs in the vicinity of 65,000 ft. 215 ft. per min.

[154]

"Climbs in the vicinity of 10,000 ft. 113 ft. per min.   . .

"It may not be within our rights to publish all of the above but would appreciate your advising me by wire immediately. . . ."

The reply was forthcoming at once:

CONFIRMING TELEPHONE CONVERSATION YESTERDAY NOT PERMISSIBLE TO GIVE INFORMATION REGARDING AIRPLANE WEIGHT SPEED WING SPREAD CREW ETC

GEORGE CREEL

Cooperation with the CPI Foreign Section loomed so large in operations of the Bureau of War Photographs that when total disbursements were added up at the end of the war the cost for work on the home front was about $100,000 but the cost for work abroad nearly $300,000. Receipts from the sale of photographs, presumably entirely from this country, came to $70,000

DEPARTMENT OF SLIDES

Another subsidiary of the Division of Films was the Department of Slides which provided schools, churches, and societies with war views for the projector at 15 cents each, which was less than half the normal cost The Signal Corps produced the slides at first, but later the CPI set up its own slide laboratory at 1820 Eighteenth Street, N.W

To begin with, unrelated pictures were turned out, but later whole sequences, following a careful "scenario," were prepared. The first of these, *The Ruined Churches of France*, was a fifty-slide set planned by Professor John Tatlock of Stanford University. It was followed by others such as *Building a Bridge of Ships to Pershing*, *To Berlin via the Air Route*, and *Making the American Army*. Seven hundred sets of these were used. George F. Zook, professor of modern European history at Pennsylvania State College and later U S. Commissioner of Education, turned out nine new series which were issued in editions of one hundred sets each, each set including from fifty to sixty separate slides. Among his titles *The Call to Arms, Airplanes and How They Are Made,* and *The Navy at Work.*

Slides, like the movies and regular photographs, found their way into other countries through the CPI Foreign Section, but the bulk of the slides were used at home And 200,000 of them were made in twelve months.

The Department of Slides and the Bureau of War Photographs helped much in the winning of the war, but the big push was for movies. The movie industry was relatively free during the nineteen months of the war, but in the very last weeks the hand of government was coming closer. It is reasonable to suppose that regimentation would have become progressively strict if the war had continued into 1919. It is noteworthy that the reason for this closing in of Washington was not any apparent new desire to control the movies as an agency of communication but the matter-of-fact and obvious wartime necessity of bringing all industry under control for efficient use of manpower and materials.

A widespread movement to close the theaters as an economy measure was reported in the spring of 1918, and although it made no serious headway, it sounded an ominous note William Brady wrote in alarm, and Secretary McAdoo, mindful of the help given to Liberty Loan drives, was also disturbed. He told Creel he would "look upon it as a misfortune if moving pictures or other clean forms of amusement should be abolished " Fuel Administrator Garfield and Food Administrator Hoover concurred, and Creel himself wrote to Charles Hart. "I believe in the motion picture just as I believe in the press, and in my work it plays just as powerful a part in the production of an aroused and enlightened war sentiment."

Late in August 1918 the War Industries Board recognized the movies as an "essential industry," at least to the extent that it helped the government and the relief agencies, "and also to the extent of its activities in supplying an educational medium in furnishing to the great masses of the people a wholesome and comparatively cheap means of recreation "

However, certain safeguards were set up by the War Industries Board. no new theaters were to be built, no new tin containers for film were to be made, only single negatives (or two if for export) were to be permitted, obsolete film was to be reclaimed, and projectors and other items of equipment were to be repaired rather than replaced.

Far outweighing these in importance, however, was the stipulation that, in the interest of conservation and efficient use of raw materials, producers should take care that only "wholesome pictures" were made.

These concessions by the industry, in return for recognition as "essential," were made in conference between Mr. Brady's National Association of the Motion Picture Industry and the Priorities Committee of the War Industries Board At the same time Mr Brady set up a fuel conservation committee to try to reduce the theaters' own consumption of coal and to spread enthusiasm for conservation among movie patrons

Still more important changes for the industry were in contemplation when the Armistice was signed George Creel wrote Herbert Bayard Swope of the War Industries Board on October 25, 1918, regarding an elaborate plan worked out by Charles Hart to save both manpower and materials and to reduce the expenses of the producing industry without cutting down on government receipts from theater taxes This plan involved sharp curtailment of production schedules, advertising, and other phases of the work, and reissue of old prints. Hart and Creel believed that it would release 10,000 people for war work, besides saving $500,000 per week in expenses

If the war had not ended when it did, the movie industry would no doubt have found itself under the strictest control from Washington, and the demand for "wholesome pictures" presented more strongly than ever before, but still on the reasonable and self-apparent grounds of economy and conservation.

[157]

Chapter 7

CLIO JOINS THE COLORS: SCHOLARS AND THE SCHOOLS

G UY STANTON FORD, the present president of the
University of Minnesota and the 1937 president of
the American Historical Association, was forty-four
years old in 1917, and held the position of professor of European history and dean of the graduate school at the University of Minnesota He had been educated at Wisconsin,
Columbia, and Berlin, receiving the Columbia doctorate in
1903, and he had taught at Yale and Illinois as well as Minnesota. His doctor's thesis had been called *Hanover and Prussia*,
and he was well versed in all periods of German history.

Except for historical reasons, however, he was not interested in Germany as he sat at his scholar's desk in Minneapolis in the spring of 1917. He wanted to build American solidarity In an attempt to further that end he took a step which
must have seemed inconsequential at the time, but which had
a profound effect on American scholarship and the thinking
of the American people.

As Dean Ford has explained to the authors, this was the
sequence of events leading up to his appointment as director
of the CPI Division of Civic and Educational Cooperation

"Early in the spring of 1917 I wrote an open letter to school
principals about the possibility of using the coming high school
commencements for patriotic purposes. I wrote it for the signature of the Commissioner of Education, but he modestly
declined to sign it and sent it out, however, over my name A
copy of that fell into George Creel's hands. I think it must
have reached him through some member of the National
Board for Historical Service, already partly formed in Wash-

[158]

ington, possibly through Professor Shotwell. Something about it made him think that I would be valuable as a writer. Presumably his earlier idea was that the Committee on Public Information would largely serve as writers, supplementing the utterances of the President and other leaders, and in doing what its name implied."

So George Creel "made one long stride by a telegram" and called this distinguished scholar to Washington Presumably, if Dean Ford had not been available some other man would have been found, but the work of Dean Ford's division bears the unmistakable mark of his personal influence, and it is doubtful whether anyone else would have done just what he did. As the chairman of the CPI made his whole great organization into something surpassing the highest hopes of the President and his Cabinet, so Dean Ford accepted his assignment and then proceeded to do one of the most stupendous jobs in "popular scholarship" that this country has ever seen

One purely statistical measure of his work is that the division which he headed put out more than 75,000,000 pieces of literature, ranging in character from the simplest four-page leaflet to an elaborate war cyclopedia and numerous heavily annotated works of research. This vast program of publication in several languages, directed to people at various levels of literacy and intelligence, was the basis of everything else that Dean Ford's office did, but it was far from being the sum of it.

Through cooperating private and government agencies he brought about a veritable mobilization of the country's scholarly resources, and made schools, colleges, and various non-educational groups among the strongest of "strong-points" in the inner lines

All this was accomplished without an elaborate administrative machine, for the division never had a large Washington staff. Samuel B. Harding, professor of history at the University of Indiana, was chief assistant, and James W Searson, professor of English and journalism at Kansas State University, did editorial work; a few stenographers about completed the permanent personnel in the office which was successively 8, 10, and 6 Jackson Place, and then 1621 H Street, N W.

Dozens of scholars from all over the country gave indispensable help, but they were not on the payroll and either worked entirely on their own campuses or came to Washington for brief consultation periods. Few of them received more than the $25 or $50 which was supposed to cover travelling expenses. Dean Ford's salary was $5,200, Professor Harding's $2,600, and the total cost of the division was $568,306.08, most of which represented the expenses of the staggering publication schedule, for though most distribution was by request, very little of it was paid.

Because of Dean Ford's familiarity with the qualifications of his own colleagues, it was natural for him to draw heavily on the services of Minnesota scholars. But Illinois had the largest representation by the end of the war, and Chicago, Columbia, Princeton, Wisconsin, and three dozen other institutions likewise contributed liberally.

The first big job, and the one for which Mr Creel wished to receive scholarly assistance in the first place, was the pamphlet The War Message and the Facts Behind It, which was the annotated text of President Wilson's speech of April 2, some forty elaborate footnotes explaining America's case against Germany and the outlines of America's foreign policy. "The plan and much of the work are due to Professor William Stearns Davis, of the history department of the University of Minnesota. He is very materially assisted by his colleagues, Professor C. D. Allin and Dr. Wm. Anderson." This pamphlet appeared June 10, 1917. The Government Printing Office alone turned out 2,499,903 copies, and reprints appeared in newspapers and magazines. Probably no man in American history had ever before put to press a scholarly work destined for a larger printing. As Dean Ford reported, on the first day after release of the pamphlet he received "a peach basket" of mail, the next day two bushels, "and then the flood just opened on us."

This launched the unparalleled printing program of the division, and it also inaugurated the plan of calling on temporary, volunteer help, rather than erecting a large and unwieldy structure in Washington. The policy was followed not only in connection with the editorial work, but also in the extensive program of "civic cooperation." As Dean Ford wrote to a friend, Howard M. Strong of the Minneapolis Civic and Commerce Association on May 25, 1917

"We must depend upon the activities of local groups who know the needs of their section and can more promptly and adequately meet them than can a temporary organization in Washington unless we build up a very elaborate machinery.

"There is no idea of propaganda other than bringing home to the great mass of people some attitude other than that of mere passiveness and acceptance of the war because it has been decreed at Washington"

On another occasion he wrote to A. C. Klumph, president of the International Association of Rotary Clubs "I distinctly hope that you can consider the possibility of organizing in each center where you have a club some active local organization of perfectly non-partisan public character that is interested in the work of publicity concerning all these questions that are back of our participation in the war and that relate to correct information concerning the issues, conduct, and necessary outcome of the struggle An informed, intelligent public opinion about these matters is vital to a democracy engaged in war."

As the division's pamphlets reached a steadily widening public and more and more people learned, or suspected, the heady circulation figures, Dean Ford's incoming correspondence increased alarmingly. Half the men of learning in the country, it must have seemed to the division stenographers, felt that they had been specially called by providence to write one of Dean Ford's pamphlets, or else that they had some strategic idea for their improvement Many folders in the CPI files are fat with essays on every subject from Plato's *Republic* to the insidious influence of Bach and Beethoven These contributors mailed their productions to the CPI confidently expecting that the Committee would publish and distribute them "by the million "

Very little of the volunteered material was usable in any way, and most of the pamphlets actually printed were first planned in Washington A wire was sent to the American scholar considered best qualified to do the particular job, and there was never a refusal.

More than a hundred separate publications were issued by Dean Ford's division, but the most important and the most influential were those in the two groups called the "War Information Series" and the "Red, White, and Blue Series" The two were published concurrently and, at least today, do not seem sharply differentiated from each other except by the tricolor band Each group contained a wide variety of material. Understanding of the work done by the Division of Civic and Educational Cooperation is gained most readily through acquaintance with these famous pamphlets.

The War Information Series ultimately included twenty-one different items, the first of which, *The War Message and the Facts Behind It,* has already been referred to. The second pamphlet was *The Nation in Arms* by Secretary of the Interior Franklin K. Lane and Secretary of War Newton D. Baker, the former assailing German feudalism for "making its last stand against oncoming democracy," and Mr. Baker explaining our own problems of finance and supply. The pamphlet had a circulation of more than a million and a half.

Charles D. Hazen, professor of European history at Columbia, was author of No. 3 in the series, which was *The Government of Germany.* This scholarly study of the "reactionary medievalism" of Germany's imperial government and of the influence of the army in German civil life was printed in an English edition of 1,798,155 and 20,500 in the enemy tongue.

Andrew C. McLaughlin of the University of Chicago (one of several future presidents of the American Historical Association who helped with the CPI work) , wrote No. 4, *The*

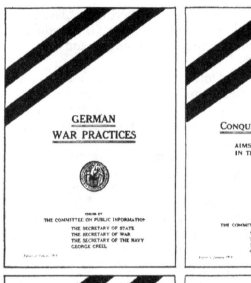

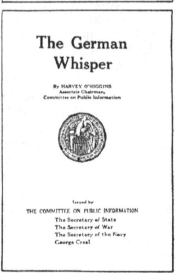

Four CPI Pamphlets
Some of the Most Famous Publications of the Creel Committee

Great War, from Spectator to Participant, which appeared in August 1917 as a reprint from the June issue of the History Teacher's Magazine He discussed German theories of Weltpolitik and Machtpolitik and told how the United States came to enter the struggle In this case, again, circulation was a million and a half.

Cabinet members were called on once more for No 5 in the series, which was A War of Self-Defense by Secretary of State Robert Lansing and Louis F Post, Assistant Secretary of Labor Mr. Post presented the argument employed in one way or another by nearly all of the CPI writers "Our problem was one of resisting conquest now, in a war in Europe and with allies, or later on in our own country and without allies." More than 700,000 copies were distributed

American Loyalty by Citizens of German Descent was No 6 in the series, and its translation (Amerikanische Burgertreue von Burgern deutscher Abkunft) was No. 7. More than 700,000 copies were issued in English and 564,787 in German, making it the largest of all the foreign language publications The contents included: "German-American Loyalty," by C Kotzenabe, "Americans of German Origin and the War," by Otto Kahn, "National Service Knows No Hyphen," by Judge F. W Lehmann, onetime president of American Bar Association, "The Spirit of '48 in 1917," by Franz Sigel, "Plain Words by a Plain Citizen," by Hans Russau, "One Answer Only," by Judge Leo Rassieur; "The Call and the Reply," by A. J. Bucher, editor of Haus und Herd, Cincinnati.

Professor Evarts B. Greene of the history department of the University of Illinois wrote No. 8, which appeared in September under the title American Interest in Popular Government Abroad. It traced American interest in the welfare of the French republic and the South American republics during the nineteenth and twentieth centuries, with many quotations from eminent Americans. Nearly 600,000 copies were issued

The War Department prepared No. 9, Home Reading Course for Citizen-Soldiers, a booklet of 62 pages of which 361,000 copies were published. This was designed to help newly enlisted men adapt themselves intelligently to army life and discipline.

A useful handbook was No 10, entitled *First Session of the War Congress*, which contained in synoptic form a history of each of the ninety-one public acts passed by the first session of the 65th Congress, lasting from April to October 1917. More than 600,000 copies were published. It was compiled by Charles Merz, at that time Washington correspondent of the *New Republic* and now editor of the *New York Times*

The German War Code was designed to show the ruthless manner in which Germany waged war. It came from the pens of George Winfield Scott, sometime professor of international law and diplomacy at Columbia, and James Wilford Garner, professor of political science at the University of Illinois About a half-million copies were issued. Germany's war code was contrasted with those of the United States, Great Britain, and France. The major part of the pamphlet was an analysis of the manual entitled *Kriegsbrauch im Landkriege* (Customs of War in Wars Fought on Land) published by the Germans in 1902, with shorter summaries of the war manuals of the other Allied powers.

A professor of English was the author of the twelfth pamphlet in the War Information Series—*American and Allied Ideals· An Appeal to Those Who Are Neither Hot Nor Cold*, by Stuart P. Sherman of the University of Illinois He quoted Cicero and Milton to prove the purity of Allied ideals More than 225,000 copies were published

Charles Altschul wrote No. 13 in the series, *German Militarism and Its German Critics*. This 48-page pamphlet appeared in March and enjoyed a circulation of 303,600 in English and a German edition of 103,300. Excerpts from German Socialist newspapers giving numerous cases of mistreatment of German soldiers by their officers, and examples of the inhumane treatment of civilians by Germans, were cited.

Arthur D. Call, secretary of the American Peace Society and editor of *The Advocate of Peace*, prepared the fourteenth number of this series—*The War for Peace. The Present War* as *Viewed by Friends of Peace*. The contents included quotations from publications of the American Peace Society, the Carnegie Endowment for International Peace, the League to Enforce Peace, the American School Peace League, the World Peace Foundation, and statements from women peace workers, churchmen, Belgian relief workers, Clarence Darrow, William Howard Taft, William Jennings Bryan, Theodore Marburg, and Samuel Gompers. Circulation was 302,370.

In the same month (March) appeared No. 15, *Why America Fights Germany*, by Professor John S. P. Tatlock of Stanford University. "The net of German intrigue has encompassed the world," wrote the author, who was professor of English. He repeated the assertion. "We must fight Germany in Europe with help, that we may not have to fight her in America without help." One passage of this pamphlet made a profound impression in 1918 and was widely quoted.

"Now let us picture what a sudden invasion of the United States by these Germans would mean; sudden, because their settled way is always to attack suddenly. First they set themselves to capture New York City. While their fleet blockades the harbor and shells the city and the forts from far at sea, their troops land somewhere near and advance toward the city in order to cut its rail communications, starve it into surrender and then plunder it. One body of from 50,000 to 100,000 men lands, let us suppose, at Barnegat Bay, New Jersey, and advances without meeting resistance, for the brave but small American army is scattered elsewhere. They pass through Lakewood, a station on the Central Railroad of New Jersey. They first demand wine for the officers and beer for the men. Angered to find that an American town does not contain large quantities of either, they pillage and burn the postoffice and most of the hotels and stores. Then they demand $1,000,000 from the residents. One feeble old woman tries to conceal $20 which she has been hoarding in her desk drawer; she is taken out and hanged (to save a cartridge). Some of the teachers in two district schools meet a fate which makes them envy her. The Catholic priest and Methodist minister are thrown into a pig-sty, while the German soldiers look on and laugh. Some of the officers quarter themselves in a handsome house on the edge of the town, insult the ladies of the family, and destroy and defile the contents of the house By this time some of the soldiers have managed to get drunk; one of them discharges his gun accidentally, the cry goes up that the residents are firing on the troops, and then hell breaks loose. Robbery, murder and outrage run riot. Fifty leading citizens are lined up against the First National Bank building, and shot. Most of the town and the beautiful pinewoods are burned, and then the troops move on to treat New Brunswick in the same way —if they get there.

"This is not just a snappy story It is not fancy. The general plan of campaign against America has been announced repeatedly by German military men. And every horrible detail is just what the German troops have done in Belgium and France."

Professor Tatlock concluded this frightening account with a call for all Americans to enlist in the fight. "We shall feel brotherly toward the German nation again if two things can be changed, their government and their spirit." Circulation was nearly three-quarters of a million copies.

One of the most important publications, because of its widespread use in schools and colleges, was *The Study of the Great War: A Topical Outline, with Extensive Quotations and Reading References*, by Samuel B. Harding, professor of European history at Indiana University. This 96-page booklet was divided into ten chapters, such as "Fundamental Causes of the War," "Historical Background of the War," "Indications that Germany and Austria Planned an Aggressive Stroke," and so on. Each chapter was a sort of syllabus for further study. The final chapter was "Proposals for Peace. Will This Be the Last War?" The edition ran to 678,929 copies.

A twenty-page discussion of the *Activities of the Committee on Public Information*, describing the work section by section, constituted No 17 in this series. Only 23,800 copies were issued.

The Adjutant General's Office prepared in chronological outline form a *Regimental History of the United States Regular Army from 1866 to 1918.*

Lieber and Schurz Two Loyal Americans of German Birth was No 19, and was printed in October 1918 Evarts B Greene was the author, and 26,360 copies of this were issued "Francis Lieber and Carl Schurz were perhaps the most notable of all those who in the middle of the nineteenth century gave up their status as German subjects to become citizens of the American Republic," began the pamphlet, which is documented with forty-five footnotes.

One of the most interesting of this series is No. 20, issued in October, and entitled *The German-Bolshevik Conspiracy.* This thirty-page 9 x 12 document has been the center of a spirited controversy which is alluded to in Chapter XIV The pamphlet consisted of the so-called Sisson Documents, the exciting history of which is described in the later chapter

The last of the War Information Series, No. 21, appeared in November 1918 It was *America's War Aims and Peace Program,* compiled by Professor Carl L. Becker of the history department of Cornell University. A big edition of 719,315 copies was printed, large numbers finding their way into schools and colleges. The pamphlet was divided into five parts, dealing with the German peace move of 1916, the Papal peace overtures of 1917; the Brest-Litovsk peace discussion, Wilson's statement on terms, and the negotiations of October and November 1918. In a prefatory note, Dr. Ford declared that the impending peace "will be a peace that conforms to the better thought of all those who have paid by sacrifice and suffering the price of the world's redemption from the imminent threat of military medievalism "

At the same time that the War Information Series appeared, the Red, White, and Blue Series was likewise making its bow. Many of the items in this latter group were much more elaborate than in the other, and some of them furnished

Bachelor of Atrocities

IN the vicious guttural language of Kultur, the degree A. B.
means Bachelor of Atrocities. Are you going to let the Prussian
Python strike at your Alma Mater, as it struck at the University
of Louvain?

The Hohenzollern fang strikes at every
element of decency and culture and taste
that your college stands for. It leaves a
track so terrible that only whispered
fragments may be recounted. It has
ripped all the world-old romance out of
war, and reduced it to the dead, black
depths of muck, and hate, and bitterness.

You may soon be called to fight. But
you are called upon right now to buy
Liberty Bonds. You are called upon to
economize in every way. It is sometimes

harder to live nobly than to die nobly.
The supreme sacrifice of life may come
easier than the petty sacrifices of comforts and luxuries. You are called to
exercise stern self-discipline. Upon this
the Allied Success depends.

Set aside every possible dollar for the
purchase of Liberty Bonds. Do it
relentlessly. Kill every wasteful impulse,
that America may live. Every bond
you buy fires point-blank at Prussian
Terrorism.

BUY U. S. GOVERNMENT BONDS FOURTH LIBERTY LOAN

Contributed through Division
of Advertising

United States Gov't Comm.
on Public Information

This space contributed for the Winning of the War by
A. T SKERRY, '84, and CYRILLE CARREAU, '04.

Appeal to the Symbols of Education
Two Graduates of New York University Contributed the Space for This
CPI Advertisement in Their "Alumni News"

the spiciest reading of any publications of the CPI Incidentally, the bands of color appearing on the cover of each pamphlet caused some difficulty, purists objecting that blue, not red, should be at the top When Marion H Brazier, member of the D A R., and according to her own description "a sort of critic on matters concerning the flag and colors," indignantly protested to Mr. Creel about this offense against "good taste, regulations, and custom," she received the following reply from Dean Ford

"I fear that as a class we are a group whose education in the proper use of colors has been sadly neglected, limited as it has been chiefly to neckties and hatbands

"We were so innocent of any idea about the arrangement of colors on the booklet that we left it entirely to the Government Printing Office and now they have committed us to something which so far as I can see, we cannot easily change. Nevertheless, the Committee is young even if the Government Printing Office is not, and has some possibilities of teachableness."

Most people, however, did not quibble about the order of colors, and the ten numbers of the Red, White, and Blue Series held the absorbed attention of a tremendous public. The first pamphlet in this group was *How the War Came to America*, and its various editions in eight languages had the breathtaking circulation of 6,227,912 copies. The forty-six pages gave the historical background of our foreign policy and our belief in the peaceful settlement of international disputes, a chronology of German-American relations, with emphasis on details of submarine warfare, and the text of three Wilson addresses, including the famous Flag Day Address. The first edition of this pamphlet, a small printing of 20,000 copies, appeared June 9 and went to the newspapers, nearly all of which reprinted it at least in part, the *New York Times*, for instance, giving it a full page and a half. Then on June 26 came the regular edition for general circulation, and still later the foreign-language printings of from 9,000 to 300,000 each, including translations into German, Italian, Bohemian, Spanish, Polish, Swedish, and Portuguese in that order of size.

The next item in the tricolor series was a 246-page *National Service Handbook*, edited by John J. Coss, assisted by James Gutmann and many others. This book, which was "suggested by the *Directory of Service* published in April in the Columbia University War Papers," discussed topically every branch of the national service—combat, industry, civil service, and so on. The book sold for 15 cents, and 454,699 copies were issued.

The Battle Line of Democracy was a 133-page collection of rousing patriotic prose and poetry relative to the World War. It proved very popular in the schools Nearly 100,000 copies were issued, and it sold at 15 cents.

No. 4 of the tricolor series issued September 15, 1917, was the *President's Flag Day Address, With Evidence of Germany's Plans*, a thirty-page annotated discussion of Germany's designs for world conquest. Twenty-four footnotes implement the address and many pages have all except two lines devoted to this documentation, which was prepared by Professors Wallace Notestein, Elmer Stoll, August C. Krey, and William Anderson of the University of Minnesota and Professor Guernsey Jones of the University of Nebraska. Distribution was 6,813,-340 copies.

Conquest and Kultur: Aims of the Germans in Their Own Words was compiled by Wallace Notestein and Elmer Stoll of the University of Minnesota This was published on November 15, 1917 "The present war is in the last analysis distinctly a war between ideals and thus between the peoples who uphold them" the foreword starts out. This book of 160 pages was divided into seventeen sections, such as "The Mission of Germany," "World Power or Downfall," "The Worship of Power," and so on Under each division were numerous excerpts from public utterances or writings of prominent Germans showing their avowed goals. General Bernhardi's book *Germany and the Next War*, for example, was freely quoted, as were Treitschke, Nietzsche, and chauvinistic politicians. Here at last was a whole arsenal of quotations for the publicist to use against the pro-German. Circulation was 1,203,607 copies.

German War Practices, also issued November 15, 1917, was a 96-page book edited by Dana Carleton Munro of Princeton, George C. Sellery of Wisconsin, and August C. Krey of Minnesota Quotations showed the glorification of war and the treatment of Belgians by Germany, and shorter accounts were devoted to practices in conquered provinces of France and Poland. Atrocity stories were repeated A total of 1,592,801 copies appeared

The War Cyclopedia, "a handbook for ready reference on the Great War," was 321 pages long, the largest publication of Dean Ford's division The first edition came out January 1918, and altogether 195,231 copies were printed. The editors were Frederic L. Paxson of Wisconsin, Edward S Corwin of Princeton, and Samuel B Harding of Indiana About fifty others contributed, including Charles A. Beard, Carl L. Becker, Sidney B. Fay, J Franklin Jameson, and St. George L. Sioussat. The volume started with "Acts of Congress" and closed with "Zimmermann Note" Such entries as "Scrap of Paper," "Spurlos Versenkt," and "Schrecklichkeit" were intended to remove all possible doubt on the subject of responsibility for the war. The cyclopedia sold for 25 cents.

No. 8 of the tricolor series was *German Treatment of Conquered Territory* (Part II of *German War Practices*). It was edited by Munro, Sellery, and Krey and, like the first instalment, quoted prominent authorities on the wholesale pillage of Northern France and Belgium Such men as Herbert Hoover, Brand Whitlock, and Hugh Gibson were used as sources, with a number of quotations from the Germans themselves More than 700,000 copies appeared

Several of President Wilson's writings made up the contents of No. 9 in the series, *War, Labor, and Peace*, which included two addresses to Congress on the subject of peace and reconstruction, and the text of Wilson's replies to peace proposals by the Pope and by Chancellor von Hertling and Count Czernin. Circulation was about a half-million, and the first edition appeared March 1918.

[172]

The last in the tricolor series was *German Plots and Intrigues in the United States during the Period of Our Neutrality*, by E. E. Sperry of Syracuse and Willis Mason West, formerly of Minnesota It was a 64-page pamphlet, and 127,-153 copies were issued It was based on Professor Sperry's previous work, for the National Security League and other groups, regarding German machinations on our soil

In all of these publications the effort was to present the Wilsonian war doctrine in a reasoned, accurate, authoritative statement that would appeal to educated people everywhere, but which at the same time would be understandable to all Americans Authorities differed as to whether this purpose was accomplished. Booth Tarkington, for instance, was a careful observer of people, and he was enthusiastic He wrote to Dean Ford·

"Thank you for having sent to me ten copies of *Conquest and Kultur* I have arranged for their distribution among the country people about Kennebunk and Kennebunk Port, copies to be in the village libraries also These people are good and loyal, but not at all clear as to what we are fighting, somewhat mystified, too, as to why Now and then a fisherman will say, 'Well, I have heard some tellin' around that it's kind of a capitalists' war: dunno whether it's so or not' Talk doesn't explain to him—not authoritatively, to his mind. But if he reads a pamphlet 'got out by the United States GUV'MENT' he is 'impressed.'"

But Harold L. Ickes, chairman of the executive committee of the Illinois State Council of Defense, was one of many who felt that Dean Ford's scholars had not yet brought themselves down to the level of the common citizen He wrote on October 24, 1917, that he had not "seen anything yet that will appeal to the farmers, to the laboring men, or to the average run of citizens who do not do profound reading" He asked if there were not a danger "of trying to over-educate the already educated, leaving the less well educated still groping as to what the war is all about?"

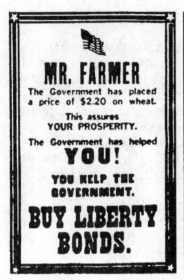

"Not Too Academic"

Appeals to the Lowest Plane of Literacy and Understanding

Once again, three months later, Mr. Ickes wrote to Dean Ford:

"Spring is almost upon us and we haven't done a thing to reach the farmer. I haven't had any literature to send to the farmers of this State, or I would have sent it long ago. I think that just like any other American citizen he needs a general appeal along patriotic lines and not merely technical documents which are often too voluminous and too prosy to get the desired results. . . .

"The criticism that is being constantly made to me, even by college professors of my acquaintance, is that much of the matter so far issued is too academic and in that criticism, which I ventured to express to you personally some time ago, you seemed to concur. Yet to date we have nothing else and the farmer from all indications will go back to his intensive farm work for the summer, short handed, with no leisure for reading, knowing almost as little about the war and what his

[174]

duty is with respect to it as at the close of the harvest season last fall."

In direct response to criticism such as that from Mr Ickes, the Division of Civic and Educational Cooperation proceeded to issue a new series, the four-page and eight-page Loyalty Leaflets, which were seven in number, had a circulation of about a half-million each, and were expressed, as to literacy, in terms of the least common denominator.

No. 1 of the Loyalty Leaflets was *Friendly Words to the Foreign Born* by Judge Joseph Buffington. Translations were available in German, Bohemian, Italian, Hungarian, and Russian.

Loyalty Leaflet No. 2, *The Prussian System*, was by Frederic C. Walcott of the U S. Food Administration and a former relief administrator in both Poland and Belgium; he described German treatment of conquered peoples.

Labor and the War, consisting of the President's address to the American Federation of Labor, was the third leaflet, and a companion piece, *A War Message to the Farmer*, gave the President's ideas as he had sent them to a farm conference at Urbana, Illinois The fifth number was *Plain Issues of the War*, by Elihu Root, former Secretary of State, and this was followed by the President's proclamation, *Ways to Serve the Nation* The seventh and last Loyalty Leaflet was *What Really Matters*, an unnamed writer's letter, which had been quoted in an *Atlantic Monthly* article by the Rev. Joseph H. Odell

One of the most ingenious devices for reaching the broad base of the people was a little booklet, *The Kaiserite in America*, which was given a circulation of 5,550,521, but which was directed to the special attention of travelling men. In response to a suggestion from Russell L. Coxe of Schuylkill, Pennsylvania, Dean Ford had written:

"It certainly seems to me that the national travelling men's organizations might well constitute themselves a flying squadron to combat idle rumors which are often the thoughtless repetition of German propaganda . I find that it does not take information but merely common sense and a sturdy squelching of those who either thoughtlessly or maliciously spread just the kind of thing which affects the morale of the nation "

In accordance with this plan, *The Kaiserite in America* was published, and fourteen of its fifty pages were taken up with a message beginning

TO THE COMMERCIAL TRAVELLERS OF AMERICA.

"Here is an opportunity for the Commercial Travellers of America to do a great work toward winning the war.

"You are summoned as specifically as if you were enlisted in the army or navy to aid the national cause.

"Our troops will meet the enemy abroad. You can meet him at home

"Throughout the land the Kaiser's paid agents and unpaid sympathizers are spreading by word of mouth rumors, criticisms and lies, that aim to disrupt our national unity and to weaken the will of our people in the successful prosecution of our task in the great world war. . . .

"It is your immediate task to 'swat the lie' Whenever you hear one of these rumors or criticisms, pin the tale-bearer down. Ask him for proof. Don't be satisfied with hearsay or rumor."

Following the introduction came the "One Hundred and One German Lies Nailed by the *St Louis Republic*." Three samples will suggest the nature of the rumors and the italicized answers:

LIE No 18 Repetitions of the lies that schools in towns at or near training camps are to be closed because girls are about to become mothers come in droves. Towns in the neighborhood of any camp site are picked by Kaiser aids for this canard. (*Investigators declare this is utterly without foundation. The morale of men at the training camps cannot be better. Schools are not being interfered with for any purpose, they declare*)

LIE No. 55. From a St Louis source comes this one· That a German doctor in the United States Army at Camp Bowie, Tex , used spinal meningitis serum instead of typhoid serum sending 1,400 men to the hospital, and that he was shot for it the latter part of last week. (Col F P. Reynolds, Surgeon General's Office, Washington, D C , had this to say of the report· "It is the most absurd and one of the wildest stories I have yet heard")

LIE No 98 A story criticising Food Administrator Hoover for "eating a $7 meal at a banquet" and rising thereafter to preach conservation and economy, is being circulated in St Louis (All such stories as this are based on exaggeration and are twisted and garbled for the purpose of creating dissatisfaction. Hoover is known to be unquestionably sincere in his work and to practise the things he urges others to do.)

But even while efforts were being made to reach the lowest intellectual ranks, Dean Ford, as the chief representative of scholarship in the CPI, was called upon to deal with questions relating to scholarly books Many a textbook fight arose during the war days. Book companies circulated rumors that their rivals' publications were tainted with pro-Germanism, and brought political pressure to have them excluded from the schools. When a book was thus under fire, and sometimes even if it was not, the publishers sought protective endorsement from the CPI In June 1918, for instance, Dean Ford wrote this letter to Allyn and Bacon, in response to a request from that publishing firm·

"Professor [Willis Mason] West's Modern History, published in 1903, was certainly the first textbook that pushed aside the German mask and showed behind it the features we now know so well as Prussian militarism with its immoral statecraft and worship of force. To have done this fifteen years ago is proof of Professor West's penetration and prevision " West's book, it seems, had been banned in Montana as pro-German and the competitors of Allyn and Bacon were making capital of this fact throughout the nation

In similar cases the drive against certain books reached such absurd lengths that standard works of history such as Robinson and Beard, Beard and Bagley, besides West, were involved. In a letter to the Secretary of the Interior, under whose jurisdiction the Bureau of Education operated, Creel wrote

"Your interest as much as my own in the schools leads me to call your attention to certain phases of the textbook question, especially in the field of history that is now precipitated by rival publishers and patriots suffering from civic shell shock. Within the past two weeks we have been appealed to by publishers and authors in three separate cases to get a reasonable hearing and treatment of school books in history, which were being thrown out of cities or whole states, for reasons essentially trivial—a picture of the present German Emperor, of Frederick the Great, that the author's son (in fact only eleven years old) had been disloyal and the father equally so, or that the text said, 'Christianity advanced from the Rhine to the Elbe,' therefore the author was trying to show that Christianity originated in Germany.

"In some cases state defense councils have been the agency appealed to, in others the Department of Justice

"Whatever the reason, and some objections are more vapid than the above, I suspect a rival book company (in a glass house) has a stone missing from its garden walk. We can hardly expect that the Department of Justice will discriminate or defend."

It was suggested that a commission be formed to adjudge such matters.

The question of banned books was a ticklish problem from every angle. By October 1918, the War Department itself had a list of seventy-five books which were banned from the army camps. Frederick P. Keppel, Third Assistant Secretary of War, and later president of the Carnegie Corporation, broached this problem to Ford on October 3, 1918:

"There is a good deal of discussion now as to the Index Expurgatorius of the War Department, for which, of course, Mr. Baker gets personal credit Would it be fair to ask your office to let me know informally the books which it might be profitable to have someone read with a view to their restoration to respectability Fred Howe, for example, writes more in sorrow than in anger on the subject, and books like Ambrose Bierce's come fairly near being classics. I assume *Le Feu* was cut off from motives of propriety"

[178]

Ford replied two days later "When the recent controversies were up concerning the textbooks in history in the public schools, I suggested that some sort of a commission ought to be formed in this matter. . . .

"I should suggest that this Commission, if it is formed, might well undertake to examine the War Department Index Expurgatorius The list made up at present seems to me a very curious one and I have wondered about its origin."

The first twenty titles on the War Department's Index Expurgatorius of September 30, 1918, were.

Name	Author	Publisher
America after the War	"An American Jurist"	Century Co
America's Relations to the Great War	John W. Burgess	McClurg
Behind the Scenes in Warring Germany	Edward Lyell Fox	McBride, Nast
Belgium and Germany	J H. Labberton	Open Court
Book of Truth and Facts	Fritz von Frantzius	The Author
Bolsheviki and World Peace	Leon Trotzky	Boni and Liveright
Can Such Things Be?	Ambrose Bierce	Neale Pub Co
Christ and War	Anonymous	Brethren's Gen Mission Board
Conquest of War	N. M. Thomas	Fellowship Press
Doing My Bit for Ireland	Margaret Skinnider	Century Co.
Disgrace of Democracy	Kelly Miller	The Author
Emden	H van Muecke	Ritter and Co.
England and Germany in the War	R J. Thompson	Chapple Pub Co.
England or Germany?	Frank Harris	Wilmarth Press
England's World Empire	A H. Granger	Open Court
European War of 1914	John W. Burgess	McClurg
German-American Handbook (1914)	F F Schrader	The Author
German Deserter's War Experience, A	J. Koettgen (tr.)	Huebsch
Germans as Exponents of Culture	Fritz von Frantzius	The Author
Germany in War Time	Mary E. McAuley	Open Court

The Book Commission was nearly rounded into shape by the middle of October, but the Armistice intervened before operations commenced, so presumably Assistant Secretary Keppel was never able to restore F. C. Howe, Ambrose Bierce, and Henri Barbusse to respectability.

But while the Index Expurgatorius was causing this work for Dean Ford, the CPI was also actively interested in a number of other books which, though published commercially, had at least the informal approval of the Committee For instance, C. E. Keck, eastern manager of Scott, Foresman and Company, wrote to Dean Ford on February 18, 1918· "You will be interested to know, in view of our conversation, that Professor [Christian] Gauss's *Democracy Today* has gone into hundreds of high schools to do its part in helping on the propaganda of patriotism 150,000 copies of this book have been sold in a month."

Many other commercially printed books were brought to the attention of the CPI, and several of the history texts included references to CPI publications This technique was followed with thoroughness in the case of American Book Company's *School History of the War*, which was written by McKinley, Coulomb, and Gerson and was widely used in the secondary grades.

Similar references appear in *The Roots of the War*, "a nontechnical history of Europe 1870-1914," by William Stearns Davis of the University of Minnesota and principal editor of the CPI's first pamphlet, *The War Message and the Facts Behind It* While the book was still in galley, Ford telegraphed the Century Company asking if he could see proof so that he could "refer to it in the forthcoming syllabus for the study of the war"—the syllabus being Professor Harding's *Study of the Great War* in the War Information Series. *The Roots of the War* was dedicated "To the great host of young men who have gone forth from the classrooms of the University of Minnesota to imperil their lives that righteousness may not perish before autocracy."

Consistent with Dean Ford's ideas of decentralization, he adopted many plans for securing active local cooperation with his division. Contact was established both directly and through a number of important assisting groups For example, here is a letter which he sent to all state superintendents of education in October 1917:

"As you may know, the Committee on Public Information published in the summer a pamphlet called *How the War Came to America* with the three great addresses of the President as a supplement. This is already being used by many schools as material in both their English and history classes.

"We have recently had this translated into German by one of the most competent translators and I am encouraged to suggest the possibility of this German translation being used as reading and supplementary material in high school classes in German."

Then a mimeographed sheet addressed "To the Teachers of America," was sent broadcast, offering two of the Red, White, and Blue pamphlets on request And more than a million and a half franked postcards, addressed to the CPI, were widely distributed, these cards likewise entitling the sender to free literature and bearing the message· "It is the earnest wish of your government that everybody be given an opportunity to learn the facts regarding the causes for America's entry into the war, to see clearly our motives and aims and to learn why this conflict must continue until our aims are achieved"

These means of reaching millions of people were effective, but it had been recognized for a long time that if patriotic ideas could be constantly repeated in the schools of the nation, it would be one of the most important avenues into the home. Much of the literature was reaching the schools already, but the approach was not systematic or regular The means of communication was provided, in the last month and a half of the war and continuing through the winter of 1919, in the *National School Service*, a sixteen-page paper, 9 x 12

NATIONAL
School Service
PUBLISHED BY THE COMMITTEE ON PUBLIC INFORMATION

| VOLUME I | WASHINGTON, D.C., NOVEMBER 1, 1918 | NUMBER 5 |

THE UNITED WAR WORK CAMPAIGN

Government Recognizes Seven Volunteer Organizations to Minister to Troops at Home and Overseas

Equalling if not surpassing in significance the world's congress of religions is

Wilson advised a joint campaign to be participated in by these seven volunteer organizations, November 11 to 18, for the purpose of raising the necessary funds.

Homes Back Clean Army

Dr. John R. Mott, international leader of the Young Men's Christian Association, is director general of the campaign acting in coöperation with a national executive

THE GERMAN SCHOOLS AS NURSERIES OF AUTOCRACY

German and American Systems of Education Contrasted

How has it been possible for the ruling class in Germany to hold seventy million

Dean Ford's Means of Access to 20,000,000 Homes

in format, established in accordance with suggestions from the Emergency Council on Education and the educational commission of the National Education Association.

The *National School Service* was attractive to children because of its liberal use of war photographs, and it gave in concise, understandable form the facts of the war as they were understood in Washington. The paper was mailed free to teachers and could be obtained by others for $1 a year. Following the original plan, it was edited so that it could be utilized in actual classroom work in a wide variety of fields from geography to arithmetic. Dean Ford was formally editor-in-chief until January 1919 (when he was succeeded by J. J. Pettijohn), but the men most directly charged with responsibility for putting out the paper were W. C. Bagley, editor; J. W. Searson, managing editor; and Samuel B. Harding, editor of the historical section. It was edited at 10 Jackson Place until the end of the year, and then the office was moved to the Bureau of Education in the Interior Building.

Through the War Department's Committee on Education and Special Training, which supervised the "War-Aims Course" required at virtually every American college and university under the Students Army Training Corps, the CPI was able to turn its pamphlets into textbooks for the higher branches of learning also. The files reveal a letter which apparently represents the start of this particular use of the publications: Frank Aydelotte, now president of Swarthmore College and chairman of the American Committee of the Rhodes Trust, was national director of the "War-Aims Course," and he wrote in July 1918 asking for a stock of CPI literature.

Other educational groups were similarly helpful, but none of them ranks with the National Board for Historical Service, either in purely scholarly assistance to the CPI in its editorial work or in its effective approach to school teachers, especially history teachers, all over the country.

Dean Ford was himself a member of this famous group, which had been formed as the result of a conference called early in the war by the department of historical research of the Carnegie Institution James T Shotwell was the first chairman, and the list of his associates fairly glitters with names renowned in American scholarship—Evarts B. Greene, Robert D W Connor, Frederick Jackson Turner, J Franklin Jameson, William E Dodd, William E. Lingelbach, Archibald Cary Coolidge, Waldo G Leland, Dana Carleton Munro, and many others.

The first object of the Board was to help the government "through direct personal service." It was also hoped "to aid in supplying the public with trustworthy information of historical or similar nature," and to encourage state and local groups. Although many scholarly contributions were published under individual bylines, or through the CPI pamphlets, the Board also had a publication schedule of its own.

The N B H.S prepared *Teachers' Leaflet No* 1, published by the Bureau of Education in September 1917, and the idea behind it was carried out in another way with great thoroughness through the cooperation of the *History Teacher's Magazine*, the September 1917 issue of which carried announcement of coming articles on adaptation of history courses to the war, these articles being in preparation by the N.B.H.S

The Committee on Public Information

Established by Order of the President, April 4, 1917

Distribute *free except as noted* the following publications :

I. Red, White and Blue Series :

No. 1. How the War Came to America (English, German, Polish, Bohemian, Italian, Spanish and Swedish).

No. 2. National Service Handbook (primarily for libraries, schools, Y. M. C. A.'s, Clubs, fraternal organizations, etc., as a guide and reference work on all forms of war activity, civil, charitable and military).

No. 3. The Battle Line of Democracy. Prose and Poetry of the Great War. Price 25 cent. Special price to teachers. Proceeds to the Red Cross. Other issues in preparation.

II. War Information Series :

No. 1. The War Message and Facts Behind it.

No. 2. The Nation in Arms, by Secretaries Lane and Baker.

No. 3. The Government of Germany, by Prof. Charles D. Hazen.

No. 4. The Great War from Spectator to Participant.

No. 5. A War of Self Defense, by Secretary Lansing and Assistant Secretary of Labor Louis F. Post.

No. 6. American Loyalty by Citizens of German Descent.

No. 7. Amerikanische Bürgertreue, a translation of No. 6.

Other issues will appear shortly.

III. Official Bulletin :

Accurate daily statement of what all agencies of government are doing in war times. Sent free to newspapers and postmasters (to be put on bulletin boards). Subscription price $5.00 per year.

Address Requests to

Committee on Public Information, Washington, D. C.

What Can History Teachers Do Now?

You can help the community realize what history should mean to it.

You can confute those who by selecting a few historic facts seek to establish some simple cure-all for humanity.

You can confute those who urge that mankind can wipe the past off the slate and lay new foundations for civilization.

You can encourage the sane use of experience in discussions of public questions.

You can help people understand what democracy is by pointing out the common principle in the ideas of Plato, Cromwell, Rousseau, Jefferson, Jackson and Washington.

You can help people understand what German autocracy has in common with the autocracy of the Grand Mogul.

You can help people understand that democracy is not inconsistent with law and efficient government.

You can help people understand that failure of the past to make the world safe for democracy does not mean that it can not be made safe in the future.

You can so teach your students that they will acquire "historical mindedness" and realize the connection of the past with the present.

You can not do these things unless you inform yourself, and think over your information.

You can help yourself by reading the following :

"History and the Great War" bulletin of Bureau of Education.

A series of articles published throughout the year in THE HISTORY TEACHER'S MAGAZINE.

You can obtain aid and advice by writing to

The National Board for Historical Service, 1133 Woodward Building, Washington, D. C.

United States Bureau of Education, Division of Civic Education, Washington, D. C.

Committee on Public Information, Division of Educational Coöperation, 10 Jackson Place, Washington, D. C.

The Committee on Patriotism through Education of the National Security League, 31 Pine Street, New York City

Carnegie Endowment for International Peace, 2 Jackson Place, Washington, D. C.

National Committee of Patriotic and Defense Societies, Southern Building, Washington, D. C.

The World Peace Foundation, 40 Mount Vernon St., Boston, Mass.

American Association for International Conciliation, 407 West 117th Street, New York City.

The American Society for Judicial Settlement of International Disputes, Baltimore, Md.

The Editor, THE HISTORY TEACHER'S MAGAZINE, Philadelphia.

For Mobilizing the Nation's Schools
Announcement in the "History Teacher's Magazine," September 1917

[184]

The same issue carried a full-page announcement (reproduced here) regarding free distribution of CPI publications

Each issue of the *Magazine* after that had a section headed "Timely Suggestions for Secondary School History," with ideas for tying up the war with school courses in Ancient, European, English, and American History. Commencing with the January 1918 number, a series of War Supplements was published, reprinting articles or pamphlets useful in the same way. The authors included Christian Gauss, George M Dutcher, Samuel B. Harding, and William E. Lingelbach

This whole program met with great success, and the *Magazine* circulation doubled during the war, making it one of the most important factors in mobilizing the history teachers of the country. The movement was further assisted by the prize contests conducted by the N B H S for teachers' essays on "Why the United States is at War."

When Dean Ford was asked by the inquisitive Congressmen in June 1918 what people had helped his division, he gave a list of more than 150 scholars and others, but prefaced this by giving credit "first and above all" to the National Board for Historical Service.

Dozens of other groups, however, cooperated with the CPI in either the "civic" or the "educational" phases of the work. In addition to chautauquas, Sunday Schools, settlement houses, and foreign-language clubs, assistance was given liberally by such other groups as the American Federation of Labor, the Red Cross, the Y.M C A , and the American Library Association. Liberty Loan solicitors and Four-Minute Men were important helpers in both advertising and distributing the publications, and the Boy Scouts of America gave out more than five million copies of the President's Flag Day Address.

Dean Ford was the leader in one of the greatest publishing ventures ever undertaken in this country. At the same time he had the task of making scholarship serve the ends of a country mobilized for war Each pamphlet was suggested by Dean Ford to Mr. Creel, never the other way around If Dean

[185]

Ford was forced on occasion to publish things that would not pass muster as scholarship in more normal times, he must also receive credit for making no more concessions to the war spirit than were absolutely necessary for the director of a government propaganda campaign. Considering all the circumstances, Dean Ford was amazingly successful in avoiding "civic shell shock," and the proof may be found in the dozens of manuscripts which would have given effective support to the war but represented a degree of hate and intolerance and hysteria which he refused to sanction. They remain in the CPI files to this day when they might, under some other leadership, have found their way into print.

Chapter 8

THE PEOPLE'S WAR· LABOR AND CAPITAL

I F there was one Wilsonian concept fundamental to all the
others it was that of a "People's War." You could differ
with the President on the ship program and complain
about living costs or the coal shortage; within limits you could
express your opinion on the freedom of the seas, Czech nationalism, the comparative virtues of the Republican and
Democratic Parties, or the ultimate fate of Bessarabia. All of
this an American citizen could do. But if he did not grant that
America was fighting by the will of the people—in contrast
to the Germans, who were fighting by the will of the Kaiser
and his coterie of Junkers—he was against Wilson and a traitor.

Nowhere was the doctrine of a "People's War" more important than in the relations between capital and labor, a
complex of problems which engaged the attention of the CPI
through its whole life.

Not everyone granted that it was a people's war Treasonous
ideas were known to persist, in spite of the fact that their expression might lead one into the toils of the federal marshal.
Pacifists, pro-Germans, Socialists, anarchists, and I.W.W.
organizers asserted, whenever they dared, that the war supposed to make the world safe for democracy was just another
in a long line of imperialist engagements; that American capitalists had forced us into war for selfish reasons, and that there
were at least as many Junkers in this country as in Prussia.

Gustavus Myers, a supporter of the war though a believer in
social democracy, wrote to President Wilson in the fall of
1917. "The real reason why certain sections of our working
and farming population are either apathetic to our part in the
war, or antagonistic to it, is the widespread conviction that

[187]

the German government has done more for its working people than any other government. This conviction is the result of more than twenty-five years of astute German propaganda in this country"

This tendency might have the gravest effects on labor, which not only saw its interest as antagonistic to that of capital but was peculiarly susceptible to the appeal of radicals, if only because it included a horde of people born in foreign countries and not yet assimilated into American life On top of all this was the fear that certain labor leaders, even with no ideological ends to serve, would seize the tempting opportunity for personal or union advantage and call their men out. Employers were racked with anxiety as to what labor might do in a period of resentment against soaring costs of living and of nationwide shortage of manpower.

But the leaders of the national government were worried, too. With industry part of the intricate mechanism of war, any serious break in production might bring disaster. A strike over wages or hours was therefore opposed not only by the employer's natural desire for docility in labor but also by the government's imperious demands for production

Labor's insistence on abstract rights might be as unpatriotic as deliberate sabotage suborned by the enemy—and might, in fact, cause even more serious damage because of the speed with which the contagion of unrest can be communicated

The whole problem was summed up in an Edgar Guest poem sent to Carl Byoir with the compliments of the Commonwealth Steel Company—unusual auspices for literature but presenting a message frequently heard during the war.

SAID THE WORKMAN TO THE SOLDIER
BY EDGAR A. GUEST

Said the workman to the soldier, as his ship put out to sea·
"While you're over there for freedom, you can safely bank on me!
I'll be just as brave as you are, in a safer sort of way,
And I'll keep production going every minute of the day."

Said the soldier to the workman, as the ship put out to sea·
"I'll be true to you, my brother, if you'll just be true to me!
Now we've got to work together, it's my job to bear a gun,
But it's yours to keep on toiling if we're going to lick the Hun."

Said the workman to the soldier· "I will back you to the last.
No more strikes for higher wages till the danger time is passed!"
Said the soldier to the workman· "I'm for you and you're for me.
Now we understand each other, let the ship put out to sea."

There were no two ways about it labor must be kept in line if the war was to be won.

That was perhaps the biggest of all the big jobs assigned to the CPI and the formal record does not even suggest the careful attention with which the campaign was followed.

This industrial-relations work of the CPI is not fully or frankly treated in any published report, because much of the effort was carried on through a technically independent organization, the American Alliance for Labor and Democracy, and because the CPI's own Division of Industrial Relations was soon transferred to the Department of Labor But in every publication of the Committee, in the appeal of its Four-Minute Men, its news stories, its posters, its movies, and its syndicate features, the effect on labor was carefully considered And, as will be seen, close contact with employers was maintained through field agents and in other ways.

The CPI, of course, was but one of the government agencies keeping a sharp eye on the movement of labor opinion and attempting to encourage it in the desired direction The Council of National Defense, the War Industries Board, the War Labor Administration, the U.S Employment Service, Military Intelligence—these and many others were vitally concerned not only with wages and hours and with regulation of manpower resources for essential industries, but with the whole great problem of labor morale.

Thus the military requirements of the government and the self-interest of capital tended to reinforce each other in seeking to ensure the patriotism of labor and to preserve industrial peace.

Employer groups such as the National Association of Manufacturers were not reluctant to tell labor where its duty lay, but the most successful patriotic education of the working masses was through labor's own recognized leaders Samuel Gompers, president of the American Federation of Labor, was a member of the Council of National Defense and tireless in persuading workers in this country (and later in other countries, too) that labor's interest would be best served through unquestioning support of President Wilson. Gompers was more important than any other man except the President himself in getting labor to accept the "People's War"

Nearly every war board included a labor member, and it was possible to say that in nearly all the details of price-fixing, labor standards, compulsory arbitration, and the policy of "work or fight" (which critics called labor conscription) labor joined in the decision. It was not until after the war that Grosvenor Clarkson, director of the Council of National Defense, said that Hugh Frayne, labor member of the War Industries Board "was not on the Board to represent labor but to manage it."

The most important of all the devices of labor control through the apparently spontaneous action of labor itself was the American Alliance for Labor and Democracy Samuel Gompers was president; J. G. Phelps Stokes, former Populist and Socialist, treasurer; and Robert Maisel, director and active organizer.

Maisel was also director of the CPI Division of Labor Publications, and the two organizations maintained joint offices in New York Among the staff members of Labor Publications were Herman Robinson, organization director; Chester M Wright, publicity director; Joseph Chykin, Jewish organizer, W. R Gaylord, field agent; George Seldes, director of speakers; and Victor H. Arnheim, assistant publicity director.

In most respects the Alliance may be considered a field organization of the CPI charged with the special responsibility of keeping labor industrious, patriotic, and quiet The Alliance had approval from high sources. When Cyrus McCormick, the Chicago manufacturer who was an old friend of President Wilson, wrote to Creel that his financial help had been solicited by Frank Wolfe of the Alliance, the chairman of the CPI replied: "The Wolfe matter . . . is very close to us, and anything that you can possibly do will be of tremendous assistance. This is our most important body, and I am eager to have it stand on its own feet If you and your friends in Chicago can help Wolfe, you will not only please me, but others who are above me "

The Alliance had departments of organization, literature, and public speaking, and through all of these it served as the "front" for a large part of the government's work with labor In its first six months the Alliance set up 150 branches in forty states, distributed 1,980,000 pamphlets, conducted 200 mass meetings, and secured 10,000 columns of newspaper publicity

But parallel CPI efforts were proceeding at the same time, one of the most interesting centering about the person of Roger W. Babson, statistician, business analyst, and employer's counsel. His private organization known as the Wellesley Associates had specialized in studying industrial-relations and other problems for large employers, and at the beginning of 1918 he began negotiations with the CPI. In February of that year he joined the Creel organization (at the modest salary of $65 a month, plus $40 expenses), as director of the Division of Industrial Relations, and he was soon turning out ideas in profusion. He wrote to Carl Byoir regarding his series of "Pay-Envelope Stories": ". . . Keep in mind that I now have a following of 200,000 workers who know me and my work. Therefore this should be put out more or less as a personal message from me. . . . My purpose of uniting with Mr. Creel is to increase my 200,000 to one or more million "

This pay-envelope plan was one of the most ingenious of the whole CPI publishing program—a minute pamphlet, $2\frac{3}{4}$ x $2\frac{1}{4}$ inches in size and containing text designed to do one of two things increase productive efficiency or provide

[191]

COMMITTEE ON PUBLIC INFORMATION
SECRETARY OF STATE
SECRETARY OF WAR
SECRETARY OF THE NAVY
GEORGE CREEL, Chairman

UNITED STATES OF AMERICA
DEPARTMENT OF LABOR
WASHINGTON, D.C.
W. B. WILSON, Secretary

Beware

of German traps and German trouble makers.

Do not let Germany even ATTEMPT over here what she DID in Russia.

When we win the war, we can settle our other disputes. If we shouldn't win the war, the Kaiser would settle them for us.

U. S. DEPARTMENT OF LABOR.

COMMITTEE ON PUBLIC INFORMATION
SECRETARY OF STATE
SECRETARY OF WAR
SECRETARY OF THE NAVY
GEORGE CREEL, Chairman

UNITED STATES OF AMERICA
DEPARTMENT OF LABOR
WASHINGTON D.C.
W. B. WILSON, Secretary

WHY

does drifting from job to job give comfort to the Kaiser?

BECAUSE

idle machines reduce production and weaken our Army.

* * *

WHY

does Uncle Sam need you on the job?

BECAUSE

the fighters for freedom must be armed and fed and clothed.

* * *

A chain is only as strong as its weakest link. You are a link in the chain of production. If you do not stay on the job you weaken the chain.

STICK TO YOUR JOB

U. S. DEPARTMENT OF LABOR

W. B. WILSON,
Secretary of Labor.

Two of Mr. Babson's Posters

patriotic inspiration and interest in the war. Mr Babson proposed that the Wellesley Associates continue to serve their clients in the efficiency campaign and that the CPI assume sponsorship for his purely patriotic messages One booklet of the latter sort under CPI auspices was *Human Bait,* which told dramatically the story of how the Germans allegedly tied an American to the barbed wire in No Man's Land to lure his comrades to destruction.

This, however, was only part of Babson's program He also put out four CPI Labor Bulletins, and material from Dean Ford's Division of Civic and Educational Cooperation was also utilized when it had labor appeal. Sometimes it was issued with a special Alliance imprint and no suggestion of government auspices—a plan agreed upon by Ford and Creel

Mr Babson also put out a series of posters, two of which are reproduced here. According to a letter from Babson to William J. Cameron, then a member of Chicago's National Security Council, the posters for the employees were supplemented by confidential bulletins for employers Presumably these were the releases of the "CPI Special Service to Employers," the first issue of which gave the results of a study by the Bureau of Labor Statistics showing that average cost of living in manufacturing centers had risen about 40 or 45 per cent from 1914 to 1917.

Babson (whose biography in Vol. XX of *Who's Who in America* says: "Served as dir. gen. information and edn , by apptmt of U.S. Govt during war period") had tremendous plans for industrial-relations work in the CPI, but they did not come to pass. After looking over Babson's past work and his new projects, George Creel wrote to Secretary of Labor William B. Wilson on March 11, 1918·

"The campaign that he contemplates is so directly concerned with matters that are fundamentally within the province of your Department that I have come to the belief that the whole work should be taken over by you .   As I have explained to Mr. Babson, there is nothing that he wishes me to do that I will not attempt to do, and this applies to the use

W. B. Wilson
Secretary

COMMITTEE ON
PUBLIC INFORMATION
Washington, D. C.

THE SECRETARY OF STATE
THE SECRETARY OF WAR
THE SECRETARY OF THE NAVY
GEORGE CREEL, CHAIRMAN

Let us Remember Russia

The Russians meant well.

But they took time to talk while the house was burning!

Of course the Kaiser encouraged them.

He knew that would be the easiest way to lick them!

We must not let him play the same trick on us.

Information and Education Service

For extra copies address: Division of Industrial Relations, 8 Jackson Place

Dept. of Labor, Washington, D. C.

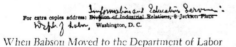

When Babson Moved to the Department of Labor

of the Four-Minute Men, the Speaking Division, and the publication of printed matter that you may not be able to issue." A first edition of *Labor Bulletin No 4* appeared with the CPI imprint, but with Babson identified as chief of the Division of Inquiry and Education, Department of Labor, and for later editions even the CPI imprint was removed From time to time the CPI made reprints of its posters for Babson, who reported that many manufacturers were requesting them to hang in their plants.

When Babson withdrew from the CPI picture, the Committee continued to work through the Labor Publications Division (which was separate from Industrial Relations) and through the Alliance Actually, representatives of the Labor Publications office did a great deal of field work bearing only the most indirect relation to distribution of literature, and in a sense it may be said that this division took over many of the functions that were handled by Mr. Babson during his brief stay with the CPI

Labor-capital relations during the World War have never been adequately reported, and there is not space here to add more than a few of the new facts that have come to light in the CPI files. But a general understanding of the approach to the great problem by labor, by capital, and by the CPI, can be gained through a series of quotations from the files, arranged roughly in chronological order from the winter to the fall of 1918

Harold L. Ickes of the Illinois Council of Defense, one of the CPI's most constant correspondents, wrote Creel on January 22 that the American Alliance should lose no time in organization, and that he feared Gompers might be the reason for the delay. In reply Creel offered to assume the expense of a Chicago office of the Alliance and the salary of an executive secretary. "I cannot afford even to seem to go into opposition to Mr. Gompers' wishes, but I do feel that the Chicago situation should have independent treatment."

At the end of March we find a letter from Dean Ford to George Creel agreeing on use of the Alliance, rather than the CPI, imprint for the leaflet *Why Workingmen Support the War* by Professor John R. Commons of the University of Wisconsin. Commons said

"This is an American workingmen's war, conducted for American workingmen, by American workingmen Never before has democracy for wage earners made so great progress as it has in the six months that we have been at war. If this continues, American labor will come out of this war with the universal eight-hour day, and with as much power to fix its own wages by its own representatives as employers have. Anybody who says that this is a capitalistic war simply does not see what is going on Capitalists are being controlled in their profits and in the wages and hours of laborers by leaders whom the workingmen themselves put on the various war boards"

But at least some people thought that capitalists were not being controlled with sufficient rigor On March 2, 1918, W. R Gaylord, field agent of the Alliance and the CPI Labor Publications Division, wrote to Gompers about evasion of the Eight-Hour Law by Milwaukee manufacturers who held contracts for 300,000 pairs of shoes "These contracts are all PURCHASE CONTRACTS [i.e treating the shoes as if already manufactured] and according to information from the War Department, the provisions of the Eight-Hour law do not apply . . Such material as this constitutes an explosive of high potential character if it should happen to be brought to light in connection with the candidacy of Victor L Berger for the U.S Senate, for instance." Gaylord also feared obstruction in the progress of the Alliance if these facts should become known, and added that if the Alliance could correct the situation it would help its popularity a great deal The letter was referred to Creel, who was informed by McConaughy that, "according to law, the government cannot insist on an eight-hour day in 'certain types of contracts,' the 'certain types' apparently covering most of the important supplies"

From the War Industries Board the CPI obtained lists of important iron, steel, copper, zinc, lead, and ammunition plants under war contract. The American Alliance for Labor and Democracy sent a letter to each employer announcing "a strong campaign of education among the war workers of America."

Carl Byoir, in outlining the plan to Walter C. Hecker of Curtis and Company, St. Louis, on April 18, 1918, proposed that a central office send out patriotic posters signed by the government, patriotic booklets, payroll inserts, an official button sanctioned by the War Department, and a service flag for workers' homes In addition, motion pictures were to be used both to bring the war home to labor, and to arouse the competitive spirit through pictures of workmen engaged in similar work in France, England, and the United States

Mr Hecker replied on April 23 in a letter to the CPI "We are endeavoring to spread among our men the real American propaganda .. It makes no difference whether a man makes munitions or whether he does not—to strike is unpatriotic If he makes munitions, it does look as though it is unpardonable If he does not make munitions, it is against the public interest, as it prevents the public having money for investing in bonds, Thrift Stamps, and other similar good causes "

Other people agreed. J. B. Haynes, "Publicity Campaigns," Omaha, had written Creel on April 20: "Millions of hours have been wasted by strikes in America on war work. . . . Shipbuilders unions have a rule forbidding a man to drive more than 75 rivets a day, when he might drive hundreds. Read General Crozier's testimony before the Congressional Committee, showing how the laborites got a rider through Congress which sanctioned such criminal sloughing as the 75 rivets a day, reducing the efficiency of the men in munitions factories 50 per cent."

A C. Hetherlin of the American Woodworking Machinery Company, Rochester, New York, sent to the CPI on April 30 a letter from Henry A. Wise Wood, chairman of the Conference Committee on National Preparedness·

[197]

"The weakest point in our war work today is the attitude of labor. . . . The United States has had an enormous number of strikes since the war started; but even if all strikes should end, if we should never have another strike . . . that unexpected condition would not be all that labor should do for victory. . . . Labor must be shown the necessity for rising above its *technical rights*, and that instead of doing its duty in a merely perfunctory manner, it must put all of its might into the work of producing. . . . The wives and daughters of workingmen constitute a force easily quickened into action to make the workingmen stick to their tasks and do more and better work There is no influence stronger than this. Women must be taught the danger to their loved ones, which lies in a strike or in shirking."

At the same time that employers were approached, the American Alliance for Labor and Democracy was writing to all of the local unions in the United States After informing those bodies that the Alliance had been called into being to unite all the workers—all the people—in support of America and America's ideals in the war, the communication declared "Nothing short of unified cooperation of both our laborers and our soldiers will win this war." But winning the war was not to be the end, for, "When this battle is won and the world, chastened and rejuvenated, will sit down to the task of readjusting social conditions on principles of universal right and justice, we have every reason to expect Labor to be an important factor, probably *the* important factor in its deliberations."

By May 1918, without waiting for responses to the above letter to labor unions, the CPI launched its workingmen's propaganda plan, working principally through employers The campaign was prosecuted by two field agents, Russell McFarland, formerly advertising manager of the Ford Motor Company of Canada, and Clifford W. Babson of the sales department, U.S. Cartridge Company, and by C. H. Howard, president of Commonwealth Steel Company, who sent letters to manufacturers of war materials. Aiding in the effort was Captain C R Dickinson of the Ordnance Department.

The first of these agents to report was McFarland, who had sounded out concerns in and around Baltimore and Philadelphia He wrote that except for "one shell-maker, who 'was too busy assimilating 1,000 new employees a month to think of anything else,' . the employer has definitely said he would appreciate further advice along this line and would like to cooperate with the government in the work"

In a memorandum to Byoir, McFarland said that all manufacturers interviewed had suffered greatly from the loss of men to the colors, or to the shipbuilding industry, or to munition plants able to pay higher wages All complained about the high labor turnover and in many cases suggested that the government do something to stop labor from drifting about

As for increasing production, the memorandum said: "Pres Wilhelm of the Eddystone Ammunition Company told of a speech Harry Lauder had made to his men urging increased production and stated the result had been a TWENTY-FIVE PER CENT INCREASE IN OUTPUT WITHOUT ANY REORGANIZATION IN THE SHOP."

As these reports and estimates of interviews began to come in, Captain Dickinson was keeping the CPI informed of other places that needed its attention. On May 11 he forwarded a letter from an inspector of ordnance stationed at Conshohocken, Pennsylvania. That officer urgently requested a prompt shipment of patriotic posters to be used and distributed through the plant of the Fisk Rubber Company. There was need for rapid delivery because labor trouble was brewing at the plant, "which in all probability will result in a strike. . . Strikes have been threatened twice which were prevented by more remuneration to the workmen of this company but the labor condition here is decidedly unsettled at the present time."

In line with the work of McFarland, Clifford W. Babson in New York was interviewing employers engaged in government war work. From his early interviews, Babson concluded that smelting companies, employing a low grade of foreign labor, would have to treat their problem along lines different from those of manufacturers who employed skilled labor. The treasurer and the chairman of the board of one concern were skeptical about increasing efficiency among workers by appealing to their patriotic sense of duty. Of those men Babson said· "Their experience had been that monetary inducement was the most positive means of obtaining concrete results. They conceded, however, that the increased wages which they had paid, had not brought about the efficiency which they had hoped to obtain."

While these field agents were at work, Mr. Howard of Commonwealth Steel sent a form letter to a selected list of employers. This letter of May 13, 1918, had received the approval of Byoir on May 4, when the latter sent Howard the list of companies having contracts with the Ordnance Department. The associate chairman wrote, "I know we are asking a great deal of you, but I do feel, that you are rendering, in this connection, a very vital patriotic service"

Howard's letter was generally similar to the one that Byoir had written to Walter C. Hecker as quoted above, but ended· "After many years of practical experience with the principles of human engineering in industry, I am convinced that the maximum of service can be unfailingly secured through a genuine Cooperative Fellowship relation between employee and employer We must have 'humanics as well as mechanics' And I believe that a conference of employers would be very fruitful in developing ideas, as well as ways and means of securing 'maximum production with minimum manpower'"

Three days after Captain Dickinson had forwarded the Conshohocken request for patriotic posters, he was sending Howard the following reactions of E. I. du Pont de Nemours & Co. "We feel that the poster will make a strong appeal to any one whose veins contain 'red blooded Americanism,' picturing as it does sturdy American manhood with sleeves rolled up determinedly doing his allotted portion The necessity of working as well as cheering is clearly shown. We believe the

[200]

effect on our workmen will be beneficial and hope they will be stimulated as much as one of our lady stenographers, who after gazing a few seconds said, while her eyes sparkled, 'My, it sends a thrill along my spine'"

In Detroit, McFarland had a chance to speak at a manufacturers' dinner and was anxious to go after big companies without regard to their connection with ordnance contracts To this suggestion Byoir was cold He told McFarland to make no more speeches and to stick to the prepared list of companies.

In St Louis, meanwhile, President Howard of Commonwealth Steel was getting a splendid response to his letter of May 13. The first reply deserves special notice not only because of chronology but because it differed so strikingly from the majority of the replies. J. E. Frederick, secretary and general manager of the Kokomo Steel and Wire Company, wrote

"If we are to make the world safe for democracy we must first democratize our industrial organizations. That this pays I am convinced, because we have been following this plan for the last eight years We have had no labor trouble during the last four years, and our production is steadily increased each year, therefore. you need not make this exclusive[ly] a labor effort, but much education could be absorbed along this line by our industrial managers"

S P Bush, president and general manager of the Buckeye Steel Castings Company, Columbus, Ohio, also felt that "the employers themselves would have to be educated," but not many of the employers recommended patriotic work in their own group

John A. Westman, general manager of the Dahlstrom Metallic Door Company, Jamestown, New York, reported discouragement with previous attempts to instruct workers, and welcomed government sponsorship of the drive, "in view of the strong Socialistic propaganda that has been carried on in this country, as well as other countries, for a great number of years, and which, in the last few years, appears to have been gradually taken up by the clergy and the professors of the colleges of the country, as a result of which there appears to be a strong antagonistic feeling towards any employers of labor "

Something was wrong with the workers in the opinion of L. J. Monahan, president of the Universal Motor Company, Oshkosh, Wisconsin "There is a contageous disease going the rounds making the men dissatisfied regardless of what is done for them There is no limit nor is there any way to satisfy them under the present conditions where they congregate evenings at their Union Hall and disgus the one side of the question The thing has gone so far that it is going to be a big job to sway the attitude by any educational system, but something should be done to show them that they should be reasonable and no better way would be than through men working within the union and swaying them at these meeting places which seems to hold their undivided interest."

A similar opinion was expressed by C. L. Coughlin of Briggs and Stratton Electrical Specialties, Milwaukee "We are at the present time in Milwaukee having propaganda spread by labor agitators and the government does not seem to take the right amount of precaution towards cutting down this sort of thing that is certainly hindering production . . We are enclosing a paragraph from a recent report received by us from our representative who attended one of these meetings " The accompanying paper read "Nicholson opened by saying that it had been said that Milwaukee was noted for its fine beers and long working hours and low wages. He said he was here to use his influence in organizing the machinists so they could demand wages that rightfully belonged to them, and that were being paid to the same class of mechanics in nearly every place in the U.S."

H. R. Wade of the Diamond Forging and Manufacturing Company, Pittsburgh, wrote: "To give you an instance [of workers' feeling about "too much officialdom"], one of our laborers called my attention to a paragraph in a Polish paper that an individual named Frankfurter, of some college, had been appointed by President Wilson to a position in the Labor

[202]

Department, and requested enlightenment as to how such a man could use any influence with common labor."

The personnel superintendent of the Winchester Repeating Arms Company of New Haven had this to say· "We have a service flag for display in the window of the home, a war medal, a factory Intelligence Bureau to which are reported disloyal utterances or actions, and conduct daily at noon and periodically during working hours, talks by prominent persons and veterans of the war to keep the matter clearly in the minds of all The response of employees of this plant to the various Liberty Bond sales has been very good, and the spirit has developed to the point where the co-workers of any slacker use the necessary moral (or physical) suasion upon those declining to participate You will note from the bracket clause that we have had to exercise care to see that the spirit developed did not get beyond reasonable bounds "

Such a worker attitude did not exist everywhere, as one could learn from the following words of F. E. Nulsen, president and general manager of the Missouri Malleable Iron Company, East St. Louis "The opinion expressed by every employer of labor is that labor with each advance in wages made is becoming more inefficient and more indifferent from day to day. It is as a rule now taking two or three men to do the work accomplished by one man before the war This is all wrong, in fact, is but little short of criminal, and I feel that if the laboring element can be awakened as to the necessity of their putting forth every ounce of strength they have, that good must be accomplished."

To deal with men and women who were receiving more money than ever before, T S Grasselli, of the Grasselli Chemical Company, Cleveland, had the following idea· "The most efficient force to correct this condition will be proper legislation from Washington, making it criminal for a man to be idle when any government work has to be done in any community, and the regulation of uniform wages for men in different sections of the country will also have to be established."

[203]

National Association of Manufacturers
of the United States of America
General Offices: 30 Church Street

NEW YORK, May 13, 1918.

E. C. Atkins & Co.,
Indianapolis, Ind.

Dear Sirs-   Attention of the General Manager.

As a patriotic and progressive industrial concern,
directly or indirectly engaged in government war contract
operations, you will be interested to know that we have
prepared for free distribution, a series (known as Series F)
of illustrated and colored educational posters, 19x25
inches in size, appealing to the workers on government
contracts to remain constantly loyal to their brothers in
the trenches by co-operating to the utmost with their
employers in maintaining and speeding up production.

These posters are available to any contractor working
on government material, without any charge whatever. All
that is asked is that you advise us of the number of sets
or specific posters desired, and we will send them to
you immediately upon receipt of your request.

It is our belief that much of the unrest in the
industrial field which has afflicted our country in the
past can be elimated by diplomatically calling public
attention to the effect thereof and demonstrating that
our industries are doing and will continue to do their
full share if all hands pull together in the common
interest.

We are sending you enclosed herein an order blank
showing in miniature reproductions of the series of posters
referred to. If you can use all of the twelve posters
in this set, or any of the same, and will advise us of
your requirements, we will send them to you. All that
we ask is that the posters be exhibited in located shop
windows, factory bulletin boards, offices, etc., where
they may be seen and read to best advantage.

Thanking you for your co-operation and awaiting your
advices in the matter, we are with best wishes

Yours very truly,

Mich. J. Hickey.

Special Representative,
Industrial Department.

MJH/AT

Help from the National Association of Manufacturers

[204]

At least two remedies for the lack of return for higher wages were suggested O. B Mueller, Mueller Metals Company, Port Huron, Michigan, after observing that at least 95 per cent of the men employees were doing actually less work than they would have done in normal times, wrote, "We have resorted to the use of women with great success."

The second remedy was suggested by H J. Wiegand, manager of the Wisconsin Gun Company, Milwaukee "Our plant is entirely owned and controlled by the government, and the labor situation so far has not been a difficult one for us to handle, due to the fact that we are working directly with the government, and turning over to them weekly reports regarding conditions of labor, fire prevention, and other protection "

As a means of increasing production the Industrial Department of the National Association of Manufacturers sent out a series of twelve posters, some of which are illustrated here.

But M. D. Baldwin, vice-president of the Oliver Machinery Company, Grand Rapids, pointed out "It is hard to talk to men about the 'speed-up' in your production to help win the war, when the same 'speed-up' in production will naturally mean a larger profit to the manufacturer, and although a larger profit to the manufacturer will result in a high wage scale, it seems a long ways around the circle to very many men."

Mutual understanding between employer and employee was advocated by J F Welborn, president of the Colorado Fuel and Iron Company, Denver: "We have for a number of years maintained a cooperative policy with our employees as to general working and living conditions "

The same idea was expressed by E. T. Weir, president of Phillips Sheet and Tin Plate Company, Weirton, West Virginia "Our own experience is that excellent results are being secured from the detailed efforts being carried on by the officers of the company with our employees. . We feel that this is a time when what is particularly needed is close personal contact on the part of the heads of a manufacturing company with the employees, that probably the influence of their own officers is greater and more lasting than any influence that might come through a centralized effort that was participated in by a great number of employees"

In one of McFarland's letters to Byoir, he said, "I've covered all kinds of shops; heard all lines of talk; from the employer that damns all his men as lunkheads to the man who thinks they are the salt of the earth"

Probably McFarland would have put in the more human category the officer of the Toledo Scale Company, George W. Hoke, who wrote to Howard "A real earnest and honest attempt to prepare a program of the things the worker ought to know will bring home to the employer many things he also should know I think that this campaign of education ought to go far deeper than stimulating posters or ginger talks for pay envelopes It also looks forward over a period of time much longer than the period of the war. It ought to be a far sighted program which would make us all more reasonable human beings."

As the spring of 1918 wore on, the CPI decided that a new effort was needed. Accordingly, at a conference on May 27 between Carl Byoir and Henry Atwater of the CPI, plans were made for resolutions to be presented in the name of organized labor at a meeting in St Paul early in June Everything went according to schedule. The meeting was held in St. Paul under the auspices of the American Alliance, and the plan for an Industrial Information Bureau adopted was substantially that drawn up in the CPI office more than a week earlier

John P Frey, editor of the *Molders Journal* and a member of the A.F. of L. mission to Europe, presented the plan at the St. Paul meeting The Industrial Information Bureau, which would help stimulate all branches of industry, was to include one representative each from the Department of Labor, A F. of L., American Alliance, War Department, Navy Department, the CPI, and the manufacturers The CPI was to be the service unit for the new agency.

As to the work which this new organization would do, Mr Frey said it would "not undertake any work in connection with the improvement of housing or working conditions, or

THE HAND THAT THREATENS OUR INDUSTRIAL LIFE

AMERICAN INDUSTRY—THE HEART OF THE NATION

More than 32,000 American industrial plants have been placed at the disposal of the government to win this war. Their effectiveness must not be hampered by enemy agitators who cause bad feeling between wage-earners and wage payers. Every community is interested in promoting industrial prosperity.

DR. UNCLE SAM

is now in charge of our industrial troubles. He has prescribed a Victory Tonic called Co-operation. It will bring better feeling among our wage-earners and wage-payers and will cure strife. Quack remedies, known as legislative ether, spirits of discontent and agitators acid, almost killed the patients. They are poisons, not remedies.

CO-OPERATION WILL WIN THE WAR!

Sample Posters Offered to Employers by the National Association of Manufacturers with adjustment of wages. It will necessarily presuppose the existence of proper conditions or that they will be secured through agencies already in existence "

Gompers was eager for the new committee to commence operations because, as Robert Maisel reported: "There are many cities and states where labor is expecting trouble, especially in the states of Michigan, some parts of Ohio, Wisconsin, and Illinois" But Mr Creel, far from being able to reassure the A.F. of L. chief, had to write that, as a result of the Congressional budget cut· "I am no longer able to extend financial aid to the American Alliance for Labor and Democracy. I am informing Mr Maisel after August 1 the existing arrangements will cease." Since Congress had not penalized the Labor Department in similar fashion, however, Creel suggested that Babson might adopt the Alliance.

Relations with the CPI were not immediately severed, but activities were greatly curtailed from that time on, though at the end of August, Chester M. Wright, publicity director, was still sanguine as to the possibilities of the Alliance. The thing that appealed to him especially was that many radical members of the Alliance could be used for speaking purposes where an admitted government agent should not appear

While the famous Alliance meeting in St. Paul was going on, the CPI had assumed an important new duty in connection with the government approach to labor—it took over the publicity work of the Labor Department. After a series of telegrams, Leigh Reilly, director of the CPI News Division, gave the assignment to William L Chenery, one of George Creel's fellow alumni of the *Rocky Mountain News* and today editor of *Collier's*

Aside from the CPI weekly labor letter, which reviewed the news of the organized workers as late as December 1918, one of the last efforts of the Creel Committee to remedy the industrial situation was undertaken by Chester Wright, who was at that time in charge of the Division of Labor Publications. After a conference with Creel, Sisson, and Frank P. Walsh, he went to Detroit in the first part of September 1918 to investigate the pronounced lapse in the work of the American Alliance for Labor and Democracy Following a personal survey, which included consultation with leaders in virtually every war trade in the city, he came to the conclusion that intolerable working conditions were to blame for the failure of active loyalty work.

According to Wright in his report dated September 27, 1918, grievances included excessive, continuous overtime work at regular rates of pay, discrimination against union members; manipulation of the draft machinery to the detriment of the unions, improper use of the Liberty Loan and other drives to make men either remain at work under unsatisfactory conditions or lose money pledged in payment; and finally, unusually low wages and unusually high prices. Wright held that "an attempt to proceed with loyalty work without an adjudication of industrial conditions would be pure waste of time."

The use of fund-raising machinery attracted his special interest. According to his information "The manufacturers subscribe for an amount computed on the payroll of the establishment This lump sum is then apportioned among the employees who in many cases at least feel under compulsion to take the amount allotted by the employer The employees make payments to the firm in instalments. . It has been the custom in many plants, I was told, for the employers to withhold the wages of an employee leaving the company to be applied on unpaid payments for bonds It is the opinion of Detroit labor bodies that this system is used by the employers, partly at least, in the hope of inducing men to remain at work under unjust conditions "

Mr Walsh had authorized Wright, according to the latter, to say to the workers in Detroit that if they had grievances, and would present them to the War Labor Board (of which Mr. Walsh was chairman) he would guarantee them a hearing But the men in Detroit were skeptical, for there had been one continuous record of disappointments. Wright telegraphed Walsh about the situation, and the latter wired to bring a delegation of as many as twelve to Washington at government expense as witnesses. Eleven of them accompanied Wright to the capital where their complaints were presented to the War Labor Board Upon the strength of that testimony, investigators were sent to Detroit, and Wright understood that Mr. Walsh and William Howard Taft were to go there to conduct a hearing.

Through all of this labor experience Creel strove valiantly to hold his balance, and to keep his office out of the hands of factionalists. Even when Edgar Sisson proposed the advantage of endorsing the British labor group which, at least today, seems closest of all to Wilson's (and Creel's) political philosophy, the chairman of the CPI wrote.

"We must stand fast at all times against imperialism and jingoism, but such a course does not compel us in any degree to veer sharply over to such groups as this headed by Henderson. As completely as possible I want to avoid any effect of intrusion in class quarrels; just as I did not think it wise for us to indorse the right wing of the labor movement in Great Britain, just so did I think it unwise to be put in the attitude of incurring favor with the left wing. We have our own aims to present and this is task enough."

At home he resisted time and again the effort to make "patriotism" serve selfish ends in dealing with labor. For instance, when F B. Johnstone, secretary of the Chicago Union League Club, called his attention to a poster entitled "What Doth It Profit a Man," Creel said he thought it did more harm than good, and that labor was "deeply resentful of the continued emphasis on the responsibilities of labor while never a word is said concerning the employer. This poster gives the idea that the working man should not concern himself about his wages, about his working conditions, or about his rights, but should toil steadily from early until late with no other thought than the National Service."

Again, he wrote to the National Americanization Committee on January 14, 1918: "The government is doing everything in its power to prevent strikes, but it avoids very carefully any suggestion that it denies the right of labor to protest against conditions "

Still another example is found in his approval in every particular of a letter from Professor S H Clark of the University of Chicago, who wrote: "My two sons in France get $33 apiece per month Why should Stone, and Armour, and Vanderlip *et al* be paid more? . . Unless we conscript wealth to the justifiable limit, all appeals whether by the Four-Minute Men or a letter from the President, to save, to give blood or money, to compose differences, to subscribe for bonds, to stand behind the President—all appeals will fall eventually on deaf ears: and we shall have a sullen, scowling, half-hearted cooperation, instead of a wholehearted, inspiring to-the-last-ditch, united democracy."

Three days later Creel wrote Mrs. Alice Kimball Godfrey of Kansas City· "The most important task we have before us today in the fight for unity is that of convincing the great mass of workers that our interest in democracy and justice begins at home."

But the most forthright statement of Creel's views on this subject was given to F. L. Collins, president of McClure Publications and editor of *McClure's Magazine*. Mr. Collins had sent the cartoon from the *Indianapolis News* which is reproduced on the next page. He asked Mr Creel. "Do you want us to build up a sentiment for the conscription of labor or do you want to prevent the necessity of conscripting labor by giving wide circulation to such sentiments as are in the enclosed cartoon? . . . Tell all the rest of us how to act It will not be an impossible task to make every industrial slacker in the United States ashamed to be seen in the company of his own dinner pail."

And George Creel replied:

"I have reason to know that the workers of the United States are bitterly resentful of this sort of thing. They feel that if they are to surrender their demands in the matter of hours and overtime, that employers, manufacturers, wholesalers, retailers, and others, should make like concessions in the matter of

[211]

There's No Question of Hours and Overtime

—From *The Indianapolis News*

The Cartoon that Aroused Creel's Anger

profits. The fact that there are so many employers who put greed before patriotism makes it very difficult to level any blanket attack against workers, who are likewise guilty of thinking of themselves before their country. This Committee cannot take part in the industrial dispute. If I were asked to suggest a policy for an editor, however, I would say that the fight should be made against both kinds of 'slacker,' so that the class line would be wiped out entirely, and suspicion removed that one side or the other was attempting to use a national emergency for its own selfish purpose."

[212]

Chapter 9

DELETING THE HYPHEN: THE FOREIGN-BORN

"HYPHENATED AMERICANISM" was one of the most familiar phrases of the war years, and, even when stripped of its emotional connotation, represented a vital problem in the mobilization of American manpower and resources for the prosecution of the war. More than 14,-500,000 residents of the country in 1917 had been born in foreign countries, and many others were but one generation removed from the status of immigrants. Foreign groups lived a life that was in many respects apart from that of the country as a whole—they held to their national customs, they spoke in a foreign tongue, they had their own churches (in many of which English was never spoken), and they had their own newspapers. The problem was to enlist the help of all these people in the common enterprise.

Large as this task was, it seemed even more forbidding to many people in 1917, because the most important group was that of the German-Americans whose homeland was the very country they were being asked to oppose. Further, Americans were reminded daily of the machinations of German agents on our soil before the war, and it was widely believed that the German-American Alliance had established a tight network of propaganda agents who had not only invaded centers of German population but also poisoned schools and colleges and the press German interest in the brewing industry also served, with the growing number of temperance advocates, to reinforce the general wartime hatred of anything connected with the name of Germany.

Even American citizenship was held to be no proof of loyalty. As Senator William H. King wrote to Creel on March

25, 1918: "There is a feeling throughout the country that there are some Prussian spies in this country who have their citizenship papers—and who should be loyal Americans I know, myself, that there are some disloyalists among our alien population and among those who have sworn allegiance to the flag."

Drastic measures were proposed by L. B. Foley of the Merritt and Chapman Derrick Company, New York, in a letter to Creel "When our government shall have *shot* or *hung* the men who are spreading anti-American propaganda, the way will be cleared for more immigrants to become citizens of our country The writer is convinced that the apathy and dilatory methods of our government, in regard to traitorous enemies within our midst, are responsible for much of the hard work in connection with Americanizing foreigners who come to our shores."

The Treasury Department received a suggestion that every bank containing the words "German-American" in its title should change its name, and many people proposed the elimination of German-language study from public schools, although in the latter case we have evidence that President Wilson, George Creel, and a number of other influential Americans thought the suggestion childish. The President had tried to distinguish between the people and the government of Germany, but not all of his fellow citizens—not even all members of the CPI—really believed in this dichotomy Many people thought the Germans had a government no better than they deserved.

The hatred of Germans in this country was generally enlarged to include hatred, or at least suspicion, of all foreigners This naturally had a reaction on the foreigners themselves

Some observers thought the country was suffering during the war for the decades of negligence during which we had refused to treat the process of assimilation as a national problem. Raymond B Price expressed this thought in the pamphlet, *Washington's Nine Months at War·*

"And what of the poor, bewildered alien himself? With no place to go for general and authoritative information, exposed to the machinations of spy and agitator, of profiteer and corruptionist—ought we not commend those great millions for their steadiness of purpose and action, their loyalty and decency under trying conditions?"

The problem was expressed simply, on the very day this country declared war when Judge Joseph Buffington addressed applicants for naturalization in Philadelphia· "Today there are fourteen and a half million men in America of foreign birth; fourteen million children of those of foreign birth. . . . I . have always said that when war faced us these foreign-born men would prove themselves Americans The crux is not the fact of the hyphen, but whether the man's heart is at the American end of the hyphen"

One thing was clear to the CPI: it could never perform effectively its assigned task of holding fast the inner lines until it had found a way of dealing with foreign elements in our population. Two methods were available. an attempt to force these groups into submission to the national will, or an attempt to explain America's war aims and make these disparate groups actively want to help. In this case, as in so many others reported in this book, Mr Creel chose the course of affirmative action, although in a small number of instances he was forced to invoke the government's legal powers under the Espionage Act and the Trading-with-the-Enemy Act.

Under the latter statute the government issued licenses for foreign-language newspapers. As W. H Lamar, solicitor of the Post Office Department, wrote to Julius Koettgen on January 29, 1918 "The German-language papers in this country were found after a careful survey to occupy a very peculiar position, practically all of them had been sympathetic with Germany before this country entered the war. Many of them, later, while declaring their loyalty to this country, continued to publish matter which not only showed sympathy with Germany, but intense hostility to the Allies. . . Many of the

[215]

German-language publishers have, from time to time, been brought to realize what their duty to their adopted country means now . . Such representations have been made to the department which has enabled us to grant quite a number of permits to these papers and I think many others still will ultimately be able to hold permits."

But in general the CPI placed its main reliance on education This was done in three ways which helped support each other—through a program of translated CPI pamphlets so that each alien, whether or not able to read English, would know the objects of democracy, freedom, and peace which President Wilson was seeking; through the work of the CPI in supplying a flood of "wholesome" news for the foreign-language press of the country, and through encouragement of societies of German-Americans, Hungarian-Americans, and so on, which sprang up all over the country with a "spontaneity" which does not seem so remarkable after examination of the CPI files as it may have appeared to the humble foreigner in 1917.

The need for all this work was clearly great. When, on February 6, 1918, George Creel sent a letter to the mayor of every city asking for a list of organizations doing Americanization work, the results were disquieting. Replies showed that few towns had records to be proud of. Although thirty-two different groups tried to help the foreign born in one way or another, there was no comprehensive or unified plan. The foreigner still looked most naturally to his own lodges, his own aid societies, and his own religious organizations.

Even before this survey, however, the CPI recognized the problem of the foreign born Eventually the work was carefully organized through a regular CPI division, as will be explained later, but to begin with the effort was directed chiefly through the various national groups

The Germans were the first to receive attention, and by October 1917 at least a beginning had been made toward organizing them into a patriotic group. The organization was originally known as the American Friends of the German

Republic, but the name was soon changed to Friends of German Democracy. Professor Otto Heller, Jacob Schiff, and others felt that the prestige of nationally known names should be added, and that membership qualifications should be broadened to include every American who wanted to join, not merely the members of old German families The changes were made, and the following became the national executive committee of the reorganized body· Abraham Jacobi, honorary president; Franz Sigel, president; Frederick L Hoffman, vice-president, Charles J Schlegel, treasurer; Frank Bohn, secretary, and Julius Koettgen, assistant secretary

Frank Bohn, the secretary, devoted most of his energy to undercover work in Europe, and the key man in the organization in the United States, in fact the active organizer and fund-raiser, was Julius Koettgen. Although a British citizen and working in an American cause, he was classed as an enemy alien because he had been born in Germany. A book which he had translated was on the War Department "Index Expurgatorius," and he was informed by the Department of Justice· "While the department appreciates your position, you will be required to register The registration, however, should not be taken as a reflection upon your good intentions or your loyalty to the United States."

Koettgen was in constant communication with Creel, and though the Friends of German Democracy was organized in the first place by private citizens and remained technically independent, actually it was little more than camouflage for the CPI. Koettgen had the official title of director of the German Bureau in the CPI Division of Work with the Foreign Born.

Financial support for the organization cannot be fully traced, but on February 24, 1918, Koettgen wrote Creel that he had $1,000 contributions from both Jacob Schiff and Otto H. Kahn This latter donation is especially interesting because German propagandists frequently tried to discredit the society by saying that it was subsidized by millionaires, and specifically by Kahn. The charge was made especially in connection with the financial contributions which the Friends of German Democracy made to the Berne newspaper *Die Freie Zeitung*, which was attempting to foment social revolution within Germany. An American scholar, Dr. George G. Bruntz, reports that Mr. Kahn consistently denied any connection with *Die Freie Zeitung* and, shortly before his death, wrote Dr Bruntz once more that he had never contributed to the Friends of German Democracy

On December 8, 1917, the Friends of German Democracy issued a manifesto to Germans throughout the world announcing the society's purpose to assist in a vigorous prosecution of the war and "to unify the people of America in the common cause as well as to arouse the people of Germany to a sense of their duty and their opportunity."

It was evident, however, that the Friends of German Democracy would have the opposition of the older German-American Alliance, and Koettgen wrote Creel on February 24, 1918: "Our movement will have to fight the German-American Alliance; we should have started that fight long ago if the leaders of that reactionary gang could be enticed out of their holes."

Creel himself had foreseen this, for he had written to Attorney General Gregory four days earlier· "The attack on it has been made by German-Americans who wanted to use it as a sort of loyalty badge without going on record for the United States and against Germany"

A less serious obstacle was encountered among the German friendly societies which declared they had not engaged in anti-American activities but had merely attempted to preserve German national customs. One such group was the Sons of Herman, and in response to a suggestion from Koettgen, Carl Byoir of the CPI wrote to the president and secretary of the society that it "might be advantageous for all concerned if the officers and members of your organization would work out a plan of cooperation with the American Friends of German Democracy." Within three weeks Koettgen informed Byoir that Richard Schaefer of the Sons of Herman had called upon him and had promised full cooperation with the CPI In addition a plan was to be adopted that would provide for the gradual substitution of English for German.

One of the great events in the life of the Friends of German Democracy was a mass meeting in Grand Central Palace, New York, on February 16, 1918. The press gave it generous publicity, and William Sleicher, brother of the editor of *Leslie's*, put up $500 to cover costs of the meeting.

A loyalty resolution adopted at that meeting was sent to every German-American society in the United States and to German social-democrats in Switzerland and other neutral countries With other meetings already held or planned, from Missouri to Brooklyn, with a bulletin being sent to the German-American papers, with promises of clippings from the press of the German Empire, and with persons of the caliber of James M. Beck, George Haven Putnam, and David Starr Jordan joining the society, Koettgen thought the battle half won.

In the final report of the CPI German Bureau, however, it was granted that although the diffusion of printed matter had been wide, membership was never large Koettgen believed that was because people of German birth were too frightened to identify themselves with a society containing the hated word in its title, and because excitable Americans of other stock were inclined to criticize everything named "German," whatever its patriotic object might be As will be seen later, however, whatever lack of success the Friends of German Democracy may have had at home was made up by its important contributions to CPI work abroad, where its finances and its moral support helped bring about the dissolution of the German Empire.

But the Germans represented only one of the twenty-three foreign groups which the CPI attempted to organize along patriotic lines. Additional field workers were engaged for several of these nationalities and the Division of Work with the Foreign Born (as it was ultimately called) came to hold an extremely important place in the CPI structure. In the beginning Creel himself was director of the CPI Foreign Section, which also encompassed the work with foreigners in this country. Later the Foreign Section was headed by Arthur Woods, Will Irwin, Edgar Sisson, and finally H. N. Rickey.

The Division of Work with the Foreign Born was headed by Josephine Roche, active then as now in a wide variety of welfare undertakings and later famous as one of the most distinguished women in American public life—Assistant Secretary of the Treasury, chairman of the executive committee of the National Youth Administration, and president of the Rocky Mountain Fuel Company.

The bureau chiefs at the end of the war were: Scandinavian, Edwin Bjorkman; German, Julius Koettgen; Hungarian, Alfred Markus (successor to Alexander Konta when the latter withdrew following a difference with the CPI over the amount of money to be spent on advertising); Italian, Albert Bonaschi; Lithuanian, Julius B. Kaupas; Polish, Ludwik Kradyna; Czechoslovak, Anna Tvricka; Yugoslav, Peter Mladineo.

For each nationality, the CPI attempted to provide speakers, press news, many miscellaneous services, and translations of the CPI's own patriotic pamphlets. Certain titles in the pamphlet series were issued in German, Italian, Polish, Hungarian, Croatian, Bohemian, Yiddish, Swedish, and Spanish.

"Hyphenated Americans" Are Asked to Buy
Special Appeals to the Poles, the Chinese, and the Hungarians

Liberty Loan and other patriotic advertising was printed in all of these languages and some others, including Chinese.

Translation difficulties were numerous. Edwin Bjorkman of the CPI Scandinavian Bureau wrote Creel that circulation in Sweden of *Hur Kriget Kom Till Amerika* (*How the War Came to America*) would be dangerous, and that its ridiculous mistakes, principally caused by "dictionary translations," and its general unintelligibility would be seized upon by German propagandists. Bjorkman said· "A retranslation of the Committee title into English would be something like 'Committee to Public Narration' The rendering of the three Cabinet titles is worthy of Hashimura Togo at his best " Ignace Paderewski was quoted in the *Philadelphia Public Ledger* as believing that certain Polish translations of President Wilson's speeches had been done by pro-Germans And in connection with the CPI's Sisson Documents, described in Chapter XIV, a scholarly board of inquiry said that bad translating "had laid bare the documents at certain points . . . to suspicions which the originals of those passages nowise warrant."

These and many other translation difficulties, however, were among the perils of war. It was generally recognized that publication in a man's native tongue gave the surest route to his heart, especially when the publication told him that he could be loyal to "the true Germany," "the best interests of the Hungarian people," and so on only by unswerving support of President Wilson and the American cause

An attempt was made to reach each of these groups, not merely with pro-American propaganda but with a message showing Wilson's special interest in the particular homeland from which the people came After the Germans the most important groups were those of "subject peoples" in Austria-Hungary—especially Hungarians and Yugoslavs. These people were enemy aliens, but their traditions or hopes of nationalism and their list of grievances against Austria and the Hapsburgs might be used to hasten the dismemberment of the Dual Monarchy.

[221]

Frank Cobb, editor of the *New York World*, had been so interested in the Hungarian-American problem that he had written directly to President Wilson, who had referred the matter to Creel. The man selected to carry on the work among Hungarian-Americans was Alexander Konta, a New York banker and broker who had been born in Budapest but had married into the family of William J. Lemp, St. Louis brewer, and had become an American citizen.

According to A B Bielaski of the Department of Justice, before the war Konta had been in close touch with agents of countries which later became our enemies, but Cobb of the *World* scoffed at this in a letter to Creel on March 27, 1918.

"The government is not going to get anywhere, dealing with this Hungarian element, if it tries to club off everybody who has influence with them I know something of the kind of work Konta is doing and it's mighty good work There is a campaign going on against Konta. Some of it originates from Bohemian and Yugoslav sources due to the inveterate enmity toward the Hungarians . . . But, from my own personal experience, I have never known Konta to do or say anything that did not measure up one hundred per cent loyalty to the United States." The previous day Cobb had written Creel, "The first information I ever had that the Austrian diplomatic crowd were playing a crooked game in the United States came from him [Konta]" Creel appears to have accepted Cobb's view, for at the end of January he wrote to Bielaski, and somewhat later to Konta himself, that Konta was officially designated to organize the Hungarians of the country. The news must have been welcome to Konta, for he had been working for some time on the basis of an informal understanding with Creel, and on December 31 he had displayed his impatience.

"We should start at once to combat the activities of those paid agents of the Austro-Hungarian consulate who, during the past two years, have been laying their plans to create restlessness among the Hungarians in American industries and a desire in the workers to return to their native country when the war ends "

Even before Creel had informed the Department of Justice of his decision, Konta had organized the American-Hungarian Loyalty League, which came into being in the first week of January 1918. Creel suggested its name, and Konta was designated chairman or director of the society. One of the earliest aims of the League was to get the Hungarians publicly to express their loyalty A second purpose was to offer to the employers of Hungarian labor, literature, speakers, and carefully selected propagandists. The object of the society, Creel told Konta, was to make the Hungarian population as much a part of the great democratic movement as if they had been "of this soil with a century of traditions behind them."

Konta attacked his assignment with great vigor, and on March 28, 1918, he wrote Creel that the organization had dues paid by 2,700 members, with 7,000 more signed up The number continued to grow and in September 1918 a drive was undertaken to enroll 100,000 members

Unlike some of the language groups which felt that the CPI connection should not be revealed, the American-Hungarian Loyalty League welcomed public knowledge of its auspices. Konta wrote·

"There is nothing that appeals so much to the Hungarian population as authoritativeness. All loyal Hungarians in the United States will give welcome to a League, which, in its promises to protect Hungarians against unjust suspicions of disloyalty, has behind it the approval and support of the government."

There was a limit, however, to the financial support which the CPI could give to the new organization, and the files reveal an inter-CPI memorandum from Carl Byoir to Arthur Woods advising that the League should stop opening new offices in various cities because Creel had offered to support only the central headquarters in New York.

As in the case of all the foreign groups, the public meeting was one of the most important devices used, and the CPI files preserve the program of one gathering sponsored by the American-Hungarian Loyalty League in Bridgeport, Connecticut, on March 10, 1918:

"Star-Spangled Banner"—First Reformed Church Choir
Opening Address—Chairman
Address—Alexander Konta, President of the American-Hungarian Loyalty League
Address—Hon C B Wilson, Lieutenant Governor of Connecticut and Mayor of Bridgeport
National Song—Recited in English and Hungarian
Address—Postmaster of Bridgeport
Address—Pastor of the First Reformed Church
Patriotic Song—Workmen's Male Quartette
Address—by an Attorney-at-Law
Address—Pastor of Holy Trinity Greek Catholic Church
American War Songs
Resolutions—Pastor, Roman Catholic Church, in English and Hungarian
Closing Address—Vice-Chairman
"America"

Eight addresses in one meeting must have been sufficient to test the patriotism of native or alien.

Occasionally Konta's League encountered difficulties with national groups already formed Thus in March 1918, Harold L. Ickes of the Illinois State Council of Defense wrote to Creel in complaint It seemed that several months prior to March 1918, Ickes's committee had authorized an organization of the Hungarians in Chicago as the New Freedom Society of America Splendid progress was being made until Konta arrived to disband it and enroll its members in his society, saying that he represented Creel. Ickes expressed doubt at that, for, he wrote, "I have known how anxious you have been not to interfere with organizations already perfected, or under way, under the direction of the various State Councils " This was directly in line with the statement made by the chairman of the CPI to James M. Curley of Boston To him Creel had written March 8, 1918, that the Committee, at all times, worked through the State Councils of Defense as far as activities in the various commonwealths were concerned

Encouragement of patriotism in Hungarian industrial labor was one of the principal objects of the American-Hungarian Loyalty League, but at least some of the employers of that labor were uncertain of the advantage to be gained Thus a Department of Justice agent reported from Pittsburgh in August 1918.

"The manufacturers seem to have no difficulty in dealing with these people at this time, and some have expressed the fear, that if they are organized in such a league they will pass from the control of the manufacturers into the control of foreigners."

But Creel continued to support the League as he had earlier. In February, George C. Foote had written him from Port Henry, New York, saying that his company had a communication from the League asking for cooperation in working among its employees "This League," Mr Foote wrote, "states that it is a branch of your Bureau. We would be pleased to receive from you information regarding the same and its objects." Creel replied·

"The Hungarian Loyalty League is an organization in which this Committee is vitally interested What we are trying to do is to form these people into a patriotic body so that we can reach them with literature, with speakers, with motion pictures, and in every other way try to bring them into closer touch with America Anything that you may do for Mr Konta will be appreciated "

While the CPI was lending its aid to the organization of the enemy-alien groups, Hungarian and German, similar attention was given to the less difficult task of ensuring the loyalty of Americans born in neutral or Allied countries Societies were formed, news bulletins prepared, speakers, films, and publications furnished. Usually there was a close liaison with the CPI office, and always Creel and his staff were prepared to render every feasible aid to the field workers

The most energetic and thoroughly organized group of neutrals consisted of people from the Scandinavian countries.

[225]

Great use was made of societies already existing or newly formed for the occasion—for instance the Sons of Norway, the John Ericsson League of Patriotic Service (Swedish), and the Jacob Riis League of Patriotic Service (Danish), the two latter directly sponsored by the CPI.

The great driving force for work among the Scandinavians was Edwin Bjorkman, who wrote Creel in November 1917 that he had just returned from Sweden where for two years he had been in full charge of all forms of British propaganda. His first object in the United States was to secure the loyalty of the Swedish-American group, but the work expanded rapidly to include other nationalities as well November 1918 saw the greatest activity of his bureau, with four organizers working in the domestic field among Swedes, Norwegians, Danes, Finns, and Hollanders. It was considered best that the CPI avoid as much as possible showing its hand in this work, but both initiative and funds were provided.

One of the efforts of Bjorkman's group was to foster among Scandinavian-Americans the sense of personal stake in the war. The leagues of patriotic service helped in this regard by serving as a clearing house of communication between American soldiers and sailors of Scandinavian origin and their home folks. But battle news proved more effective than anything else.

Writing from Minneapolis, during an organization trip, Bjorkman stated that there had been a marked change of sentiment among the Swedes in the Northwest recently. German activities in Russia and Finland seemed chiefly responsible. "News of the killing and wounding of Minnesota and Iowa boys at the front has helped too. Noted pacifists and pro-Germans are coming around in great shape."

Diplomacy was frequently needed in dealing with foreign groups. For instance, the immigrants from Alsace-Lorraine objected to being classed as alien enemies. Charles Blumenthal, of the World League for the Restitution of Alsace-Lorraine, commenting upon the Attorney General's ruling, stated that it had led to loss of jobs by Alsatians. In explanation, Attorney

General Gregory sent Creel a photostat of his letter to the French Ambassador:

"As I understand the situation, a non-official committee of French people in New York City, acting with the sanction of the French Embassy, makes inquiry into the antecedents of Alsatians resident in the United States and if satisfied of their loyalty to France, issues a document certifying in each individual case that the person is entitled to the protection of France, this being accompanied by a photograph and description of the individual. I am informed that the organization in New York City and the French Embassy ask that persons

Germans Learn How the War Came to America

holding these certificates be not designated or treated as alien enemies."

Perhaps the outstanding event in all the work among the foreign born under Miss Roche was the series of patriotic rallies held by forty-four organizations, representing twenty-nine nationalities, on July 4, 1918. Slavs, Teutons, Scandinavians, and so on—each held an Independence Day meeting, and at least partial indication of the success of the occasion is found in the report that 750,000 Americans of Scandinavian blood participated

An interesting phase of the CPI work with all foreign groups was the effort, seemingly contradictory to the function of a government propaganda agency, to secure news from the homeland for the foreign-language press—even the enemy-language press—in this country

Koettgen of the Friends of German Democracy early saw the advantage of this policy. He wrote to the CPI in December 1917 requesting items in papers from Bavaria, the Palatinate, Baden and East Prussia, because the most clannish people came from those regions, and they were "perhaps more interested in German events than those coming from other parts . . Local, sentimental and humorous matter, murders, accidents, etc., should be well represented " William Churchill, director of the Division of Foreign Language Newspapers, told Creel:

"For three years the German-American papers have been cut off from their foreign exchanges, always the most important part of the papers. If we undertook to let them have this look-in they will feed out of our hands on all the propaganda that we supply."

At the end of February 1918 Koettgen was able to promise clippings from the German Empire to cooperating newspapers. The American-Hungarian Loyalty League established a regular news service furnishing daily and weekly items from the press of the homeland. General news was interspersed with information of American propaganda value, for example the big losses of the Austro-Hungarian army; the ill-treatment of Hungarian soldiers by Austrian generals, the hopeless economic conditions in the Dual Monarchy; the pitiful condition of the people at large.

A few months later, however, the CPI found it advisable to cut down on items from the German press, because the German censorship was effectively concealing the signs of unrest and despair which it had been hoped the clippings would indicate. But in greater or less degree the maintenance of a foreign news service was an essential part of the CPI strategy to the end of the war.

The whole subject of securing news from abroad for the foreign-language press of this country is intimately connected with another great phase of CPI activity—the work of the Committee in the foreign countries themselves An indication of the scope and nature of the latter undertaking will be given in following chapters, but it should be noted here that the help of foreign-born Americans was an integral part of the plan

It was of critical importance, of course, that the right personnel should be selected for the work. In December 1917 Harold Ickes was noticing the great number of Russians who had returned to their native land from the United States, many of them not too well disposed toward us and the American government. As a result a great deal of damage had been done to our cause, in the opinion of Mr Ickes This same thought came from William M Leiserson of Toledo University, who urged that Russians of long residence in the United States be sent back as emissaries.

Later, in November 1918, we find record of a body of Yugoslavs whom their associates in the United States wished to send back to their home country to carry the message of America. Creel assured William Phillips of the State Department that they were patriotic and trustworthy Meanwhile Bjorkman's bureau was maintaining two representatives in the Scandinavian countries, and the foreign and domestic services were being overlapped.

[229]

Encouragement of civil discontent and the advancement of separatist movements in enemy lands formed part of the CPI effort abroad, and Americanized foreign groups here were able to give important assistance, through resolutions of support, through secret agents abroad, and through financial help. Koettgen of the Friends of German Democracy wrote to Professor Otto Heller on October 9, 1917, that his group "has established relations with a group of exiled German democrats in Switzerland, who under very trying and difficult conditions are attempting to carry the message of democracy into Germany, and who are looking upon the elements of German birth and descent in the United States as their natural support." Frank Bohn, secretary of the Friends of German Democracy and in later years a lecturer at the University of Southern California, was a leader in this work When peace came, Koettgen reported that everything possible had been done to support President Wilson in his effort to drive a wedge between the imperial German government and the German people.

The doctrine of self-determination, as one of President Wilson's war aims, bulked large in the campaign among the foreign-born in this country, and workers here helped to disseminate the message in the homeland This is well illustrated in the case of the Hungarian group. Konta wrote to Creel with respect to a forthcoming convention in Cleveland·

"Specifically, the point is whether the attempt to break up Austria-Hungary, which, from current published newspaper reports, is now beginning abroad, shall be supported at this meeting in Cleveland. In other words, shall an American movement in support of an independent Hungary be initiated here, and expedited to the limit at next Sunday's gathering. There can be no doubt that the people there will be ready for it—will support it enthusiastically—but will it be prudent?" Creel telegraphed him: "Follow your own judgment and go the limit. You are best judge and have my entire confidence."

And when the convention was held on January 27, the resolutions were adopted and Creel had them cabled to Russia for clandestine introduction into Hungary. Even more direct contact might be established, Konta thought, and he wrote Creel on July 31, 1918.

"I have thought, and still think, that the change of attitude which has been taking place in the Hungarian mind in America, is gradually bringing about a change of attitude in the Hungarian mind at home regarding Austria and her German ally. By seizing the occasion opportunely, and by broadening the scope of our organization, it should not be impossible for this League working in connection with the leaders of the Independent Party in Hungary, to deliver a very powerful stroke towards the complete dismemberment of the Dual Monarchy"

Similar help was given to many Teutonic and Slavic groups, which were urged to compose their minor differences and unite on the one important issue of freedom from oppression The contributions of American residents toward the creation of Czechoslovakia, Yugoslavia, and the Baltic States constitute whole chapters in wartime history which cannot be examined here in detail. As one example, it will be recalled that President Wilson's support of Thomas Masaryk, then in Washington, was crucial in the founding of the Czechoslovak Republic.

When the Armistice came and the CPI prepared for its part in the Peace Conference (and both the joys and sorrows which it brought to foreign groups in this country), additional emissaries were sent from the United States to their homelands to help spread worldwide knowledge of America's program of reconstruction. But it was with evident regret that Creel saw cessation of the work. He wrote to Koettgen on March 19, 1919, six weeks before final dissolution of the Foreign Section of the CPI:

"Much remains to be done. There is still a fight to be made against the tendency toward segregation, in the defense of American ideals and institutions, and to bring the mass of people of German descent closer to their American neighbors and fellow citizens." Creel would have been glad to know that, for five years after the Armistice, Josephine Roche was to be director of the Foreign Language Information Service, and that this would be only one expression of the great new interest in "Americanization" developed under the CPI during the war.

Part III

ADVERTISING OUR MISSION ABROAD

Chapter 10

"THE FIGHT FOR THE MIND OF MANKIND"

GEORGE CREEL's first job was to win the battle of the
inner lines Incidents in that triumphant campaign
have been described in preceding chapters, and it is
that work for which the CPI is best known—with reason. If
the Wilsonian doctrine had not won at home, Marshal Foch
might conceivably have lost in France—or at least would have
confronted a situation vastly different from that which he saw
when the German envoys, under a flag of truce, pushed
through the forest of Compiègne to learn the Armistice terms
of the Allies.

The battle at home was the crucial battle for the CPI to
win.

But mobilization of public opinion in this country was but
part of the great undertaking. When George Creel said he was
engaged upon a "fight for the mind of mankind," he was not
merely boasting. The CPI extended its work of education, its
propaganda for the Wilsonian world program, straight around
the globe. In little more than a year Creel and his associates—
notably Arthur Woods, Will Irwin, Edgar Sisson, and H. N.
Rickey, successive directors of the CPI Foreign Section—built
up a worldwide system of foreign agents and kept them supplied with a steady stream of American news and other American propaganda By the time of the Armistice, the name of
Woodrow Wilson, and a general idea that he was a friend of
peace, liberty, and democracy, were nearly as familiar in some
of the remote places of the earth as they were in New York,
St. Louis, or San Francisco.

The adulation that the President received en route to the
Peace Conference was at least in part a tribute to the thor-

oughness with which the CPI Foreign Section had done its work.

George Creel's letter to the authors, quoted in Chapter I, suggests that he had the foreign program in mind from the very beginning, but there is no indication that the President or his Cabinet conceived, except vaguely, of the work in other lands at the time the CPI was established. One reason for this, no doubt, was the popular fear of the word "propaganda," and its association in the minds of most people with the German secret agents and saboteurs who were providing daily copy for the newspapers. Gradually, however, it became clear that at least "information" must be sent to other countries, and by the early fall of 1917 serious plans for a comprehensive program were made.

Many members of the CPI recognized that "propaganda" is not a term of opprobrium, and although all of them believed that the American propaganda was more truthful than that of other countries and consecrated to a higher cause, the word was used without value-judgment in much of the correspondence. In public statements, especially for consumption in neutral countries, it was frequently necessary to deny the intention of propagandizing—sometimes even to deny all connection with the CPI.

By whatever name it was called, this activity took various forms according to the needs in particular countries. In the work directed against Germany and Austria-Hungary, the object was to encourage separatist movements and to destroy civilian morale, "to break the war-will" as the Germans themselves would have put it; if this could be accomplished, the contribution to the winning of the war would be almost as direct as Pershing's. In other countries, Spain being an obvious example, the object was to urge that neutral country into belligerence on the side of the Allies, or at least to prevent alliance with the Central Powers. And in still other countries, such as England and France, the object was almost entirely political—to win support, over the heads of the government if

[236]

need be, for the Wilsonian program of peace and reconstruction.

Commercial overtones and other irrelevancies to the central problem were not lacking in all of this, but the main object was to convince all the world that hope for the future lay in Wilson alone.

In this work of foreign propaganda, as in the domestic program of censorship and counter-espionage, the CPI was in the closest relationship to the intelligence branches of the army and navy Because the war was predominantly a struggle on land, Military Intelligence was by far the more important of the two service groups with which the CPI worked. By the end of the war an interesting division of labor had been worked out, whereby the CPI had actual administration of propaganda into Allied and neutral countries, while the Military Intelligence Branch had executive charge for enemy countries But in each case the non-executive agency had responsibility to help provide the information on which all propaganda must be based, and to offer suggestions

At many of our diplomatic posts the military or naval attaché served as CPI representative during emergency periods, and in some other cases the CPI men did work which normally would have fallen to the lot of Military Intelligence. Also, it was occasionally charged by the diplomatic corps that the CPI was attempting to usurp State Department functions. Some indications of this inter-service cooperation—and misunderstanding—will be noted in later chapters.

The very beginning of America's foreign propaganda campaign may be said to date from long before 1917. President Wilson had a good world press almost from the outbreak of war in 1914; foreign papers might twist his thoughts, but at least they knew who he was and that he was a symbol of an important force in the world. After we had entered the war, and before the CPI was making a formal effort at work abroad, the Committee's pamphlets found their way into other countries through our diplomatic representatives, and quotations from them were filed by the regular news services. It was not

[237]

until the end of 1917, however, that the CPI Foreign Section commenced work in earnest. One of the first steps was to send agents abroad.

These foreign representatives were charged with acting as jobbers or retailers of the news, feature stories, pamphlets, movies, and other propaganda material received from Washington. But they interpreted their orders in such a wide variety of ways that the record of the CPI Foreign Section shows everything from the straight and unimaginative relaying of the material to an espionage program in the approved style of the cinema—tapped wires, midnight meetings, and a general effort at political intrigue and melodrama.

In spite of uniform instructions to all CPI agents that they were to spend no money on bribery, subsidizing newspapers, or other secret activities, the files show that this rule was not strictly enforced. Sometimes Washington merely winked at the transgressions, but in a few cases the CPI headquarters gave specific permission to break its own rules. In more than one case our agents also broke the laws of neutral countries.

Development of the Foreign Section was about as impromptu as that of the domestic unit of the CPI, but in spite of the apparent lack of plan the work followed closely a Military Intelligence report that was not issued until several months after the Committee had started work in the foreign field. This report, *The Psychologic Factor: Its Present Application,* published by the General Staff April 19, 1918, recognized that in the "strategic equation" of war there are four factors—combat, economic, political, and psychologic—and that the last of these is coequal with the others.

Although the Germans had long recognized this, the report continued, the Allies and America had been inclined to belittle the importance of the psychologic factor, thus making the other branches carry an unnecessarily heavy burden. The memorandum held that to attack the enemy's political homogeneity and national morale it was necessary first to discover his points of political and social weakness. To defend our own morale against enemy attacks it was necessary to understand our own weak points. In short, both the offensive and defensive use of the psychologic factor rested on intelligence of social, political, military, and economic conditions in all countries. The report concluded that to be effective the psychologic effort must be worldwide, continuous, definitely related to the combat-strategic needs of the situation, and, in methods, adapted to our war aims.

Military Intelligence, however, did not consider that the actual planning of a propaganda campaign lay within its province Specific methods were not suggested, though media were listed, including news, mail service, movies, exhibits, lectures, interchange of correspondents, distinguished visitors, airplane and balloon leaflets, secret agents, and so on Examination of the CPI files shows that each of the media listed by Military Intelligence was at least tried by the Creel Committee, and many of them extensively used.

As far as positive propaganda was concerned, the first and most pressing need was to get American material into the countries in usable form Three methods were utilized, representing the three main branches of the CPI Foreign Section: (1) Wireless-Cable Service; (2) Foreign Press Bureau; (3) Foreign Film Division.

In the matter of news, the basis of all other propaganda, usability is directly proportional to freshness—as German propagandists in this country had found to their sorrow during our neutrality. they might have reams of stories by mail, but the newspapers were not greatly interested in this German material when the British-controlled cables were bringing in contradictory stories bearing date lines two or three weeks later. The assignment of the Wireless-Cable Service was to get the news abroad so quickly that foreign papers would want to use it, perhaps to give it a bigger play than later stories coming in by the regular news services.

The Wireless-Cable Service was directed by Walter S. Rogers, and the news was prepared by Paul Kennaday. As described in Chapter XV, Edward L. Bernays was placed in charge of news for Latin America.

Until the war the United States was almost alone among the great powers in having no means either of spreading propaganda or of controlling news channels. England through Reuters and France through Agence Havas had been able to carry their story far and wide, and, besides the news service, England had developed a worldwide propaganda which excites admiration to this day. The notorious pre-1917 propaganda machine of Germany had been seriously handicapped but by no means destroyed by Allied seizure and cutting of cables, and the powerful wireless station at Nauen was in constant communication with German agents in distant countries.

The United States, too, wanted its story to be told abroad, but the cables were congested and, though under friendly auspices, were not actually in our own hands. The need was for a regular daily news dispatch which would tell all the people on earth what President Wilson was saying about the war and what the aroused American people were doing to win it.

Help came from the Navy Department which, at President Wilson's order, had seized all wireless establishments upon the outbreak of war. Arrangement was made for a daily news dispatch from the United States station at Tuckerton to the French station at Lyons, where, through the cooperation of Agence Havas and Agence Radio, it was relayed to Italy, Spain, Portugal, Holland, Switzerland, and other nearby countries.

Next, it was arranged that our naval operators should intercept the Tuckerton-Lyons dispatch and pass it on to London for the British press and eventually for Scandinavia Other links in the globe-girdling news circuit were added from time to time, with cable, land-telegraph, and even couriers supplementing the radio where necessary The wireless system was never thoroughly satisfactory, and the CPI Foreign Section would have been unable to do its job without the cables

Navy wireless operators at San Francisco sent 500 words a day to the Pearl Harbor station at Hawaii, and from there it went on to the Orient. The message was intercepted at Guam, and there put on the cable for China, where Carl Crow distributed it to some of his four hundred million customers, and to Japan, where it was given to the news agencies. Darien, Panama, was the distributing point for the Central American republics, and direct contact was maintained with Rio de Janeiro, Buenos Aires, and other key cities in South America. Mexico had a special 300-word dispatch for the afternoon papers each day.

Russia was approached from both the Atlantic and the Pacific, but as the tide of revolution closed in on the CPI offices, communication became more and more difficult. The Tuckerton-Lyons-Moscow route was frequently used, but often the CPI agents in Russia were lucky if they were able to get a few words of instructions from Washington, let alone news dispatches.

Various difficulties were encountered in other countries besides Russia—not overlooking difficulties raised by our comrades in arms—but for a large part of the time official United States news was available to many of the most important papers in the world, and it was then up to the ingenuity of our resident agents to see that it was used.

Effective as the Wireless-Cable Service proved to be, however, it could not begin to carry all the information and propaganda that America was eager to give the world. Accordingly, the Foreign Press Bureau was established in November 1917 under the direction of the novelist, Ernest Poole, who became one of the key figures in the Foreign Section.

The Foreign Press Bureau prepared and sent abroad by mail "short articles, descriptive of our development as a nation; our social and industrial progress, our schools, our laws, our treatment of workers, women, and children " The articles were from 100 to 1,000 words long, and many of them were written by the famous authors already at work with the CPI's domestic Division of Syndicate Features.

A pictorial service was added, utilizing material from the domestic Bureau of War Photographs At the high point, more than 1,500 photographs for window display, besides captioned photographs, mats, and cuts for newspapers, were sent to thirty-five countries each week. Besides this, a total of 60,000 large "news pictorials" were exported for display in foreign shop windows, especially by firms with American connections, and 650 foreign agents of American exporters kept their windows filled with CPI material.

War posters produced by Mr Gibson's artists were shipped in great quantities, and literally millions of picture postcards were likewise sent For the Orient, special material was prepared, including window hangers with legends in various languages, and display sheets without imprint for Russia, China, Japan, Korea, and parts of India.

The Foreign Press Bureau, as well as the Wireless-Cable Service, were attempting to invade a field long since preempted by other countries. But in the third foreign unit of the CPI, the Foreign Film Division, America had the inside track to begin with, for even in that day the movie capital of the world was in southern California. American films were known wherever a projector could be set up

With film on the export conservation list toward the end of the war, and with the power of censorship granted by the Trading-with-the-Enemy Act anyway, the government could bring whatever pressure might be necessary to make the movie industry serve the cause. As the reader has seen in Chapter VI, exporters sent CPI movies with every consignment of commercial film George Creel said in his *Complete Report*.

"When our propaganda films began to go abroad it was found that the Germans had bought up practically all the moving-picture houses in some of the neutral countries. They were busy with German propaganda films. They would not take American war pictures on any terms. It looked like a complete blockade for the Committee's films, but a way was found to submarine it The heads of the American exporting companies met with the Committee's officers and agreed that no American films should be exported unless a certain amount of American propaganda film was included in the order The foreign movie houses could not live without American film.

[242]

The war had reduced the output of the foreign film companies to a minimum. The German-owned movie houses had either to capitulate or starve to death Some took one alternative, some the other, but practically all gave up the fight "

Jules Brulatour and Lieutenant John Tuerk, respectively a volunteer from the movie industry and an officer assigned by the War Department, handled the control of film export. The total that they passed ran to 6,200 reels, and along with it went Delco plants, projectors, projection booths, and an endless number of other accessories. They went everywhere from upland cities in South America to Archangel, Vladivostok, and Harbin.

These three phases of the Foreign Section's work—Wireless-Cable Service, Foreign Press Bureau, and Foreign Film Division—presupposed Committee representatives in the various countries to handle local distribution of the material. Such agents were appointed, and they are a famous group.

Personnel changes were bewildering, and the fact that some people were appointed from Washington, some retained by field workers, makes it impossible to list the entire staff of the Foreign Section Even payroll records, which solve many similar problems for the domestic division, are of only partial help here, as several important workers are not listed at all. As nearly as can be determined, however, the following were the principal figures in the CPI campaign abroad Diplomatic, military, and naval officers are named only in those cases where they did actual CPI work, not in the numerous cases in which there was cooperation with Committee agents on the ground.

Propaganda into Enemy Countries—James Keeley, European director, G H. Edgell, commissioner to the Padua conference, assisted by Lieutenant Walter F. Wanger, John Bass, and others on the Italian front; Hugh Gibson (first secretary of the Paris embassy, on loan to the CPI) and Frederick Palmer (war correspondent and Signal Corps officer) were active in France.

[243]

England—successive directors: H N. Rickey, Henry Suydam, Charles Edward Russell, John Russell, Perry Arnold, Paul Perry, John L. Balderston in charge of news for British press.

France—successive directors James Kerney, W H. Lewis; aided by Hugh Gibson, Frederick Palmer, and many others, various phases of the film campaign handled by H. C. Hoagland, E B. Hatrick, and Frank Fayant, head of Paris Wireless-Cable office, A M Brace, in charge of CPI news from France, Maximilian Foster and Perry Arnold

Italy—successive directors Ambassador Thomas Nelson Page, Charles E Merriam, John H. Hearley, director of speaking, Rudolph Altrocchi, succeeded by Sergeant Kingsley Moses and assisted by Fiorello LaGuardia, S A Cotillo, Vincent Auleta, Arthur Benington, Albert Spaulding, and others, Byron M. Nester in charge of postcard and photographic section

Russia—nearly two dozen men might be listed, but among the most important were Edgar Sisson, Arthur Bullard, Guy Croswell Smith, Malcolm Davis, Read Lewis, Phil Norton, and Consul Maddin Summers

Spain—Frank J Marion, director, Irene Wright, business manager and editor of the *American News*, succeeded by Seward Collins, Romera Navarro was one of the most important lecturers.

Switzerland—successive directors Vira B Whitehouse, Guy Croswell Smith, in charge of Wireless-Cable Service, George B Fife; agents of the Friends of German Democracy and the Lithuanian Bureau, Frank Bohn and Lieut. B. F. Mostowski, respectively.

Sweden—successive directors: Naval Attaché E. B Robinette, Eric H. Palmer, in charge of films, Guy Croswell Smith

Netherlands—successive directors. Ambassador John Work Garrett, Henry Suydam

Denmark—Edward V. Riis.

China—Carl Crow.

Latin America—organization trips made by Lieutenant F. E. Ackerman in South America and S. P. Verner in Central

America; Latin American news directed by Edward L. Bernays

Mexico—Robert H Murray, director; film program inaugurated by George Mooser, George F Weeks in charge of news bulletins

Brazil—Ambassador E V. Morgan

Argentina—H H. Sevier

Chile—A A Preciado.

Peru—C N. Griffis

Panama—S. P Verner

Many other countries received CPI material through embassies and legations, through expatriated American businessmen, and through British agencies.

The Military Intelligence Branch sent seven officers (including Walter Lippmann, Heber Blankenhorn, and Charles Merz) to the A E F. to acquire all possible information regarding the propaganda situation They commenced their investigations in France July 18, 1918, but even before this Colonel Marlborough Churchill, head of the MIB, and Will Irwin, director of the CPI Foreign Section, inaugurated plans for a more thorough cooperation between their two offices. When Irwin withdrew in July to resume his work as a correspondent in France, Edgar Sisson, new director of the Foreign Section, continued the consultations with Churchill, and the result was an agreement between MIB and CPI, signed July 23, 1918. The two organizations recognized that the Committee was equipped to prepare and manufacture the propaganda product, utilizing its own and MIB sources of material The mechanical responsibility for manufacture was upon the operating forces of the CPI in France and Italy. The responsibility for distribution, both as to mechanical means and choice of operating field at the fronts, was upon Military Intelligence, since that problem was wholly military.

The CPI's Dr. G. H. Edgell, a young Harvard architecture teacher who later became dean of the faculty of architecture, and in 1935 director of the Boston Museum of Fine Arts, was appointed U.S commissioner to the Inter-Allied Com-

mittee for Propaganda into Enemy Countries, which met at
Padua At the same time, James Keeley, former editor of the
Chicago Herald and after the war an official of the Pullman
Company, was placed in charge of all CPI propaganda against
the enemy in Europe

One of the most tangible products of joint work by CPI
and MIB was the interesting series of "Psychological Estimates" of various countries prepared by MIB on the basis of
information coming in from all sources Each of these analyses
had separate headings for historical background, objectives,
controlling factors, propaganda status, and the American Program. Two brief quotations will suggest the nature of these
reports, and the service they were able to give to both MIB
and CPI:

"Argentina's economic importance   to the Allies makes
it almost imperative that the affairs of the country be in a
tranquil state. . . . Labor disorders of all kinds . . . are largely
fomented by German propaganda, playing on grievances often
legitimate, often grievances against American capital"

"The Austrian government has testified to its dread of the
entrance of Bolshevism It is greatly to the interest of the
United States to bring to fulfillment the most pessimistic of
these Austrian anticipations."

Military men since the war have sometimes said that the
CPI was inefficient in its cooperation with MIB, and that the
members of the Creel Committee, most of them inexperi-
enced, appropriated the glory for hard work performed by
MIB. Major E Alexander Powell of MIB, for instance, said
in his *The Army Behind the Army* "Despite the vast amount
of publicity which has been given to the work of Mr. Creel's
organization, truth compels me to assert that it was very far
from being the success which the public has been led to believe" It is true that there was occasional jealousy between
the CPI and MIB field men, but at least in Washington the
relationship seems to have been cordial and fruitful The records leave no doubt that it was advantageous to both offices

not only in furthering worldwide acceptance of the Wilson program but also in helping to win the victory that would make that program possible.

Reduced to its simplest terms, the foreign mission of the CPI was to convince the people of the world:

(1) That America could never be beaten; and therefore that it behooved them to join the winning side;

(2) That America was a land of freedom and democracy; and therefore that it could be trusted, however faithless imperialist rulers might be;

(3) That, thanks to President Wilson's vision of a new world and his power of achieving it, victory for the Allied arms would usher in a new era of peace and hope in which armaments could be forgotten, all mankind would gather around a council table of the nations, minorities would be released from oppression, and the sovereignty of every country would be returned to the people.

Chapter 11

CROSSING THE ENEMY LINES

THE first and most obvious purpose of American propaganda abroad was to reach the enemy country itself, for military leaders have long recognized that in a struggle between foes at all equally matched the victory is not finally won until the war-will of one civilian population is destroyed. Since the beginning of the World War the Allies and the Central Powers had tried various means of accomplishing this purpose. As early as August 1914, the very first month of the war, both the French and the Germans were dropping propaganda leaflets, but it was not until the German drive gathered in the spring of 1918 that the Allies recognized the full importance of propaganda warfare and gave it the earnest attention which it had received from Germany all along. Not until the tide of battle was actually turning in the summer of 1918 did the Allies plan a unified and large-scale attack on the propaganda front, and, in the opinion of Americans at least, actual unification was never achieved.

The United States, as a late-comer to the war, lacked even the somewhat limited experience of the Allies, and, except in the very last weeks, this country's chief function was to assist the British, French, and Italians. Even when American propaganda material was used, it was frequently transmitted to the Germans by Allied, not American, agencies Apparently because of the opprobrium attaching to the word "propaganda," as well as honest skepticism in certain quarters regarding its effectiveness, American representatives were not at first permitted to join wholeheartedly in the work, though the symbols of Wilson and America were used in all Allied appeals to the peoples of Germany and Austria-Hungary

[248]

But if America was not especially active in actual trench propaganda, realism would have shown that much of the work in Switzerland and the Netherlands was aimed not at the citizens of those countries but across the frontier into Germany and Austria This effort on neutral soil was readily approved in Washington, and though many rules of propriety were set up they were not impossible of circumvention.

In the work from neutral bases, the CPI was the important American group, but for straight trench propaganda and for aerial operations the CPI was ancillary to the Military Intelligence Branch The story of the latter organization has been interestingly sketched in such popular books as Heber Blankenhorn's *Adventures in Propaganda* and E Alexander Powell's *The Army Behind the Army*, while a more systematic picture of the whole broad campaign is given in Harold D. Lasswell's *Propaganda Technique in the World War* and the recent Hoover War Library book, *Allied Propaganda and the Collapse of the German Empire*, by George G. Bruntz. This chapter will not attempt to retrace the same ground but to keep the focus of interest on the rather modest contributions made to this particular phase of the propaganda war by American agencies, and on the new information regarding Inter-Allied "cooperation" that has come to light in the CPI files

One of the earliest items in the files on this subject is a report from the Military Intelligence Branch informing the CPI of French methods of aerial propaganda over the enemy lines and the captive territory of Alsace-Lorraine, including the use of Russian appeals to the German workers to throw off the yoke of oppression This was but one of many reports given to the CPI by Military Intelligence. Sources of information regarding conditions within Germany included German, Swiss, Scandinavian, and Dutch newspapers; reports from agents inside Germany, interviews with travellers; mail censors' findings; cross-examination of prisoners and deserters; reports from patrols and raiding parties. With this information from MIB, plus the CPI's reports from its own representatives, the Committee was supposed to ascertain the enemy's weak points—for example, the critical food situation, friction between infantry and artillery, jealousy of Bavarians for Prussians, and so on.

When these points had been determined by exchange of information and advice between CPI and MIB, the latter was to determine the best methods for distributing the propaganda material—such as airplane, balloon, trench mortar, rocket, rifle grenade, agents in the enemy ranks. Not only the contents but the size and make-up of the printed material had to be carefully considered: the document must be small not only so that large numbers could be carried in one device but so that the leaflet could be easily concealed, because of reported

Tägliche Portionen der amerikanischen Soldaten.

Die deutschen Kriegsgefangenen erhalten dieselben Portionen.

	Gramm			Gramm
Ochsenfleisch . . .	567		Zucker	91
oder			Milch	14
Büchsenfleisch. . .	453		Salz.	18
Mehl oder Brot . .	453		Pfeffer.	1,18
Backpulver. . . .	2,25		Zimt.	0,4
Hülsenfrüchte. . .	68		Speck.	18
oder			Butter.	14
Konservengemüse .	142		Gewürzsauce . . .	0,4
Reis.	17		Zuckerwaren (wöchentlich). . . .	227
Kartoffeln oder anderes frisches Gemüse	567			Liter
Pflaumen u.f.w.. .	86		Essig.	0,019
Bohnenkaffee. . .	31,75		Sirup	0,068

An American "Paper Bullet"

Aerial Propaganda Leaflet Showing a Doughboy's Food Rations

German army orders to shoot upon sight any soldier reading an Allied bulletin.

The message carried by these leaflets was designed either to aggravate the defeatism or to inspire the idealism of the Germans. In the first category were the leaflets presenting by pictogram the growth of the American army in France, figures on destruction of U-boats, maps of ground taken from the Germans by American troops, and, perhaps most important of all, assurances that if German soldiers would surrender, their troubles would be over and they would be well fed. A few samples of these American propaganda documents (all dating from late in the war) are reproduced here But at the same time both the Allies and the Americans made every effort to capitalize on President Wilson's interest in the future of the German people and his assurances that when the war was over the true Germany would at last find itself

One of the propaganda channels was amazingly direct and simple, and in this case the CPI was in complete charge. This was the utilization of newspapers and press services in neutral countries to introduce American news directly into the newspapers of Germany. Hendrik Willem Van Loon advised the CPI in the winter of 1918 that news straight from the CPI office in New York would reach Frankfurt, Cologne, Berlin, and Hamburg if printed in the newspapers of the Netherlands, especially Amsterdam and Rotterdam Walter S Rogers, head of the CPI Wireless-Cable Service in New York, forwarded this suggestion to Creel on March 7, 1918. This plan was followed, and not only did the CPI message reach Germany via the cross-border circulation of papers printed in Switzerland, Scandinavia, and the Netherlands, but on occasion German correspondents themselves filed to their home papers CPI stories picked up in neutral papers or from neutral press associations.

The propaganda situation on March 30, 1918, was analyzed for Creel in a letter from Frederick Palmer, war correspondent and officer of the Signal Corps, who was working closely with the CPI in Paris. He said: "What we can do in Germany

depends entirely upon the progress of this [German] offensive.
. . . If the offensive halts and German casualties are heavy,
then will be the time to bring home our message to the Germans." But Palmer cabled the CPI three days later "Strongly
suggest concentration educational facts on enemy country
immediately. German soldiers and people begin to feel effect
of heavy casualties and failure of offensive. [Hugh] Gibson,
who is making remarkable progress and thoroughly familiar
European methods, should, I think, be given authority and
support to direct this work in cooperation with [James] Kerney
with whom he has established cordial working relations"
Besides recommending continued use of tested methods of
trench propaganda, Palmer proposed reaching the enemy's
civilian population across Swiss and Dutch frontiers through
social-democrat agencies.

Will Irwin, in charge of the Foreign Section of the CPI,
thought that Kerney, CPI commissioner in Paris, should not
attempt to carry both his regular job and the new propaganda
into enemy countries, but Kerney answered that he could
handle both phases of the work, and that he could find all the
help that he needed in France This caused Irwin some concern, as he felt it essential that the Paris office be adequately
staffed not merely to get propaganda into Germany, but to
have it of exactly the right kind He wrote Hugh Gibson on
April 12, 1918 "If we send over matter poorly written, or
written in such manner as not to reach the intelligence of the
German people, it is better not to have done it at all. . . . We
ought to have on that job the best brains we can get—men who
know how to write, men who understand Germany, men
who have the genius for writing what might be called 'advertising copy.'"

Meanwhile Gibson himself had consulted Lieutenant Tonnclat and his assistant, Hansi, the Alsatian cartoonist, who
were in charge of French trench propaganda and the smuggling of papers into Germany These two were convinced that
the only good means of transmission was the airplane, but
the War Office had not been willing to assign machines ex-

clusively for the work Also, "the flyers who have been required to carry bundles of papers with their bombs are usually filled with disgust by the idea and dump their load overboard as soon as they get out of sight of their starting point, often into French trenches or No Man's Land "

Although balloons had been suggested, Gibson reported that they were not completely successful because "they say the winds on the Western Front have been arranged for the benefit of the Germans " He wrote· "So far no system has been devised for controlling the flight of the balloons and a large proportion of them float down into Switzerland and some of them even to Italy and Spain, while the French peasant in the Midi is frequently enraged by picking up in his fields what he believes to be Boche propaganda."

The authors have just received dramatic confirmation of this failure to recognize the origin of propaganda A friend, learning of our interest in the war, presented us with four tattered pieces of "German propaganda" that he had picked up in the front-line trenches when a member of the A E F twenty-one years ago Each of those sheets was a propaganda leaflet directed against the Germans by his own army!

In spite of the uncertainty of the winds, the balloon was an important vehicle of propaganda to the end of the war On April 17, 1918, Irwin wrote Gibson about experiments on a new balloon which was nine feet in diameter and would carry 10,000 leaflets, releasing them at the rate of twelve to twenty-four per minute, with a bomb to destroy the entire apparatus when the last leaflet was gone. It was possible to control the time when the leaflets would start to drop, and, in theory at least, the balloons would be over enemy territory before the "paper bullets" were released It was claimed that the cost of distributing leaflets in this way would be only about a dollar a thousand

Five months later, September 1918, after a long series of tests of balloons by Military Intelligence, 500 were ordered, the President providing the money from the National Security and Defense Fund The MIB intended to secure 6,000 more,

Der Bogen, wo sich die Deutschen
4 Jahre lang behauptet hatten, wurde in **27** Stunden
von den Amerikanern eingenommen.

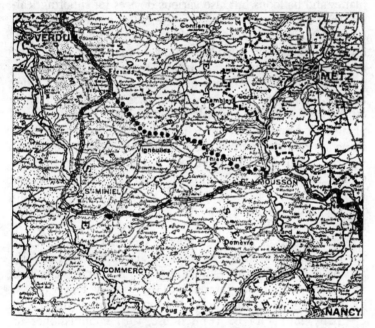

Front am 12. September früh.
Front am 13. September früh.

390 Quadratkilometer wurden erobert
Die Zahl der Gefangenen beträgt **15.000**

To Encourage German Defeatism

A Balloon-Carried Broadside Reporting American Reduction of the
St. Mihiel Salient after Four Years in German Possession

but the program was necessarily curtailed when it was estimated that by April 1919 the total amount of gas available for this purpose in France would have been 2,240,000 cubic feet, whereas the full number of balloons would have required ten times that amount.

The methods of trench propaganda included not only airplanes and balloons but also various devices for shooting leaflets into the German lines—rifle grenades, rockets, and mortars. The difficulty here was that enemy artillery promptly brought reprisals against the sector from which the propaganda had come—which is as impressive testimony as may be presented that the Germans held the paper bullets in higher respect than those of metal. Gibson wrote Irwin from Paris on April 17 of a way around this difficulty. "There is a new plan to use Seventy-Fives which can be fired at the same time along a wide front, and in this way reprisals will be prevented. For this method special shells will have to be prepared, so it cannot be put into effect immediately. . . The shell is designed to carry a package of small pamphlets or tracts, and the explosion spreads them in a radius of several kilometers behind the lines."

For reaching civilians behind the German lines, air raids were carried on at frequent intervals, but some of the CPI personnel thought that smuggling was the most effective method of getting the material into the country. Edgar Sisson set up arrangements for wholesale smuggling from Russia into Germany, and Vira B. Whitehouse, CPI commissioner in Switzerland, recommended similar procedure to Colonel Godson, military attaché at Berne. Also a systematic attempt was made to provide German soldiers interned in neutral countries with CPI literature, some of which, it was hoped, would reach the interior of Germany when prisoners were released or exchanged

How much of this attempted smuggling was successful may never be known, but reports of Military Intelligence at least suggested good results For instance, an intelligent Roumanian officer who had returned from Germany was the authority for a report by our military attaché at Jassy. "American propaganda in both interior and front has excellent effect, and German soldiers and civilians are getting our ideas."

While the American MIB and CPI were planning their various assaults on German morale, our comrades in arms were likewise active, but in April 1918 Henry Suydam of the CPI, then in London, reported that as yet there was no genuine co-operation among the Allies. Two meetings had been held (with U S. representatives only as observers) in an attempt to block out a unified program, but the only result had been the dispatch of a "special British mission to Italy to get simple direct propaganda before Austrian troops" Although other CPI correspondence confirms Suydam in his opinion of the London meeting, one result of the British mission to Italy was establishment of the Padua headquarters of the International Committee for Propaganda into Enemy Countries.

It is evident from the CPI files that in the opinion of Americans none of the attempts at Inter-Allied cooperation was as harmonious or as productive of results as one would gather from popular accounts by Allied apologists such as Sir Campbell Stuart, author of The Secrets of Crewe House The high command of each army properly considered that propaganda objectives, if achieved, would have an important bearing on the terms of peace Everyone wanted to beat Germany, but no one wanted to do it in such fashion that territorial or other aspirations would be disappointed at the Peace Conference

Even by July 9, 1918, when Will Irwin said he believed that the United States should join in the Inter-Allied effort, Charles Edward Russell, CPI agent in London, reported that if there had been any joint action to that date he was not aware of it.

Padua, London, and Paris were the three centers of all attempts at cooperation, but the "Padua Board," as it was called, seemed to cause the most difficulty Colonel Siciliani, in charge of enemy propaganda for the Italian army, was president of the board, and other nations or would-be nations

[256]

represented were France, England, Roumania, Poland, Bohemia, and Yugoslavia, with at first only observers from the United States Obviously, the purpose of defeating the Central Powers would be served best by encouraging both social revolution and political separatism within Germany and Austria-Hungary But, to cite only one example of the difficulty encountered in reaching agreement on precisely what should be done, Italy had eyes that could see across the Adriatic, and had more than a strictly military interest in the political status of Yugoslavia and other Austrian territory.

Nevertheless, dissident groups within Austria were of such great potential use to the Allies that in spite of Italian hopes, secret treaties, and everything else, the Padua group had to cooperate with them. One of the plans employed was to select Yugoslavs, Bohemians, Poles, and Irridenti Italians (some of whom were probably deserters) from prison camps in Italy, put them through a training course, and then have them work on the Italian-Austrian front, entering into communication with Slav-Austrian troops across the lines and trying to persuade them to meet in No Man's Land for a conference.

The CPI was directly concerned with this work of splitting apart the enemy countries, and not only through our representatives abroad but also through the groups of Hungarians, Bohemians, Czechs, Yugoslavs, and other subject peoples organized in the United States through Josephine Roche's Division of Work with the Foreign Born Resolutions passed by national groups in this country were distributed abroad, helping greatly to hearten their fellow countrymen engaged in underground activities at home or plotting on neutral soil

Our encouragement (and eventually our military support) of the Czech Legions in Russia represented one form of this American participation in the Allied campaign, but there were many others. An important incident was the announcement of the Secretary of State, May 30, 1918, of American interest in the Congress of Oppressed Peoples of Austria-Hungary, meeting in Rome, and his statement of our sympathy with the national aspirations of Czechoslovakia and Yugoslavia.

That statement seemed so useful, in fact, that American help assumed a new importance in Allied eyes, and in July 1918 James Keeley, the Chicago publisher, was placed in charge of all CPI propaganda work against the enemy, with G. H. Edgell, the Harvard architecture teacher, serving under him as U.S. commissioner to the Padua Board. Later Edgell was joined by Lieutenant Walter F. Wanger, and that future movie producer had an important part in aerial propaganda work at the Italian Front.

Keeley soon learned, however, that the organization with which he was supposed to cooperate was cooperative largely on paper. He reported on August 18:

"We expected to find three organized and working Inter-Allied Propaganda Boards, one in Paris, one in London and one in Padua, which would be landmarks in the fields, with which we would have to deal and to which we would immediately designate liaison officers. Those boards are ghosts. This afternoon we sat in at a session of the so-called board here [Paris]. It is essentially the new French Army Board for propaganda into enemy countries, headed by Commandant Chaix, and international only by the virtue of the fact that an Italian, an Englishman, three Belgians and three Americans (Hugh Gibson, Lippmann, and I) were present to hear what the French had done and were planning."

Keeley continued his report: "The French at last are doing quite a good deal of propaganda in a precise, intelligent fashion, freely playing the American card as their trump, and mainly through the energy of Major Chaix, a Clemenceau personal appointee, attempting to expand their efforts with an intensified air program, greater use of smuggling through Switzerland, and reaching out to touch off Albania and Bulgaria. . . . The British are also doing a good bit, mainly with balloons but not with aeroplanes. The Belgians are anxious to have the whole program center around the distribution of Belgian newspapers and literature. . . . All this means that there is considerable stirring of the ground but no clear and scientific ploughing and not an American machine on the whole farm."

Finally, during the middle of August 1918, the long expected Inter-Allied Conference on Propaganda in Enemy Countries met in London. Its copious minutes reveal little actual work in addition to points already mentioned. Those present thought that Austria-Hungary was the country toward which most of the Allied propaganda should be directed As for Germany, "the effect of raids on such towns as Essex, Frankfurt and all the Rhine Towns and the munition centers is very great." The conference closed after adopting resolutions favoring a permanent Inter-Allied Committee

As the Allies pushed through their victory drive in the late summer of 1918, Edgell reported from Rome that the situation on his front seemed satisfactory, though distribution of material had decreased somewhat, with the civil population of Austria-Hungary virtually ignored except for sporadic raids such as those of D'Annunzio over Vienna On August 29, however, Edgell told of an ugly controversy which had grown out of proposed use of Yugoslav soldiers The English and French backed the Serbs in their desire to recruit Yugoslav prisoners (former Austrian soldiers) for fighting on the Saloniki front, but the Italians wanted to use them for pushing the Austrian army out of Italy. In the meantime the Yugoslavs already employed at the Italian Front were making trouble as a result of their dubious standing—sometimes being regarded as prisoners of war and sometimes comrades in arms Yugoslav soldiers who did not please the Italians were returned to prison camps, and under these circumstances the Serbs refused to recognize or officer the Legions.

As that antagonism grew, other signs of disintegration of the Padua Board increased, although the United States, through Mr. Edgell, Lieutenant Wanger, and others, increased its own efforts Edgell's recommendation was sent to Edgar Sisson on October 7 He said that the Austrian "must be made to believe that America is after him as much as the German

The rations of Prisoners of War are

exactly the same

as those of the american troops

Auszug aus der
Rede des Präsidenten Wilson

vom 27 September 1918

White bread, meat, bacon, lard,
marmalade, tobacco, etc. are included in the daily rations of the
American soldiers and, therefore,
also in the rations of the prisoners

Wir sind uns alle darüber einig, daß kein Friede geschlossen
werden kann durch irgendwelche Verhandlungen oder Uebereinkommen
mit den Regierungen der Zentralmächte   Denn wir haben schon
mit ihnen verhandelt und sie mit anderen Regierungen, die an
diesem Kampfe beteiligt waren, in Brest Litowsk und Bukarest
verhandeln sehen   Sie haben uns überzeugt, daß sie jeder Ehre
bar sind und nicht nach Gerechtigkeit streben   Sie setzen sich über
Verträge hinweg und kennen keinen anderen Grundsatz als Gewalt
und Eigennutz   Wir können mit ihnen zu keinem Ziele
kommen   sie haben jedes Einverständnis unmöglich gemacht
Das deutsche Volk muß sich nunmehr vollkommen darüber klar sein,
daß wir das Wort derer, die diesen Krieg über uns herauf-
beschworen haben, nicht annehmen können   Was Verträge
anlangt, so denken wir nicht dieselben Gedanken und sprechen nicht
dieselbe Sprache wie sie

Es ist von höchster Wichtigkeit, daß wir uns vollkommen
darüber einig sind, daß kein Friede geschlossen werden kann, durch
irgendwelche Art von Uebereinkommen oder Abweichen von den
Grundsätzen, für deren Durchführung wir kämpfen   Hierüber
darf kein Zweifel bestehen

The treatment of prisoners prescribed above
must be obeyed to the letter of the law   Good
treatment is assured to every German Soldier
who gives himself up

(1 a)

Invitation to German Deserters

Text of Pershing's Order on Treatment of Prisoners, and German
Translation of a Message from President Wilson

fighting in France. He must be convinced of the effort in
America . . but also of the effort America is to make here.
Any announcement of an American effort in Italy, such as
the sending of troops here or the announcement of any steps
taken to strengthen the Italo-American entente must be played
to the limit. Another point, the material must be extremely
pertinent. For example, the photograph of 10,000 American
soldiers at Camp Grant is great material. It carries a kick and
embodies a threat that the commonest soldier can understand "

With additional reports of military victory, James Keeley
suggested from Paris on October 10 a plan "To establish and
cause to be accepted by the enemy peoples the ideas of new
organizations . . . for all peoples following the modified con-

ditions in international life " He thought that if the Central Powers were flooded with literature explaining German responsibility for starting the war, and the advantage to the people to be gained from German democracy, the effect on the enemy population during peace negotiations would be good.

Keeley touched here upon the most delicate point of the whole propaganda effort against Germany and Austria Every speech of President Wilson's, every piece of literature put out by the CPI, was in effect an incitement to both political and social revolution: the people of Germany were told that the United States had no quarrel with them but only with their tyrannical government, that the Germans had been systematically robbed, misruled, and lied to by the Junker class. And when armistice negotiations began, the Germans were told that we could not accept an engagement from the existing government. in other words that a revolution must take place before peace could be concluded.

Similarly, America's promises to Czechs, Yugoslavs, and other minorities could not be made good without the dismemberment of established governments.

Yet both Mr Wilson and many people in the CPI believed that the United States differed from other belligerents in not encouraging revolution, in not doing anything "that would directly or indirectly bring about revolution, even in an enemy country." When Mr. Wilson used that last phrase it was in advising caution regarding plans of Frank Bohn, an agent of the Friends of German Democracy But very shortly after this, on September 20, 1918, George Creel introduced to President Wilson at the White House the president of the Czechoslovak Republic, Thomas Masaryk, whose country as yet existed only on paper. This was of course consistent with Wilson's faith that autocratic governments could be liberalized by orderly representative processes; but by the enemy it was called revolution.

Besides Mr Wilson's own part in urging the peoples of Germany and Austria-Hungary to democratize their governments and to seek political self-determination, many agents of the CPI in many countries were in secret or open alliance with separatists and social revolutionaries of the enemy powers, and Military Intelligence even suggested direct incitement of labor trouble with a secondary system of secret agents to guard against treachery by the primary agitators.

All of this is customary in warfare and no different from the plotting and propaganda of many other countries, but it should be remembered that the expatriated Germans through whom the Americans worked in Switzerland and elsewhere were called traitors at home, and that to pro-Germans among the neutral populations the work of our Military Intelligence and CPI appeared similar to that of German propagandists in this country during the years of our neutrality. Certain phases of the work on neutral soil will be examined in the next chapter.

Chapter 12

IN THE LAND OF THE NEUTRALS

IN propaganda against enemy countries, as the reader has
seen, part of the campaign was directed over No Man's
Land, and carried by various ingenious devices straight
into the heart of the German army. But part of the attack was
launched from neutral countries bordering on the Central
Powers, and from there the major effort was made toward
breaking down the political integrity and the civilian morale
of Germany and Austria Separatist movements in the two
countries were developed on neutral as well as on Allied soil,
and the forces of social revolution given encouragement

The mere geographical convenience of certain non-bellig-
erent countries such as Switzerland, Holland, and Denmark,
therefore made them attractive to MIB and CPI, as well as
to a host of espionage and counter-espionage agents of both
the Allies and the Central Powers.

But the World War was not given that name lightly The
theater of active operations for all forces except those of combat embraced the entire world. Even those neutral countries
hundreds or thousands of miles from the German border had
a place in the strategic situation Spain, for instance, was of
slight potential use as a base of propaganda operations into
Germany, but the question of Spain's continued neutrality (as
opposed to possible belligerence at the back door of France)
was so important that both the Allies and the Germans waged
a bitter and spirited campaign of publicity and intrigue.

In other countries, such as Sweden, the pro-Ally or pro-
German disposition of the people and their government might
be a serious factor in economic warfare, and especially in rela-

tion to the Allied blockade, which the Swedes were in a position to help or hinder.

In Latin America there were special reasons of commerce and politics why the CPI should find it wise to operate there, and in Russia (which after the Bolshevik Revolution and the Peace of Brest-Litovsk was never satisfactorily defined as enemy, ally or neutral) there were still more complicated forces at work. These two special cases receive treatment in the final chapters of this section

And in all neutral countries, whether or not touching the territory of our enemies, President Wilson, and hence the CPI, were concerned with preparing the way for the Peace Conference—with convincing everyone that a peace such as was in his mind was the only hopeful peace for the world, and with establishing America's right as an unselfish, peace-loving, forward-looking democracy, free from the "age-old prejudices of Europe" to step forth as the friend of all mankind and lay down the program

As in so many other phases of the CPI, the work in neutral countries is of amazing ramifications, and merits far more extended study than is possible here. However, as an illustration of how the CPI conducted its operations of this sort this chapter will be devoted to special aspects of CPI work not already familiar through the work of other writers

Spain was the first of the European neutrals to receive the direct and forceful attention of the Creel Committee. On November 14, George Creel notified Frank J Marion, president of Kalem Company, that he had been selected to distribute CPI movies in Spain and Italy. Before sailing he received a letter from President Wilson warning him to abstain from intrigue and simply to carry out an honest educational mission in a frank and open way Marion wrote to the CPI in March 1918 that he had carried out these instructions literally

"I have not assumed that it has been in my province to conduct any active anti-German campaign, but rather to confine

[264]

myself to the clear instructions of the President—namely, to make the people of Spain better acquainted with the United States, the people and their resources, in an entirely friendly way Acting upon this assumption I have not been able to cooperate very closely with similar offices of the Allies ... I have not made any attempt to answer the anti-American propaganda of the enemy, and will not do so unless so instructed by you"

But Marion and those associated with him found that the Germans had been long in the field Irene Wright, an American girl engaged in research at Seville, was among the very first to offer her services to the American Embassy, and after she became assistant to the naval attaché she wrote to Marion "The enemy has long conducted, and is still conducting, a careful and clever campaign of propaganda in this country. It is directed by men who thoroughly understand the character of the people with whom they are dealing. . . . Germany had prepared this field. . . . Her best agents were her accommodating business men."

To the American sitting at home, constantly reading the varied messages of the Creel Committee, it must have been hard to imagine what the Germans could find to use in their propaganda against us in Spain, but a brief catalog was given in a message from the Madrid naval attaché to Marion·

" Readers in southern Spain are eternally reminded that the English took and kept Gibraltar, readers in northern Spain are eternally reminded of what was suffered during the Napoleonic invasion, readers in all Spain are not permitted to forget that it was the Americans who bereft Spain of the last of her colonial glory. Catholics are incited against the heretic English, against the godless French, and the gross materialistic Yankee"

General discouragement with previous attempts to combat the German propaganda in Spain was indicated in various ways. Hugh Gibson in the Department of State at Washington wrote Creel on December 3, 1917 "We have been hearing a good deal lately from Madrid as to the need for propaganda in Spain The Germans are apparently having things pretty much their own way and have built up a strong press with such papers as *La Tribuna*, *A B C* and so on. . . . A letter which has just reached me says, among other things· 'It is absolutely necessary for us to combat this influence with all our power, and it seems as though we alone of all the co-belligerents, can do it. From what I learn the English and French have undertaken to control certain papers here but have failed, they did not go about it in the right way, although they offered large sums of money for the control of certain periodicals ' "

A little later, on January 4, 1918, the American Ambassador in Madrid, Joseph E Willard, sent some clippings from *The Times* of London to the Secretary of State with the observation: "The Embassy's views on this subject are quite accurately expressed by these articles Independent propaganda on our part at this time, unless handled on a very large scale and with the utmost tact (and there is no person now here competent to take charge of the necessary organization), is extremely dangerous.   The Embassy therefore suggests that no independent American propaganda be undertaken, but that we lend quiet support to the propaganda work of the Allies, if and when that propaganda becomes intelligent."

Before Ambassador Willard had written this letter, however, Marion's film campaign had started, and by January 2, 1918, a naval attaché was reporting· "Showing preparedness pictures to large gathering army officers at their request. Leading labor union sending fifty men each show Madrid Start showing Salamanca and Bilboa next week Confident our work important and beneficial."

In February 1918, while Marion was absent from Spain, the naval attaché, Captain (later Rear Admiral) Burton C. Decker, continued showing the films, reporting mild success and recommending to Washington that the campaign be continued independently of the Allies.

[266]

First American news dispatches reached Spain via the Tuckerton-Lyons wireless toward the end of February, as arranged by Marion The naval attaché had the dispatches translated and turned over to the Fabra news agency, setting up an office in a house opposite the American Embassy in Madrid and placing Irene Wright in charge of the service. Miss Wright did not limit herself to straight news work, however, and on March 9 recommended to Marion that the Singer Sewing Machine Company and American automobile concerns operating in Spain be asked to put CPI displays in their windows, although she thought the quality of the pictures then available would have to be improved The files reveal a letter, dated June 7, 1918, from C. P. Adcock, Singer representative in Spain, asking for 200 sets of CPI photographs "to display in the shops of the Singer Company in Madrid and the Provinces," and offering to assume the cost of distribution.

Meanwhile the news service was operating under difficulties, the most embarrassing of all being the failure of the supply in the middle of March when telegraph and mail communication with Spain was suspended Marion, however, attempted to carry on in spite of this obstacle, and we find him writing on March 18, 1918 "We are scraping together from every available source items with which to fake a service to Fabra during the present suspension of communications. Our supply is very limited. You will therefore appreciate the advisability of your getting material to us through any channel that may be open."

But even with a steady flow of news, Marion felt seriously handicapped because of the pro-German attitude of many Spanish editors. One means of pressure that occurred to him was suggested to CPI headquarters: "A crisis is impending here, which, if we can control the supply of print paper to Spain, will enable us to control the Spanish press . . I believe that at this moment I could alter the complexion of the most influential journal in the country (A B C) if I could assure its owners of a supply, or a lack of supply, of print paper, depending upon their attitude toward the United States."

Operative No. 52 of Naval Intelligence suggested the same weapon to his headquarters in Washington, and added that American manufacturers might give further incentive by placing advertising in Spanish papers friendly to our cause

When Marion returned to the United States in April, Irene Wright was left in charge of the news service and the general CPI program was given into the hands of Lieutenant George A Dorsey, U.S.N R., assigned by Captain Decker. Miss Wright was authorized by Marion "to make payment for articles, after some have been published, to reputable writers whose work benefits the educational campaign of this office "

Dorsey summed up Marion's work to that date and suggested future action in a letter to Creel on May 13, 1918

"Marion has done remarkably good work, considering his handicap. . . Re handicaps. The change in attachés is bound to make Marion's work easier and smoother—Captain Crosley [succeeding Decker] will get along with the Ambassador, which means in my opinion that Publicity will get along Another handicap may be removed if your office will be more prompt in replying to Marion's cables and letters   There must be, for telling work, cooperation here among War, Navy, War Trade Board and Embassy on the one hand and the . . . representatives of the Committee on Public Information on the other—even if the President has to order such cooperation . . . I believe we can bargain Spain to a showdown—in which case she will see her destiny on the Allies' bandwagon But we cannot get a showdown by trading oil for provisions or even good will. Spain respects force and must be shown—we have things to show her, but we have asked her to peep through the keyhole rather than open wide the door."

Meanwhile, an attempt was made to gain the help of influential Spanish writers, and the CPI office in Madrid wrote Rafael Atlamira on June 4, "It occurred to me that you . . might be able wisely to advise the office of this representative how best to proceed to acquaint Spain with American life, aims, and ideals." When Mariano Alarcon was approached on the subject of lecturing in Spain on behalf of the United States he was indignant, suggesting that he was being treated cheaply His objection was at least apparently misunderstood, and he was told that the rates proposed were normal and that there was no thought of trying to buy his good will. "What we do hope to do is to make ourselves known as you, for instance, know us. Knowing us, Spain will form her own opinion, as you have yours . . . Inquire and you will find that the American government has no propaganda office, that we have subsidized no newspapers, that we have no notion of buying Spanish opinion for cash "

The extant files of the CPI do not reveal whether the arrangement with Señor Alarcon in particular was completed, but regarding Altamira and other leading writers the result was successful Miss Wright wrote to Will Irwin, director of the Foreign Section in Washington, on June 18

"He [Altamira] agrees with me that it were better that the two gentlemen you name should arrive in Spain without apparent close connection with this office—rather, in their proper capacity of 'friendly intellectuals.' As such, they will be met by a young Spaniard whom Dr. Altamira will select . who, between now and their arrival, will have arranged bookings for them in those cities which Dr Altamira's experience leads him to think suitable . . . In brief, the idea is to make this lecture work look as unlike propaganda as may be—to make it appear to be an intellectual treat, among friends, quite apart from war or rumors of war. In each city the club or organization likely to drum up the largest and most influential audience will be selected."

But even more direct action was resorted to, as is evidenced by a number of letters in the files One, for example, is from the CPI office in Madrid to the American Consul at Santander, the legible part of which is reproduced on the next page.

GEORGE CREEL, CHAIRMAN
THE SECRETARY OF STATE
THE SECRETARY OF WAR
THE SECRETARY OF THE NAVY

COMMITTEE ON PUBLIC INFORMATION
WASHINGTON, D. C

DIVISION OF FOREIGN SERVICE

WILL IRWIN
CHAIRMAN

FRANK J MARION
REPRESENTATIVE
FOR
SPAIN

Turbane 14, Madrid, June 19.

TO : The American Consul, Santander.

FROM : Madrid Office, Committee on Public Information.

SUBJECT: Friendly Newspaper.

1. Referring to conversations between you and Lieutenant Dorsey:

2. Monthly, beginning the reckoning from next Saturday, there will be sent you 500 pesetas from this office, which it is requested that you see delivered to the editor in question.

3. Beginning on Saturday, the Fabra agency in this city will send that paper a daily 15 minute news service, to consist of one domestic item, one allied item, and the rest American news. It is requested that the editor communicate direct with Fabra as to hours, etc., just as though he were a regular subscriber, which, indeed, he has become.

Special Inducements Were Sometimes Necessary

The Madrid office also wrote, on June 29, to the American consul at Coruna. "In one port in Spain, whenever a vessel puts in from America, certain newspaper correspondents (for the Madrid press and agencies which serve the provinces) invariably hear a lot of cheerful talking about war activities in America . . . It is earnestly requested that you discover who at Coruna represents *Radio,* . . . *La Correspondencia, El Mundo* . . . and see to it that whenever a ship comes in from America he hears the same sort of good news. . . . It is requested that you advise us what connections the man discovered has, for in some instances tolls will have to be prepaid, and we would expect to gratify the correspondent modestly. . . . When this gets to working, we would also like you to tip this office off whenever a ship with talkative passengers or crew comes in that from this end we may aid them to become

[270]

even more communicative . . . This is a good stunt and it works, and therefore we beg you to aid us to establish it there "

Utilization of the American colony in Madrid and elsewhere for propaganda purposes was aided by establishment, in July 1918, of a newspaper, about 9 x 12 in size, called the *American News* and distributed without charge each week to every American citizen in the country whose address was known. Simultaneously the distribution of photographs was improving, and apparently Miss Wright's objections of poor quality had been overcome, for on July 11 the Madrid office was writing Will Irwin for "twenty times what we are now getting "

Marion's return to Spain was not viewed with approval by some of our representatives there Miss Wright had told Irwin that Marion would continue to encounter the opposition of the Embassy, and that what was needed for CPI chief in Spain was "a man competent to chat with the King while still acting as unofficial ambassador to the Lefts." Miss Wright's prophecy of friction was fulfilled two weeks later, for the files show a letter of July 26 from Marion to Major John W. Lang, military attaché and later chief of public relations of the General Staff·

"In reply to your memo asking 'just what the object of this office is,' I beg to quote you the following from President Wilson's letter to me of last November 14 . . . Will you now, be good enough to let me have similar information concerning your office—what relation, I mean, it has to the general matter of publicity in Spain?"

Relations with Naval Intelligence in Spain continued to be cordial, but Marion complained to Sisson on July 26: "I find on my return that the Navy Department has not allowed the attaché here money enough to enable him to develop his system of agents in Spain, nor even enough, it appears, to enable him to maintain it as it now exists . . But for these agents we would not have got as far as we have in our enterprise."

In August, Miss Wright resigned, and Professor Romera Navarro of the University of Pennsylvania took her place for a short time, after which the office was turned over to Seward B. Collins, then a Princeton undergraduate, now editor of *The American Review*.

Professor Navarro then continued on the lecture tour for which the CPI had sent him to Spain A typical report on the success of this latter effort was given by the American Consul at Vigo on September 4

"The address of Professor Romera Navarro which was given here on the 2nd instant was very well received and the audience, which consisted of about 300 persons, mostly business men and others of local prominence, was very enthusiastic over same I may add that some of the auditors who had anticipated a highly literary lecture which would be over the heads of most of the auditors spoke enthusiastically of the popular manner in which the lecturer treated his theme of 'American views about Spain.' ['Spain in America' according to Navarro.] It flattered them to learn of the broadminded and liberal attitude of Americans towards the work of their countrymen in discovering and settling America and the keen interest of Americans to learn the Spanish language and the literature of Spain."

At the same time Jose M Gay was touring the peninsula with CPI films and announcing good results. The favorite reels, he said, were *Making an Automobile*, *A Glass of Beer*, *Making of Shoes*, and *The Queen of the Rails*. The MIB was somewhat skeptical of the movie campaign: free admission, they thought, attracted a large crowd of good-for-nothings but failed to draw the influential section of the population As a more promising venture the MIB proposed sending Spanish journalists to the front to see for themselves the might of the American military machine—a project that was carried out, though Marion suggested careful chaperonage next time, as the returning travellers were more impressed with Parisian dinners and joy rides than with the grim matter of war

Marion appreciated the value of news from France and on August 8 complained to Edgar Sisson, the newly appointed director of the CPI Foreign Section. "I have appealed to

Washington and Paris at almost weekly intervals for six months for suitable material from our front, but cannot get it. There is no propaganda like a victory in Spain, and now that we are winning [Marion was writing on 'the Black Day of the German Army'], all I can get in the way of news is how many Sam Browne belts have been issued to the Y.M C.A"

For a month Marion continued to complain that news was coming into Spain from every source except the CPI, but when the CPI finally sent Maximilian Foster to join the A.E.F. and prepare special CPI dispatches from the front, Marion wrote to Sisson in delight: "The new special service of Maximilian Foster from the front is working fine and *all* the papers are using it Please notice that '*all!*' That means the pro-German press as well. It is just the dope I have been shooting for, for months. I am getting good stuff also from the for

Copy for PUB.

June 30th 1918.A.M.

From agent at Santander.

The Diario Palentino of Palencia will use service but they want Five hundred Pesetas per month. If agreeable to you begin at once. = 13229.

ToG
    Crosley,
        Naval Attache.

WFB
A *Memorandum from the Spanish Office Files*

[273]

eign press bureau and using it to good advantage. The cable is now coming from London, greatly condensed and reduced, to save tolls, but is all right—just about what I need to augment the Foster stuff."

In Spain, as in every other country, the two potent items of propaganda were military success of the Allied arms and the idealism of Woodrow Wilson. With the tide of battle clearly turned in the fall of 1918, the post-war program became more and more important. W. F. Alcock, American Consular Agent at Huelva, wrote Marion. "Of all the Public Information copy that has been distributed round here, I can safely say that President Wilson's *La Liga de Naciones* has eclipsed everything," and Marion himself was writing to A. M Bracc in Paris on October 11, "Wilson's speeches are the biggest features of the day, far ahead of the Spanish 'Crisis' or the 'epidemic.' Anything and everything about Wilson goes"

One of Marion's final reports before the Armistice was hopeful· ". . . All the papers of Spain are coming out strongly for President Wilson and his policies, and by the time this letter reaches you, it may be that 'the message of democracy' will have done its work here as in other oppressed countries of Europe A change here is inevitable I think it will be peaceful"

But an ominous note for the future had been sounded by Marion in a letter to Sisson on October 25, a fitting quotation with which to close this hasty survey of CPI work in Spain:

"Daily evidence is accumulating in my office that the British and French are trying in many ways to offset the growing influence of President Wilson. It is reliably reported to me that a member of the French Embassy said to a prominent Spaniard yesterday, 'President Wilson may think he is going to be the arbiter of this war but he is fooling himself. When the time comes, the French and the British will settle it as they please' . . . The use of the word 'Yanqui,' which always appears in the press material given out by the French office, is used with malice aforethought, for they know it is a term of opprobrium in Spain."

Switzerland was similar to Spain in that German propagandists had a long head start, and in that the CPI representative encountered opposition from some other American agents in the country. But because of Switzerland's large German population, as well as its geographical position, many special problems were encountered The CPI agent was Vira B. Whitehouse (Mrs. Norman de R. Whitehouse), and her interesting story has been told in her book *A Year as a Government Agent*. She had been an active suffrage worker, and was as devout a believer in the Wilson program as Creel himself, to whom her book is dedicated.

Before her work in Berne was finished she engaged in certain secret operations, but her principal difficulties came about because of her desire for full and frank announcement of her mission, whereas legation officials, for a variety of reasons, favored as little emphasis as possible on Mrs. Whitehouse and her work She was eager to carry out her mission openly, and made a great play of submitting her literature to Swiss government officials with the CPI imprint prominently displayed

Mrs. Whitehouse was given her assignment in December 1917. She was barely out of the country when the Department of Justice informed Creel in confidence that Mr and Mrs. Whitehouse had repeatedly visited Germany before the war and had received many attentions from the Emperor. Creel was able to reply that the Whitehouse visits had been to Ambassador Gerard "Whitehouse himself belongs to one of the oldest and wealthiest families in New York, and is one of the truest Americans I know" And Ambassador Gerard himself wrote· "Congratulations on your sagacity in sending Mrs. Whitehouse to Switzerland."

Another difficulty arose when it was reported that Norman Whitehouse was going to conduct a propaganda campaign in Switzerland and our State Department announced that, far from this being the case, Mrs. Whitehouse was on a tour to study conditions relating to women and children. Mrs. Whitehouse protested indignantly, but was told that the announcement was only camouflage and to proceed with her mission.

[275]

But when she arrived at Berne, Chargé d'Affaires Hugh Wilson showed little enthusiasm for the extra-diplomatic addition to the group of American representatives. Mrs. Whitehouse told Creel on February 18 "Wilson still holds on to the wireless news, apparently not using much of it, although on receipt of your telegram saying I was to handle it, not Wilson, he wrote that he would turn it over to me."

Even before Mrs. Whitehouse's arrival, the legation officials had established contact with two German-language papers, *Die Freie Zeitung* in Berne, and *Das Deutsches Wort* in Geneva. Dr. Rösemeier, a leading contributor to the former, was thought (probably inaccurately) to be the author of *J'accuse* and, according to William Phillips, Assistant Secretary of State, in a report to Creel "has been of much assistance to our legation in Berne in furnishing information of a valuable nature, while the paper itself is regarded by the legation as a valuable medium for American educational publicity." But all of our agents seemed to feel that the German propaganda machine was firmly entrenched both as to newspapers and as to movie houses, which were believed to have been purchased in great numbers by a German trust

In March Mrs. Whitehouse left Berne for Paris and the United States because of legation antagonism, but on June 24 she was back on the job again, this time armed with a special letter from President Wilson, who also wrote Minister Pleasant A. Stovall While Mrs Whitehouse was away one of the most active American propagandists was Frank Bohn, who handled some of the CPI publicity work but was chiefly concerned with "political" undertakings.

One of Bohn's suggestions, tangible support for *Die Freie Zeitung*, was also made independently by Mrs. Whitehouse "I have seen Dr. Schlieben, editor-in-chief of the *Freie Zeitung*, and have had two long interviews with him and he has made out a budget for the activities of the German democrats here in Switzerland." As to handling money, she said, "It is of absolute importance . . . that it should come to them not from any government fund but from friends of German Democracy—whom they believe in—connected with our Committee." The contribution to *Die Freie Zeitung* was needed to make up the monthly deficit caused by free distribution in Germany and among German prisoners interned in Switzerland Another justification of the contribution was that it would pay for the unsold copies of any issue of the paper containing American news—the copies supposedly being bought to send to German-Americans across the Atlantic.

By the middle of July Mrs Whitehouse's campaign in Switzerland was making rapid advances on many fronts. She sought permission to join with Allied agents in seeking to gain control of commercial moving pictures, and she persuaded Agence Télégraphique Suisse to use the COMPUB news service, which was handled at the Swiss end by George B. Fife, on "loan" from the Red Cross

The chief need was for translators, and Mrs. Whitehouse asked especially for Dr. Heinecke, regarding whom the CPI wrote Secretary Lansing on July 27 "We are very much in need there of some one who writes good literary German and at the same time has the American point of view . . His loyalty has been thoroughly investigated by the Intelligence Department of the Army. The French, before giving him permission to cross France, wish to have assurances from you that Dr Heinecke is needed by the United States in Switzerland. Would you be good enough to send such assurances at your earliest convenience to Monsieur Jusserand, the French Ambassador?" The French consented, and sent Heinecke across their territory, as the Germans had sent Lenin on a very different mission to Russia.

While on her sabbatical from Berne, Mrs. Whitehouse had asked permission to send some Swiss journalists to the United States, and on her return to Switzerland this was arranged.

On several occasions Mrs. Whitehouse reported, both directly through CPI and sometimes by furnishing information to MIB agents (which information was then forwarded to Washington, turned over to CPI, and sent back to Mrs. Whitehouse once more) that the best of all propaganda would

[277]

be provision of food for hard-pressed Switzerland. The news service was not entirely certain, and until Maximilian Foster began his reporting from the front was not entirely satisfactory, the film program was not running smoothly, partly, Mrs Whitehouse believed, because of War Trade Board embargo. But short-term arrangements for getting grain into Switzerland would far outbalance this in the minds of the Swiss.

Arrangements for victualling the country would also have an effect on the government, and that might be useful in view of the fact that propaganda was going to the interned Germans against the order of the Swiss authorities. Mrs. Whitehouse wrote to Edgar Sisson on October 7, 1918: "Part of the $2,500 you send me in cash goes into this work. Bank accounts in Switzerland and bank transactions are not confidential as in America. I therefore thought that it was wiser to do all such necessary but illegal work with the money that comes in cash and cannot be traced."

One of Mrs Whitehouse's last important acts before the Armistice was to transmit to the Swiss press and the press of the defeated Austro-Hungarian Empire, President Wilson's appeal for moderation and order. After an exciting time (during which she says the Legation officials, military attachés, and Allied representatives were completely uncooperative) she tried all normal means of communication into the onetime Dual Monarchy, and finally dispatched the pacifist Hungarian, Rozika Schwimmer (who later was refused American citizenship in a famous Supreme Court decision), over the border with translations of President Wilson's message, which read.

"May I not say, as speaking for multitudes of your most sincere friends, that it is the earnest hope and expectation of all friends of freedom everywhere, and particularly of those whose present and immediate task it is to assist the liberated peoples of the world to establish themselves in genuine freedom, that both the leaders and the peoples of the countries recently set free shall see to it that the momentous changes now being brought about are carried through with order, with moderation, with mercy as well as firmness, and that violence and cruelty of every kind are checked and prevented so that nothing inhumane may stain the annals of the new age of achievement. They know that such things would only delay the great things we are all striving for and they therefore confidently appeal to you to restrain every force that may threaten either to delay or discredit the processes of liberty."

In Scandinavia the propaganda work of the United States had a later start, but under the urging of Military Intelligence, Naval Intelligence, and our regular diplomatic representatives the need for activity was brought forcefully to Washington's attention. On March 18, Colonel Van Deman of MIB wrote Creel:

". . . Following are the current expenditures for propaganda in Denmark, Sweden and Norway, according to figures just received by the General Staff. . . In Denmark, by Germany about $40,000 a month; by England about $2,000 a month; by France a little less than the English. . . In Norway Germany spends probably little less than in Denmark In Sweden Germany spends much more. Sweden's domestic press propaganda is helped by German money. . . The United States representatives in Scandinavia strongly urge that all possible support be given the Naval Attaché and his assistants in Copenhagen, in their efforts to maintain a foreign information service in all the northern neutral countries Experts and money should be sent."

Naval Attaché Robinette represented the CPI in Stockholm while the CPI was beginning its foreign work, but in April 1918 Eric H. Palmer was appointed as regular CPI commissioner, and began using the propaganda channels already employed in other countries A special phase of Palmer's work, however, came about through the great activity in the United States of Edward Bjorkman in the CPI domestic Division of Work with the Foreign Born and the numerous contacts between Sweden and America. On May 7 Palmer wrote Creel for statistics on the number of Scandinavians in our army and navy, the names of Swedes holding public office in the United States, and similar material

On the same day Will Irwin was cabling him from Washington, "Will allow you $20,000 for your work with usual understanding that none of it shall be spent for bribing officials, secretly influencing the press, buying space in newspapers, or for any other method which would not bear exposure " Nevertheless, Palmer sent a number of suggestions regarding the possibility of buying certain newspapers. These were discouraged by the Washington office, but Bjorkman wrote to Palmer just before the Armistice·

"The British have apparently made a muddle of that thing but we can do nothing about it. . . . During the last few days I have been discussing with proper people here the possibility of directing legitimate American business advertising into Scandinavian countries, not for the sake of bribing or buying up the press, but to show that we are interested in them and the markets they offer us Right through the war the Germans have been scattering advertising of this kind throughout the Swedish press . "

The film campaign was perhaps the most successful of all phases of CPI work in Scandinavia and the principal obstruction to its operation came from our own Allies. Guy Croswell Smith, who had taken films to Russia the previous year, was placed in charge of all film work in Scandinavia He wrote to Sisson from Stockholm on August 16, 1918.

"We now absolutely control Scandinavia, 90 per cent of the films shown being American. . . . The attitude of the British toward films amounts almost to stupidity They are unable to appreciate the propaganda value which nearly every film carries, whether commercial or official, and insist upon regarding them as flour, cotton or other commercial commodities. Instead of aiding the circulation of the Allies films they constantly put restrictions in their way. They had an idea that no printed or raw film should be permitted to come to Scandinavia for fear it would reach Germany where it would be used for areoplane

[sic] wings It has taken me two months to convince them that they were wrong I had a chemical analysis made of two pieces of German and American film and the test showed that they were almost identical in composition "

Stockholm was important not only for CPI work in Sweden but for that in all of Scandinavia, and in Finland and other Baltic regions, where the results of the Brest-Litovsk Treaty were anxiously watched by the Allies. Looking toward the coming peace, Bjorkman wrote to Eric Palmer on September 9, 1918·

"What we want is, first to keep Finland from electing a German monarch; secondly to keep her from taking part in any German expedition against the Murman coast, and thirdly to draw her away from German control as speedily and as completely as possible. These aims cannot be announced publicly, but when Finlanders ask for American sympathy and support, it is proper to let them understand that neither can be had if Finland goes against our wishes along one of the three lines suggested above "

In Denmark, the principal United States representative was Edward Riis, son of the famous Danish-American, Jacob A. Riis He reported to Sisson in August 1918 that although the Germans had been hard at work ahead of him, "Apart from the Socialist and some of the radical papers, the Danish press is fairly disinclined to publish material from German sources " On August 24, however, MIB told Washington headquarters that the Germans were spreading news of a reported billionaire dinner in New York with service from plates of solid gold. The object, the operative related, was to hold up before all Europe "American capitalism in all its atrocity for the edification of the European laborers, and to show that American capitalists provoke war in order to make money "

Sisson at once cabled Riis to get in touch with the military attaché in Copenhagen, and Riis replied that he was aware of the situation but that CPI should be cautious in attempting to counter enemy propaganda by direct attack. He did ask, however, for continuation of the news service, and for more films and window displays He said the CPI should "wave Danish flag little more and show them benefit which comes to Denmark by sticking with Allies."

After conference with the attaché, Riis made some additional requests American books for pro-Ally Danes to review in Danish newspapers, full orchestra sets of American music, and illustrated material on the Liberty Motor and the Browning machine gun. He said that 150 newspapers were receiving his material and that the news agency was using his CPI daily dispatch And in September the campaign was going so well that Riis apparently decided there had been an excess of waving the Danish flag: he warned Sisson to tone down the praise of Danes in America—"Looks too much like obvious propaganda." Besides, it was unnecessary. "Papers all swinging our way as long as we winning," he cabled on September 1.

In the Netherlands, as in Sweden and Denmark, propaganda assistance from the United States was requested by diplomatic and Military Intelligence agents before the CPI began work there In February H. N. Rickey, CPI commissioner at London, arranged to distribute feature material in Holland through the British Information Service, but the American Minister at The Hague, John Work Garrett, reported that the news arrived so late or in such mutilated condition that the Dutch papers would not use it. He informed the American Embassy, London, that a daily CPI news dispatch should be sent, as well as films and a special agent Rickey then arranged to send Henry Suydam of the *Brooklyn Daily Eagle* to set up a CPI office in the Netherlands. Because of shorthandedness in London, however, it was May before Suydam finally took his post

He requested editorial comment from the Dutch-language press of the United States on Holland-American relations and certain other approved items from America's German-language press. He also asked that Hendrik Willem Van Loon contribute a series of special articles to a Rotterdam paper on Dutch settlements, and to have him visit "chief Dutch towns, especially in Michigan, New Jersey, and Illinois."

Suydam wrote to Paul Kennaday, who prepared CPI foreign news in New York: "To think of getting dyed-in-the-wool propaganda articles accepted is absurd The articles must have a distinct news value . . . a description of life on an American farm seemingly means more to these people than other things which you and I might deem much more interesting."

Suydam's post at The Hague was pivotal in that the Netherlands was perhaps the most important of all German sources of knowledge regarding America and the Allies German correspondents would frequently send to their papers items of news which originally had been prepared in New York by Paul Kennaday. But the German correspondents knew that an American was at work in The Hague, and Suydam therefore requested the American Embassy in Paris to "get into touch with Dutch newspapermen in Paris through French Foreign Office and cultivate them so that they will telegraph American news to Holland " He continued, "I am especially anxious to get as much independent Dutch testimony about our war effort as possible in order to translate into German for pamphlets to be circulated in German army."

While this effort for the nurturing of "independent Dutch testimony" was going forward, Suydam was fretful about the non-appearance of promised movie films, but was prosecuting the news campaign energetically. In this connection he worked closely with the British, notably the Reuters news service. A forecast of the worldwide communications struggle after the war, and of England's assumption that America would naturally wish Great Britain to have supremacy, came in a note to Suydam on September 22, 1918, from William J. Maloney, head of Reuters office in Amsterdam. The CPI news was reaching rival agencies from some unknown source, and Maloney wrote· "I should like to have another chat with you on the subject of giving news to agencies which are rivals of Reuters. The point which I should most like to impress on you is that every advantage given to these agencies strengthens them for the after-the-war competition against a purely British agency."

CPI work with neutrals embraced far more than Spain, Switzerland, Scandinavia, and the Netherlands. The special cases of Latin America and Russia (if Russia be considered a neutral) will be noted later, and whole chapters could be written on American wartime propaganda in China and many other countries. But in all neutral lands the CPI agents discovered the same thing—that the Germans were not their only opponents on the propaganda front. The letter from Maloney to Henry Suydam quoted above typifies the grave problem that confronted the CPI Foreign Section if British and French agents did not naively assume that America's sole wish was to further their own political and economic ends, they recognized the incompatibility of President Wilson's war aims with their own and then proceeded to take definite steps to counteract the work of the CPI.

This anti-Wilson program, later made evident in the skilful maneuvering of the Wilson entourage before the Peace Conference, as well as in the negotiations of the Conference itself, was intensified in the fall of 1918 as the German defeat drew closer A few CPI agents abroad failed to recognize it until the very final days of the war, though President Wilson himself knew through Colonel House, through General Pershing, and through other sources, that his victory over the Allies might be a harder one to win than that over the Germans.

Chapter 13

EDUCATING OUR COMRADES IN ARMS

IN Woodrow Wilson's first political adventure, the campaign for the governorship of New Jersey, he accepted the help and the sponsorship of politicians of whom he cordially disapproved During the campaign he said he was going to do things that the political machine would not like, but the bosses did not worry because they knew that the college professor was drawing votes that way. And Mr. Wilson did not worry about the obviously cynical applause of the politicians, because he thought that once the election was won he, not they, would control the state

That was what happened, and much of his progressive program went through in spite of their opposition

But in Mr Wilson's greatest of all political ventures the cards were turned the other way He had a progressive program for all mankind in 1917, and he was finally persuaded that it could never be inaugurated unless he joined forces with the Allies. And the Allied governments, like the New Jersey bosses in 1910, cheered loudly for each of his idealistic pronouncements, while knowing full well that Wilson could never have what he wanted if what they conceived as their national interests were to be served

The debate of a few years ago as to whether Wilson knew the provisions of the Allies' secret treaties before the end of the war is almost unimportant in view of the full evidence made available by Ray Stannard Baker and many others that Wilson realized the Allies were with him only until the last shot was fired, and that then they were to be against him.

He knew that they would be against him, but he thought that he could win.

[285]

He knew that the fight would be violent, however, and it is reasonable to assume that he was anticipating the post-Armistice disputes of the victors when he gave his endorsement to the program of CPI work in the land of our Allies. It is customary for allies to lend more or less perfunctory help to each other in sustaining civilian morale, but the CPI program in England, France, and Italy was not limited to that. The attempt was to acquaint the people of those countries with the war aims of America, and to gain their support, over the heads of their own governments, for a peace of moderation and hope, not a peace of vengeance and Old World nationalism.

France, England, and the United States felt that in Italy they had an uncertain ally. Pre-war wobbling between Triple Alliance and Triple Entente did not inspire confidence in the first place, and by October 1917, with disaster apparently overtaking the Italian armies and civilian morale shaky at best, it was feared that Italy might soon be out of the fight Charles Edward Russell wrote Creel on October 29, 1917:

"Italy has collapsed, that is the plain truth of it, and the consequences that open before us are enough to sober us all with a good, full view of the abyss. It is of no use to try to fool ourselves If Germany overruns Northern Italy, as she can easily now, she can strike France in the back and have both France and England practically licked before we can get ready to do any real fighting. . . . Germany could never have crushed Italy if Russia had stood up to the line "

In November 1917, as noted before, Frank J. Marion was dispatched on his mission to Spain and Italy, planning to visit the countries in that order and bearing President Wilson's personal warning "Please bear in mind always that we want nothing for ourselves, and that this very unselfishness carries with it an obligation of open dealing. Guard against any effect of officious intrusion, and try to express a disinterested friendship that is our sole impulse."

Italy apparently was not eager for this display of disinterested friendship, however, for on December 27 Creel received a message from Marion in Madrid· "American, French, and Italian naval attachés all think I should work Spain, postponing Italy. Italian attaché queried his government and today has answer from representative of propaganda· Quote Preferable Marion remain Spain instead of proceeding to Italy at present Unquote."

But Ambassador Thomas Nelson Page in Rome did not share this opinion The State Department's paraphrase of his cable in the middle of January was: "The effective propaganda [of pro-Germans] which has been used against England is now extending against America, whose aims and intentions are being misrepresented with marked results. . As a medium of propaganda the Red Cross is proving excellent, as it reaches the people directly, but beyond this is the need of information for soldiers and civilian population in the form of regular news in newspapers, pamphlets, letters, books, lectures and motion pictures to create a better understanding of America's part in the war and her reason for being in " Page also asked for public speakers, especially Captain (later Major) Fiorello H La Guardia, who was enjoying a thrilling sabbatical from politics as an aerial bomber.

On March 11, 1918, Military Intelligence informed Creel that the Central Powers were spending $5,000,000 a year in Italy It was just four days later that Ambassador Page received a CPI cable advising him that Captain Charles E Merriam, professor of political science at the University of Chicago and future president of the American Political Science Association, was being detached from the Red Cross to take charge of American propaganda work in Italy. He said he wished to retain the staff Page had selected in Rome. At the same time Professor Rudolph Altrocchi, of the University of Chicago, was being sent to help Merriam, and especially to have charge of speaking activities. Altrocchi held the position until the first week in October, when he was succeeded by Sergeant Kingsley Moses of the Air Service.

Captain Merriam reported to Creel from Rome on April 23 that Altrocchi and his associated speakers were making good progress, but that a great deal more work was needed "Unless action is taken very promptly it will not tell. Elaborate plans maturing late this fall or next year will probably be *too late* to do any good." Merriam constantly urged speed and forceful action and, at his end, pushed many plans He arranged for American visits by Italian journalists, he sent Italian postcards and propaganda pamphlets which the CPI might use as models, and he called for American photographs and films, including one request for 500 pictures of Wilson, Washington, Lincoln, and Martha Washington.

On May 24, Merriam received a highly effective piece of propaganda material in the form of a special message from President Wilson to the people of Italy "I am sure that I am speaking for the people of the United States in sending to the Italian people warm fraternal greetings upon this the anniversary of the entrance of Italy into this great war in which there is being fought out once for all the irrepressible conflict between free self-government and the dictation of force The people of the United States have looked with profound interest and sympathy upon the efforts and sacrifices of the Italian people, are deeply and sincerely interested in the . . security of Italy, and are glad to find themselves associated with a people to whom they are bound by so many personal and intimate ties in a struggle whose object is liberation, freedom, the rights of men and nations to live their own lives and determine their own fortunes, the rights of the weak as well as of the strong, and the maintenance of justice by the irresistible force of free nations leagued together in the defense of mankind "

By July 2, John H. Hearley, Merriam's assistant (and later his successor) was able to report to the Rome office· "America and things American have been featured in both the editorials and news of this past week's press. The principal reason has been the arrival of the American ambulance corps at Genoa and the announcement of the immediate coming of American fighting troops from France." A short time later one of Hearley's own propaganda ideas was carried out—the visit of twen-

[288]

ty-three wounded American soldiers of Italian extraction, who were honored in their home towns

Fourth of July saw the showing in eight theaters in Rome of the first CPI films, and Merriam reported that 50,000 American flags had been distributed and widely displayed Three weeks later, reports came in of the great success of the speaking tour of S A. Cotillo, New York State Senator who was working under Altrocchi

Captain Merriam's idea of using picture postcards was an immediate success in Italy and elsewhere, for on August 13 he wrote Creel from Rome that 2,000,000 cards were already allotted and 5,000,000 more could be used ". there is a very large correspondence carried on between the soldiers and their families entirely by means of cards . Excellent propaganda as they pass through many hands" The picture and movie program was perfected when H C Hoagland, a travelling expert for the CPI, came to Rome and helped the resident contingent during August.

The Y M C A and Red Cross proved steadily cooperative in Italy, the latter organization providing the CPI with mailing lists of prominent Italians, as well as putting up posters and distributing literature But these and the Naval Attaché seemed to be exceptions among the various Americans in Rome, for Captain Merriam encountered many difficulties. He wrote to Creel on July 2, for instance "There is no disguising the fact that the diplomats of career look askance at the COMPUB everywhere. I have done and will continue to do all in my power to cooperate with them cordially, but without surrendering the essential purposes for which I was sent."

Merriam wrote again on August 29, that a change was needed in either the spirit or the personnel of certain American groups in Rome, and it was in response to this complaint that the Military Intelligence Branch on September 9 issued an order to all attachés that, except with relation to propaganda into enemy countries, CPI had charge of preparation and distribution of all propaganda material. "Military attachés in particular, have no authority whatever to initi-

[289]

ate propaganda nor to interfere with or criticize the work, methods or personnel . You are to cordially assist the representatives of the Committee on Public Information."

Apparently even this order was not sufficient to end the constant difference of opinion between Captain Merriam and the army officers, and on September 30, MIB headquarters wrote to the Military Attaché at Rome, "Plainly speaking, what we want is that you and Captain Merriam get together and iron out all difficulties or misunderstandings that may possibly exist"

But on October 9, George Creel advised Brigadier General Marlborough Churchill, head of MIB· "I am bringing Captain Merriam home from Italy He did a remarkable job and I do not know how to replace him, but whether rightly or wrongly he became involved in disputes with General Treat [major general in charge of American military mission to Italy] and Ambassador [Thomas Nelson] Page to such an extent that I deemed it wise to make a change."

In Italy, as elsewhere, the CPI viewed with envy and some suspicion the activities of their French and British colleagues, the latter being reported as spending $400,000 a year on propaganda in Italy And Hearley said on September 20, "Certain Italian journalists are receiving monthly checks from the British and French Embassies."

But most of CPI's difficulties in Italy arose from the political situation of the country itself, and the fact that Italian Socialists, probably aided by actual German Social Democrats or by German propagandists posing as such, regarded the United States as an imperialist nation and no friend of the workers When Samuel Gompers reached Italy on his European tour designed to inspire labor in Allied Countries, Hearley, who had succeeded Merriam as CPI representative on October 4, reported: "I have . . . been occupied in making proper contacts for Mr. Gompers and his party This was not immediately easy owing to the vigorous and malicious campaign against the president of the American Federation of Labor on the part of *Avanti*, the anti-war organ of the Socialists [once edited by Benito Mussolini]."

And even more determined opposition came from journals very different from *Avanti*, for as far back as the previous April, Hearley had reported "Individual industrials either own journals 'outright' or have the controlling stock in them or 'reach' them through newspaper proprietors and stockholders who are either politically or industrially bound to their monopolistic interests Apart from their agreement on a program of protectionism, the trusts have plenty of superficial discords. It is not impossible that there will be a fight of particular interests after the war."

Whatever the political commitment or economic philosophy of newspaper owners, however, certain public men have a way with reporters, and it is of more than passing interest to note this report from Captain Merriam, dated Rome, August 13, 1918:

"Our best news story of the week was that given out by Asst Secy. [Franklin Delano] Roosevelt. I arranged to have him receive the Italian journalists at the Grand Hotel and provided suitable refreshment! Twenty-two of our twenty-three invited were present, and the occasion was a great success. The press representatives were delighted with the frank statements of the Secretary, and the further fact that he invited them to ask him questions. The result was that he was handsomely treated by the Italian papers personally and that most of his remarks were printed in practically all of the papers."

But the final note in this brief series of quotations on the CPI effort in Italy should reflect the anxiety for the future which was felt by many of our representatives abroad. Hearley wrote to Creel on October 25:

"In these confused and confusing days, amid the evasive declarations of the Central Powers and the hypocritical comments of the Allied governments, the thought of a well seasoned politician comes back to me: 'President Wilson can win and will win if he has the courage and the nerve But he has first to conquer the Old World's two thousand years and more of governmental traditions and class and political prejudices.' "

France did not receive major attention from the CPI until the winter of 1918, though of course as the chief battleground of the war it was occupied by intelligence officers from the first, and as an important European distributing center for information, and as the source of battle news and battle pictures, it was at all times an important link in the CPI circuit. James Kerney, publisher of the *Trenton* (N.J.) *Times* and friend of President Wilson, was sent to Paris as resident CPI commissioner in February 1918 and promptly swung into action in spite of his feeling, as Mrs. Whitehouse reports it, that "there was a great difference between Paris and Trenton and you noticed it more in Paris than in Trenton."

Kerney had difficulties of supply similar to those of other CPI men, movie film being the principal lack Thanks to the Tuckerton-Lyons wireless dispatch and the cables, he had the COMPUB news service, but apparently was not uniformly successful in getting the French papers to use it At least there is a note from Paul Kennaday to Will Irwin on March 15 "You will note that *Figaro's* only American news consists of a four-line announcement that Mr. Gerard has had an operation performed on his right eye."

The general propaganda condition, as it related to American participation, was summed up in a message to Creel from Frederick Palmer, writing from Paris on March 30

Hatrick was "running about the Army at top speed making photographs. Someone cabled him to get pictures of the German offensive, which rather discouraged the boy, as the German offensive is being made entirely in British territory . . We have to be careful in our educational work just at this time when our soldiers are in a quiet sector not to give the impression that we are trying to substitute words and promises for the sacrifice of blood. . . . So far as the Allied countries are concerned, French morale is splendid. . . . The announcement which was made today that our troops are at the disposal of the Allies to be used against the German offensive in Picardy is the greatest possible propaganda for Europe. We shall see that both Allies and neutrals have full information"

Kerney and other CPI men in Paris were in close touch with MIB regarding propaganda against the Germans, in which undertaking MIB was the executive organization, but Kerney was also concerned with reaching the French people themselves In accordance with a suggestion from Irwin on March 19, a great deal of emphasis was placed on public speaking, in the belief that the impact of printed propaganda was becoming less forceful all the time. Irwin wrote

". . . Word-of-mouth stuff is infinitely more valuable I also know that the French are great on *conférences*, and that public lecturers are excellent propagandists Much was done in an organized way last winter by such speakers as Herbert Adams Gibbons I think you should do all you can to organize the Americans capable of making an acceptable speech in the French language, and sending them forth with the general ideas which we wish to implant"

In line with this idea, Kerney was able to report back that Firman Roz had been engaged for a seven-weeks series of lectures at French universities And later Kerney told General Pershing that the CPI lecture series was to open at the Sorbonne on May 23. He cabled Irwin that the whole program had been gone over with Clemenceau, who strongly approved

At last, on June 26, Kerney received his first copy of the CPI feature film, *America's Answer to the Hun*, and it was given a preview to a private group in a Gaumont theater in Paris A few days later the Comité des Forges volunteered to arrange showings of the movie to munitions workers in every part of France. Other industrialists were similarly enthusiastic, and in many cases a CPI lecturer went along with the films. Kerney reported on the joint appearance of *America's Answer* and Herbert Adams Gibbons at the motor and munitions plant of Louis Renault, where the speech was placed on phonograph records:

[293]

"The film and lecture will thus be repeated forty times in the Renault factories for the benefit of 25,000 workmen M Renault said that this film and the lecture meant for him the postponement of any possible strike for six months. The Renault factories turn out aeroplane motors, motor trucks, tanks, cannon, and shells"

French enthusiasm for public speaking and pictures placed a heavy load on the CPI Paris staff, and in September, II. C Hoagland, the film expert, returned from Rome to help with one phase of the work, while the lecture program required addition of other CPI speakers and a cooperative arrangement with established French groups Herbert Adams Gibbons wrote to a friend on September 10, "Our work in France has grown to such proportions that we have been compelled to carry our lecture work through certain organizations" And in a note on the following day he said, "Our films will be shown in France exclusively by Pathé Frères and Gaumont, and, in connection with conférences, by the organization 'La Conférence au Village.' "

Intrigue and jealousy were not unknown in Allied propaganda circles in Paris Kerney had written to Creel on March 23 regarding his colleagues from other countries, "They are, of course, very much out for themselves." Although he added that "The French really treat us more liberally in their news columns than the English," in another letter he admitted that "publication of any matter describing America's great efforts in this war is badly received by the French at the present moment [with the German drive getting under way]."

In one of Irwin's earlier messages to Kerney, written on March 19, he gave a warning regarding the complications of French politics "If I were you, I should avoid the mistake of allowing myself to be closely connected with what we call 'the ex-patriot bunch' in Paris. . . . Europe is getting very radical, and what is whispered among the submerged classes today may be the dominant thought of the governing classes tomorrow, so even in friendly France we cannot overlook the working and peasant classes"

And on May 5 the CPI representative in Paris was returning comparable advice to Washington. Kerney wrote Irwin.
"You ought to warn all missions with official or semiofficial
status to soft-pedal on Joffre and otherwise get their bearings
on delicate governmental situation here Have had discreet and
well known man attached as conducting officer to American
Labor Mission to keep them straight on the situation which
is very critical in some of the larger French cities"

Apparently Hugh Gibson, on loan to the CPI from the
American Embassy, had found new propaganda channels, for
he sent a note to Will Irwin via the Department of State on
April 18· "If I can feel free to spend some occasional cash to
feed one or two people when it seems desirable I think it
would get very good results I don't need to tell you about
the returns on that sort of an investment but I have never seen
a place where such investments are more necessary or more
repaying than here. I have been bankrupting myself trying
to get the right sort of people lined up to help on our game but
can't carry the whole load very long"

By the end of July, as the tide of battle was readying for the
turn, the whole CPI program of news, lectures, films, and displays was proceeding under full steam H N Rickey reported
to Washington on July 24: "With the machinery we have in
motion, we seem to be reaching the intellectuals and the industrial workers as well as the middle classes, about the only
folks we don't get to are the peasants, who really are the most
pathetic of all because all they know of the war is that their
boys are taken off for the slaughter"

But in spite of this success, there was work yet to be done,
as clearly foreseen in a dispatch from A. M Brace, head of
the Paris office of the Wireless-Cable Service, to Walter
Rogers "News regarding the American steam roller, the tremendous gathering of the great industrial and military machine set in motion by an aroused and powerful people—it all
has been invaluable, whether viewed from the standpoint of
weakening enemy morale or bolstering the morale of the Allies
But we must watch out for the kick-back. I know that there

is the belief in some quarters in France that the American industrial machine (and military machine) are a power that may some day wish to dictate terms. . . .

"I suppose peace isn't very far off. But after the military battle will follow the diplomatic battle, with the old selfish groups in every Allied capital, working for the antebellum status quo, and with so-called 'practical' politicians and statesmen sneering at sun-kissed diplomacy, at the ability of Poland and other small countries to handle their own affairs, at a new régime of free trade, free seas, and free accesses to the seas And it impresses me that then, if ever, will be the golden hour of the Division of Foreign Press Cable, to hammer home American ideals and America's will to see them through. It will be a fight in the bourgeois capitals of Europe and we should prepare for it."

The London office of the CPI was never stabilized, either as to personnel or as to program. H. N. Rickey, who later became director of the whole CPI Foreign Section, was the first resident commissioner, and he began work in February 1918, receiving the Wireless-Cable news which was picked out of the air on its Tuckerton-Lyons journey and forwarded to Rickey—if everything worked properly. If the news came through, it was then released to the British press and an attempt made, not always successfully, to forward it to our representatives in Scandinavia and the Netherlands.

When Rickey resigned "for personal and official reasons" in April, Charles Edward Russell, the former Socialist who had been helping the CPI in a number of ways, was chosen as his successor. However, Russell was not yet in London after his Russian tour with the Root Mission, and Henry Suydam, youthful veteran of war correspondence, was given temporary charge of the London office before proceeding to his own assignment at The Hague.

But after Russell arrived and had been a short time at work he too asked to be removed from a "distasteful" situation, and Creel told him to turn the office over to his son, John Russell

British Detachments with the 27th and 30th American Divisions Sending Propaganda Balloons to the Germans

Public and Private Enterprise Aid the Cause

Above: Charlie Chaplin's "Shoulder Arms." Below: Introduction of the
CPI's Feature "America's Answer," Filmed by the Signal Corps
and the Photographic Section of the Navy

He was succeeded almost immediately, however, by Perry Arnold, who in turn gave way to Paul Perry Edgar Sisson, associate director of the CPI, also passed through the London office, and still another man entered the picture when John L. Balderston, expatriated American playwright (*Dracula, Berkeley Square*), made himself responsible for getting American news to the British press. Balderston was also successful in placing CPI feature material, notably articles by Booth Tarkington, several of which appeared in *The Field*

There were other comings and goings among members of the staff, and although an attempt was made to turn London into a European distributing center for all Allied and neutral countries, the task was a forbidding one because of communications difficulties

And the task of presenting the American story to the British public itself was little less difficult, perhaps chiefly because of the incompatibility of certain English and American war aims It was obvious, for instance, that American interest in the freedom of the seas was not likely to arouse enthusiasm in the homeland of the British Navy, and even discussion of our modest part in naval operations might be received unkindly. Henry Suydam wrote Walter Rogers on April 19 that Admiral Sims and H N. Rickey had previously agreed to use few naval stories because the "British have had almost nothing concerning their own naval operations, and publicity concerning ours might arouse jealousy if overemphasized." The British also felt an obligation to censor our movies, according to word from Creel to Rickey, the information probably coming from MIB

Further, in a letter of March 5, Creel wrote Captain E G Lowry, military attaché at London, that certain publications, consigned to neutral countries and passed by our Censorship Board, were being thrown out of the mails by the British censorship Two days later Creel was writing to Frank Polk, counsellor of the State Department, that according to our minister at The Hague, John Work Garrett, President Wilson's messages and speeches, relayed through London, arrived so late or in such mutilated condition that the newspapers could not use them And even as late as July 19, Perry Arnold, then in charge of the London office, reported to Walter Rogers· "Until the last few days COMPUB never saw our wireless, it being intercepted by British Admiralty and turned over by them to British ministry of information, which used articles it saw fit."

Charles Edward Russell thought he knew a reason for British lack of cooperation He had written Creel on June 19 "I don't see much use in trying to cut a wide swath here anyway, even if it could be done We are not getting much into the British papers and never will get much. . . . The British are not interested in bringing about a closer working understanding with America for the winning of the war only. . . . What they want and are all obsessed about is a permanent Anglo-American alliance . We have had two dinners of Newspaper editors and proprietors for the purpose of discussing the best ways to make Great Britain acquainted with America's efforts in the war, and both have drifted off into discussions of the best way to form an enduring Anglo-American league to control the world."

And the hopelessness of trying to gain acceptance of the whole American program in England was forcefully presented by John Balderston, who sent a message to Sisson on August 10 presenting a scheme for counteracting the illiberalism of American expatriates moving in High Tory circles In this cable he said that until July all that had been required was to cheer up British spirits, but that now, with the Allies succeeding on the battlefield, the CPI propagandists should concern themselves "*with nothing to which all factions in this country do not offer lip service. . . .* There exists a large imperialist class here that is secretly hostile to all international ideals and regards our policies with the deepest hatred; e.g. Curzon, Milner, Northcliffe, the *Morning Post,* indeed the whole high Tory party. . . . While no propaganda could do any good among this class, there exists a very large public in this country that is traditionally Tory in politics, but has been caught by

[298]

the new liberalism of America, and hesitates, puzzled, between the two schools of thought. We can help to make converts in this class of wobblers and thus help to draw the fangs of the reactionaries, who boast (verbally) everywhere (I have heard scores of them) that after using America to win their war they will crush all our aims and ideals at the Peace Conference."

Chapter 14

THE CPI AND RUSSIAN CHAOS

O N June 19, 1918, Secretary of War Newton D Baker
wrote to President Wilson· "If I had my own way
about Russia and had the power to have my own way,
I would like to take everybody out of Russia except the Russians, including diplomatic agents, military representatives,
political agents, propagandists, and casual visitors, and let
the Russians settle down and settle their own affairs." Mr
Baker acknowledged that his wish was impractical, but he
suggests here the incredible extent to which Russia was over-
run with the political agents and armed forces of other countries.

Aside from the Russians themselves, split into monarchists
and several special brands of revolutionists, there was a whole
array of other military forces at one time or another on Russian soil—British, French, American, Japanese, German, Austrian, Czechoslovak, Roumanian, Polish.

And the complexity of foreign interests was similarly bewildering Imperial Russia had been a member of the Triple
Entente with England and France, and had been the first of
the three to declare war on Germany. The Russian army failed
to sweep down into Germany in the advertised "steam-roller"
fashion, but as long as Russia was in the war Germany had to
keep divisions on the Eastern Front, making the task of England, France, and Italy just that much easier in the West. The
"Kerensky Revolution" in the spring of 1917 dethroned the
Tsar, but both under Prince Lvov and later under Kerensky
himself the government tried to keep on fighting for the Allies

The Germans, however, had permitted Lenin to return to
Russia, correctly believing that a Bolshevik revolution would

put Russia out of the "imperialist war " That is what happened. On the night of November 7-8, 1917, the Congress of Soviets vested power in a Council of People's Commissars, with Lenin as premier and Trotsky as foreign commissar. Soon afterwards Trotsky invited all belligerents to conclude an armistice, and, after protracted and involved negotiations, the Bolsheviks themselves signed with Germany the treaty of Brest-Litovsk.

That treaty and the events leading up to it, gave a certain coherence to the intervention plans of all countries, since it was of obvious interest to the Allies to dislodge the Bolsheviks from power and put a Russian army in the field again. But each foreign country had its own special purposes to serve. Dismemberment of Russia was the clear object in certain cases. Even among technical allies such as the Americans and Japanese suspicion if not actual antagonism was the rule The Germans, while interested in extending their own influence to the East, were by no means friendly to Bolshevism as such, and some of the Allies, though opposing Bolshevism in Russia and their own countries, would have been willing to see it destroy the industrial machine of the Central Powers Meanwhile social revolution, with all of its violence and bitter hatred, seethed throughout the onetime Russian Empire

It was in this chaotic situation that the CPI attempted to carry out its most ambitious and perhaps its most interesting foreign assignment.

At first America had been delighted with the overthrow of Tsarism The idea of another great democracy joining in the struggle against autocracy was attractive during pre-Bolshevik days in the spring and summer of 1917, and the CPI was one of many American agencies anxious to show its friendship for the new order in Russia, and to lend moral support On June 18, 1917, George Creel wrote to the director of the Petrograd Press Bureau

"This letter will introduce to you Mr. Arthur Bullard and Mr Ernest Poole who have been my associates here in Washington in organizing the work of the Committee on Public

Information and are now leaving this country to follow their profession as journalists in Russia. They will be writing of Russian affairs in some of the most important of our newspapers and reviews. I have asked them to call on you to present my cordial greetings. If there is any way in which the Press Bureaux of our two countries can cooperate, I hope that you will explain your wishes to them and they will report to me. It is our belief that the free exchange of news for the informing of the public, made possible by the printing press and the newspapers, is the foundation stone of Democracy And I am sure that I speak for all American newspaper men in expressing the most hearty good wishes to the Press of Russia "

Shortly before this, President Wilson had sent a special commission headed by Elihu Root, and this group arrived in Petrograd June 13 and left Vladivostok July 21 Trouble for the future might have been foreseen in an article from the September 1917 issue of the Petrograd *Commune*, which Naval Intelligence sent to Creel The paper referred to the "commission formed of prominent and well known millionaires, bankers and capitalists, as Elihu Root, [Cyrus H.] McCormick, [Charles R.] Crane, [John R.] Mott, [Samuel R] Bertran and other parasites . . . to acclaim the rising of the Russian nation. .   To mask the capitalistic lot of the commission, serving as a lightning rod, were the leader of the American Labor Federation, Jas. Duncan, and the 'prominent socialist,' Charles E. Russell "

Charles Edward Russell himself wrote to Creel on October 29, explaining at length his estimate of the whole situation. "Russia would never have daddled around about the war if there had been efficient publicity work last summer There would have been efficient publicity work last summer if the Commission had insisted upon it. . . We knew perfectly well what was needed We had been on the ground and we knew. . . . Two or three things . . . are absolutely essential to us in Russia.

"First, the cable news service distributed through the Russian news agency will do very little good. Few Russian papers take it. What is needed is a complete news bureau of our own with a service that all the papers will take and publish We need a force of men in Russia to get up and distribute the kind of matter that will stir Russia to fight . . . We need a cut and editorial service like the N E A We need handbills and dodgers. We need an immense film service at work now in every part of Russia. . . . If the United States had begun in July when we wanted it to begin and had spent $10,000,000 on publicity in Russia it would have been the best investment it ever made. . . . The commission, merely by being too regardful of etiquette and position, made a hash of this part of its work. . Don't you make any such blunder . . . Get your men out, get something started. . . . I tell you frankly that if Russia is not aroused this winter it will not be aroused at all and the game is up so far as it is concerned."

Even before receipt of that letter, however, Creel had written on October 24, 1917, to Colonel William B. Thompson, head of the American Red Cross Mission to Russia, that President Wilson had turned over to the CPI the formal report of the Root Mission, and had asked Creel to take charge of publicity work in Russia The letter was carried by Edgar Sisson, associate chairman of the CPI, who, after personal conference with Mr. Wilson, was dispatched to Petrograd "Mr. Sisson," wrote Creel, "with full authority, is acting on the scene for us."

But while Sisson was en route, the Bolshevik Revolution took place, and on November 9 Creel was telegraphing to Bullard in Petrograd· "Handle Russian situation firmly stop United States hoping Petrograd local disturbance unaffecting great freedom-loving Russian people stop Trusting nation to understand that the Bolsheviki success menaces revolution and invites return autocracy stop Russian and Italian situation only nerves America to greater determination, creating more solemn realization of greatness of task and arousing sterner determination stop America at war for certain great fundamental principles and neither reverse nor desertion will cause surrender stop Only possible peace based on justice with guarantees of permanence stop Give this as coming from high official sources."

Bullard, however, was having his own difficulties, and, a week after Creel's message, was informing the CPI from Moscow: "For a week we have been marooned in the consulate, most of the time without any telephonic communication The only papers now issued are the revolutionary ones They do not have any general news."

More discouragement came to Creel from Ernest Poole, then back in New York, who wrote on November 20· "If the present extreme government stays in power, there will be little use in sending over many war items. Of course, we hope for a more moderate government. But in either case, as Bullard and I both discovered, the main thing they want to know about us is what kind of a nation we have tried to build . . . especially in the last few years." One of the few rays of hope came from Albert J. Nock, who told Creel on November 26 that there was good stuff in the Slavs if America could understand them, "and it is conceivable that they may succeed, after a fashion, in doing something important"

Bullard was instructed to get the widest possible distribution for the daily news dispatch (which was now coming by wireless from Lyons), but he himself was worried lest the United States might be forced into recognizing the Bolshevik régime. He warned, however, that: "Our refusal to recognize . . . should be based on sound democratic grounds, not on distaste for their fantastic social experiments"

Meanwhile, Sisson had reached Petrograd on November 25, and on December 2 Creel advised him "Drive ahead full speed regardless expense stop Coordinate all American agencies in Petrograd and Moscow and start aggressive campaign stop Use press billboards placards and every possible medium to answer lies against America stop Make plain our high motives and absolute devotion to democratic ideals. . . . Engage speakers and halls. . . . Cable if send motion pictures"

Without waiting for a reply on that last point, Creel dispatched a reported 500,000 feet of film via Sweden, only to learn a few days later that the frontier was closed Sisson himself reported from Petrograd on December 22 that the news was not coming through either by wireless or cable, but that a million copies of President Wilson's speech to Congress had been printed and that CPI offices in both Petrograd and Moscow were in operation under the respective directorship of Graham Taylor, Jr , who had a background of work in the German prison camps of Russia, and Read Lewis, special assistant to the American Ambassador and former relief administrator in Russia

On December 30 Bullard announced from Moscow that 300,000 posters and handbills had been lost in transit, but that the first number of the CPI's *Russian News-Letter* would be ready shortly, and that he wanted to open new CPI offices "in Rostov on the Don in the South . . in Kiev in the Ukraine, and later one or two in Siberia "

But Russia was no easy place for operations of this sort, as Bullard feelingly told Creel· "Besides decreeing that all the world shall ride in box cars, the Bolsheviki have closed all the banks There is a great fight on between the financiers and the de facto government By refusing to operate under the new regulations the bankers hope to bring on a revolt against the Bolsheviki. If the banks are closed no one can cash checks and no one can draw money to meet his payroll This, the bankers hoped, would make the Proletariat mad at the Bolsheviki, but on the contrary it seems to make them all the madder against the Bourgeoisie. I have about 7,000 roubles in the safe here, which I drew out yesterday, just before the axe fell. . . . It is unfortunate that we did not get started sooner, so that our organization might have been on its feet."

Still unsuccessful in the effort to get CPI films into Russia, Creel tried a new device. On December 31 he wrote Hugh Gibson of the State Department that Herman Bernstein, *New York Herald* correspondent, was going to Russia ostensibly merely as a reporter but actually "to serve the Committee in our publicity division in Petrograd." The films which Bernstein carried were "not propaganda in any sense of the word, but are merely a frank presentation of American life in its various aspects "

A possibly boastful summary of CPI accomplishments in Russia through December and January was given in a letter which Creel wrote on February 5, 1918, to R G Hutchins, Jr., of the National Bank of Commerce, New York. "We are working through three mediums The printed word—one thousand words a day of cable service and feature service, consisting of short articles from a hundred to a thousand words, illustrated by photographs and sent by mail——the motion picture, showing the social, industrial, and war progress of the United States, and outdoor advertising. Sisson has practically every theater in Petrograd and Moscow for the exhibition of our motion pictures He has over fifty thousand billboards in the cities, he circularizes the German prison camps to the extent of millions, and on the Russian Front and on the Roumanian Front, we are using aeroplanes for a systematic bombardment of the enemy lines, and enemy country, with special literature specifically designed to encourage revolt against the military clique "

Unfortunately for the CPI, the signs of this revolt were not pronounced in Petrograd, and the German army was approaching the city, following Russian hesitancy about signing the treaty of Brest-Litovsk Sisson cabled on February 23 "in contingency of German entry plans made to transfer a part of equipment to Vologda on Embassy train, sending [Graham] Taylor. In same contingency Moscow office will go with [Maddin] Summers to Samara. Bullard has developed practical idea of greeting Germans if they ever arrive Petrograd with billposted copies President's messages of February 8 and February 11 in German. Copies ready. Bill posters keen for job. Germany's new and increased peace demands received today."

On February 28 came the report that the American Embassy, consulate, military mission, and Red Cross mission had left for Vologda two days before, and on March 8 Bullard cabled from Petrograd· "Sisson left last night via Finland stop We stay as long as possible then move base to Moscow."

Sisson did not leave the country without difficulty, however, and a possible reason for this was suggested in his message to Creel from Norway on April 8. "I have in my possession documents proving completely and conclusively that the German government not only created the government of Bolshevik commissars, but that during the whole farcical negotiations for peace this government was operated by the German General Staff." More attention will be given to these documents later in the chapter.

Herman Bernstein arrived in Petrograd on March 11, but minus the movies, and to remedy the situation the CPI sent Guy Croswell Smith to Helsingfors to see if the films could be shipped by boat Smith had originally gone to Russia taking D W. Griffith movies on behalf of the Department of State, but he was now made CPI cinema director for Russia.

Shortly after reporting the movie difficulties, Bullard asked for a 50,000-word popular history of the United States, translated into Russian, and on April 13 he cabled to Sisson, by that time in London on his way home, begging his help in persuading Washington to give more support to the Russian work:

"It is not impossible that diplomatic relations will be broken off with former Allies but I do not consider this likely . . Smith informs me by cable that he is coming with films, but I have notified him that the route by Archangel is difficult and unsuited to his purpose . . . [William Adams] Brown and [Malcolm] Davis are in Western Siberia and Taylor is in Petrograd. The remainder are at Moscow in good health . The censorship of the press becomes increasingly strict and in addition there is further suppression of provincial papers. We must therefore depend mainly on our own pamphlets and bulletins . . Please inform me immediately when you expect to reach Washington. I look to you to push my request for material and recruits "

But Sisson feared that the Bolsheviks would hold Bullard as a hostage, and the following cable went from Will Irwin in

Washington to Bullard by a special ambassador's code on April 24:

"On information and advice from Sisson who understands aspect of situation of which you are probably ignorant and with endorsement of Creel you and your American assistants ordered immediately and with all possible secrecy to leave for the present all territory controlled by Bolsheviki stop Leave your Russian assistants in control of office for the present and report final whereabouts pending orders stop Should by all means be out of Bolsheviki territory by about May 5."

Bullard obeyed the order, withdrawing to Archangel, but under protest, as this May 6 cable suggests "I cannot imagine the facts to justify this move stop Unless some of us at least are allowed to return to Moscow at once the continuation of the work we have developed will be impossible stop Luckily the holidays give some cover to our absence for a few days but it will soon be noticed and we will have seemed to run away from charges which have not been made."

When five more days had passed, Bullard tried once again "We have received no news which gives slightest reason for believing any danger in returning to Moscow stop [Read] Lewis, [George] Bakeman and [Otto] Glaman at least are in no way involved in Sisson's anti [Bolsheviki] activities stop Lewis, Bakeman and [Graham] Taylor have diplomatic commissions from Lansing."

And still again, on May 13. "Our withdrawal seems expression of guilty conscience. This is the only organization engaged in placing the liberal democratic viewpoint of the Allies before Russia and our withdrawal means that it is scrapped Its work must be the foundation of any successful Allied policy in Russia . . It will be impossible to act intelligently without further orders Please reply at once, care of the American Consul at Archangel, stating the reasons for the order of withdrawal and the nature of danger, so that we can return to work or understand why it is necessary to wreck it."

After Bullard's withdrawal, Russian assistants had carried on the CPI work, but: "We cannot leave the work to any Russian Mr [Consul Maddin] Summers' death has made it impossible to turn it over to the Consulate General without help " And the Consulate General told Bullard, "Hope to see you or in any case [Read] Lewis back here soon."

Eventually, permission came, and Read Lewis returned to Moscow on June 22, finding DeWitt Clinton Poole, the young consular officer in charge, anxious to continue publicity in place of the CPI if the Committee itself did not wish to stay. Lewis wished to remain, but on September 2 the Bolsheviks closed down the CPI office, and Lewis cabled from Stockholm on August 26 that he had left Moscow in company with practically all Americans then remaining in Bolshevik Russia, the exception being Poole who, for the sake of Allied solidarity, stayed in Moscow until the British and French representatives were ordered to leave.

Lewis wanted to go back to Moscow once more, or at least to establish a base at Ekaterinburg in back of the Czechoslovak (anti-Bolshevik) lines, but he was ordered to Archangel where, at last, CPI films were available and *Pershing's Crusaders* and *America's Answer* were shown to audiences on the shores of the Arctic Ocean

Guy Croswell Smith at Stockholm was also impatient, and was told by Sisson from Washington on August 29. "Keep on the job in spite of any homesickness you may have I need you where you are. I am planning for you too, and at your need will send you an assistant to break in. This is preparation for the time when you may be able to join forces with the Russian group, which now is a large party of sixteen or eighteen persons, still under Bullard, prepared to work its way through Siberia as fast as it can open up stations. I hope some members of it will be operating offices in Irkutsk and Chita this winter."

This message introduces the Siberian phase of the far-flung CPI venture in Russia. As early as March 4, 1918, Major C. H Mason of Military Intelligence had informed Creel: "The urgent necessity for a systematic effort to combat prejudices in the minds of Siberians against Americans is pressed upon the administration by American officials in the Far East . . . The people there refer to the coldness of Americans, their aloofness and their failure to understand Russians . . . Definite suggestions are made that the needs of the United States there are full discussion in the newspapers, lectures on American affairs and personal contact with the people. The names of organizers are suggested to engage the corps of Russian teachers who are close to the people and pay them to deliver lectures on the war. The expenditures are described as insignificant and the results predicted as of great importance."

Operations in Siberia had both military and political implications. A force of 50,000 or more Czechoslovaks, largely Austrian soldiers who had deserted or been imprisoned in Russia, had formed a Czech Legion, just as Yugoslav Legions had been assembled from other Austrian prisoners in Italy, as noted in Chapter XIII. After the revolution, the Czechs in Russia started with a supposed Bolshevik safe-conduct for the Pacific Ocean. Squabbles with local soviets over food supplies and right-of-way for trains soon developed into something more serious, and by June the Czechs were fighting the Bolsheviks openly, with their force strung out in detachments along several thousand miles of railway from Kazan to Vladivostok By the end of July large sections of Siberia were under the control of the Czechs or of various anti-Bolshevik governments, and foreign intervention in support of the Czechs, and of a great variety of White Armies, was becoming an important reality. When Chita was captured on September 6, 1918, organized Bolshevik government east of the Urals seemed to have disappeared.

American intervention in Siberia (which was distinct from our participation in the Allied landing at Archangel and Murmansk), was not dictated solely by America's genuine sympathy for Czechoslovak nationalism and our wish to see the Czechs fight their way back home, but also by eagerness to keep an eye on some of our Allies, especially the Japanese.

[310]

As the situation in the heart of western (Bolshevik) Russia had become more and more untenable for the anti-Bolshevik CPI in the winter of 1918, Arthur Bullard had prepared to shift his base to the east, reporting to Creel on March 11 that he was ready to send Malcolm W Davis and William Adams Brown to Siberia

Then, on March 22, Colonel R H. Van Deman of Military Intelligence advised the CPI. "Siberia is now our last hope on the Eastern Front, and it is there that we can work with reasonable security I suggest that you send at once a publicity agent to Siberia to establish a newspaper etc." On that very day Will Irwin cabled Bullard in Petrograd "Go ahead establishing yourself in Harbin if Moscow becomes untenable stop If you need assistance in men wire designating how many and what sort and we will send them as we have many volunteers here "

To facilitate the work in the Orient, the American consul at Harbin was authorized to spend $5,000, to be charged against the CPI, and on July 9 Malcolm Davis reported "Propaganda for America and the Allies can certainly be carried on in Harbin. Most of the people are with us anyway, and there is no real opposition. Our news is at once taken up by all of the daily papers, and the motion pictures go well It all may conceivably have some influence toward creating friendly relations for Americans in Siberia and Russia after the war. It is, however, too far from the real field to have any effect upon the issue of the war itself, unless there is a great change in the circumstances here "

Bullard had crossed the Atlantic after leaving North Russia, and in August was at Victoria, British Columbia, preparing to go to Vladivostok. As he left Canada, he urged that a second CPI party follow him, bringing movie films, especially *Intolerance*, *Hearts of the World*, *The Birth of a Nation*, and anything starring Theda Bara, Geraldine Farrar, or Mary Pickford Pending Bullard's arrival in the Orient, Davis and Brown were using such films as they had, and were distributing CPI news, received via the wireless on the U.S S *Brooklyn*.

When Bullard reached Tokyo he was apparently impressed anew with the vagueness of Allied objectives in Siberia, for he wrote Sisson on September 11. "We are rather in the position of advertising something and not knowing what it is. Buy it! Buy it! What is it? We don't know, but we are sure it will do you good." Bullard also realized that American interest in Japan's activities in Asia was reciprocated He and Ambassador Roland S Morris visited the Japanese Foreign Office, with the result that a Japanese was assigned to work with the CPI. As Bullard said, it would "save our ally a large expense in espionage. And as my work will be watched carefully, I would much rather have the guy inside looking out than outside looking in."

Units of the CPI were started westward (toward Bolshevik territory) from Vladivostok, and Professor William Fletcher Russell began active CPI educational work in Eastern Siberia He asked for more and more films, dealing with agriculture, industry, mining, forestry, and fisheries

By the end of 1918, plans had been completed for establishing CPI offices at Chita, Irkutsk, and Omsk, with Franklin Clarkin of the *Boston Transcript*, George Bakeman, and Robert Winters as the respective directors

On November 5, Bullard received word from Sisson· "If Germany accepts armistice terms, Committee work of news distribution in foreign countries will still continue . through-out peace conference. . . . Keep your news-distributing organization at high pitch of efficiency " During December actual improvement in the news service was reported, with connections established with Rusta, the Siberian government agency, and news reaching Omsk both by wireless from Lyons and by COMPUB wire from Vladivostok The result was "as good as could be expected in these unsettled conditions, and the reports from our men along the line show steady improvement." To Chita and more remote points the service was carried in cooperation with the Czechs.

While the Siberian unit of the CPI was thus extending its lines, Read Lewis at Archangel was aided by the arrival of

Harry Inman, who arranged with the educational department of the Russian Cooperative Union, a powerful organization, for wider showing of the CPI films

Arthur Bullard at Vladivostok, however, was in poor health, and by the end of December turned the office over to Phil Norton Norton's summary of the Siberian work of his predecessor was that Bullard, with a skeleton organization, had covered all possible lines of communication as far as Ekaterinburg and Cheliabinsk without "even the good will of the people, opinions to the contrary in the United States notwithstanding."

Norton's effort to expand Bullard's work was terminated abruptly on February 4, 1919 when he received this cable from H. N. Rickey, in charge of the CPI Foreign Section "Begin demobilizing all activities under your jurisdiction at once stop Make adequate arrangements with consuls for distribution all pamphlets etcetera which are left over or which arrive after you leave stop This includes Russian translation Sisson's Bolshevik pamphlets which are being shipped this week addressed to American Consul Vladivostok stop Also arrange with consuls for continued distribution presidential communications and such other cable and wireless news as may be sent . . Cable at once film situation . . Bring with you to Washington complete files and final accounts "

The American vice-consul at Ekaterinburg wrote to William Adams Brown, CPI head in that place "It has been a great surprise and in some ways a discouragement to learn that the work of the Committee on Public Information is suddenly stopped in our territory. When this work first started I was not very optimistic as to its influence but since I have learned further of the ideas involved and the manner in which it was intended to carry them out I have come to thoroughly believe in it. . . . I personally was in hope that this work would be continued through the troubled times and gradually connected up with and fused into the commercial end with whatever organization might be established, and have felt sure that the friends you have made and the larger number you

[313]

certainly would have made would have become one of the greatest buying fields for American products that has ever been known. It certainly seems a pity to drop this valuable work just at the most critical moment."

Bullard, also, was opposed to cessation of the work, but the best the CPI headquarters could offer was the State Department's promise that consular officials would continue distributing CPI material as long as the supply lasted The Russian adventure of the CPI seemed to be at an end

But actually, one activity of the Russian section was destined to influence the thinking of Americans and Russians for many years to come. The so-called "Sisson Documents" which the associate chairman of the CPI brought back with him from Petrograd in the spring of 1918, and which the CPI published in the fall of that year, are capable of arousing lively debate even today.

The controversy which has raged about this fascinating material has enlisted the emotions and the polemical energy of many people. Only a master of several languages, of Russian and German history, and of the science of manuscript study should attempt to pass judgment on the charge of forgery which started the commotion in the first place But as part of the history of the CPI the controversy itself must be at least reported

Edgar Sisson obtained the documents in Petrograd under dramatic circumstances which he describes in his book *100 Red Days*, published in 1931. Sisson accepted the documents in good faith as proving that "the present Bolshevik government is not a Russian government at all but a German government acting solely in the interests of Germany and betraying the Russian people, as it betrays Russia's allies, for the benefit of the Imperial German Government alone."

Sisson's report was in President Wilson's hands on May 9, 1918. Presumably with Wilson's approval, the "Sisson Documents" were released to the papers on September 15. Nearly everyone took them at face value, as indicated by the New York *Times* headline, but the New York *Evening Post* headline of a few days later shows that opinion was not perfectly unanimous.

The Evening Post	The New York Times
## CALLS SISSON PAPERS "BRAZEN FORGERIES"	# DOCUMENTS PROVE LENINE AND TROTZKY HIRED BY GERMANS
### S. Nuorteva Says They Were Proved False	
Creel Committee's Russian Revelations, He Asserts Were Revived After Inquiry and Rejection.	Communications Between Berlin and Bolshevist Government Given Out by Creel.

On September 16 the *Post* (with the interest of the editorial writer, Henry Alsberg, who has recently been director of the WPA Writers Project) charged that the Sisson material had been published in Paris months earlier and had "on the whole been discredited." The charges were renewed on the following day, and alluded to briefly once more on September 18. Then on September 21 came the most important of the *Post's* attacks, the statement from Santeri Nuorteva, who described himself as head of the Finnish Information Bureau of New York.

Nuorteva said that the documents had been first delivered to Raymond Robins (the Red Cross administrator with whom Sisson had had a well publicized feud in Russia), and that "Mr. Robins, assisted by William B. Thompson and Mayor T. Thatcher, all of whom were connected with the American Red Cross, investigated the truth of the statements made in the documents and decided they were forgeries." Even Sisson, Nuorteva said, was at first convinced of their falsity. No responsible critic, it should be added, has suggested that Mr.

[315]

Sisson had anything to do with the forgery—if forgery there was. He merely secured the documents and brought them to Washington.

In Sisson's book, *100 Red Days*, he declares that Nuorteva was brought to Washington on September 23, 1918, and "examined by me " He admitted, again according to Sisson, "that he had no personal knowledge upon which to base any such accusations," and that he had not even met two of the three Red Cross men whom he quoted Thompson and Thatcher denied knowing Nuorteva, and Raymond Robins, when found by a reporter in Arizona, said he was under State Department orders not to talk.

Although Nuorteva was regarded as a Bolshevist sympathizer, and therefore an incompetent witness, his charges had made sufficient headway to require answer. Mr Creel decided to place the matter in scholarly hands, and at his request the National Board for Historical Service undertook to investigate the documents. Their committee for this purpose was composed of Professor Samuel N. Harper, experienced University of Chicago student of Russian language and history, and J. Franklin Jameson, managing editor of the *American Historical Review* and later chief of the manuscript division of the Library of Congress.

This committee, after study of the papers and interrogation of Mr. Sisson, decided in favor of authenticity for the great majority of the sixty-eight documents, though pointing out significant peculiarities which cast at least some doubt on some of them.

With the report of the National Board for Historical Service, the "Sisson Documents" were published by the CPI as *The German-Bolshevik Conspiracy*, pamphlet No. 20 in the War Information Series, and over 137,000 copies were issued.

By the great majority of Americans they were accepted as proving not only German connivance in the Bolshevik Revolution (which connivance nearly everyone was prepared to grant on the grounds of reasonableness if not actual proof)

[316]

but also that Lenin and Trotsky were serving only a German cause. Sisson, in addition to other defense of his work in *100 Red Days*, adduces a 1919 affidavit by Eugenie P Semenov through whom he obtained the documents, explaining how they were secured with the help of spies in offices of the Bolshevik government.

But many attacks have been made on the documents, and perhaps the most usual current attitude of scholars is represented by the statement of Frederick L. Schuman in *American Policy Toward Russia Since 1917*, published in 1928. "They were pronounced forgeries by Soviet representatives soon after their appearance and have been regarded as such since, even in many anti-Bolshevist circles . . . While perhaps not entirely spurious, they show many evidences of crude fabrication and their genuineness is most questionable."

The vast majority of comments on *The German-Bolshevik Conspiracy*, however, are of interested authorship A new example has just come to light in the Library of Congress among some material turned over to the library many years ago when the Kerensky embassy in Washington closed Dr Nicholas R. Rodionoff, chief of the Slavic division of the library, who brought this document to the attention of the authors, believes it may be a unique copy, at least in America. It was printed in Russian at Vladivostok in 1921, bearing the title *Historical Forgery: American Forged Documents*, by B A Panov He was a former officer of the Imperial Russian Navy and implicated in Documents 9 and 29 of the Sisson collection. His motives, therefore, are not above suspicion, but his arguments, which he says he presented without effect to the American consul at Vladivostok, are at least superficially important.

Much more significant than the Panov brochure, however, was a letter of September 20, 1918 (more than a month before publication of *The German-Bolshevik Conspiracy* though after the newspaper instalments had appeared) from Philip Patchin of the State Department to George Creel:

[317]

PART I
The German-Bolshevik Conspiracy

A REPORT BY
EDGAR SISSON

Special Representative in Russia of the Committee on Public Information in the Winter of 1917-18

CHAPTER I.
THE BASIC CONSPIRACY

Three groups of documents are subjected to internal analysis in the material that follows. One group consists of originals, one group consists of photographs of documents believed still to be in the file rooms of the Russian Bolsheviki, and the third (Appendix I) of typewritten circulars that have not been traced to their originals except perhaps in the case of two of the number. The chief importance of the third group is that its appearance inspired the efforts that led to the uncovering of the other groups. And they fit into the fabric of the whole.

The first set of these appendix circulars came into my hands on February 2, in Petrograd. An additional set appeared the following day at an office where I frequently called. A third appeared in another quarter a day afterwards. One set was in Russian and two in English. On February 5 I held all three sets. A possible explanation for their appearance at this time and their intent is given in Appendix I.

By themselves they were plausible but not substantiated. Having first performed the obvious duty of analyzing them for surface values and transmitting them and the analyses to Washington, I turned, therefore, to the task of further investigations.

It is not yet possible to name those who helped, but in three weeks' time the judgment of facts became apparent.

The text of the documents discloses both the methods and the effects of the German conspiracy not alone against Russia but the world. With each document is the indication of whether it is an original or photograph. With each document is an interpretative note.

DOCUMENT NO. 1

People's Commissary for Foreign Affairs.
(*Very Secret*)
Petrograd, November 16, 1917
TO THE CHAIRMAN OF THE COUNCIL OF PEOPLE'S COMMISSARS:

In accordance with the resolution passed by the conference of People's Commissars, Comrades Lenin, Trotsky, Podvoisky, Dybenko, and Volodarsky, the following has been executed by us:

1. In the archives of the Ministry of Justice from the dossier re "treason" of Comrades Lenin, Zinovieff, Koslovsky, Kollontai and others, has been removed the order of the German Imperial Bank, No. 7433, of the second of March, 1917, for allowing money to Comrades Lenin, Zinovieff, Kameneff, Trotsky, Sumenson, Koslovsky and others for the propaganda of peace in Russia.

2. There have been audited all the books of the Nia Bank at Stockholm containing the accounts of Comrades Lenin, Trotsky, Zinovieff, and others, which were opened by the order of the German Imperial Bank No. 2754. These books have been delivered to Comrade Müller, who was sent from Berlin

---

Authorized by the Commissar for Foreign Affairs.
E. POLIVANOFF.
F. ZALKIND.

NOTE.—*The Russian Council of People's Commissars was dominated by the president, Vladimir Ulianov (Lenin); the then foreign minister, Leon Trotsky, now war minister; and the ambassador to Germany, A. Joffe. The marginal indorsement in writing is: "To the secret department, B. U." This is the fashion in which Lenin is accustomed to initial himself. The English equivalent would be V. U., for Vladimir Ulianov. So, even if there existed no further record of German Imperial Bank order No. 7433, here would be the proof of its contents, and here is the link connecting Lenin directly with his action and his guilt. The content matter of the circular exists, however, and herewith follows:*

Order of the 2d of March, 1917, of the Imperial Bank for the representatives of all German banks in Sweden:

Notice is hereby given that requisition for money for the purpose of peace propaganda in Russia will be received through Finland. These requisitions will emanate from the following: Lenin, Zinovieff, Kameneff, Trotsky, Sumenson, Koslovsky, Kollontai, Sivers, and Merkalin, accounts for whom have been opened in accordance with our order No. 2754 in the agencies of private German businesses in Sweden, Norway, and Switzerland. All these requests should

---

bear one of the two following signatures: Dirshau or Milkenberg. With either of these signatures the requests of the abovementioned persons should be complied with without delay.—7433, IMPERIAL BANK.

I have not a copy of this circular nor a photograph of it, but Document No. 2, next in order, proves its authenticity at once curiously and absolutely. Particular interest attaches to this circular because of Bolshevik public denial of its existence. It was one of several German circulars published in Paris in the "Petit Parisien" last winter. The Petrograd Bolshevik papers proclaimed it a falsehood. Zalkind, whose signature appears not only here but on the protocol (Document No. 3), was an assistant foreign minister. He was sent in February on a mission outside of Russia. He was in Christiania in April when I was there. Have photograph of the letter.

DOCUMENT NO. 2

G[reat] G[eneral] S[taff], Intelligence [Nachrichten] Bureau, Section A. No. 292.

(*Secret*)

February 12, 1918.
TO THE CHAIRMAN OF THE COUNCIL OF PEOPLE'S COMMISSARS:

The Intelligence Bureau has the honor to inform you that there

Facsimile of Document Number 2

First Page of the "Sisson Documents" Pamphlet

"The Secretary directs me to send you the following paraphrase of a telegram from Ambassador Page, contained in the Embassy's No 2044, September 19, 8 p m

"The Ambassador states that he had learned that the British War Office had received from a War Office agent named Maclaren the same photographic copies that were taken to America by Sisson He adds that the War Office, the Foreign Office, the Postal Censor and the Admiralty examined the material carefully and in a general way reached the decision that the documents which appeared to be genuine were old and not of any particular value, and those which had propaganda value were of a doubtful character He says that, for instance, Dansey (Major Dansey, British Military Intelligence Service), who had just been to see him, and who is the only one with any knowledge of the matter whom he had been able to see since he received the Department's telegram, said that very careful tests were made by the Postal Censor, who found that the same typewriting machine, with the same faults, must have been used to type original documents coming from different offices or sections of the same city Dansey also said that one Bauer, who is supposed to have signed several documents, never wrote his name the same way The inference from this is that all or most of his alleged output are forgeries Dansey added further that Maclaren was 'hipped' on the matter of buying documents, and anything offered him he would take.

"Dansey further stated that he had a long talk with Sisson in London last spring and expressed to Sisson a fear that many of the documents were forgeries and urged Sisson to go slow with them. The Ambassador adds that if this is true he thinks that Sisson would have been wise to have let the American government know before the documents were published that the genuineness of some of the papers was doubted by the British authorities, who might, therefore, naturally object to publication in England."

Creel replied to Patchin the same day that he had reached Sisson by long-distance telephone and had secured a denial

[319]

"specifically and absolutely" that he had held any such conversation with Major Dansey, whom he claimed to have seen only briefly. And Creel added that the British opinion of the documents "was not based entirely upon the question of genuineness but on their ideas as to what constitutes effective propaganda." Buttressed by the National Board for Historical Service, the CPI went ahead with publication

Whether true or false—a question that may never be solved to the entire satisfaction of all the scholars who have worked on the problem—*The German-Bolshevik Conspiracy* was widely distributed in this country and in Russia, not only giving a definite "set" to American ideas regarding the Bolsheviks but also making sufficient impression in Russia itself so that certain people have returned to the "Sisson Documents" in seeking an answer to the enigma of the famous Moscow Trials of a few years ago. Even more recently observers have gone back to the conclusions of these documents in considering the Reich-Soviet Treaty of 1939.

It is of ironical interest that the one CPI pamphlet which met with spirited and responsible criticism has proved to have the greatest survival power of them all.

Chapter 15

BELOW THE RIO GRANDE

WARTIME propaganda of the United States in the other countries of the Western Hemisphere is of exceptional interest today because of the importance which "hemisphere solidarity" has assumed in the power politics of the whole world The contemporary Division of Cultural Relations of the Department of State is attempting, on a modest scale and in unostentatious fashion, to continue a campaign for Pan-American friendship which was started as a governmental activity twenty-two years ago by the CPI, and which had been carried on even before that by the Pan-American Union.

And Latin America commands special attention in the CPI story for an additional reason· in no other part of the world was the relation between Wilson idealism and commercial interest more intricate or more pronounced. American businessmen helped the CPI in all countries, but in Latin America they carried the chief burden of our national propaganda.

The two most important figures in the CPI invasion of Latin America were Lieutenant F. E. Ackerman and Edward L. Bernays.

Ackerman, who was attached to Ernest Poole's Foreign Press Bureau in New York, was dispatched on an organizing trip to South America in the winter of 1918, reaching Pernambuco on March 1 and continuing from there to Rio de Janeiro and then other leading cities of the continent. At each place he set up a CPI office In Brazil the work was left in the hands of Ambassador E V. Morgan, with the feature service supervised by Lieutenant William Y. Boyd, assistant naval attaché. II. H. Sevier, former publisher of the Austin (Texas)

American and future ambassador to Chile, was appointed director of the Buenos Aires office and also covered Paraguay and Uruguay, receiving help from private citizens in Asuncion and from the American minister, F. C. Crocker, in Montevideo. A A. Preciado was in charge for Chile, and C N Griffis, a Lima publisher, for Peru, Ecuador, and Bolivia An organization trip similar to Ackerman's but not nearly so productive of results was undertaken in Central America by S. P. Verner, who made Panama his base.

The other key man in the Latin American work was Bernays, who today is widely believed to have succeeded the late Ivy Lee as No. 1 public-relations adviser of American businessmen. He came to the CPI in 1917 as a young Vienna-born New Yorker who had served as press agent for the Russian Ballet, Enrico Caruso, and other top-rank artists His most important work with the Committee was the conception and execution of plans for enlisting the help of American business firms Toward the end of the war he was also in charge of the whole Latin American news service, and following the Armistice he went to Paris with the CPI delegation Creel was not uniformly pleased with the post-Armistice work of Bernays, but everyone granted the importance of his contributions while we were still at war.

Ford, Studebaker, Remington Typewriter, Swift, National City Bank, International Harvester, and many other corporations were persuaded by Bernays to turn their Latin American branches into veritable outposts of the CPI. Pamphlets and other publications were distributed to customers, and posters and photographic displays filled windows Advertising was sometimes given or denied to Latin American papers in accordance with the editorial attitude toward the war

Study of the Committee's work in every country below the Rio Grande brings important results, but the most comprehensive picture of objectives in all Latin America is given by the record of experience in Mexico, where the program was the most elaborate and where the general nature of the whole problem was perfectly illustrated.

Mexico was not an easy place to convince people of America's nobility of purpose. It was not forgotten that the commander of the A.E F , supposedly fighting for the rights of small nations, had gone to France almost directly from his military expedition on Mexican soil. And American seizure of Vera Cruz at President Wilson's order, as well as the countless actual and alleged sins of American capitalists and the widespread suspicion of "dollar diplomacy," did not make the task easier Further, it was recalled, at least in educated circles, that Mexico had certain "lost provinces" within the borders of the United States—territory which had been taken during a special manifestation of American big-brotherliness seventy years before, and which was offered back to Mexico in the Germans' notorious Zimmermann Note.

German propagandists had been active in Mexico City at least since 1914, and, although the Allies had made some effort to oppose them, nothing serious was done until 1917, when the British established a central committee under H A C Cummins, chargé d'affaires, with orders to counteract and if possible destroy the German propaganda machine

When the United States entered the picture, it was proposed that our agents cooperate with the British, but, for a variety of reasons, the relationship was never close and sometimes not even cordial. One reason was the CPI belief, at the outset, that we were furnishing "information," not "propaganda," as Creel explained to John Barrett, director of the Pan-American Union, in a letter on May 24.

A general analysis of the Mexican problem was given to Creel on February 27, 1918, by Robert H. Murray, who had been about a month at work as director of the Mexico City office·

"We have to deal with a fanciful revolutionary government which conservatively may be assumed to be at least passively anti-American and pro-German. We make our appeal to a densely ignorant population. The proportionately small educated, reading and theoretically thoughtful part of this population is inclined by instinct, racial traits, and the example

[323]

and influence of the past generation to distrust us and our government and to dislike Americans in the mass. There always is in Mexico more or less latent anti-American sentiment This may be dormant, or become active as it serves the purposes of politicians and chauvinistic agitators, either in or out of the government, to fan and excite it. Thus considering the people and the government, we are compelled to realize at the outset that we are working in territory which normally is antagonistic."

Murray was staff correspondent of the New York World, and apparently continued in this private employment throughout the CPI work, though at one point the World objected to his double assignment. There was certainly no suggestion on the part of the CPI that he was not giving proper attention to the government job He was not only an experienced newspaperman but familiar with Mexico, where he had lived for seven years. Editor and Publisher said on March 29, 1919 "Mr. Murray is the only foreign correspondent who has witnessed and covered every stage of the Mexican revolution from its beginning in 1910 to the present. He has known personally and interviewed all of the ten presidents from Diaz's time. . . . He has also known and interviewed Villa and Zapata."

On the basis of his knowledge of Mexico, Murray advised Creel that the CPI should steer clear of the British and operate independently. But George Mooser, who had been sent with a consignment of films via Vera Cruz, and was apparently slated to be CPI commissioner in Mexico, disagreed. He favored working through George T. Summerlin, counsellor of the American Embassy, and Mr. Cummins, the British chargé After study of both Murray's and Mooser's reports, Creel decided in favor of Murray and named him head of all CPI work in Mexico

Murray was not hopeful of results at first, and his principal desire was merely to show United States colors in the field· "This service will obtain merit not so much through what it may be expected really to accomplish or that it is vitally necessary to influence public sentiment, but because it will indicate that we are at least as enterprising as the Germans. . . . I think news, movies ample for start, reserving other proper measures as experience and opportunity dictate."

To be as enterprising as the enemy was a strenuous assignment in Mexico City, for German agents found ready allies in native haters of the Gringo. It seemed reasonable to many Mexicans when they were told that the American army in France was merely sharpening a knife that ultimately would be turned against Mexico. Stories of American atrocities against Cubans, Filipinos, and Porto Ricans were widely distributed, and an attempt was made to persuade Mexico that all was not happy achievement north of the Rio Grande.

One of the most resourceful and urelenting of the opposition papers was *El Democrata*, which resisted all blandishments and threats of *force majeure* and cheerfully continued to belabor America and Americans. For instance, the March 23, 1918, issue reprinted a Hearst editorial from the *Los Angeles Examiner* of a fortnight earlier, under the head: "North America Confesses Its Evident Defeat in Europe and Considers Annexing Mexico to Recoup Itself" Another number carried a translation of William Hard's article "Is America Honest?" from the March 1918 issue of the *Metropolitan*, explaining that the original had been smuggled through the censorship, the article was printed again in an extra edition and still once more on the next day. And on March 22 *El Democrata* came out with "The Downfall of the United States Announced by an American . . . a notable editorial from the *Metropolitan Magazine*, edited by Theodore Roosevelt" *El Democrata's* introduction of this typical anti-Wilson editorial read: "Without any comment whatever on our part, we present to the Mexican public the apocalyptic picture which a great North American paints of the corruption of his people and the chaotic state of its administration. Read and ponder, you Yankee-lovers!"

[325]

Perhaps goaded by such activities of the opposition, or perhaps merely encouraged by his own success, Murray rapidly warmed to his task. His initial hesitancy gave way to determination and finally frank enthusiasm His office force grew to eight, then to more than twenty, with sixty-seven "correspondents" scattered throughout Mexico, including American consuls and vice-consuls, Allied and American businessmen, and friendly Mexicans Military Intelligence reports confirmed Murray's own belief that he was "getting the Germans on the run," though certain intelligence officers retained something of the British skepticism regarding Murray's principal assistant and office manager, Arthur DeLima, whose father was on the Allied blacklist of "Enemy Traders " Murray explained the whole situation to CPI headquarters, and the Committee loyally upheld him, H. N. Rickey, for instance, writing to Rear Admiral Roger Welles of Naval Intelligence on October 29, 1918, of the Committee's satisfaction with Murray and his work.

The first medium planned for the CPI campaign in Mexico was the moving picture. George Mooser had thought of giving exhibitions on certain public squares, but Major R. M Campbell, military attaché, advised that the appearance of propaganda would be avoided if the CPI films were quietly introduced into the programs of regular movie theaters The problem, here, however, was that most of the theaters in Mexico City were owned by an American who was on the Allied blacklist. Mooser advised that the name should be restored to respectability for the sake of the film program, and, although the files do not show whether this was done, in two weeks Allied films were running, while Mooser himself was anxiously awaiting arrival of his own pictures from Vera Cruz.

When, some months later the first full-length CPI film arrived, it proved to be *Pershing's Crusaders*. Murray had it tactfully renamed *America at War*, but enemy agents saw to it that the earlier title was made known in the country from which some other Pershing crusaders had withdrawn scarcely a year before. Some of the exhibitors raised a point of delicacy

about showing this particular picture, and Murray felt obliged
to remind them of the blacklist which would cut them off from
future film supplies.

In spite of difficulties such as this, however, the CPI movie
effort was considered a great success, reaching an estimated
4,500,000 people by the end of the war. When the Armistice
came, the CPI was in virtual command of the whole movie
situation, and plans had been made for the final domination of
the business through a central film exchange controlled by
the United States government As Robert Murray said in his
final report to Creel

"It goes almost without saying that among a population in
which illiterates unfortunately predominate, motion pictures
possess an enormous influence.   . German agents saw to
it diligently in the beginning that [our pictures] met with an
uproariously hostile reception from the audiences to which
they were shown Frequently the police were summoned to
restore order. Complaints to the authorities were made by our
opponents that our pictures were inciting riots, and that the
screening of portraits of the President, Gen. Pershing, and
other notable personages and of the American flag floating at
the forefront of marching troops or at the masthead of naval
units, constituted an insult to the Mexican government and
people and were in violation of Mexico's neutrality On various occasions our displays were halted until the local authorities could be convinced by tactful explanations, and by private
exhibitions given for their benefit, that the pictures might
properly be allowed on view

"Gradually the demonstrations in the cinés lessened, and
finally ceased The pictures won their way. The attitude of the
public altered until after a few months we were repaid for our
persistence by reports from our agents, telling of cheering and
applause in place of hoots and yells, and even of 'Vivas!' being
given for the flag, the President, American war vessels, and
American soldiers."

The visual appeal was also made through posters (printed
both in Mexico and the United States) and large "news pic-

[327]

torials " The latter device had been suggested bv William P. Blocker, vice-consul at Piedras Negras, and billboards and window displays were constructed to show twelve pictures at a time. They were kept well filled, though the material was not always perfectly adapted to the CPI purpose In the beginning there were more pictures of Poilus than of Doughboys, and even the most intuitive Mexican must have had trouble in discovering the message for him in pictures of a Lithuanian celebration in McKinley Park, Chicago, or of logging operations in the Northwest.

In the field of pamphleteering, so important in all countries where the CPI worked, Murray's first production was a translation of Brand Whitlock's *Belgica* in an edition of 10,000, and this was followed by *How the War Came to America* By the end of the war, the Mexico office had distributed more than 985,000 pamphlets through its own agents, and at least 100,000 leaflets without imprint had been broadcast through insertion in patent-medicine packages.

A mailing list of Americans and influential Mexicans was maintained, and every message went to them on a special letterhead which significantly omitted the names of the three Cabinet members of the Committee. Murray wrote Creel on March 13, 1918· "It would not do to give our German friends and their Mexican friends a chance to shout that the American War, Navy, and State Secretaries were trying to influence public sentiment in Mexico." So only Creel's and Murray's names appeared on the letterhead, but the threat of force was not overlooked even here, for at the bottom of each sheet was the legend· "THE WAR. REMEMBER: THE UNITED STATES CANNOT LOSE!"

Though movies and pamphlets were vital in the Mexican work, the reader will not be surprised to learn that here, as elsewhere, news was the chief vehicle of propaganda, or at least the basis for everything else. Besides the daily cable service, which brought a total of more than 4,400,000 words, the CPI maintained a system of daily and weekly news bulletins which the Mexican government carried post-free through the mails These bulletins were under George F. Weeks, director of the Mexican News Bureau, who also inaugurated one of the most unusual of all CPI publishing projects—a small English-language news-letter for circulation in the United States, in the belief that our own misunderstanding of the Mexican situation was at least partly to blame for difficulties between the two countries. This paper, something like an *Official Bulletin*, for Mexico, was published from October 3, 1918, to January 30, 1919.

Neutral and pro-Ally papers in Mexico were delighted to receive the CPI news service, which was not only free but also timely and interesting But for some papers special inducements seemed necessary

When Creel sent Robert Murray the first check for $2,000 for expenses on February 21, 1918, he cabled "Under no circumstances subsidize papers either directly or indirectly Make no financial arrangements with Allied committees until submitted to me." But just two days later Murray was proposing that papers in the interior should be helped in buying the Associated Press service, he suggested that the offer might come through the American Chamber of Commerce in Mexico City so that the United States government would apparently not be involved It is not certain whether this plan was carried through, but Creel did not raise objection when informed that George Agnew Chamberlain, the novelist who at that time was our consul-general in Mexico, planned to canvass the American colony for $7,500 monthly to be used largely for advertising

And on March 15, 1918, when Creel was informed that pro-Ally papers in Guadalajara and Monterrey seemed to be weakening, he specifically told Murray to use his own judgment about contributing. This was not to be regarded as a precedent, but at the same time Creel offered to help arrange another form of subsidy without cost to the CPI "We can exert pressure here to have American firms place advertising under control American Committee and greatly enlarge appropriations."

[329]

Again, when German propagandists attempted to convince Mexico that the Fourth Liberty Loan had failed, Creel authorized an extra appropriation of $2,000 for straight newspaper advertising, which read in part "From the time that the Kaiser forced the United States to enter the war to make the world safe for democracy, the government has requested loans of $15,000,000,000. The American people have contributed $18,-972,955,650 If it were necessary in order to conquer the Kaiser, they would contribute $100,000,000,000. And in order to gain the victory they will send to Germany 10,000,000 soldiers."

But some papers remained stubborn in spite of the bait of advertising, the threat of newsprint embargo, and the cutting of communications. El Democrata, for instance, survived all of these attacks and continued to show a news-gathering ability that bordered on the supernatural It offered its readers what purported to be up-to-the-minute reports of German victories in France, in spite of the fact that no such messages were coming over the Allied-controlled cables Creel told George Weeks on April 11, 1918 "None of El Democrata's cables go from this country at all They are faked in Mexico City We are watching El Democrata's mail and telegraph very closely, and have practically shut them off from communication with this country." And still the German victory news appeared in El Democrata's columns as long as there was a German army in the field, and then the attack was shifted to the terms of peace.

One of the special approaches to the Mexican press was a United States tour, similar to those for other foreign journalists as planned by Perry Arnold, but in this case especially elaborate The CPI kept in the background, but made all arrangements and paid the bill, which was nearly $10,000 Wilfred E. Wiegand of the Associated Press Mexican bureau accompanied the group of editors, who were transported in a special Pullman car from Laredo to New York to Seattle and return, with the tour under the direction of Lieutenant P. S O'Reilly, U.S N.R. El Democrata was not invited.

Perhaps the most "Wilsonian" of Robert Murray's projects for winning the sympathy of the Mexican people was establishment of American Reading Rooms in seven cities, with approved literature, newspapers, and periodicals always available. Growing out of this scheme was the even more ambitious one of American classes in English, French, bookkeeping, and shorthand. This was immediately popular, and it was reported that 30,000 students were enrolled. It was with the greatest reluctance that Murray gave up this particular phase of the work when the general demobilization order for his office was received toward the end of January 1919. He thought there was still work to be done in Mexico.

It was not until twenty years later, however, with establishment of the Division of Cultural Relations in the Department of State, that the American government once again frankly addressed itself to the problem of educational propaganda in Latin America. But Ernest Poole, director of the Foreign Press Bureau, pleaded that the work of the CPI might not be ended with the war. In a long, careful, and thought-provoking report to Creel on December 30, 1918, he urged continuation of a government bureau to employ the media of news, films, and features, and keep the official picture of the United States before the masses of the world, ". . . to clear away all points of misunderstanding or misconception that already prevail or that will arise in foreign countries in regard to this nation, its life, work, ideals, and opinions, its purposes both here and abroad."

* * *

But as Poole was writing that report, CPI offices were making ready to close, one by one, throughout the world. The last far-flung outpost would not cease propaganda work until the Committee itself went out of existence in June 1919, but almost from the moment of the Armistice CPI agents in various countries raised new anxious questions for the future.

On November 14, Mrs. Whitehouse in Berne told Edgar Sisson about the attempted Bolshevik strike: "Official of Swiss government suggests that it would be most helpful to

[331]

have items from our service to the effect that such disturbances in Europe, especially Switzerland, would interfere with or even halt plans made by United States for feeding Europe."

CPI affairs themselves were not proceeding smoothly. On November 15 Creel applied for passports for the group he was sending to the Peace Conference (including Sisson, Byoir, Bernays, Charles Hart, Carl Walberg, Major H. E. Atterbury, and E H. Shuster), but shortly he was cabling about his high displeasure with the way Bernays was handling publicity for the group, and on November 25 said:

"Contrary to the press, the people that I sent abroad were part of the Foreign Section, and will have nothing to do but purely mechanical work in connection with distribution. I will have absolutely nothing to do with the publicity of the Peace Conference, nothing to do whatsoever with the organization of any personnel that will go from here, and am going myself in a capacity personal to the President . . The House Committee [The Inquiry?] in New York had entire charge of getting the organization of experts together, and the State Department is looking after others."

Meanwhile, the intentions of our comrades in arms received new scrutiny. Hearley reported from Rome that England was trying to persuade Italians that Britain was their only true friend. Rus said that Copenhagen newspapers feared the Peace Conference would leave open wounds and cause enduring bitterness. Mrs. Whitehouse described on December 10 the significant emphasis by both Reuters and Agence Havas on reports of Senate opposition to President Wilson. And Paul Perry cabled Sisson from London on December 12:

"The different views concerning the President's attitude are still those of expectancy and they are being very much discussed particularly those referring to the freedom of the seas The opinions the most often expressed are that Wilson came to France with certain definite ideas founded on too small an appreciation of the situation in Europe and that he is very likely to change his views when he meets and confers with

[332]

statesmen who have the proper European outlook. Many criticisms are also expressed here in regards to the increase of the navy, but opinions are heard that the proposed addition to the navy would be an asset if it insures cooperation with the navy of Great Britain in preserving world peace. The press is in favor of the utmost publicity in regards to the peace conference . . . but the majority of the officials do not approve of the idea."

From another source Sisson was informed on December 20 "The French are supposed to be planning for the President, with very great ability, fêtes and entertainments to distract him from the object of his mission as much as possible, and to be planning as many postponements and delays in conference as divergence of President's opinion may warrant, with the object of forcing his premature departure."

Then on January 7, 1919, Walter Rogers in Paris reflected Peace Commission anxiety regarding the tides of opinion at home He advised Perry Arnold

"Peace Commission wants following wireless so as to be received here daily not later than 7 00 a.m Paris time substance front page news American press stop Editorial comment dealing primarily with peace conference and problems of peace stop Comment desired from not only leading Republican and Democratic papers but also from papers like *New York Call* and from weeklies like *New Republic*, *Collier's* etcetera stop Also want brief review proceedings of Congress with special reference to international affairs stop . . you personally prepare biweekly diagnosis state of mind of country about Peace Conference and policies which country wants adopted for instance in regard to sending American troops Russia stop . . . All material requested herein is part COMPUB service and should be addressed to COMPUB "

The CPI office in Berne on February 4 reported that Swiss papers doubted the permanence of the new world order They believed "it is almost certain so called World War not last war stop Without total revolution naive to believe shall see formed great family Europeans of London Paris Madrid Rome Vienna Berlin Petrograd ...." And on February 15, Guy Croswell Smith, who had succeeded Mrs Whitehouse at Berne, paraphrased a Basel newspaper: "Impression prevailing Wilson gave way to French English imperialistic pressure stop Germany driven desperation. . . . Hopeless Germany dangerous to European peace stop Germany and Entente policies responsible for coming catastrophe by refusing listen Wilson."

Disquieting reports increased as the winter wore on to Europe's first peaceful spring since 1914. French farmers might try to turn battlegrounds into wheat fields once more, but only in Russia, where armies still held the field and even "civil" life was on a wartime basis, and in Latin America, where the prize of war-won trade outshone everything else, were the agents of the Creel Committee sanguine for the future.

While the United States prepared for its repudiation of Woodrow Wilson, for Teapot Dome and the Big Bull Market, Europe also was on its way back to normalcy

Some happy chapters were to be unfolded—the Nansen Office, Near East Relief, Bryan shouting for joy from the press table at the Washington Conference, Briand and Streseman walking arm in arm at Geneva, Locarno, the International Labor Office, the Pact of Paris. . . .

But also there were the chapters on Reparations, debt-defaults, inflation, famine, the Ruhr, the Riff, book-burning, race hatred, mass trials, concentration camps, Manchuria, China, Ethiopia, Austria, Spain, Czechoslovakia, Albania, Poland. . . .

President Wilson was given the military victory he wanted on November 11, 1918, and it seemed that his spokesmen of the CPI had likewise triumphed. But in those final weeks of the Committee on Public Information the realistic members of the staff asked themselves if, after all, they had won their fight for the mind of mankind.

Part IV

THE FUTURE

Chapter 16

BLUEPRINT FOR TOMORROW'S CPI

Six days before the end of the World War and the supposed victory in the fight for the mind of mankind, George Creel received this letter from William Allen White, Republican editor of the *Emporia Gazette*:

"November 5, 1918

"Dear George·

"Pardon me for neglecting your letter of October 29, but I have been a very busy little person since it came, saving our beloved country from the slimy clutches of your Democratic Party, and now that the country is saved again I take up your letter with joy.—I say joy because your letter discloses a situation which comes to every man more or less, and I have just been going through a parallel experience.

"I have on the *Gazette* one of those safe editorial writers who confines himself to lambasting the Turk and soaking the Kaiser and estimating the relation of the corn to the population, and who never has made me trouble. He takes his typewriter in hand about a month ago and writes what seemed to be a harmless editorial calling attention to the fact that in the new reorganization of society men were getting paid for manual labor, which requires little training, as much as college professors used to get, who spent years in training.

"I was in New York making Liberty Loan speeches when he sent it to me, and as I thought that it was a good thing that labor was coming into its own, and that the laborer and the college professor were getting about the·same, I glanced through it hurriedly, put a head on, 'The Grand Shake-Up,' added a three-line cracker at the end, saying that in the grand

[337]

shake-up that was coming society was going to be reorganized and justice would edge up a little closer to the millennium.

"I sent it back with a bunch of copy, it lay on the dead hook until three or four days before the election, was printed, and WHIZZ-BANG! the Third Ward blew up, down where the railroad boys are getting two hundred bucks per month for fairly common labor The editorial was taken to mean a dirty Republican protest against the Democrats paying the railroad men their hard-earned wages, which was not my thought at all. . . ."

Mr White's engaging reflections on the danger of writing for publication, and the almost certain misunderstanding of motives, must have struck a responsive chord in the heart of George Creel. Plenty of evidence may be found of his mistaken snap judgments and his needless exuberance of invective, but most frequently he was attacked either for total irrelevancies or for sins which he had not committed For instance, he was often accused of "Kaiserism," yet the record seems to show that he withstood the temptation to dictatorship not only with courage but with considerable success And he was accused of cynicism and insincerity, whereas actually he was one of the most "oversold" men in America on the very doctrines which he preached.

This book is not meant to defend Mr Creel as a person, but to show the CPI for what it was—a social innovation brilliantly conceived and in many ways brilliantly executed. Its work is with us today.

One measure of the impact of the CPI on American life is the persistence through two decades of the stereotypes which it gave us during the war. Some of these are still accepted by scholars, some rejected, but for the public mind the great majority are as clear today as when they were vividly presented by Dean Ford's pamphleteers, Charles Dana Gibson's artists, and Ernest Poole's feature writers For instance—the World War was a "People's War" and a "holy war of ideas"; America, alone of all belligerents, was disinterested, conscription was more democratic than voluntary service, but the Liberty Loans were more democratic than taxation; the Allies observed international law; unrestricted submarine warfare was adopted because of German liking for *Schrecklichkeit*; Germany alone conducted propaganda against our neutrality; England and France were committed to President Wilson's program . . and so on.

Some of the CPI stereotypes, such as the cruder pictures of German atrociousness in the field of minor tactics, have become blurred even in the popular mind, while disillusionment has wiped away, for many, the last trace of Wilson internationalism, perhaps the most important idea conveyed by the Committee. But by and large the American people today hold the articles of faith which the CPI, as spokesman for President Wilson, drew up in 1917 and 1918.

The stamp of the CPI is visible, however, not only in the popular conception of World War history but also in official thinking about "holding fast the inner lines" if America should become involved in the new European War.

Dozens of writers recently have told what will happen to American life with the advent of "M-Day." Some accounts are based on government reports, some place greater reliance on the imagination, but in neither case has anyone suggested a technique or a channel of propaganda which was not at least tried by the CPI. Even radio broadcasting, unknown in 1918, was at least simulated by the Four-Minute Men, and of course point-to-point wireless was important for the Foreign Section.

Most people believe that if the United States should find itself in another war we would have conscription of labor and wealth and an industrial mobilization more immediate, more inflexible, and more complete than during the World War. If so, the CPI formula could not be followed exactly. We could not afford to have a "George Creel" mediating between stern military necessity and the normal procedure of civil life. Whether we should have the earlier type of committee on public information, and what sort of man would head it—those are questions on which the American people have not yet spoken.

But whether the main pattern were "totalitarian" or "democratic," the objectives sought and the general procedures followed would be those of the CPI.

Contrary to naïve opinion, conscription of wealth would not decrease the need for propaganda of the "Fight or Buy Bonds" variety. As Goebbels and his colleagues demonstrate, the "hammer and anvil of propaganda" must be pounded even more noisily to gain popular acquiescence in policies imposed from above Whatever change might come over our state in a new war, a "propaganda ministry" would hold a vital place in the government.

It is clear, for instance, that the present Division of Cultural Relations in the Department of State needs only the stimulus of increased international excitement to push it into frank continuation of work begun by the CPI Latin American branch. And there is an authentic Creel flavor in the Senate bill, introduced in January 1938 by Senator Chavez of New Mexico and Senator McAdoo of California, for construction of a superpower broadcasting station near San Diego "to transmit programs upon high frequencies to all the nations of the Western Hemisphere," the programs to be "particularly designed to strengthen the spiritual, political, and historical ties between the United States and such other nations of the Western Hemisphere."

Perhaps the Division of Cultural Relations would be absorbed into a committee on public information upon declaration of war, perhaps it would continue independently, but either way it would follow in the steps of the Creel Committee's Foreign Section, though presumably avoiding some of the errors of that hastily contrived organization.

Similarly on the home front, the CPI is the clearly recognizable model for practically every plan of government public relations in the event of war. The most important blueprint has been prepared by a joint committee of the army and navy. An understanding of its auspices and significance requires a general statement of peacetime public relations of the War

Department and the Navy Department, and of the changes which they envisage in the event of war.

In the War Department, the key unit is the Military Intelligence Division (G-2) of the General Staff, charged with responsibility for public relations, intelligence, and censorship. The Public Relations Section and the Press Section maintain relations with the press and with comparable offices in the navy. During peacetime, the War Department decentralizes its public relations as much as possible, allowing the various Corps Areas and other field offices to have direct access to the press, and to carry on their own public relations according to general rules of policy Thus, during peace, the Public Relations Section in Washington is largely concerned with routine duties of gathering, examining, and mimeographing press material from various sections of the War Department, receiving the help of an officer assigned from each section of the department As in all offices of both the army and navy, every effort is made to deal with all civilians courteously and, within the limits of policy, to give all possible assistance.

Navy publicity is handled by a branch of Naval Intelligence, which, in turn, is under the Chief of Naval Operations The present unit grew out of the Information Section established in 1922, and at present is known as the Public Relations Branch with Lieutenant Commander Leland P. Lovette in charge. Two officers serve under him, one an assistant and the other a director of press relations with a clerical staff of three. A news room, commodious and well equipped, is maintained for reporters, and releases are furnished with amazing speed The Public Relations Branch also cooperates with motion picture producers and magazine writers, and undertakes ghost-writing assignments.

This office also keeps close tab on everything about the navy printed in more than 400 newspapers in several languages, and from time to time makes reports on the state of public opinion. The Secretary of the Navy recently issued a memorandum which read in part· "Officers of the several Bureaus and activities of the Navy Department designated as liaison officers with the Navy Department Public Relations Branch will maintain close contact with the Press Section and furnish such items as are suitable for publication. . . . Where circumstances make departure from this procedure advisable, the responsible officer who releases information . . . should communicate to the Public Relations Branch the substance of his remarks."

Recently the navy has been less openhanded in its release of significant news, one of the reasons for the change of policy being a desire to "amortize the shock of censorship" in the event of war. Since the beginning of 1937, progress reports on naval construction have not been released, and correspondents are no longer permitted to go with the fleet on maneuvers with the former frequency.

Both the army and the navy realize that in the event of war their public relations programs would undergo change, and that the problems to be faced would be common to the two branches of service. Accordingly, the two departments have brought their public relations programs closer together since January 1937, when a Special Joint Army and Navy Public Relations Committee was appointed to investigate the entire field, work out peacetime coordination of the two services, and draw up the public relations part of the Industrial Mobilization Plan.

After four months of research, the committee reported to the Army and Navy Joint Board The report was approved with minor changes on August 11, 1937. One of the recommendations was establishment of a Continuing Joint Army and Navy Public Relations Committee, and this was formed toward the end of 1937 with a membership of eight, divided equally between the army and navy. It is a planning unit, not administrative. Four sections, each comprised of one army and one naval officer, deal with publicity, censorship, organization, legal matters. The committee is now engaged in perfecting the general plans suggested by the Special Committee.

The Industrial Mobilization Plan covers far more than public relations. It provides for other control units which are descendants of the War Trade Board, the War Industries Board, and other emergency establishments of the World War The Public Relations Administration provided in the plan would be the successor of the CPI. Its functions would be

1. To coordinate publicity programs of government departments and agencies.

2 To serve as an information bureau to which the nation and the world might look for accurate and unbiased facts regarding war aims.

3 To combat disaffection at home.

4. To counteract enemy propaganda both at home and abroad.

5 To organize all existing propaganda media for the prosecution of the war.

6 To secure the cooperation of the press, the radio, and the film industry

7. To formulate and administer rules of censorship.

Plans have been drawn for securing the instantaneous backing of individuals and groups in the fields of newspapers and magazines, advertising, pictures, radio, civic cooperation.

The organization of the Public Relations Administration, shown by the chart on the next page, is more than merely reminiscent of the CPI and the Censorship Board.

This proposal comes from the army and navy, but if it should seem like military infringement on the domain of the civil government, two things should be remembered: (1) That the distinction between civil and military government can be all but obliterated in time of war, and (2) that even at the present moment of American neutrality certain legislators are willing to go at least as far as the fighting men.

The well known May Bill, for instance, introduced March 1, 1938, by Representative Andrew Jackson May of Kentucky, would establish price-fixing, control of property and services, a system of priorities in all trade and industry, and limitation of profits The May Bill has received considerable support, though attacked by liberals The comment of the *Philadelphia Record* was typical of the opposition attitude· "In the first

Public Relations Administration

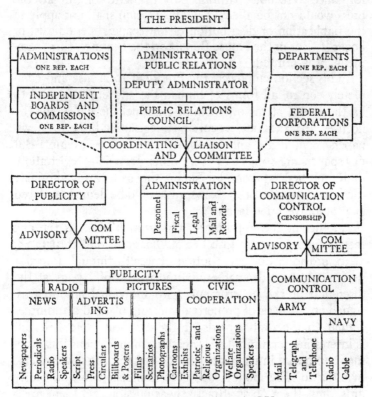

One Blueprint for Tomorrow's CPI

place, the new bill . . . doesn't take the profits out of war. In the second place, after ducking this basic issue, the bill goes on to reduce these United States to a dictatorship, going far beyond anything we have ever tried or needed in our greatest war emergencies." The minority report on the May Bill said it proposed "Congressional hara-kiri."

Section 6 of the May Bill, providing a system of "universal licensing," is important. No person in industries named by the President could do business without license from the government, and of course the license could be revoked if performance were not "patriotic." By the letter of the law the press would not be affected ("This section shall not apply to the publication or distribution of newspapers, periodicals, or books"). But in the *House Report* on the hearings, this "comment" was printed:

"This section empowers the President to license and completely control all forms of human life and endeavor and to fix the terms, at his own whim, on which he will grant the licenses. It makes one exception—a legislative bribe to 'newspapers, periodicals, and books,' which shall be exempt. But newspapers are subject to every other provision—registration, draft, and hedged around in such a way as to easily eliminate the freedom of the press. Newsprint could be denied or placed at prohibitive price levels."

Another of the important "mobilization" bills is the one introduced by Senator Josh Lee of Oklahoma on February 28, 1939, providing for conscription of wealth through forced 1 per cent loans redeemable anytime within fifty years at the discretion of the government, with individual amounts assigned on the basis of property ownership by local committees similar to the draft boards of the last war. The Lee Bill is interesting for a number of reasons, among them this argument advanced in its favor: "In the last war the government, in order to raise money, was even compelled to find pretty girls, dress them up as attractively as possible, get them to go out in front of the curtains in theaters, and make four-minute speeches begging for enough money to buy food for the soldiers who were at that time facing death in the trenches."

Though the Veterans of Foreign Wars endorsed the Lee Bill, the Treasury, War, and Navy Departments seem to have turned thumbs down. Conscription of lives and dollars and resources and labor may well be expected in any lengthy war, but the realistic officers of the fighting service recognize the problems that would arise in a "totalitarian democracy." And whatever the structure of the wartime state may be, and whatever degree of civilian control military men would like to see, they know as George Creel did that man does not live by bread alone—that publicity and propaganda must keep alive the fires of patriotism however stern the laws may be.

As the war to end war recedes into the past, America's fighting men turn back to the CPI. Improvements on the Creel Committee would undoubtedly be made, but if another war should come to this country, no American would need to read the story of the CPI. He would relive it

NOTES

NOTES

THE one great reservoir of material for this book has been the hitherto unexplored files of the CPI. These have yielded such an embarrassing wealth of information that a book might well be written on each of the score or more of divisions in the Committee. The task of selection has been difficult, and the authors realize that in attempting to give a rounded picture of the whole undertaking they have done less than justice to certain of its phases and its personnel. Temptation has been great to include many more documents than could be included in this space; selection has been weighted in favor of material not already familiar through the work of other authors.

For the great majority of facts adduced here, the source is a document in the CPI collection of the National Archives To footnote each document according to the classification scheme of the Archives would be not only meaningless to the vast majority of readers but completely useless to a scholar in any other library In nearly all cases, however, identification through names and dates is supplied in the text

The authors will be more than pleased to furnish direct key reference numbers to any qualified scholar communicating with them.

Many persons in the National Archives, the Library of Congress, and other institutions have given valued help without which the book could not have been possible In addition to the persons named in the Preface, the authors thank particularly· Frank Hardee Allen, Marilynn Allen, Robert G Ballentine, Elizabeth Bethel, Mr. and Mrs. Martin P. Claussen, Jesse S Douglas, G Vinton Duffield, Elizabeth B Drewry, David C. Duniway, Robert A. East, Edward Epes, May E. Fawcett, Miles McP Fitch, Herman Friis, Bess Glenn, Vladimir Gsovski, Philip M Hamer, Roscoe R Hill, Elbert L Huber, Helen Hunter, Dorsey W. Hyde, Dallas D Irvine, Edwin Justice, Mrs Margaret V. Kettler, Ralph H Lutz, David C. Mearns, Leland D Norton, Donald G. Patterson, Marcus W. Price, Martin A Roberts, Dorothy Shorb, Harold H. Sprout, Charles L. Stewart, S F. Stoudenmire, Jr , Margaret Farrand Thorp, Frederick P. Todd, Karl Trever, Edna F. Vosper, Arthur E. Young, Malcolm O. Young, and the editorial staff of the Princeton University Press

Thanks are also due to the publishers who have permitted quotations from their books, as indicated in these notes

[349]

GENERAL SOURCES

Aside from the files in the National Archives, on which this book is based almost entirely, the three most important sources of information regarding the CPI are George Creel's *Complete Report of the Chairman of the Committee on Public Information, 1917 1918 1919.* Washington, 1920, his more popular *How We Advertised America.* New York: Harper, 1920, and the hearings at which CPI personnel was interrogated by a House of Representatives committee (U.S. Congress House Committee on Appropriations. 65th Cong 2 Sess. *Hearings before the Subcommittee of the House Committee on Appropriations in Charge of Sundry Civil Appropriation Bill for 1919.* Pt 3. Washington, 1918).

Background atmosphere has been gained from a wide range of books, some of the most useful including Ray Stannard Baker, *Woodrow Wilson, Life and Letters* (especially Vols. 7 and 8). New York: Doubleday, Doran, 1938-1939, George G. Bruntz, *Allied Propaganda and the Collapse of the German Empire in 1918* (Hoover War Library No 13) Stanford University Press, 1938; Will Irwin, *Propaganda and the News* New York McGraw-Hill, 1936, Harold D. Lasswell, *Propaganda Technique in the World War.* New York Knopf, 1927; Waldo G. Leland and Newton D Mereness, *Introduction to the American Official Sources for the Economic and Social History of the World War.* New Haven: Yale University Press, 1926, Frederic L. Paxson, *American Democracy and the World War* Boston Houghton Mifflin, 1936 and 1939; Hans Thimme, *Weltkrieg ohne Waffen* Stuttgart. Cotta, 1932

Throughout the work, constant use has been made of the files of the *Congressional Record* and of many House and Senate documents, including bound copies of original bills and amendments

In the following notes, general references are given for certain of the chapters Specific facts are annotated here only if the source lies outside the CPI files and is not given in the text:

PREFACE

Pages viii-ix Harold D Lasswell, *Propaganda Technique in the World War* New York Knopf, 1927.

CHAPTER 1

Page 5 Among the important special interpretations are Newton D Baker, *Why We Went to War* New York· Harper, 1936; Charles A. Beard, *The Devil Theory of War* New York: Vanguard, 1936; C Hartley Grattan, *Why We Fought.* New York Vanguard, 1929; Walter Millis, *Road to War.* Boston· Houghton Mifflin, 1935, Horace C. Peterson, *Propaganda for War.* Norman University of Oklahoma Press, 1939,

Charles Seymour, *American Diplomacy During the World War* Baltimore· Johns Hopkins University Press, 1934; and U.S. Congress. Senate. Special Committee to Investigate the Munitions Industry. 73rd Cong *Hearings Pursuant to S Res.* 206. Washington. Government Printing Office, 1934 et seq. (22 vols)

Page 15 John Lord O'Brian in *New York State Bar Association Report*, Vol. 42 (1919), p. 280. U S Department of Justice *Annual Report of the Attorney General,* 1917.1918 1919

Chapter 2

Among the most useful books on censorship are Zechariah Chafee, Jr, *Freedom of Speech.* New York Harcourt, 1920 Leon Whipple, *The Story of Civil Liberty in the United States* New York· Vanguard, 1927; and Ernest Sutherland Bates, *This Land of Liberty,* New York· Harper, 1930 All three are in popular style, though Chafee's is essentially a work of legal scholarship All three argue against censorship, but open up more avenues of thought than more conservative works

Page 22 Webb Bill: H R 20757 Overman Bill: S 8148. 64th Cong 2 Sess.

Page 23. U S. Congress House Committee on the Judiciary. 64th Cong 2 Sess. *To Punish Espionage . . . Hearings . . on S* 8148, Serial 53, February 22, 1917.

Pages 23-4. Webb Bill H.R 291 Culberson Bill: S 2 65th Cong 1 Sess.

Page 24 When section 4 was stricken from the bill, another provision was of course moved up to take that number. In this book "section 4" means the defeated section which the press called "censorship," not section 4 as it appears in the *Statutes at Large*

Page 30 U.S Congress House Committee on the Judiciary. 65th Cong. 1 Sess. *Espionage and Interference with Neutrality, Hearings . . . on H R.* 291, Serial 53, pt 2, April 9 and 12, 1917.

Page 38. Wilson to conferees: Ray Stannard Baker, *Woodrow Wilson, Life and Letters* New York: Doubleday, Doran, 1938. Vol. 7, p 83

Page 39. As passed, the Espionage Act had thirteen titles: I, Espionage; II, Vessels in Ports, III, Injuring Vessels; IV, Interference with Foreign Commerce, V, Enforcement of Neutrality; VI, Seizure of Arms, VII, Certain Exports in Time of War Unlawful, VIII, Disturbance of Foreign Relations; IX, Passports, X, Counterfeiting Government Seal; XI, Search Warrants; XII, Use of Mails, XIII, General Provisions.

Page 42. Title I of the Espionage Act was largely incorporated into chapter 4, Title 50 (War) of the U S Code. See *U.S Code Annotated,* Title 50, secs. 31-42 (especially 31-3)

Page 43 Oswald Garrison Villard, *Fighting Years*. New York: Harcourt, 1939, pp. 340-1, 354-5.

For Title XII see *U S Code Annotated*, Title 18 (Criminal Code and Criminal Procedure), secs. 343-5.

For Title XI see *U S. Code Annotated*, Title 18, chiefly chapter 18.

Page 44. Schenck decision: 249 U.S 52

Page 45. For section 19 of the Trading-with-the-Enemy Act see *U S Code Annotated*, Title 50, pp. 300-1.

Page 46. The following is the text of section 3, Title I, of the Espionage Act of June 15, 1917, as amended by the so-called "Sedition Act" of May 16, 1918. The 1918 amendments, which were repealed by act of March 3, 1921, are shown in italics

"Whoever, when the United States is at war, shall wilfully make or convey false reports or false statements with intent to interfere with the operation or success of the military or naval forces of the United States, or to promote the success of its enemies, or *shall wilfully make or convey false reports or false statements, or say or do anything except by way of bona fide and not disloyal advice to an investor or investors, with intent to obstruct the sale by the United States of bonds or other securities of the United States or the making of loans by or to the United States, and* whoever, when the United States is at war, shall wilfully cause, or attempt to cause, or incite or attempt to incite, insubordination, disloyalty, mutiny, or refusal of duty, in the military or naval forces of the United States, or shall wilfully obstruct or attempt to obstruct the recruiting or enlistment service of the United States,* and *whoever, when the United States is at war, shall wilfully utter, print, write, or publish any disloyal, profane, scurrilous, or abusive language about the form of government of the United States, or the Constitution of the United States, or the military or naval forces of the United States, or the flag of the United States, or the uniform of the Army or Navy of the United States, or any language intended to bring the form of government of the United States, or the Constitution of the United States, or the military or naval forces of the United States, or the flag of the United States, or the uniform of the Army or Navy of the United States into contempt, scorn, contumely, or disrepute, or shall wilfully utter, print, write, or publish any language intended to incite, provoke, or encourage resistance to the United States, or to promote the cause of its enemies, or shall wilfully display the flag of a foreign enemy, or shall wilfully by utterance, writing, printing, publication, or language spoken, urge, incite, or advocate any curtailment of production in this country of any thing or things, product or products, necessary or essential to the prosecution of the war in which the United States may be engaged, with intent by such curtailment to cripple or hinder the United States*

* At this point the 1917 form of the law included the phrase "to the injury of the service of the United States"

[352]

in the prosecution of the war, and whoever shall wilfully advocate, teach, defend, or suggest the doing of any of the acts or things in this section enumerated, and whoever shall by word or act support or favor the cause of any country with which the United States is at war or by word or act oppose the cause of the United States therein, shall be punished by a fine of not more than $10,000 or imprisonment for not more than twenty years, or both Provided, That any employee or official of the United States Government who commits any disloyal act or utters any unpatriotic or disloyal language, or who, in an abusive and violent manner criticizes the Army or Navy or the flag of the United States shall be at once dismissed from the service. Any such employee shall be dismissed by the head of the department in which the employee may be engaged, and any such official shall be dismissed by the authority having power to appoint a successor to the dismissed official "

Chapter 3

One of the best things written on Creel as a person is the "profile" in the San Francisco magazine, The Coast, Vol. 1, no. 10 (September 1938), pp 30-3 The structure of the CPI is described in the general sources mentioned above.

Page 54 George Creel, Quatrains of Christ New York P. Elder and Co , 1908

Page 59. George Creel, Wilson and the Issues New York Century, 1916

Page 61. Ray Stannard Baker, op cit , Vol 8, p 156.

For Congressional investigation see Sundry Civil Bill Hearings listed under general sources

Page 62 George Creel, "The 'Lash' of Public Opinion," Collier's, Vol 74, no 21, p 46 (November 22, 1924)

Page 67. Byoir's public relations projects Public Opinion Quarterly, Vol. 3, no. 3 (July 1939), pp 513-15; U.S. Congress House. Special Committee on Un-American Activities 73rd Cong 2 Sess Hearings, No 73-DC-4 The latter reference is to the "Dickstein Committee." On June 5, 1934, Carl C Dickey of Carl Byoir and Associates testified that their firm was receiving $6,000 per month from the German Tourist Information Office of New York. George Sylvester Viereck (wartime German propagandist) was expert adviser to the Byoir firm at $1,750 per month, Byoir maintained a Berlin office at a cost of $1,000 per month, up to the time of the hearings the firm had received more than $100,000 for promoting German-American goodwill in the interest of American tourism in the Reich

CHAPTER 4

In addition to the general sources, the student will be aided by the *Preliminary Statement to the Press of the United States.* Washington· Government Printing Office, 1917, and the *Report of the Director of the Official U S. Bulletin to the Chairman of the Committee on Public Information* Washington, 1919.

Page 102 *New York Times,* January 20, 1918, sec 8, p 11.

Page 104 Fairfax D. Downey, *Portrait of an Era as Drawn by Charles Dana Gibson* New York: Scribner's, 1936. pp 322, 324

CHAPTER 5

Files of the *Four-Minute Men News* (nos A-F) and the *Four-Minute Men Bulletins* (nos 1-46) give the readiest understanding of the work. Also see "The War Work of the Four-Minute Men," *The Touchstone,* Vol 3, no 6 (September 1918), p 507; Glenn N. Merry, "National Defense and Public Speaking," *Quarterly Journal of Speech Education,* Vol 4, no 1 (January 1918), pp 58-9, and Bertram G Nelson, "The Four-Minute Men" in *What Every American Should Know About the War* (Montaville Flowers ed) New York. Doran, 1918

Page 114. George Creel, *How We Advertised America* New York. Harper, 1920 p 84

Page 130. Nelson, *op. cit*, p. 252

CHAPTER 6

Files of *Exhibitor's Trade Review, Moving Picture World, Hearst's,* and *Variety* are the most important sources outside the CPI files.

Page 145 Maximilian Foster was later the highly successful and uniformly praised head of the CPI news service with the A E F

Page 146. U S Congress. Senate. Committee on the Judiciary 65th Cong. 2 & 3 Sess. *Brewing and Liquor Interests and German Propaganda, Hearings   Pursuant to S.Res.* 307. Washington, 1919. Vol 2

Page 150. R. S. Baker, *op cit*, Vol 8, pp. 65-6

Page 153. R. S. Baker, *op cit*, Vol. 8, pp. 213, 441

CHAPTER 7

Publications of Dean Ford's division are the most important sources Files of the *History Teacher's Magazine* are likewise useful, as are Parke R Kolbe, *The Colleges in War Time and After* New York· Appleton, 1919, and Charles F. Thwing, *The American Colleges and Universities in the Great War* New York Macmillan, 1920 Sharp criticisms of wartime scholarship may be found in Charles Angoff, "The Higher Learning Goes to War," *American Mercury,* Vol 11 (June 1927), pp 177-91;

Harry Elmer Barnes, "The Drool Method in History," *American Mercury*, Vol 1, no 1 (January 1924), pp. 31-8, C. Hartley Grattan, "The Historians Cut Loose," *American Mercury*, Vol 11 (August 1927), pp 414-30, and Upton Sinclair, *The Goose Step* Pasadena: the Author, 1922. The problem of suppressed and "revised" textbooks is brilliantly and comprehensively treated in Bessie Louise Pierce, *Public Opinion and the Teaching of History in the United States* New York Knopf, 1926

Chapter 8

Page 188 The poem bears the printed notation "Compliments of Commonwealth Steel Company, St. Louis, Mo.," and in longhand "Byoir: This is one of the best and should be given great publicity— C H H [C H Howard, president of Commonwealth] "

Page 190 Grosvenor Clarkson, *Industrial America in the World War*. Boston Houghton Mifflin, 1923 p. 276.

Page 210 In the Detroit case formal specific complaints were never filed, and on January 29, 1919, the National War Labor Board (Docket 439) said it could only conclude that "the difficulties complained of no longer exist, or that the complainants do not care to press the case, and therefore recommend that it be dismissed without prejudice "

Chapters 9-15

In addition to the general sources, see Heber Blankenhorn, *Adventures in Propaganda* Boston Houghton Mifflin, 1919. Rear-Admiral Sir Douglas Brownrigg, *Indiscretions of the Naval Censor* London Cassell, 1920, Major E Alexander Powell, *The Army Behind the Army*, New York Scribner's, 1919, Sir Campbell Stuart, *Secrets of Crewe House*, London Hodder and Stoughton, 1920, and Vira B Whitehouse, *A Year as a Government Agent*, New York Harper, 1920 None of these latter is intended as scholarship, but all are valuable for background information regarding the CPI's foreign campaign

Page 218. George G Bruntz, *Allied Propaganda and the Collapse of the German Empire in 1918* Palo Alto Stanford University Press, 1938. "In a personal letter to the writer, Mr. Otto H. Kahn shortly before his death again denied any connection with the *Freie Zeitung* or that he had given money to the Friends of German Democracy" (p 37 n)

For German-American Alliance, see U S Congress Senate Committee on the Judiciary. 65th Cong. 2 Sess Hearings . . . on S. 3529, *a Bill to Repeal the Act Entitled, "An Act to Incorporate the National German-American Alliance . . ."* Washington, 1918. Also see *Brewing and Liquor Interests* hearings listed under Chapter VI

Page 246 Powell, op cit , pp 348-9

Page 261 Wilson on fomenting revolution; a probably unused memo-randum to Tumulty R. S. Baker, op. cit, Vol. 8, p. 389.

Page 267. Irene Wright is now a member of the staff of the Division of Cultural Relations in the Department of State.

Page 275 For cablegrams on the "camouflage" incident and a special interpretation of it, see Whitehouse, op cit, appendix.

Page 278. Schwimmer incident: ibid, pp. 232 ff.

Page 292 Kerney on Paris: ibid, p 81.

Page 300 For general background of the CPI work in Russia, see James Bunyan, *Intervention, Civil War, and Communism in Russia.* Baltimore. Johns Hopkins University Press, 1936, William Henry Chamberlin, *The Russian Revolution,* 1917-1921. New York· Macmillan, 1935, Frederick L. Schuman, *American Policy Toward Russia Since 1917.* New York: International Publishers, 1928, George Stewart, *The White Armies of Russia.* New York. Macmillan, 1933, Leonid I. Strakhovsky, *Origins of American Intervention in North Russia* (1918). Princeton: Princeton University Press, 1937. The story of a principal in the CPI Russian work is given in Edgar G Sisson, 100 *Red Days* New Haven: Yale University Press, 1931. For an interesting Russian estimate of the Root Mission and the background of CPI effort, see D Fedotoff White, *Survival Through War and Revolution in Russia* Philadelphia· University of Pennsylvania Press, 1939.

Page 317. Schuman, op cit., p. 152.

CHAPTER 16

Page 340 Chavez-McAdoo Bill: S 3342.

Page 341 For peacetime public relations of Army and Navy see Senate Report 1275, 75th Cong 1 Sess Investigation of Executive Agencies of the Government [Byrd Committee] *Preliminary Report of the Select Committee to Investigate the Executive Agencies of the Government.* . Washington, 1937 For plans in the event of war see *Industrial Mobilization Plan,* Washington, 1936 and the 1939 revision, also literature on May Bill (1938) and Lee Bill (1939). Also Leo M. Cherne, *Adjusting Your Business to War.* New York Tax Research Institute of America, 1939, Rose M Stein, *M-Day.* New York Harcourt, 1936; Larry Nixon (editor), *When War Comes.* New York· Greystone, 1939

Page 343 May Bill H R 9064.

Page 344 Chart reproduced through courtesy of AIC Library

Page 345. Comment (summary of argument) on Section 6 of May Bill: House Report 1870 75th Cong 3 Sess pp 24-6.

Lee Bill. S. 1650.

INDEX

INDEX

Abbott, Lyman P , 27
Ackerman, F. E., 244, 321, 322
Adams, Herbert, 102
Adams, Samuel Hopkins, 110, 119, 145
Adcock, C P., 267
Addams, Jane, 30
Adjutant General's Office, 168
Advertising Division, 72, 96, 97, 99, 105, 109
Advocate of Peace, 165
Agence Havas, 240, 332
Agricultural Publishers Association, 99
Agriculture, Department of, 97
Aircraft Production, Bureau of, 150
Alarcón, Mariano, 269
Alcock, W F , 274
Aliens, see Foreign Born, 232
Allen, Frank Hardee, ix
Allin, C D , 160
Alsberg, Henry, 315
Altamira, Rafael, 268, 269
Altrocchi, Rudolph, 244, 287, 289
Altschul, Charles, 165
Aluminum Cooking Utensil Company, 99
American Alliance for Labor and Democracy, 70, 189-91, 193, 195-8, 206, 208, 209
American Association of Advertising Agencies, 96
American Association of Teachers of Journalism, 28
American Banker's Association, 134
American Book Company, 180
American Chamber of Commerce, 329
American Defense Society, 9

American Federation of Labor, 23, 185, 190, 206, 208, 290, 302
American Friends of German Democracy, 218
American Friends of the German Republic, 216, 217
American-Hungarian Loyalty League, 223, 224, 225, 228
American Labor Mission, 295
American Library Association, 185
American News, 244
American Newspaper Publishers Association, 28
American Peace Society, 165, 166
American Press, 97
American Protective League, 83
American Rights League, 27
American School Peace League, 166
American Union Against Militarism, 23, 24
American Weekly, 86
American Woodworking Machinery Company, 197
Amidon, Charles F., 44
Anderson, William, 160, 171
Arabic, 128
Argentina, 246
Argentina, CPI in, 245
Armament, French Ministry of, 86
Armed Ship Bill, 27
Army Bulletins, 125
Arnheim, Victor H , 190
Arnold, Perry, 244, 297, 298, 330
Artists, 102
Ashurst, Henry Fountain, 37
Associated Advertising Clubs of the World, 96
Associated Business Papers, 97
Associated Press, 329, 330

[359]

Association of National Advertisers, 96
Atrocity stories, 12, 13, 123
Atwater, Henry, 67, 206
Auleta, Vincent, 244
Austria, 246
Austria-Hungary, Penetration of propaganda into, 257-62
Avanti, 291
Aydelotte, Frank, 183
Aylward, William J, 106

Babson, Clifford W, 198, 199, 200, 208
Babson, Roger W., 70, 94, 95, 191, 193
Babson Institute, 95
Bagley, William C., 177, 182
Bakemen, George, 308, 312
Baker, George Barr, 63
Baker, Newton D., 49, 50, 51, 150, 162, 300
Baker, Ray Stannard, 61, 150, 153, 285
Balch, Emily Green, 30
Balderston, John L., 244, 297, 298
Baldwin, M. D., 205
Baltimore Sun, 32
Bara, Theda, 131, 135, 311
Barrett, John, 323
Bass, John, 243
Bates, Blanche, 57
Batten, George, 96
Beach, Rex, 110
Beard, Charles A, 5, 172, 177
Beck, James M, 219
Becker, Carl L., 168, 172
Belgian Legation, 127
Benington, Arthur, 244
Benson, William F, 88
Berg, Clare de Lissa, 137
Berger, Victor L, 43, 196
Bernays, Edward L., 239, 245, 321, 322, 332
Bernhardi, Friedrich, 171
Bernstein, Herman, 305, 307
Bernstorff, Count von, 21, 25

Bertran, Samuel R, 302
Bestor, Arthur E, 72, 126
Bielaski, A B., 222
Bjorkman, Edwin, 220, 221, 226, 229, 279-81
Black Tom Explosion, 144
Blair, William McCormick, 72, 118, 120
Blankenhorn, Heber, 245, 249
Blashfield, E H., 102
Blocker, William P., 328
Blue Devils, 128
Blumenthal, Charles, 226
Bohn, Frank, 217, 230, 244, 261, 276
Bonaschi, Albert, 220
Boston Post, 132
Bowles, George, 140
Boy Scouts of America, 185
Boyd, William Y., 321
Brace, A M, 244, 274, 295
Brady, William A, 118, 134, 135, 156, 157
Brazier, Marion H, 170
Brazil, CPI in, 245
Breed, Donald L., 110
Brest-Litovsk Treaty, 281, 301, 306
Briand, Aristide, 334
Briggs and Stratton Electrical Specialties, 202
British Information Service, 282
British War Mission, 127
Brisbane, Arthur, 37, 80
Brown, L Ames, 72, 110
Brown, William Adams, 307, 311, 313
Brown Brothers, 153
Brulatour, Jules E, 74, 142, 243
Bruntz, George G, 218, 249
Bryan, William Jennings, 117, 166, 334
Bucher, A J, 164
Buckeye Steel Castings Company, 201
Buffington, Joseph, 175, 215
Buffington, Ora, 12

[360]

Bullard, Arthur, 244, 301, 303, 304, 305, 306, 307, 308, 309, 311, 312, 313
Burleson, Albert S , 41
Bush, S. P , 201
Business Management Division, 67
Butler, Ellis Parker, 110
Butler, Nicholas Murray, 26
Byoir, Carl, xi, 3-4, 66, 72, 73, 94, 97, 105, 110, 136, 148, 149, 188, 191, 197, 199, 200, 201, 206, 218, 223, 332

CALL, ARTHUR D , 165
Cameron, William J , 193
Campbell, R. M., 326
Capital, 196-210
Carnegie Endowment for International Peace, 26, 166
Carnegie Institute of Technology, 15
Carnegie Institution, 183
Cartoonists, Weekly Bulletin for, 72
Cartoons, 105
Cartoons, Bureau of, 72, 108-9
Caruso, Enrico, 322
Casey, Frank De Sales, 102
Castle, Irene, 143, 144
Catt, Carrie Chapman, 73
Censorship, 11, 19, 20, 21, 22, 23, 24, 28, 36, 37, 38, 39, 42, 45, 46, 47, 78, 79-80, 81, 82, 85, 156
Censorship Board, 20, 44, 46, 80, 84, 297
Central America, 244-5
Chafee, Zechariah, Jr , 44
Chaix, Commandant, 258
Chambers, Ernest J , 143, 145
Chamberlain Bill, 115
Chamberlain, George Agnew, 329
Chaplin, Charles, 142, 151
Chatterton, Ruth, 131
Chautauquas, 127
Chavez, Dennis, 340
Chenery, William L , 208
Chester, C L , 140

Chicago Herald, 90, 246
Chicago Herald and Examiner, 69
Chicago National Security Council, 193
Chicago Tribune, 24, 66
Chicago Union League Club, 210
Children in Bondage, 57
Chile, CPI in, 245
China, CPI in, 244
Christian Science Monitor, 15
Church, S H , 15
Churches, 26
Churchill, Marlborough, 86, 87, 150, 245, 290
Churchill, William, 68
Chykin, Joseph, 190
Civic and Educational Cooperation, Division of, 68, 101, 111, 158-86, 193
Clark, S. H., 16, 119
Clarkin, Franklin, 312
Clarkson, Grosvenor, 13, 190
Clawson, Elliot J , 151
Clemenceau, Georges, 293
Cleveland Plain Dealer, 129
Cobb, Frank, 15, 222
Cochrane, R H , 149
Cohan, George M , 131
Collier's Magazine, 66, 208, 333
Collins, James, 110
Collins, Seward B , 244, 272
Colorado Fuel and Iron Co , 205
Comité des Forges, 293
Committee on Public Information, Congressional attitude toward, 60-1, creation of, 4, 48-52, finances of, 67, 92, 126, 129, 141, 160, 223, 280, organization of, 48, 65-74, 96-130, 133-86; publications of, 120-1, 160, 191-3, 220, 316; records of, vii, salaries in, 67
Commons, John R , 196
Commonwealth Steel Company, 188, 198, 200, 201
COMPUB, 277, 289, 292, 298, 312, 333

Conference Committee on National Preparedness, 197
Congress of Oppressed Peoples of Austria-Hungary, 257
Connor, Robert D. W., 96, 183
Contracts, 196
Coolidge, Archibald C, 183
Coolidge, Calvin, 43, 93
Correspondencia, La, 270
Corwin, Edward S, 172
Cosmopolitan Magazine, 66
Coss, John J., 171
Cotillo, S A, 244, 289
Coughlin, C L, 202
Coulomb, Charles A, 180
Council of National Defense, 72, 92, 97, 115, 127, 149, 189, 190
Courtivron, Marquis and Marquise de, 128
Coxe, Russell L, 175
Crane, Charles R, 302
Crawford, Arthur W, 90
Creel, George, vii, ix, xi, 10, 16, 17, 18, 33, 44, 46, 47, 48, 52, 54-5, 57-9, 73, 77, 80, 83, 84, 92, 97, 101, 111, 135, 136, 142, 148, 149, 150, 153, 156, 157, 158, 159, 170, 177, 191, 193, 195, 196, 197, 208, 210, 213, 214, 215, 216, 217, 218, 220, 221, 222, 223, 224, 227, 229, 230, 231, 235, 236, 241, 242, 251, 261, 264, 275, 279, 286, 287, 289, 290, 291, 294, 297, 298, 301, 303, 304, 305, 306, 307, 316, 317, 319, 320, 322, 323, 324, 328, 329, 330, 331, 332, 337, 338, 339, 346, appointed chairman, 4, 11, 49, 50, 51; attitude of toward censorship, 11, 28, criticism of, 11-12, 13; influence of on Censorship Board, 20, post-war career, 74
Crocker, F C, 322
Crosley, Walter S, 268
Crow, Carl, 244
Crozier, William, 197

Cuddihy, R J, 15
Culberson, Charles A, 24
Cummins, Albert B, 29
Cummins, H A C., 323, 324
Curley, James M, 224
Current History, 41
Curtis and Company, 197
Curzon, Lord, 298
Cusack, Thomas, 96
Czernin, Count Ottokar, 172

D O.R.A., see Defense of the Realm Act
Dahlstrom Metallic Door Company, 201
Daniels, Josephus, xi, 28, 49, 51, 79
D'Annunzio, Gabrielle, 259
Dansey, Major, 319-20
D'Arcy, William, 96
Darrow, Clarence, 166
Davis, Malcolm, 244, 307, 311
Davis, William Stearns, 160, 180
Davison, Henry P, 118
Dayton-Wright Company, 150
De Lima, Arthur, 326
Debs, Eugene V, 43
Decker, Burton C., 266, 268
Defense of the Realm Act, 34
Democrata, El, 325, 330
Denmark, CPI in, 244, 279-82
Denver Post, 54, 55
Deutsches Wort, 276
Diamond Forging and Manufacturing Company, 202
Dickinson, C R, 199, 200
Dixon, Frederick, 15
Dodd, William E., 183
Domestic Section, 68-73
Dorsey, George A, 268
Doubleday, Page & Company, 96
Douglas, Charles E, xi
Downey, Fairfax, 104
Draft, Selective, 115
duPont de Nemours & Company, E. I., 200
Duncan, James, 302

[362]

Dunn, Harvey, 106
Durant, Kenneth, 90
Dutcher, George M , 185

Eastman, Max, 43
Eastman Kodak Company, 96
Eaton, Horace A., 30
Eddystone Ammunition Plant, 33, 199
Edgell, G. H , 243, 245, 258, 259
Editor & Publisher, 28, 90, 324
Education, Bureau of, 183
Educational Institutions, 158-63
Eight-Hour Law, 196
Emergency Council on Education, 182
Emergency Peace Federation, 25, 33
Employment Service, 189
Emporia Gazette, 337
England, CPI in, 244, 296-9
Enright, Walter J , 106
Ericsson, John, League of Patriotic Service, 8
Erskine, John, 110
Espionage, 15, 22, 33, 37, 38, 39
Espionage Act, 19, 20, 36, 37, 41, 42, 43, 44, 45, 80, 147-8, 153, 215
Espionage Bill, 1917, 24, 33, 34, 36 38
Everybody's Magazine, 56, 64, 145
Executive Division, 66, 70, 108
Exhibitor's Trade Review, 132, 134, 152

Fabra News Agency, 267
Fairbanks, Douglas, 135
Farm, Stock and Home, 85
Farrar, Geraldine, 132, 311
Fay, Sidney B , 172
Fayant, Frank, 244
Federal Register, 96
Fife, George B , 244, 277
Film Division, 68, 69, 131, 136-53
Finland, CPI in, 281
Finnish Information Bureau, 315

First National Pictures Company, 137, 153
Fisk Rubber Company, 199
Foley, L. B , 214
Food Administration, 92, 97, 100, 118, 127
Foote, George C., 225
Ford, Guy Stanton, 5, 68, 77, 92, 136, 158, 159, 161, 167, 175, 177, 180, 181, 183, 185, 196, 338
Ford, Henry, 322
Ford Motor Company of Canada, 198
Foreign-born citizens, 213-32
Foreign Film Division, 74, 137, 141, 239, 242, 243
Foreign-Language Information Service, 232
Foreign-Language Newspaper Division, 68, 228
Foreign-language press, 45
Foreign Press Bureau, 74, 77, 239, 242, 243, 331
Foreign Section, 73-4, 155, 220, 235-334, 339
Foster, Maximilian, 91, 145, 244, 273, 278
Four-Minute Men, 72, 112, 113-30, 185, 189, 195, 339
Four-Minute Men Bulletin, 116, 119, 127
Four-Minute Men News, 115
Fox, Albert W., 88
Fox, Edward Lyell, 146, 148
Fox, William, 135
France, CPI in, 244, 292-6
Frankfurter, Felix, 202
Frayne, Hugh, 190
Frederick, J E , 201
Free-Speech League of America, 30
Freie Zeitung, 276, 277
French High Commission, 127
Frey, John P , 206
Friends of German Democracy, 8, 127, 217, 218, 219, 228, 230, 244, 261

[363]

Friends of Irish Freedom, 30
Frost, Wesley, 128-9
Fryatt, Charles, 84
Fuel Administration, 97, 100

Gallagher, Patrick, 110
Gallatin, Albert E , 106
Gard, Warren, 36
Gard Amendment, 36, 38, 39
Garfield, Harry A , 156
Garner, James Wilford, 165
Garrett, John Work, 244, 282, 297
Gaumont Film Company, 138, 293,
    294
Gauss, Christian, 185
Gay, José M , 272
Gaylord, W R , 190, 196
General Staff, U S , 341
Gerard, James W , 152, 275, 292
German-American Alliance, 25,
    213, 218
German-American Organizations,
    25
German-Americans, 214-21
German-Bolshevik Conspiracy, 317-
    18
German propaganda, 145, 146
German Social Democrats, 290
German Whisper, 66
Germany, Penetration of propagan-
    da into, 251-7, 260-2
Gerson, Armand J , 180
Gibbons, Herbert Adams, 293, 294
Gibson, Charles Dana, 71, 77, 101,
    102, 104, 106, 242, 338
Gibson, Hugh, 172, 243, 244, 252,
    253, 255, 258, 265, 295, 305
Gilbert, Cass, 102
Glaman, Otto, 308
Glenn, Bess, xi
Goebbels, Paul Joseph, 340
Goethals, George W , 88
Goldman, Emma, 33
Goldstein, Robert, 147
Gompers, Samuel, 43, 71, 166, 190,
    195, 196, 208, 290
Good Housekeeping Magazine, 144

Grannon, Ryley, 87
Grasselli, T. S., 203
Grasselli Chemical Company, 203
Greene, Evarts B , 164, 168, 183
Gregory, W D., 45, 218, 227
Griffis, C N , 245, 322
Griffith, D W , 135, 147, 307
Grissom, Arthur, 52
Grover, Oliver Dennett, 102
Guest, Edgar A , 188
Gutmann, James, 171

Hale, Robert L., 23
Halloran, Charles T , 23
Hand, Learned, 44
Hanover Film Company, 132
Hansi (cartoonist), 252
Hard, William, 325
Harding, Samuel B , 159, 160, 167,
    172, 182, 185
Harding, Warren G., 10, 43, 93
Harn, O C., 96
Harper, Samuel N , 316
Harris and Ewing, 153
Hart, Charles S , 69, 136, 148, 156,
    157, 332
Hartford Courant, 32
Hatrick, E B , 244, 292
Haus und Herd, 164
Haynes, J. B , 197
Haywood, William D , 16, 17, 43
Hazen, Charles D , 162
Hearley, John H , 244, 288, 290,
    291, 332
Hearst, William R , 146, 148, 150
Hearst papers, 143, 144
Hearst-Pathé Film Company, 138,
    148
Hearst's International Magazine,
    143
Hearst's Magazine, 136
Hecker, Walter C , 197, 200
Hecht, George J , 109
Heinecke, Dr , 277
Heller, Otto, 217, 230
Henderson, Arthur, 210
Hertling, Georg F. von, 172

Hetherlin, A C , 197
Hexamer, C. J., 25
History Teacher's Magazine, 164, 183
Hitchcock, Gilbert M., 27
Hittinger, Joseph H., 70
Hoagland, H. C., 244, 289, 294
Hodkinson Picture Company, 140
Hoffman, Frederick L., 217
Hoke, George W , 206
Holder, Arthur E , 23, 30
Holmes, Oliver Wendell, 44
Hoover, Herbert, 85, 118, 156, 172
House, Edward Mandell, 284
Houston, Herbert S., 96
Howard, C. H , 198, 200, 201, 206
Howard, Edward Percy, 97
Howard, Roy W., 15
Howe, Fred, 178
Hrdlicka, Aleš, 3
Hughes, Rupert, 61
Hughes, Hugh J , 85
Hungarian-Americans, 222
Hungarian Loyalty League, 225
Hunt, Henry T., xi, 15
Hutchins, R. G , 306

ICKES, HAROLD L., 173, 195, 224, 229
Igoe, William L , 30
Illinois Council of Defense, 195
Ince, Thomas H , 135
Independent, 53, 54
Industrial Information Bureau, 206
Industrial Mobilization Plan, 342
Industrial Relations, Division of, 70, 189, 191
Industrial Workers of the World, 16, 43
Ingersoll, William H , 72, 120
Inman, Harry, 313
Inter-Allied Committee for Propaganda into Enemy Countries, 245-6, 256, 259
International Film Service Corporation, 146

International Harvester Corporation, 322
International Labor Office, 334
Irwin, Wallace, xi, 107, 110
Irwin, Will, 73, 220, 235, 245, 252, 253, 255, 256, 269, 271, 280, 292, 293, 294, 295, 307, 311
Italian Embassy, 127
Italy, CPI in, 244, 286-92

JACOB RIIS LEAGUE OF PATRIOTIC SERVICE, 226
Jameson, J Franklin, 172, 183, 316
Jewel Productions, 151
Joffre, Joseph, 295
John Ericsson League of Patriotic Service, 226
Johns, William H., 72, 77, 96, 105
Johnson, Hiram, 37
Johnstone, F. B , 210
Jones, Francis C , 102
Jones, Guernsey, 171
Jones, Lewis B , 96
Jordan, David Starr, 25, 219
Julian, Rupert, 151
Jusserand, Jules, 277
Justice, Department of, 16, 20, 43, 45, 46, 83, 84, 89, 149, 178, 217, 222, 223, 275

KAHN, OTTO, 164, 217, 218
Kansas City World, 52
Kaupas, Julius B., 220
Keck, C E , 180
Keeley, James, 243, 246, 258, 261
Kennaday, Paul, 238, 283, 292
Keppel, Frederick P , 178
Kerensky, Alexander, 300
Kerney, James, 59, 244, 252, 292, 293, 294, 295
King, William H , 213
Kirby, William F , 29
Kirby Amendment, 80
Kirby, Rollin, 64
Kitchin, Claude, 61
Klein, Arthur J., 71
Klumph, A C , 161

Koettgen, Julius, 215, 217, 218, 219, 220, 228, 230, 231
Kokomo Steel and Wire Company, 201
Konta, Alexander, 220, 222, 223, 224, 225, 230, 231
Koons, J. C., 78
Kotzenabe, C., 164
Kradyna, Ludwik, 220
Krey, August C, 171, 172

LABOR, 26, 188-212, 225
Labor and Democracy, American Alliance for, 70, 189, 190, 191, 193, 195, 196, 197, 198, 206, 208, 209
Labor Bulletins, 193
Labor Department, 94, 97, 127, 189, 202-3, 206, 208
Labor Publications, Division of, 71, 190, 195, 196, 208
Labor Statistics, Bureau of, 193
Laemmle, Carl, 135
LaFollette, Robert M., Sr., 27
LaGuardia, Fiorello, 34, 244, 287
Lamar, W H, 215
Lamont, Thomas W., 16, 17, 315
Lamson-Scribner, Frank, 70
Lane, Franklin K, 43, 162
Lansing, Robert, 51, 164, 277
Lasky, Jesse L, 135
Lasswell, Harold D, viii, 249
Latin America, CPI in, 244
Lauder, Harry, 199
Lawrence, David, 96
League to Enforce Peace, 9, 166
Lectures, 126
Lee, Clayton D, 67
Lee, Ivy, 322
Lee, Josh, 345
Lehmann, F W, 164
Leicht, Gretchen, 109
Leiserson, William M, 229
Leland, Waldo G, 183
Lemp, William J, 222
Lenin, Nicolai, 300, 301, 317
Leslie's Magazine, 218

Lester, George G, 146, 147
Lewis, Read, 244, 305, 308, 309, 312
Lewis, W. H, 244
Liberty Loan, 97, 100, 105, 116, 125, 128, 134, 135, 156, 203, 209, 330
Lichnowsky Memoir, 110
Lindsey, Ben B., 55, 57
Lingelbach, William E, 183, 185
Lippmann, Walter, 245, 258
Literary Digest, 24, 25, 26, 32, 33-4, 41, 83
Literary societies, 127
Lithuanian Bureau, 244
Lodge, Henry Cabot, 88
Loew, Marcus, 135
Long, Frank E, 99
Los Angeles Times, 31
Lovette, Leland P, 341
Lowry, E. G, 297
Loyalty Leaflets, 175
Loyalty League, American-Hungarian, 8
Lusitania, 69, 128, 129, 152
Lyons, Maurice F., 66

McADOO, WILLIAM G, 134, 135, 156, 340
McConaughy, John W, 68, 90, 91, 196
McCormick, Cyrus, 191, 302
McCormick, Medill, 115
McFarland, Russell, 198, 199, 201, 206
McFarlane, Arthur E, 110
McIntyre, Frank, 78
McKinley, Albert E, 180
McLaughlin, Andrew C, 162
McLean, Edward B, 87
McReynolds, Frederick W., 71
Madden, Martin B, 34
Maddox, R L, 20
Maisel, Robert, 70, 71, 190, 208
Maloney, William J, 283, 284
Marburg, Theodore, 166

Marion, Frank J , 244, 264, 266, 267, 268, 271, 272, 273, 274, 286, 287
Markham, Edwin, 54, 57
Markus, Alfred, 220
Marshall, Thomas, 127
Martin, Frederick Roy, 28
Masaryk, Thomas, 231, 261
Mason, C. H., 309
Masters, G. L. R., 154
Matthews, Arthur T., 102
Maxim, Hudson, 132
May, Andrew Jackson, 343
Merchant ships, Legislation to arm, 26
Merriam, Charles E., 244, 287, 288, 289, 290, 291
Merritt and Chapman Derrick Company, 214
Merz, Charles, 165, 245
Metropolitan Magazine, 325
Mexican News Bureau, 329
Mexico, CPI in, 245, 323
Military Intelligence, viii, 15, 20, 46, 61, 86, 87, 146, 150, 189, 237, 238, 239, 245, 246, 249, 250, 253, 255, 262, 263, 272, 277, 281, 282, 287, 289, 290, 293, 297, 309, 311, 326, 341
Millis, Walter, 5
Milner, Alfred, 298
Minneapolis Civic and Commerce Association, 161
Missouri Malleable Iron Company, 203
Mladineo, Peter, 220
Molders Journal, 206
Monahan, L J , 202
Mongolia, 79
Moore, John D., 23, 30
Mooser, George, 245, 324
Morgan, Dick Thompson, 35
Morgan, E V., 245, 321
Morgan, J P , 26
Morgan, Wallace, 106
Morgenthau, Henry, Sr , 153
Morning Post (London), 298

Morris, Roland S., 312
Morrison, Martin A , 71
Moses, Kingsley, 244, 287
Mostowski, B. F , 244
Motion Pictures, 43, 131-57, 242-3, 272, 281, 293-5, 304, 305, 307, 309, 311
Motion Picture Industry, National Association of, 118, 157
Motor, 144
Motor Boating, 144
Mott, John R , 302
Moving Picture World, 141
Mueller, O. B , 205
Mueller Metals Company, 205
Mundell, Mrs. William A , 72
Mundo, El, 270
Munro, Dana Carleton, 172, 183
Munsey's Magazine, 90
Murray, Mae, 131
Murray, Robert H , 245, 323, 324, 326, 327, 328, 329, 331
Mutual Pictures Company, 138

NATION, 43
National Academy of Design, 102
National Americanization Committee, 210
National Archives, viii, ix, 150
National Association of Manufacturers, 190, 205, 207
National Bank of Commerce, 306
National Board for Historical Service, 158, 185, 316
National City Bank, 322
National Conference of American Lecturers, 127
National Education Association, 182
National School Service, 68
National Security League, 9, 13, 173
Naval Intelligence, 20, 46, 271, 302, 326, 341
Naval Oil Leases, 62
Naval Operations, Chief of, 341
Navarro, Romero, 244, 271, 272
Navy Department, 77, 79, 85, 153, 206, 240, 341, 345

Navy League, 9
Neal, Jesse H., 96
Nearing, Scott, 43
Neel, John D , 93
Nelson, Bertram G., 130
Nester, Byron M , 244
Netherlands, CPI in, 244, 282
New Freedom Society of America, 224
New Republic, 57, 89, 165, 333
News Division, 68, 73, 77, 89, 90, 91, 92, 96, 111, 208
New York American, 146
New York Call, 333
New York Evening Mail, 90
New York Evening Post, 16, 24, 43, 88, 314, 315
New York Federation of Churches, 26
New York Herald, 305
New York Journal, 52
New York Sun, 27, 110
New York Times, 31, 39, 40, 41, 59, 60, 64, 102, 105, 165, 170, 314
New York World, 15, 32, 222
Newspapers, see Press
Nicholson, Meredith, 110
Nock, Albert J., 304
Notestein, Wallace, 171
Northcliffe, Lord, 298
Norton, Phil, 244, 313
Norway, CPI in, 279
Nulsen, F E., 203
Nuorteva, Santeri, 315, 316
Nye Committee, 5

O'Brian, John Lord, 15
Odell, Joseph H , 175
Official Bulletin, 68, 92, 93, 94, 95, 96
Official War Review, 138, 141
O'Hare, Kate Richards, 43
O'Higgins, Harvey, 5, 66, 72, 110
Oland, Warner, 143, 144
Oliver Machinery Company, 205
Omaha World-Herald, 32

Ordnance Department, 136, 199, 200
O'Reilly, P. S , 330
Overman, Lee S , 22, 24

Pacifists, 25
Paderewski, Ignace, 221
Page, Thomas Nelson, 244, 287, 290
Page, Walter Hines, 319
Palmer, Eric H , 244, 279, 280, 281
Palmer, Frederick, 243, 244, 251, 252, 292
Panama, CPI in, 245
Panov, B. A , 317
Papen, Franz von, 146
Paramount-Bray Pictograph, 139
Parker, Sir Gilbert, 90
Patchin, Philip, 148, 317, 319
Pathé Company, 137, 139, 143, 294
Patterson, T. M., 55
Paxson, Frederic L , 172
"Pay-Envelope Stories," 191
Peace Conference, 95, 231, 235, 264, 284, 299, 332, 333
Pearson's, 56
Peixotto, Ernest C., 106
Pennell, Joseph, 102, 106
Perigord, Paul, 128
Perry, Paul, 244, 297, 322
Pershing, John J , 87, 106, 128, 284, 293
Peru, CPI in, 245
Petrograd Press Bureau, 301
Pettijohn, J. J., 126, 182
Pew, Marlen E , 90
Philadelphia Public Ledger, 31, 221
Philadelphia Record, 343
Phillips Sheet and Tin Plate Company, 205
Phillips, William, 229, 276
Photographic Association, 153
Photographs, 153-5
Pickford, Mary, 135, 142, 311
Pictorial Publicity, Division of, 71-2, 101-8
Picture Division, 68, 74, 153
Pinchot, Amos, 17

Pittsburgh Post, 31
Pittsburgh Press Club, 83
Polignac, Marquis and Marquise de, 128
Polk, Frank, 297
Poole, DeWitt Clinton, 309
Poole, Ernest, 74, 77, 241, 301, 304, 321, 331, 338
Post, Louis F, 164
Post Office Department, 20, 80, 215
Powell, E. Alexander, 246, 249
Preciado, A. A., 245, 322
Press, 28-34, 40, 41, 43, 62, 77, 83, 84, 86, 88, 90, 215-16, 229, 276, 280
Press censorship, 28, 29
Press, Regulations for the, 81-3
Price, Raymond B, 214
Production and Distribution, Division of, 67
Propaganda into enemy countries, 243
"Psychological Estimates" of MIB, 246
Publications, Division of, 153
Publications of CPI, 220
Public Relations Administration, 343
Public Relations Branch, 341
Putnam, George Haven, 219

QUATRAINS OF CHRIST, 54, 55

RADIO, 270
Railroad Brotherhoods, 26
Raine, William MacLeod, 72, 110
Rassieur, Leo, 164
Red Cross, 97, 100, 116, 118, 125, 127, 185, 287, 289, 315
Red Cross Mission to Russia, 303
Red, White and Blue Series, 162, 167, 170, 181
Reed, John, 30
Reilly, Leigh, 68, 90, 208
Remington Typewriter Company, 322

Renault, Louis, 293, 294
Reuterdahl, Henry, 105
Reuters News Bureau, 240, 283, 332
Rickey, H N, 73, 220, 235, 244, 282, 295, 296, 297, 313, 326
Riis, Edward, 281, 282, 332
Rinehart, Mary Roberts, 110, 111
Robinette, E B, 244, 279
Robins, Raymond, 315, 316
Robinson, Herman, 190
Robinson, James Harvey, 177
Roche, Josephine, 73, 220, 228, 232, 257
Rochester, E. S., xi, 68, 93, 94, 95
Rocky Mountain News, 32, 55, 56, 57, 208
Rodionoff, Nicholas R, 317
Roe, Gilbert E, 30
Rogers, Walter S., 238, 251, 295, 297, 333
Roosevelt, Franklin D, 49, 291
Roosevelt, Theodore, 26, 88, 325
Root, Elihu, 175, 302
Root Mission, 296, 303
Rosemeier, Hermann, 276
Rosten, Leo, 90
Rotary Clubs, 127, 161
Roz, Firman, 293
Rubel, Lawrence, xi, 154
Russau, Hans, 164
Russell, Charles Edward, 244, 256, 286, 296, 298, 302
Russell, John, 244, 296
Russell, William Fletcher, 312
Russia, CPI in, 244, 300-18
Russian Cooperative Union, 313
Russian News-Letter, 305
Ryerson, Donald, 72, 114, 115, 116, 118, 120

ST. LOUIS GLOBE-DEMOCRAT, 31
St Louis Republic, 176
San Francisco Chronicle, 31
San Francisco Examiner, 86
Sanger, Margaret, 56
Saperston, Alfred M, 72, 108
Schaefer, Richard, 218

Scandinavian Americans, 226
Scenario Department, 69, 139, 140
Schenck, Joseph M , 135
Schenck v United States, 44
Scherer, James A B , 149
Schick, Mary E , 71
Schiff, Jacob, 217
Schlegel, Charles J , 217
Schlieben, Hans, 276
Schuman, Frederick L , 317
Schwimmer, Rozika, 278
Scott, Foresman and Company, 180
Scott, George Winfield, 165
Searson, James W , 159, 182
Seattle Post-Intelligencer, 32
Secret Service, 144
Sedition Act of 1798, 21-2, 34
Sedition Act of 1918, 45, 80
Seldes, George, 190
Sellery, George C , 172
Selznick, Louis J , 135
Semenov, Eugenie P , 317
Service Bureau, 71
Sevier, H. H , 245
Shaw, Dr Anna Howard, 73
Sherman, Stuart P , 165
Shipping Board, 97
Shotwell, James, 159, 183
Shuster, E H , 332
Siciliani, Colonel, 256
Sigel, Franz, 164, 217
Signal Corps, 69, 136, 138, 140,
   149, 153, 155, 243, 251
Silver Bell, 85
Sills, Milton, 143
Sims, W. S , 297
Sinclair, Upton, 33
Singer, Caroline, 72
Singer Sewing Machine Company,
   267
Sioussat, St George L., 172
Sisson, Edgar, 5, 66, 73, 148, 208,
   210, 220, 235, 244, 245, 255, 271,
   272, 273, 278, 280, 281, 297,
   298, 303, 304, 305, 306, 307, 308,
   309, 312, 314, 315, 316, 318,
   319, 331, 332, 333

"Sisson Documents," 88, 167, 221,
   314-20
Sleicher, William, 218
Slides, 124, 155-6
Slides, Department of, 69, 155
Smith, Mr and Mrs Datus C., Jr ,
   xi
Smith, Guy Croswell, 244, 281, 307,
   309, 334
Smith, J. André, 106
Socialists, 25, 33, 201, 290
Society of American Artists, 102
Songs, 124
Sons of Herman, 218
Sons of Norway, 226
Spain, 263
Spain, CPI in, 244, 264-74
Spaulding, Albert, 244
Speakers' Bulletins, 127
Speaking Division, 72, 126-30, 195
Sperry, E E , 173
Spirit of '76, 43, 147
Standard Aircraft Corporation, 154
State Councils of Defense, 117,
   127
State, Department of, 48, 77, 92,
   128, 153, 229, 265, 275, 287, 295,
   297, 305, 313, 316, 317, 321,
   331, 332, 340
State Fair Exhibits, Bureau of, 70
Steele, Rufus, 139
Stenography and Mimeographing,
   Division of, 67
Stokes, J G Phelps, 190
Stokes, Rose Pastor, 43
Stoll, Elmer, 171
Stone, William J , 27
Stovall, Pleasant A , 276
Streseman, Gustav, 334
Strong, Howard M , 161
Stuart, Campbell, 256
Studebaker Motor Corporation, 322
Summerlin, George T , 324
Summers, Maddin, 244, 306, 309
Sunday, Billy, 26
Supreme Court, 20, 43-4

Suydam, Henry, 244, 256, 282, 283, 284, 296, 297
Sweden, CPI in, 244, 263, 279-81
Swift Packing Company, 322
Swiss Telegraphic Agency, 277
Switzerland, CPI in, 244, 275
Swope, Herbert Bayard, 157
Syndicate Features, Division of, 72, 74, 109-10, 145, 241

TAFT, WILLIAM HOWARD, 166, 210
Tanguay, Eva, 131
Tarbell, Edmond C , 102
Tarbell, Ida, 73
Tarkington, Booth, 110, 173, 297
Tatlock, John, 155, 166, 167
Taylor, Clara Sears, 72
Taylor, Graham, Jr , 305, 306, 307, 309
Thatcher, T , 315, 316
Theaters, 113 ff
Thomas, Norman, 23
Thompson, William B , 303, 315, 316
Thrift Stamps, 197
Todd, David W., 78, 85
Toledo Scale Company, 206
Townsend, Harry, 106
Trading-with-the-Enemy Act, 20, 44, 80, 142, 215, 242
Training Camp Activities, 97
Treasury Department, 127, 214, 345
Trenton Times, 292
Trotsky, Leon, 301, 317
Tuerk, John, 74, 142, 243
Tumulty, Joseph P , 12, 43
Turner, Frederick Jackson, 183
Tvricka, Anna, 220
Tynan, Jim, 55

UNDERWOOD AND UNDERWOOD, 153
United States Cartridge Company, 198
United States Chamber of Commerce, 128
United States Bulletin, 95

United States Daily, 96
United War Work Drive, 97
Universal Motor Company, 202
Universal Picture Company, 138, 139, 148, 150
Useless Papers Committee, viii

VAN DEMAN, R H , 311
Van Loon, Hendrik Willem, 251, 282
Vance, Louis Joseph, 143, 146
Veiner, S P , 244, 245, 322
Victory Loan, 135
Vigilantes, 110
Villard, Oswald Garrison, 24, 43
Volk, Douglas, 102
Vrooman, Carl, 63

WADE, H R., 202
Walberg, Carl, 332
Walcott, Frederic C , 175
Walsh, Frank P , 208, 209, 210
Wanger, Walter F , 243, 258, 259
War Cooperating Committee, 135
War Department, 77, 97, 149, 164, 178, 179, 182, 196, 197, 206, 217, 243, 340, 341, 345
War Expositions, Bureau of, 69
War Industries Board, 156, 157, 189, 190, 197, 343
War Information Series, 162, 165, 167
War Labor Administration, 189
War Labor Board, 209, 210
War Message and the Facts Behind It. 67
War News Digest, 91
War Office, French, 252
War Photographs, Bureau of, 69, 153, 241
War Savings Stamps, 97, 123
War Trade Board, 73, 80, 84, 92, 142, 268, 278, 343
Washington Herald, 79
Washington Post, 87, 88, 93
Wear-Ever Magazine, 99
Webb, Edwin Yates, 22, 23, 35, 38

Webb-Culberson Bill, see Espionage Act
Webb-Overman bill, 22-23
Webster, N. P , 67
Weekly Bulletin for Cartoonists, 109
Weeks, George F , 245, 329, 330
Weinberger, Harry, 30
Weir, E T , 205
Welborn, J. F., 205
Welles, Roger, 326
Wellesley Associates, 94, 191, 193
West, Willis Mason, 173
Western Newspaper Union, 153
Western Photoplays Company, 151
Westman, John A., 201
Wharton, Leopold, 143
White, Eugene, xi
White, William Allen, 337
Whitehouse Vira B., 244, 255, 275, 276, 278, 292, 331, 332, 334
Whitlock, Brand, 172, 328
Wiegand, H J, 205
Wiegand, Wilfred E , 330
Willard, Joseph E , 266
Wilson, C. B , 224
Wilson, Hugh, 276
Wilson, William B , 193
Wilson, Woodrow, viii, 4, 10, 11, 12, 17, 18, 21, 23, 27, 28, 37, 38, 39, 47, 48, 50, 56, 79, 80, 88, 101, 126, 147, 150, 153, 160, 172, 190, 191, 202, 210, 214, 216, 221, 222, 230, 231, 240, 247, 261, 264, 274, 284, 285, 286, 288, 291, 292, 300, 302, 303, 305, 314, 323, 332, 334, 339
Wilson and the Issues, 59
Winchester Repeating Arms Company, 203

Winters,' Robert, 312
Wireless-Cable Service, 73, 239, 241, 242, 243, 244, 251, 295
Wisconsin Gun Company, 205
Wolfe, Frank, 191
Women's Division, Four-Minute Men, 124
Women's Division, Council of National Defense, 72
Women's Peace Party of America, 30
Women's War Work, Division of, 72-3
Wood, Henry A Wise, 197
Wood, Lee B , xi
Wood, Leonard, 9
Woods, Arthur, 73, 220, 223, 235
Wooley, R. W , 118
Work with the Foreign Born, Division of, 68, 73, 217, 219-32, 257, 279
World Film Company, 137
World League for the Restitution of Alsace-Lorraine, 226
World Peace Foundation, 166
Wright, Chester M , 190, 208, 209, 210
Wright, George, 106
Wright, Irene A , 244, 265, 267, 268, 269, 271
Writers, 109-12
Wyeth, N C , 105

Y M C A , 100, 185, 289

Zook, George F , 155
Zukor, Adolph, 135

CPSIA information can be obtained
at www.ICGtesting.com
Printed in the USA
LVHW011410200121
676966LV00007B/381